THE VEGETARIAN CRUSADE

The Vegetarian Crusade

The Rise of an American
Reform Movement, 1817–1921

ADAM D. SHPRINTZEN

THE UNIVERSITY OF NORTH CAROLINA PRESS   Chapel Hill

The paper in this book meets the guidelines for permanence
and durability of the Committee on Production Guidelines for
Book Longevity of the Council on Library Resources.

The University of North Carolina Press has been
a member of the Green Press Initiative since 2003.

Library of Congress Cataloging-in-Publication Data
Shprintzen, Adam D.
The vegetarian crusade : the rise of an American
reform movement, 1817–1921 / Adam D. Shprintzen. — 1st edition.
pages cm
Includes bibliographical references and index.
ISBN 978-1-4696-0891-4 (cloth : alk. paper)
ISBN 978-1-4696-2652-9 (pbk.: alk. paper)
1. Vegetarianism—United States—History. 2. Vegetarians—
United States—History. 3. Vegetarians—United States—
Biography. I. Title.
TX392.S446 2013
613.2'620973—dc23 2013010472

THIS BOOK WAS DIGITALLY PRINTED.

PUBLICATION OF THIS BOOK IS ENABLED BY A GRANT FROM

Jewish Federation of Greater Hartford

FOR MY WIFE, *Rachel,* AND OUR DAUGHTER, *Aviva*

Contents

Illustrations

Acknowledgments

Work on this project began innocently enough nearly seven years ago, after I noticed a brief mention of the existence of vegetarians in the antebellum United States. Having recently converted to a vegetarian diet, I was intrigued to find out more about the history of this movement in the United States. Never could I have imagined that simple decision would lead to such rich, evolving research. Certainly I could not have predicted that I would still be researching the subject many years later.

The process of putting together this manuscript has benefited considerably from the professional and personal guidance I have received from innumerable sources. My work on vegetarianism began in a research seminar on nineteenth-century America taught by Tim Gilfoyle. An incredible historian, teacher, and writer, Tim has offered advice, care, and guidance throughout the process of writing this book, focusing and sharpening my research and writing considerably. I consider myself truly lucky to have Tim as a mentor, and any success I may have with the book owes much to his advice.

My years of historical study have put me in contact with incredible scholars whose influence—either directly or indirectly—can be found in this book. In particular, I would like to thank Harold Platt and Susan Hirsch, whose meticulous review and comments on early drafts of the manuscript were invaluable. I owe them a debt of gratitude. In addition, I would like to express my deepest thanks to teachers and advisors over the years, including Jack Salzman, Robert Seltzer, and Lawson Bowling, all of whom have enthusiastically encouraged my studies and provided advice long after my years in their classroom.

I consider myself truly lucky to have received such careful analysis from the University of North Carolina Press's readers during the process of completing this book. The detailed feedback and advice of Andrew Haley and James McWilliams helped strengthen the manuscript considerably and provided fresh perspective. Most of all, I was honored to have my work reviewed by accomplished scholars whose work I admire greatly. To them, I owe a considerable debt of gratitude.

The staff of UNC Press has been incredible to work with and particularly patient given the numerous questions of a first-time book author. Mark Simpson-Vos took an early interest in my work and helped me navigate through the publishing process. His knowledge of the time periods involved in the book helped me further contextualize my research. My thanks to Mark for being such a true pleasure to work with. Alex Martin's copy-editing of the manuscript provided significant clarity and strengthened the narrative considerably. I owe Alex many thanks for his time, patience, and efforts. In addition, I thank others whose assistance was vital, including Zachary Read, Paula Wald, Susan Garrett, and Beth Lassiter.

I am also indebted to friends and family for their support and patience through the years. My sister, Jodi; brother-in-law, Evan; mother-in-law, Jane; grandparents, Milton, Florence, Shirley, and Jesse; and in-laws from the Hakimian family have been constant sources of support and motivation. To all of you, I express my gratitude. I am particularly indebted to my parents, Deborah and Robert, who have never wavered in their support of my academic pursuits as well as all of my life decisions. They have always gone out of their way to encourage and foster critical thought and creativity, qualities that have served me well in my historical studies. Thank you for always being there.

Most important, I would not have completed this project without the support of my wife, Rachel. We began dating soon after I started researching this topic. Her love, patience, good humor, and warmth have nourished me through times of self-doubt, frustration, and writer's block. I consider myself truly blessed to have found her. Thank you, Rachel, especially for the many nights and weekends I have spent reading old vegetarian magazines instead of enjoying my time with you. I love you with all my heart. In September 2012 Rachel and I welcomed our daughter, Aviva, into this world. To Aviva, I thank you for all the joy that you have brought into my life. I look forward to watching you grow, and please know that your dad will always be proud of you.

THE VEGETARIAN CRUSADE

Introduction

::

We are urged to write a history of Vegetarianism. —Henry S. Clubb,
"History of Vegetarianism: Chapter 1," Vegetarian Magazine (October 1907)

In December 1988, *Vegetarian Times*—a popular national magazine devoted
to vegetarian living, food, and culture—reflected on the growth of vegetarianism in the United States. The cover of the magazine noted the increasing
number of vegetarian celebrities, including former Beatle Paul McCartney,
"King of Pop" Michael Jackson, teen heartthrob River Phoenix, and children's television icon Fred Rogers. The issue included a reflection on the
comparative history of the vegetarian movement in Great Britain and the
United States.

The article's author lauded British vegetarianism, noting that it had a
longer and more prominent history than its U.S. counterpart. The article
concluded, however, that it was ultimately unfair to compare the history
of vegetarianism in the two countries because "few Americans have ever
been inspired to vegetarianism by any national society."[1] Two years later
the magazine devoted an entire issue to celebrating "how far we have come
but also to put[ting] the success of the vegetarian 'movement' in some sort
of historical and social context."[2] The issue only covered developments in
American vegetarianism starting in the 1970s, thus ignoring the vast majority of the movement's history in the United States.

Abstention from meat became a vital ideological and political movement
in the United States in the early nineteenth century. But all too often vegetarianism has been presented—even by its proponents—as a product of
twentieth-century modernism, reflecting a rise in ethical consumer awareness.[3] Dietary choices regarding meat consumption were, in fact, connected
with larger nutritional, social, and individual goals for vegetarian reformers
in nineteenth- and early twentieth-century America. At the center of the relationship between food choices and political ambitions surrounding meat
abstention was the organized vegetarian movement, which formulated and
shifted significantly during this period.

But how can a movement be defined? Not every person abstaining from meat during this period was involved in the vegetarian movement. Some individuals ate a meatless diet for stretches of time out of pure economic necessity. Others, including some Shakers, lived a vegetarian lifestyle by ideological choice but remained largely disconnected from the vegetarian movement.[4] In the case of American vegetarianism, a movement formed around a singular idea imported from abroad, eventually leading a variety of practitioners to formal organization. The movement was supported and spread by a national association, a proliferation of literature, and the words of popular orators whose message appealed to interested reformers.

The history of movement vegetarianism in the United States—the institutions, organizations, prominent advocates, and publications aligned with the creation of a community based on the idea of abstaining from meat—illustrates how a singular idea proliferated into a nationwide movement united through a common culinary practice. The motives, methods, and goals of individual vegetarians throughout the country shifted significantly over time and were often shaped by the values and ideals espoused by the vegetarian movement. American vegetarianism developed within a larger cultural milieu that affected understandings of social and political reform. As a result, tracing the development and evolution of the vegetarian movement provides insight into the changing nature of reform in the United States from the early nineteenth through the early twentieth century.

From 1817 until 1921, movement vegetarianism shifted its aims from conquering social ills and injustice to building personal strength and success in a newly individualistic, consumption-driven economy. Until the Civil War, the vegetarian movement saw the diet as the catalyst for a total reform ideology, including abolitionism, women's suffrage, pacifism, and economic equality. In the postbellum years through the Progressive Era, individuals embraced the lifestyle under the promise of creating healthy, vital bodies best prepared to advance socially and economically. How did this shift occur, and what were the implications of these changes?

While the history of vegetarianism as a movement in the United States can be traced to proto-vegetarian groups arriving in 1817, they were not the first in North America to consider the implications of meat consumption for moral and physical health. Native American tribes such as the Osage acknowledged their ancestors as peaceful farmers who ate no flesh.[5] Some early European migrants to North America also followed meatless dietetics. In Lancaster County, Pennsylvania, German immigrant Johann Conrad

Beissel led a group of followers in 1721 living in a meat-free community as a means for spiritual and moral cleansing.[6]

William Dorrell, a former British soldier who fought for the Crown during the American Revolution, repatriated to Vermont after the war and founded a settlement of religious perfectionists who refused to utilize animals for food, dress, or labor.[7] Some members of the Society of Friends in Philadelphia—commonly known as the Quakers—practiced a meatless diet as a means to respect the souls of animals, who they believed would, like humans, become liberated from their bodies at the time of ultimate judgment.[8] Americans by the turn of the nineteenth century were exposed, in small doses, to ideas regarding vegetable-based dietetics. However, unlike the dietary reformers who would eventually coalesce into a vegetarian movement, these meat-abstaining groups remained isolated and disconnected from one another.

In Great Britain, meatless dietetics had deep roots in the eighteenth century as well. Swedenborgian churches popped up throughout London in the 1770s and 1780s, preaching Christian mysticism through meat abstention.[9] Disgruntled ex-followers of Emanuel Swedenborg eventually gave birth to the religious movement that led British dietary reformers to migrate to the United States. Led by physician William Lambe in the 1790s, British medical care began flirting with meatless dietetics as a means to cure patients.[10] The famed romantic poet Percy Bysshe Shelley speculated in 1813 on the coming of an age of peace, when humans would no longer give in to their violent desires for flesh foods.[11] Meat abstention as a communal movement found its way from England to the United States by 1817. But despite their frequent transatlantic exchange, American vegetarianism diverged significantly from its British counterpart in its demographics, goals, and methods.

Widespread belief in the prevailing nutritional and medical theory of the body's functions during the period largely inspired proto-vegetarian ideologies in the United States. The ancient Greek physician Hippocrates first expressed the humoral theory of the human body in the fourth century BCE. In early nineteenth-century America, the fundamental underpinnings of the theory remained largely accepted.

The humoral theory held the human body contained four humors, or fluids, paralleling the four earthly elements of earth, air, water, and fire. The four humors in the human body were black bile, blood, phlegm, and yellow or red bile. Individuals each had their own humoral constitution, it was believed, and the proper balance of these humors ensured health; an imbalance created disease. Each bodily humor was associated with one of the four seasons and had similar characteristics of warmth and cold, wetness and dryness. In order to keep bodies in a state of equilibrium, treatments were advised to rid the body of an imbalance, including bloodletting, enemas, and purgatives to induce vomiting.[12]

In colonial America, dietetic practices were particularly connected to ideas of the humoral body. With settlers concerned about the availability, security, and scarcity of food products, ideals linking food with health and virtue suffused English North America. Popular theories linked certain foods with specific aspects of the humoral body, as bread, meat, fish, dairy, fruits, and vegetables were all believed to interact with specific humors in varying ways. Balancing a proper diet of delicate, fresh foods was believed to ensure humoral balance.[13] While the humoral theory's popularity began waning with increased food security, the integration of new foods into common diets, and the scientific revolution, the notion that foods had stimulating characteristics remained common in the United States when the first proto-vegetarians appeared in the second decade of the nineteenth century. The idea that the human body needed to remain in balance largely motivated and informed the dietary theories of early proto-vegetarians.

American movement vegetarianism's history can be traced directly to these proto-vegetarian movements. Groups such as Bible Christians, Grahamites, water curists, residents of Fruitlands, and physiologists exposed increasing numbers of Americans to the potential benefits of a meatless diet. Eventually, by 1850, these various interests conjoined to propagate a new term and movement in the United States, forming as the American Vegetarian Society (AVS).

During this period, vegetarianism was visualized as a catalyst for total social reform, including the emancipation of slaves, the extension of suffrage to women, and the end of oppressive economics. This period was marked by a belief in the power of personal food choices to benefit society at large. Vegetarian reform during this period was similar to abolitionism in that both were radical appeals for fundamental changes in American culture and society. Given the nature of these aims, the movement met significant resistance, as the popular media presented vegetarians as frail, weak, and sexually impotent. The movement depended on individual actions but was communal and utopian in its goals and activities. Ultimately, however, with the dissolution of the AVS, the failure of an attempted vegetarian colony in prestate Kansas, the increased importance of abolitionism, and the coming of the Civil War, the vegetarian movement fractured, allowing the ideology to be redefined.

Immediately following the Civil War, the American vegetarian movement experienced years of transition without a national organization. The ideology itself did not disappear, and individual vegetarians sought ways to keep the movement alive. These efforts eventually led to a new movement as well as greater popularity and renown. By the late nineteenth century, movement vegetarianism gained its greatest recognition from normative culture by embracing the domestic sciences, consumerism, physical culture, and athletics. Vegetarianism became intertwined with the burgeoning movements of muscular masculinity, organized sports, home economics, and health advocacy, in each instance connecting these ideologies with the power of product consumption. The new vegetarian movement's larger ideology was a response to a newly mature corporate culture that focused on individualized success while simultaneously producing anxieties about the weakening and feminizing of male workers.

Vegetarianism emerged as a viable way to build individual character and personal health in order to succeed in a society driven toward personal gain and monetary advancement. The purported benefits of a vegetarian lifestyle included physical strength, a muscular physique, health, and vitality. These values were exalted by American vegetarianism's most renowned advocate, J. H. Kellogg, and were espoused by advocates at the World's Vegetarian Congress, which met at the Columbian Exposition in 1893. The vegetarian movement's national organization, the Vegetarian Society of America (VSA), also embraced the new association of vegetarianism with normative values.

Not coincidentally, vegetarianism also became a growing commercial venture during this period. Food products, meatless restaurants, and vegetarian kitchen equipment were marketed to consumers interested in purchasing the promise of health, happiness, and strength. These new products helped shift the nature of movement vegetarianism. Practitioners became indelibly linked to commercial market forces, individuals interested in consuming products with the promise of personal success and social advancement. During this period, the popular press largely extolled the virtues of vegetarianism as promoting healthy, successful living aimed at personal development. By the turn of the twentieth century, the vegetarian movement had shifted from being a source of radical critiques of social injustice to being an advocate for "the strenuous life" described by Theodore Roosevelt as a means to ensure American strength at home and abroad.[14] This shift parallels the evolving nature of reform from the early nineteenth century into the twentieth.

In order to fully explain the development of the vegetarian movement, it is important to begin with proto-vegetarian groups, as the term *vegetarianism* did not enter popular use in the United States until 1850. Accordingly, chapter 1 examines the roots of dietary reform in the United States, focusing on the first groups to place meat abstention at the center of their identity and activities. The Bible Christian Church—whose members were immigrants from England—established meatless living in a growing Philadelphia metropolis filled with reform movements. The group met significant resistance from flesh-eaters but grew steadily in Philadelphia's middle-class reform community.

Soon after, Sylvester Graham appeared on the American reform scene, preaching against the horrors of overtaxing the body with alcohol, processed bread, tobacco, masturbation, and flesh foods. Graham's followers—known as Grahamites—placed dietary reform at the center of their identity, publishing periodicals spreading the gospel of bran bread and dietary reform while living in communal boardinghouses throughout the Northeast. Through the 1830s Grahamites held the mantle of dietary reform in the United States.

Other meatless reform movements challenged the Grahamite identity by the 1840s. Chapter 2 explores movements that emphasized meatless dietetics. William Alcott's publication, *Library of Health*, presented dietary reform from a distinctly physiological perspective, helping to broaden the appeal of meatless identity away from the sole realm of Grahamism through the notion of medical authority. New opportunities opened for dietary reformers interested in proving that meatless living could stand at the center of social reform. Bronson Alcott—William's cousin and father of Louisa May—attempted to make dietary choice central to his utopian Fruitlands, a community free of oppression and flesh foods, a working model of how to live a morality-driven life. The difficulties incurred by the settlers at Fruitlands in finding a balance between intellectual, spiritual, and agricultural pursuits, however, illustrated the contradictions and limitations faced by dietary reformers. Other meatless ideologies also appeared during this time, including that of the water curists, further expanding the possibilities for those interested in living flesh-free diets.

Chapter 3 analyzes the rise of the American Vegetarian Society, the first national organization of its kind in the United States. The group popularized and defined the term *vegetarian* in the United States, using it is a means to unify meatless dietary reform into a singular identity. The AVS brought together the full spectrum of reformers interested in flesh-free dietetics under a single umbrella. Most important, the group connected a vegetarian diet with the great social reform movements of the time, including abolitionism, women's rights, and pacifism. Vegetarianism was presented as a means to free the slaves, liberate women from the kitchen, lessen violence, and promote greater economic equality for all. Members of the AVS shifted vegetarians away from their previous identities, even making a conscious effort to distance the diet from the shadow of Sylvester Graham.

Although the AVS was relatively short-lived, the movement remained connected with the larger political issues of the day, in particular abolition. In fact, the sectional crises and eventual Civil War helped ensure that the larger issues facing the Union made vegetarianism lose some of its distinctiveness. Vegetarians under the leadership of AVS member Henry S. Clubb headed westward to colonize Kansas, to do their part to ensure that the state would enter the Union free of slavery. The group quickly disbanded. However, in the aftermath of the colony's demise, settlers remained, even taking up arms to resist forces favoring the spread of the slave system. As events progressed and vegetarians became involved with Union forces, the pacifism that helped define vegetarianism came into direct conflict with a dedication to abolition.

Vegetarians faced harsh personal attacks during this period, as detractors focused on the purported physical, mental, and emotional frailty of reformers. Chapter 4 describes the construction of the image of vegetarians, whom the popular press as well as the scientific and medical communities cast as weak, enfeebled faddists worthy of constant mockery. These attacks were hardly surprising, given the radical nature of vegetarians' politics and dietary choices. However, the common themes of antivegetarian missives indicate that vegetarians offended deeply held social, political, and culinary normative values. With the dissolution of the AVS and continued assaults by mainstream society, individual vegetarians sought to prove the physical benefits of their diet to the public at large. While the attempts made some headway during the years leading up to the Civil War, the connection of vegetarianism with muscular, strong individuals would eventually resonate with a new generation of movement vegetarians.

These new movement vegetarians initiated their activities in the years following the Civil War. Chapter 5 explores the transformative role of John Harvey Kellogg in creating a new vegetarianism that corresponded with a new style of diet. Through his work at the Battle Creek Sanitarium, Kellogg marketed the first products explicitly labeled meat substitutes. Vegetarian products such as Protose, Nuttose, and Granose were sold to customers with the promise of tasting, feeling, and smelling like meat, qualities that previously would have raised the ire of dietary reformers. Thanks to the rise of these new vegetarian success foods, vegetarianism began to be embraced by the public as a means to prepare individuals for competitive modern life. Vegetarianism became a capital enterprise, and with this came wider social acceptance and a depoliticization of the identity.

The dietary shift for vegetarians led to a larger change in the movement as it separated itself further from its previous radical politics. Chapter 6 examines the formation of the Vegetarian Society of America—a new national organization—and the role of vegetarians at the Columbian Exposition, which vegetarians used to promote a new spirit of vegetarianism connected to notions of modernity, culture, and social advancement. Chicago became a center of the new vegetarianism, supported by the city's wealthy philanthropic class, whose members believed that the diet produced morally and socially industrious individuals. Vegetarianism, as a result, became a profitable commercial venture. Vegetarian restaurants, clubs, publishing houses, and grocery stores opened in the years following the group's appearance in the "White City," reflecting a new vegetarian lifestyle focused on the benefits of the diet to the individual rather than to society at large. Different groups competed over vegetarianism during these years, as some continued to tout the diet's connection with political and social reform. The vegetarian movement, however, largely ignored these alternative groups.

Chapter 7 concludes with vegetarianism's connection to the growing physical culture, fitness, strength, and bodybuilding movements of the early twentieth century. Vegetarianism's most widely read advocate became fitness guru Bernarr Macfadden, in the pages of his flagship magazine *Physical Culture*. Macfadden emphasized a vegetarian diet as a way to gain physical strength, a muscular body, and powerful vitality. Macfadden was not alone in these efforts. Other bodybuilders and athletes experimented with vegetarianism, believing that it maximized strength and endurance. The vegetarian movement used these advocates as living proof of the diet's benefits and promoted them as evidence that individuals could utilize vegetarianism to create social and economic success. Mass audiences embraced vegetarianism's connection to these normative values.

Movement vegetarianism changed significantly in the first century of its development in the United States, shifting from an identity that was connected to radical political reform to one that was commercialized and that focused primarily on benefits for individuals. During this period vegetarians witnessed widespread changes in American society. From the time of the Bible Christians through the Civil War, the group fought against main-stream social norms. Following the war and through the Progressive Era, movement vegetarianism and its adherents touted the diet's benefits as a means to build legitimacy.

The arc of the movement's history from the early nineteenth century through the early twentieth century allowed vegetarianism to occupy a unique space in American food culture and reform—neither pure subculture nor mainstream ideology. And yet movement vegetarians, precisely because of their transition in the nineteenth and early twentieth century from being targets of ridicule to being accepted cultural actors, were able to question American dietary practices and the effects of these food choices. At first this ideology manifested itself by connecting dietary choice with other social and political reform causes. Eventually the movement's impact was felt through the glorification of meat substitutes, nuts, and other marketed healthy fare that was linked to and promoted normative cultural values. In this sense, movement vegetarianism of this period cannot be classified as a pure alternative food way or countercuisine.[15]

Movement vegetarians never came close to their utopian goal of mass conversion of the meat-eating population. However, the movement was able to develop into a recognizable, visible, and growing community during the nineteenth and early twentieth century. It won this recognition by questioning dietary practices and expanding the public dialogue on the implications of food choices. Through these years, movement vegetarianism also succeeded in illustrating—to vegetarian adherents and detractors alike—that there was "plenty to eat without any meat."[16]

CHAPTER ONE

Proto-vegetarianism

::

And the cow and the bear shall feed: their young ones shall
lie down together: and the lion shall eat straw like the ox. —Isaiah 11:7

It was the early morning of March 29, 1817. A cool breeze wafted through the foggy Liverpool air along with an overriding sense of excitement, anxiety, and anticipation. The Reverends William Metcalfe and James Clarke gazed out on their gathered flock, surveying the situation before them. Inspired by the providential timing—it was, after all, near the time of the year when the ancient Israelites made their exodus from Egypt—forty-one followers of the fledgling Bible Christian Church boarded the majestic *Liverpool Packet*.[1] For months church members had discussed rumors of religious freedom and abundant providence in the new American republic. With a radical religious and political spirit that had led to isolation and intimidation in England, Bible Christians saw the nascent American experiment as fertile ground where their independent lifestyle could flourish. The fear of political persecution combined with a burgeoning industrial society pushed Bible Christians westward to Philadelphia.

The Bible Christians' decision to leave England for the United States would eventually have larger social and cultural implications than the group could have imagined. The activities of this small band of dissidents would lead to the development of a much larger movement in the United States, focusing on one particular component of the church's doctrine, the abstention from meat. Proto-vegetarianism—the individuals and groups who would lay the foundations of a vegetarian movement in the United States—began with the arrival of the Bible Christians.

The group was the first to adopt meatless dietetics at the center of its members' lives while also advocating for this lifestyle in American society at large. The Bible Christians, however, were not the only group to introduce the principle of meat abstention to Americans in the early years of the republic. Within years of the group's establishment in Philadelphia, another movement, known popularly as Grahamism, inspired larger groups of interested reformers to abandon their carnivorous practices.

In the first decades of the nineteenth century, multiple groups and individuals experimented with meatless diets, driven by a desire to create moral, social, and political reform. Proto-vegetarian movements in the United States were marked by outreach to meat-eaters through speeches, publications, newspapers, and public meetings that sought to illustrate the larger social and political implications of dietary choices. These early developments set the stage for a larger movement to mature outside of Philadelphia and eventually gave rise to American vegetarianism.

The Bible Christians migrating to Philadelphia did so with the full support of the movement's founder, William Cowherd, who preached that it was only possible to live an authentic religious life in an agricultural society.[2] In 1793, Cowherd, tired of the sectarian quibbles and professional jealousies that seemed to pervade Anglicanism, left his pulpit and became the spiritual leader of the Swedenborgian New Jerusalem Church in Manchester. He embraced the radical politics of the movement, including its Christian spiritualism, pacifist worldview, and meatless dietetics. Cowherd quickly realized, however, that even the Swedenborgians were afflicted by interpersonal conflict and power plays. Influenced by the radical politics of Thomas Paine and William Godwin, Cowherd decided to start his own movement.[3] At the heart of the Bible Christian Church were three guiding principles: temperance, pacifism, and a meatless diet.

In the early years of the nineteenth century, Cowherd's church grew, primarily drawing members of Manchester's working class with the promise of salvation for their souls and free vegetable soup for their stomachs. The church's activities attracted the attention of William Metcalfe, a fellow former Swedenborgian. Metcalfe had already adopted a meat-free diet in 1810, viewing it as the most natural of human states. Many of Metcalfe's friends and colleagues disagreed, urging him to give up what they referred to as his "foolish notions of a vegetable diet," fearing for his strength and general well-being.[4] To the contrary, Metcalfe pointed out; the effects of a meat-free diet had quickly led to an increase in weight and strength.[5] Things were looking up considerably. With his health intact, Metcalfe even married; something he felt was highly unlikely just a few years earlier.

In 1811, Metcalfe was ordained as a Bible Christian minister. Soon after he began looking toward the United States as a new potential home where the group could grow. An increasingly oppressive political environment in

England at the end of the Napoleonic Wars led to organized attempts to quell radical reformers. Bible Christians—sympathetic to the Luddite spirit of the times—were, in the words of one church member, "obnoxious not only to the hired minions of power, but also to our relatives."[6] The notion of emigrating enjoyed significant support among church members, who frequently discussed the opportunities for civil and religious freedom in the United States. What better place than America, Metcalfe argued, to present a nascent, radical religion?[7]

Under the guidance of Metcalfe and Clarke, the Bible Christian immigrants arrived on the shores of the United States on June 14, 1817. The group had survived a difficult seventy-nine-day voyage at sea, presumably made even more objectionable by the liberal consumption of meat and alcohol by the ship's crew, non–Bible Christian passengers, and even by a few renegade church members.[8] Yet the group arrived in Philadelphia well-funded and determined to "stand still and do good" with faith in the notion that "verily thou shalt be fed."[9]

Immediately, however, the group split along ideological lines. Clarke and his followers viewed agriculture as the key to the growth of the church. Metcalfe—cosmopolitan and decidedly more modernist—saw the city as the location with the greatest potential for expansion. In August 1817, Clarke and his family settled in Elkland Township, Pennsylvania, establishing a small church and Sunday school based on the principles of akreophagy, the habitual abstention from meat-eating. However, the agricultural life would not lead to the growth of the Bible Christians as Clarke and Cowherd had planned. In 1823 Clarke and his family—having lost the few followers they had accrued—resettled in Shelby County, Indiana, living out their days tilling their farm, disconnected from the Philadelphia Bible Christians.[10]

The path of William Metcalfe and his followers differed significantly from that of the Clarke family. Philadelphia originally attracted the group because of its available land and passable roads connecting the church to the rest of the city.[11] Philadelphia was the country's second most populous city, and the Bible Christians saw it as an ideal location to gain converts amid a growing urban reform spirit.[12] In Philadelphia, popular fears of perceived new dangers including prostitution, pornographic writers, and other corrupting influences led older citizens to attempt to guide the younger generation toward moral piety. Through reform institutions, pamphlets, and novels these reformers sought to quell youthful intemperance.[13] Bible Christians' attempts at converting individuals to a meatless diet fit seamlessly within the larger reform milieu that took hold in Philadelphia during the early nineteenth century. Individuals free of the overly invigorating influence of meat, Bible Christians believed, were more apt to make morally sound decisions.

In July 1817, the Bible Christians established a day school and informal worship space, inviting Philadelphia's churchgoing public to join. Metcalfe's entreaties were based on the desire to "not form a sectarian church, deriving their doctrines from human creeds." Instead, the Bible Christians promised to "become more efficiently edified in Bible Truths" and "the literal expressions of Sacred Scripture."[14]

A meatless lifestyle, the Bible Christians believed, was the true heavenly inspired diet, present in the garden of Eden and promised during the messianic era. At the heart of the Bible Christian ideology was the notion that biblical truths were to be revealed to humanity progressively over time. Only through dedicated study of the Bible's tenants could individuals truly understand divine providence. Under Metcalfe's guidance, the group preached that Jesus himself was a vegetarian and that any stories of his eating meat were misinterpretations.[15]

The group rented a back room in a schoolhouse at 10 North Front Street, providing daily schooling along with Sabbath morning services that featured intensive text study. The church's space quickly became too expensive, however, particularly after a handful of founding members perished during a yellow fever epidemic in the fall of 1818. With dwindling membership and an unpopular philosophy of meat and alcohol abstention, Metcalfe sought to reinvent the Bible Christian Church while holding on to its core principles of pacifism and meatless dietetics. In 1820, Metcalfe began trying to appeal to a wider audience, utilizing the development of the printed press while connecting the ideas of the Bible Christian Church with those of a variety of reform movements.

Under Metcalfe's guidance, ten prevailing principles of the Bible Christian sect were codified in a constitution, emphasizing the real world applications of a biblically guided life. While existing biblical interpretations were invaluable and even prophetic, Bible Christians argued that continued study and interpretation was necessary to avoid the pitfalls of narrow, sect-driven loyalties. The Bible, when approached with an open, scientific mind would continue to reveal new secrets to healthy, ethical living. The Bible Christians emphasized the power of revelation through concerted study rather than blind adherence to the dictates of religious leaders or sects. Meat abstention, temperance, and moral living served to transform an individual "conjoined to the Lord, and the Lord to him." Thus believers had the capacity to be reformed, regenerated, and finally saved.[16]

The Bible Christians argued that religion, like science, could be rationally understood—emphasizing the power of individual, lay study over bombastic sermonizing. The group downplayed the idea of heavenly revelation in favor of learned epiphany, even questioning the ultimate divinity of Jesus Christ in favor of strict monotheism. The group emphasized that right living in body, mind, and soul ensured salvation for the individual as well as the community at large. The words of the Bible, Bible Christians believed, clearly called for the abstinence from the flesh of animals as food, intoxicating liquors as beverages, as well as war, capital punishment, and slavery. The second coming of the messiah was not a literal, physical event but rather the personal attainment of the divine truths revealed by concentrated study.[17]

There were, of course, ironies in the principles of Bible Christianity. At the same time that the Bible Christians criticized established churches led by cults of personality, the group was led by a vocal, gregarious personality in Metcalfe. And as church ranks grew, the group sought to build institutions that provided social legitimacy. While the religious and political views of the Bible Christian Church were radical, the group was decidedly conservative in its structure and notion of self-righteousness, sharing these values with other more established Philadelphia churches.

Metcalfe's exhortations met harsh responses from Philadelphia's established religious elite. Warning of the dangers of "wolves in sheep's clothing," one Philadelphia religious body accused the Bible Christians of having "attacked the most plain and important doctrines of our holy religion" while seeking to "impose their own creed upon mankind, and take away from us the doctrines for which martyrs bled."[18] Bible Christians were often met in the streets with accusations of heresy. It seemed apparent to the Bible Christians that meat did, in fact, stir up animalistic responses in its consumers.

Despite the angry reactions, the church and its membership continued to grow, thanks in part to a series of articles published in *The Rural Magazine and Literary Evening Friend*, an agricultural and literary-themed periodical headquartered in Philadelphia.[19] In a series of "Letters on Religious Subjects" published throughout 1820 and 1821, Metcalfe expounded on a variety of reformist ideals, connecting them with religious justifications and explanations. In "The Duty of Abstinence from All Intoxicating Drinks," he offered one of the first arguments in the United States for total avoidance of alcohol.

Metcalfe followed his protemperance essay in 1821 with *Bible Testimony: On Abstinence from the Flesh of Animals*, his first piece articulating the moral, religious, and health justifications of a meatless diet.[20] At the heart of Metcalfe's argument in favor of a flesh-free lifestyle was his interpretation of the biblical commandment against killing, whose application he believed "was benevolently intended to reach the animal creation." The fact that the prohibition had not been understood as such was proof of humanity's degradation. Humanity, however, had the power of reason to follow such prohibitions.[21]

Metcalfe equated meat consumption with violent, cruel tendencies, appealing to the most uncontrolled whims of human aggression. Even more than alcoholic spirits, a carnivorous diet was deleterious to the soul, an affront to the natural forces of life. Further, meat consumption was a violent rejection of God itself, a notion expressed by one Bible Christian hymn that warned, "Hold daring man! From murder stay: God is the life in all, You smite at God! When flesh you slay: Can such a crime be small?"[22]

It was the Bible Christians' goal to "instruct . . . to correct general sentiment and to determine the principles of public habits so as to cherish universal humanity." Metcalfe placed abstention from meat at the center of a plan for total reform. Once the church accomplished its goal of converting nonbelievers to its violence-free diet, Metcalfe believed that individuals would "withdraw themselves from a system of cruel habits . . . which has unquestionably a baneful effect upon the physical existence and the intellectual, the moral and religious powers of man." The benefits of a vegetable-based diet—mental clarity, a sense of morality, and an adherence to nonviolence—allowed individuals to lead lives of "benevolence," caring for the "souls of all men."[23]

Metcalfe's pamphlet was the first published creed in favor of total avoidance of meat in the United States. The booklet helped spread the idea of a meatless diet to the general public, connecting food choices with a variety of reform principles ranging from pacifism to antislavery. And while Metcalfe was fundamentalist in his religious outlook, he utilized modern technologies and an Enlightenment-inspired emphasis on rational study to spread the word of his church. What started as a group of twenty families had nearly doubled by 1825, garnering increased attention among interested social reformers in Philadelphia.[24]

The Bible Christians came to the United States as a largely working-class group, drawn toward a meatless diet in cities like Liverpool and Manchester because of its affordability. While the group advocated for dietary reform while in England, it did little to reach out beyond its own small community.[25] However, once in the United States and under Metcalfe's guidance, Bible Christians began to branch outward. While many of the church's original settlers left Bible Christianism after arriving in Philadelphia, the group's reform-oriented ethos appealed to sectors of the city's growing middle class.

Spurred by Metcalfe's growing visibility, and despite the group's avowed antisectarian principles, the Bible Christians began to formalize their organization. In May 1823, they purchased a plot of land in Philadelphia's Kensington neighborhood on the north side of the city. On December 21, the Bible Christian Church opened its doors for the first time on North Third Street and Girard Avenue. With a new, more visible presence the group continued to grow, welcoming in a combination of converts and recently arrived British Bible Christian migrants. In 1830, the group was formally incorporated by the Pennsylvania state legislature. As the Bible Christians' constitution specified, "none can be members . . . but those who conform to the rules, regulations, and discipline of said Church; which rules require abstinence from animal food."[26]

Metcalfe's increasing public presence helped spread the vegetable diet gospel outside the walls of the Bible Christian Church, introducing the notion to a general public that was becoming increasingly interested in reform. With its evangelical, reformist tradition, Philadelphia was the perfect city for the Bible Christians to attempt their experiment in meatless living.[27] Knowledge of the Bible Christians' creed continued to grow, even beyond Philadelphia.

A young Presbyterian minister named Sylvester Graham was among the reformers who became aware of the Bible Christians' philosophy of abstaining from meat. Graham was born in Suffield, Connecticut, in 1794, the youngest of seventeen children. His childhood was filled with strife, instability, and illness. At the time of Sylvester's birth, his father, the Reverend John Graham Jr., was already seventy years old and in poor health. Just two years later, John Graham passed away.[28]

The discord apparent early in Sylvester's life did not end with his father's death. His mother, Ruth—John Graham's second wife and mother of seven of his children—was wracked with debt and unable to access funds from the Graham estate for lack of a will. Under the pressure of raising seven children on her own, and with little support or income, Ruth Graham was overcome by an unknown mental illness. At age three, Sylvester was sent to live with a neighboring family and continued to bounce around among various community households. In 1799, he became seriously ill and spent the next two years living under the care of one of his married half-sisters.[29]

In 1801, the tattered remnants of Sylvester's family structure fell apart as the county probate court of Suffield deemed Ruth to have been "in a

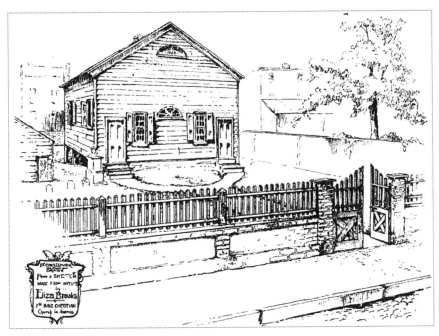

First church edifice of the Philadelphia Bible Christian Church, 1823–44.
From Maintenance Committee, Bible Christian Church, History of the Philadelphia
Bible Christian Church for the First Century of Its Existence (1922).

deranged state of mind" and incapable of caring for her children.[30] Ruth spent the remainder of her years in and out of various mental asylums throughout the Northeast; the court's ruling placed Sylvester in the hands of a local farmer. Thereafter, Sylvester went from home to home, those of various relatives and complete strangers, all the while battling crippling physical ailments and mental dissatisfaction.

By the time he was twenty, it was clear that Sylvester Graham was different. Constantly fighting a variety of illnesses, he shunned the routine alcohol consumption that was a nearly unavoidable fact of life in the early American republic.[31] Viewed as odd, feeble, and preachy by many of his peers, Graham managed to pull his life together working a variety of farming and teaching jobs through his mid-twenties. In 1823 at the relatively late age of twenty-nine, Graham entered Amherst College intent on studying to become a minister and continuing the tradition of both his father and grandfather. Yet, as happened in his early life, Graham's trajectory would not be simple or straightforward. After just one semester at Amherst, Graham dropped out after suffering from exhaustion and a nervous breakdown. This time, transition became a catalyst for a life change. Graham married one of his caretakers, Sarah Earle, in September 1826. At the same time Graham was studying to receive ordination as a Presbyterian minister. With a new family to support, Graham became a full-time minister in Bound Brook, part of the Presbytery of Newark in New Jersey's Berkshire Valley.[32]

Motivated by his own constant health difficulties, Graham—much like the Bible Christians in Philadelphia—believed physical and moral health were closely linked. But through the 1820s he was little focused on the perils of consuming meat; instead, he preached about the evils of alcohol abuse. This war on alcohol led Graham to venture outside of the walls of his church and the safe protection of his community in New Jersey. A gifted public speaker, Graham decided that his talents were best utilized as a champion for social reform rather than as a congregational leader. Just as William Metcalfe moved outside of the church pulpit in order to spread his message of healthy living, Sylvester Graham began to publish and give public lectures in order to gain converts to his cause.

Graham began the process of building a public persona by enlisting in the growing temperance movement. In early 1830, he became a general agent for the Pennsylvania Society for Discouraging the Use of Ardent Spirits. Originally propagated primarily by local clergy, the temperance movement began the process of formalized organization, culminating in the founding of the American Temperance Society (ATS) in 1826. Based in Boston, the ATS—under the guidance of its founder, Lyman Beecher—pressed for the voluntary suppression of alcohol, encouraging its members to sign pledges to abstain from the use of demon rum.[33] In addition to printing pamphlets and statistical studies highlighting the dangers of alcohol, the ATS created a network of localized affiliated societies that utilized the lecture circuit to spread the message of abstinence. Within three years, the ATS had grown to include 229 affiliated, local temperance societies, adding another thousand by 1830.[34]

Within this growing temperance environment the Pennsylvania Society for Discouraging the Use of Ardent Spirits was founded in 1827.[35] The name of the organization says much about its methodology, its attempt to *discourage* the use of alcohol through lectures, pamphlets, and education rather than advocating for the ban of spirits through legislation. Fear of alcohol abuse, including its medical, spiritual, and social effects, was widespread among members of Philadelphia's medical elite, who saw the abuse of spirits as the primary cause of mortality and poverty in the 1820s and 1830s.[36] Though reticent to legislate absolute prohibition, the society worked with local magistrates to prosecute public drunkenness, gambling, and Sabbath violations.

The group warned against the destructive lives of both the "habitual drunkard" as well as the equally pernicious "occasional drunkard."[37] The society advocated for stiff punishments under existing laws and believed in the need for internment in hospitals, almshouses, and prisons to reform alcohol abuse.[38] In addition to its published reports, the Pennsylvania Society aimed to curb alcohol consumption through a network of agents and lecturers sent out to spread the gospel of sobriety, temperance, and clean living.

In June 1830, Sylvester Graham set out to reach the masses, lecturing throughout Pennsylvania connecting alcohol consumption with both physical and spiritual debasement. Graham peppered his speeches with compelling evidence, anecdotes, and scientific reasoning, all under the umbrella of religious imagery. This methodology was part of Graham's attempt to avoid "mere declamation against drunkenness" and instead provide his audiences with "the reasons why they should not use intoxicating drinks."[39] During this period Graham became fascinated with studying human physiology, connecting physical health with ethical development. Not surprisingly, given his existing preoccupation with the connections between alcohol and physiology, Graham eventually turned his attention to dietary habits.

While Graham lectured throughout Philadelphia in 1830, he was introduced to members of the Bible Christian Church, beginning a correspondence with William Metcalfe that continued for most of their lives.[40] Graham later claimed that his dietary decisions were "neither . . . founded on, nor suggested by, the opinions of others who have taught that vegetable food is the proper aliment of the human species," though this was more a rhetorical device aimed at building personal credibility. The growing Bible Christian movement undoubtedly influenced Graham's own dietary conversion, given his connection to Metcalfe.[41] Graham's specious claim that his vegetable diet was based purely on experimentation reflected his methods as a lecturer, emphasizing rational science rather than loyalty to a mere philosophy.

Graham's time working solely on temperance was short-lived, and he resigned from his post after just six months. But his life as a public reformer and lecturer was established. By the spring of 1831, Graham began delivering a series of lectures at the Franklin Institute in Philadelphia on what he labeled "the Science of Human Life," including instruction on meat-free living, temperance, and the dangers of masturbation. Despite these other concerns, Graham's philosophy of healthy living hinged on the adoption of a meatless diet; of the twenty-four lectures included in the *Lectures on the*

Science of Human Life, fourteen focused on food, digestion, and the benefits of avoiding flesh foods.[42] At the core of this lecture series—which Graham delivered in New York City immediately after lecturing in Philadelphia—was the notion that the human body could be controlled and maximized through the mechanism of deep self-awareness. In this sense Graham's lectures offered a democratic notion of personal health care, arguing that it was the individual's responsibility to understand how the human body functioned and to react by initiating the healthiest path of living.

Graham presented a vegetable diet as "the diet of man," proven by a combination of anatomical and historical study.[43] The fact that most Americans lived omnivorous lives was not proof of the dominant diet's validity; rather, it reflected a general disconnect between humans and their natural, physiological state. Graham recognized the potentially controversial nature of his dietetics. A vegetable diet was not antireligious, he assured his audiences. Rather, there was "the most entire harmony between the Sacred Scriptures, and the dietetic and other principles" that he advocated.[44] While Graham's ideas about meat were radical, the traditional awareness of the need to keep the humoral body in balance provided some familiarity and legitimacy to Graham's dietary dictates, as he claimed that meat overheated the body.

In the *Science of Human Life* lectures Graham presented the first unified theory of a meatless diet to general audiences, expunging the notion from the purely religious and placing it within the temporal and physical. Even though Graham's dietary principles were controversial, they offered practical advice and reasoning on how to improve day-to-day life. Connecting the benefits of a vegetable diet to a variety of social changes, Graham successfully exploited the social reform spirit of the 1830s.

This historical moment was the right one for Graham's message to win converts. In the nineteenth century, ideals of republicanism congealed and political parties evolved, providing the opportunity for individual philosophies to coalesce into larger, political movements. Movements like abolitionism and women's suffrage in the 1830s indicated a larger shift in political consciousness in the United States. As the nation and industry expanded, personal choices—and the ethical and political implications of those choices—grew in importance.

Food choices were infused with inherent political power, an idea that proto-vegetarians sought to explore. For example, the famed abolitionists Sarah and Angelina Grimké avoided using food products produced by the slave system in the United States, such as coffee, tea, and sugar.[45] With the geographical growth of the nation also came an increased regional connectedness, more expansive foodways, and a rise in social migration. Graham's dietary advice sought to relieve the tensions inherent in these changes, offering a seeming cure-all for the fears and difficulties wrought by an increasingly urban, industrial society.

Graham's lectures emphasized the naturalness of a vegetable diet based on the study of physiology, arguing that the human dental and alimentary systems were constructed to chew and digest only vegetable-based products. Carnivorous members of the animal kingdom had sharp, elongated teeth, perfect for chewing through flesh and sinew. Humans, in contrast, were blessed with flat teeth, perfect for the grinding necessary to break down fruits, vegetables, and grains.[46] The goal of a meatless diet was a "more healthy, vigorous and long-lived" life, allowing for a "more active and powerful" intellect able to develop the most "moral faculties . . . rendered by suitable cultivation." A moral and intellectually driven individual would not debase him- or herself with the evils of stimulants such as meat. History, Graham argued, pointed toward the benefits of a vegetable diet. Ancient Romans, Greeks, Phoenicians, and Jews all expounded on the virtues of the "natural diet." A vegetable diet worked for Plutarch, Ovid, Hesiod, and Pythagoras; it was only logical that Americans, the torchbearers of modern republicanism, should follow this lead.[47]

Graham, however, was not arguing for animal rights. In fact, he referred to nonhumans as "the lower animals," driven strictly by instinct, a quality to be managed and sublimated by humanity.[48] Meat abstainers feared humanity's inclination to act like the rest of the animal world. Exposure to all kinds of sensory experiences—whether culinary, alcoholic, or sexual—worried dietary reformers, who believed that Americans had relinquished themselves to the most primal, animalistic urges. Proto-vegetarianism put little emphasis on the effects of meat production on the animals themselves, focusing instead on human ethics and their effect on physical functions.

The concept of overstimulation was at the center of Graham's antimeat doctrine, an idea derived from the traditional view of the balanced humoral body. Humanity's natural state—which included a meatless diet—kept the body in a mode of regulated stasis. Substances such as meat, alcohol, and spices served to throw off this natural balance, overstimulating and overheating the human body, mind, and soul. Once the body was out of balance it would become susceptible to any number of serious physical and moral maladies.

Graham's claims about the dangers of meat and other stimulants gained more traction with the outbreak of a mass cholera epidemic. The simultaneous growth of American cities and waves of new immigrants entering urban areas contributed to overcrowding. A lack of available municipal services ensured that impoverished urban areas remained dirty and disease-ridden. By June 1832 cholera appeared in North America in Quebec and quickly spread to the United States before the month was over. In just two months nearly 3,500 New Yorkers—primarily working-class inhabitants of the crowded slums—died from the epidemic. Diarrhea, vomiting, and intense stomach cramping culminated in the eventual collapse of the circulation system. Cities large and small along the East Coast were gripped by fear and hysteria. Wealthy citizens fled to the countryside fearing the spread of the disease, leading one New York reporter to reflect that "the roads, in all directions, were lined with well-filled stagecoaches, livery coaches, private vehicles and equestrians, all panic-struck, fleeing the city, as . . . the inhabitants of Pompeii fled when the red lava showered down upon their houses."[49]

The medical response to the epidemic was slow and usually ineffective. In a pre–germ theory generation, cholera was not perceived as being communicable via interpersonal contact; rather, it was seen as an airborne illness, apt to attack the physically and morally weakest in the cities.[50] Mercury chloride was given out to those afflicted as a strong purgative to induce purification, while laudanum—a powerful opiate that includes opium and morphine—was administered in a glass of hot brandy to treat intense stomach pains. On a federal level, all that Congress could offer was Senator Henry Clay's call for a national day of fasting and prayer for a providential cure.[51]

As these treatments proved to be ineffective and Americans struggled to understand the reasons for the epidemic, Sylvester Graham offered strikingly different advice on how to best treat and avoid cholera. Graham argued that a combination of factors contributed to the epidemic, especially diet and overstimulation. Americans, Graham preached, were detached from and ignorant of the natural laws that regulated the human body, and drunk from a diet heavy in stimulants. Animal flesh was essentially rotting and inorganic, leading to impure blood and the draining of vital power in order to digest unnatural substances.

Laying the blame squarely on meat-eating and alcohol consumption, Graham pointed toward "dietetic intemperance and lewdness" as the primary causes of the spread of cholera.[52] Only by adhering to natural laws—a flesh- and alcohol-free diet; cold, pure water; frequent bathing; exercise; and fresh air—could one avoid contracting the disease.[53] Graham pointed further toward emotional strength as a weapon in the fight against choleric agents. Fear of the disease weakened the body's constitution, making it

A

LECTURE

ON

EPIDEMIC DISEASES GENERALLY,

AND PARTICULARLY

THE SPASMODIC CHOLERA,

DELIVERED IN THE CITY OF NEW YORK, MARCH, 1832, AND
REPEATED JUNE, 1832, AND IN ALBANY, JULY 4, 1832,
AND IN NEW YORK, JUNE, 1833.

WITH

AN APPENDIX,

CONTAINING

SEVERAL TESTIMONIALS, AND A REVIEW OF BEAUMONT'S
EXPERIMENTS ON THE GASTRIC JUICE.

New Edition, revised and enlarged.

BY SYLVESTER GRAHAM,

PUBLIC LECTURER ON THE SCIENCE OF HUMAN LIFE.

BOSTON:

PUBLISHED BY DAVID CAMBELL,
No. 9, Washington Street.
1838.

Title page of Sylvester Graham's
A Lecture on Epidemic Diseases
Generally, and Particularly the
Spasmodic Cholera *(1838). Courtesy
of U.S. National Library of Medicine
Digital Repository Project.*

more apt to overtax itself.[54] Only through strength of mind, body, and soul could individuals avoid the importation of impurities. Through a vegetable diet and mastery over the laws of nature, Graham argued, individuals could avoid the perils of illness.

Graham's medical advice was not limited to the disease itself; he decried the efforts of medical practitioners who had created "medicines which are more to be dreaded than any pestilential cause of cholera." Doctors and druggists caused an "arsenal of self-destruction," leading patients to "vomit out the lava of death."[55] Graham's attack on the medical establishment's response to the epidemic was legitimate; increased vomiting caused by purgatives undoubtedly led to dehydration and increased death rates.[56]

The cholera lectures gained new converts to the cause of meatless living and garnered praise in some circles of the established medical profession. A group of physicians in Maine reported that "we entertain a high sense of our obligations to Mr. Graham for his Lectures on the Science of Human Life, in which the laws of the vital economy have been explained and elucidated by a great variety of original, striking and happy illustrations."[57] Similarly, John Bell—a Philadelphia medical doctor who later became a harsh critic of Grahamism—reported that Graham "speaks like a man who has earnestly and carefully examined his subject" while claiming to "known of no lecturer or writer out of the profession, who is, in the main, so well informed in physiology."[58]

A key component of Graham's meat-free diet was a reevaluation of the bread consumed by Americans to accompany nearly every meal. In the early nineteenth century most bread was baked at home and comprised of corn or rye meal.[59] However, as the decades progressed, cities grew, and men and women joined the industrial workforce, more and more Americans purchased their daily bread from a local baker. Produced in mass batches, this bread differed in composition, often whitened through the process of bolting, which removed the outer casing from grains and with it much of the nutritive value.

The bolting process often utilized chemicals such as chlorine in order to whiten grains. As a result, white bread was less expensive and in greater abundance, particularly with the spread of large farms into western New York and the Midwest that provided cheaper, abundant wheat.[60] The bread was also produced outside of the household. As Americans were shifting from producers to consumers, Sylvester Graham offered a critique of the increasing disconnect between individuals and their food sources.

With a heavy dose of nostalgic yearning, Graham hearkened back to "those blessed days of New England's prosperity and happiness when our good mothers used to make the family bread."[61] Bread baked at home, according to Graham, was crafted with care and control over its ingredients, while the wheat used to make bakers' white bread was inferior, aimed at maximizing profits rather than dietary excellence. These principles led to the development of what became known as Graham bread, "coarse wheaten bread" that was "the least removed from the natural state of food" and "best adapted to fulfill the laws of constitution and relation."[62]

Throughout his cholera lectures in 1832, Graham labeled bread as "the most important article of artificially prepared food used by civilized man" and warned of "the pernicious effects of superfine flour bread." Graham pointed to the greedy motives of bakers who "make bread and sell it for the profits of the business, and not for the sake of promoting your health."

When it came to bread and diet in general, individuals had a responsibility to regulate their own bodies by taking control over what was ingested. Graham's attacks on bread offered a harsh critique of the rise of industrial capitalism in the United States, warning against the profit-driven motives of bakers and farmers, looking to "extort from those acres the greatest amount of produce, with the least expense of tillage, and with little or no regard to the quality of that produce in relation to the physiological interests of man."[63]

Although Graham first advocated for wheat bread as a pulpit minister in New Jersey, broader audiences began to become aware of its existence as his activities gained attention. Frequently the coverage was negative. As early as July 1832, Atkinson's Casket—a humor magazine published in Philadelphia—mocked Graham bread as indigestible and hard enough to break a window.[64] However, the journal's use of the term *Graham bread* without a precise definition illustrates that the product was already known in some circles. One publication described Grahamites as appearing too thin and irrationally inflexible in their dietary ideals.[65] Another pleaded for the "speedy extinction of Grahamism," an event that "should be witnessed by every lover of mankind."[66] The *New York Mirror* labeled Grahamites as being filled with "humbug" and the system as filled with "absurdities[,] . . . perversion and folly."[67] One medical journal said Graham was "entirely out of his element" in discussing matters of health and driven by "pride and vanity."[68]

Other publications mocked the culinary choices of Grahamites. New York's *Morning Herald* described Grahamites as clinging to a "crusty morsel like half starved dogs, and prefer[ing] sawdust bread to fresh, superfine flour." The author stated that a bachelor friend was lonely not because of inherent personality flaws but rather because of "the awful catastrophe" known as Grahamism.[69] The *New England Review* described the "first Grahamite" as "the man who fed on husks until he lost all his flesh." The individual, however, reportedly soon found his way, and "was very glad to make public confession of his folly for the sake of a cut from the falled calf."[70] The *New York Review* was explicit in its rejection of a Grahamite, meatless diet, referring to it as "dietetic charlantanry."[71]

Not all attention was negative. In 1834, an advertisement for Graham bread appeared in *New-York as It Is*, a manual and guide to living in New York City. The guide pointed interested parties to Pierce and Luke, bakers who sold the bread at their bakery located at the intersection of Broadway and Leonard Street.[72] The first published recipe for Graham bread appeared in 1835, emphasizing the use of finely ground, pure wheat meal.[73] In that same

year the *Minnesota Farmers' Institute's Annual* reported on the differences between Graham and white bread, recommending "the use of some graham
bread in families of growing children," though warning that the bran in the
bread could be "irritating to a delicate digestive system."[74]

In 1835 Graham furthered his development of a unified theory of diet,
publishing *A Defence of the Graham System of Living*. Poor diet was endemic
in America, a result of the malevolent effects of "Luxury, soft enervating
Luxury," which had "lulled her victims into a fatal security" that would ultimately lead to self-destruction. Graham warned that the effects of a pernicious diet went further than just the individual. The nation itself was at risk
of becoming degraded by overindulgence and luxury that had "destroyed
our health, perverted our morals, debased our intellects, and, in its prevalence[,] . . . may foresee the downfall of a people, once famed for their
intelligence, their virtue, and their freedom."[75] American opulence created
moral and social ills, Graham argued, including "our diseases, our deformi-
ties, our poverty, and our slavery."[76]

The city brought forth "the noxious effects of impure air, sedentary habits, and unwholesome employments," all of which pulled individuals further from physical and mental health. The growing metropolises of antebellum America were filled with a variety of urban amusements that Graham
viewed as threatening vices. Saloons, brothels, and dining establishments
with their alcohol, sex for gratification, and overly taxing foods all provided
services that Graham warned against as causing moral and physical failure.[77] These distractions not only led individuals to falter but also ensured
that they would remain disconnected from their natural physical state.

Graham's attacks resonated in the rapidly developing industrial capitalist
society of the Northeast, which freed individuals from the rigors of farm life
yet at the same time destabilized the very social structures that had previously provided stability and comfort. The ascendance of the self-made man
was contrasted among concerned politicians with the foppish aristocrats
who purportedly composed the European ruling class, described by John
Adams in 1819 as "producing effeminacy, intoxication, extravagance, vice
and folly."[78] Free individuals had the opportunity and ability to create their
own identities and build their own lives; however, with this freedom came
the opportunity to fail as well as succeed.[79] The same stark choice, according to proto-vegetarians, applied to dietary practices, which could influence
and even dictate moral and physical well-being.

Animal foods were primarily to blame for personal vice, according to
Graham, causing "a coarseness and ferocity of disposition" that rendered

"the temper irritable and petulant; the passion of anger is either induced or strengthened by its use."[80] Meat consumption made humans no better than the violent members of the animal kingdom that fed on the flesh of other animals. This distinction helps explain Graham and his followers' lack of interest in animal welfare. Meatless dietary reform was predicated on the notion that humans had the ability and responsibility to use logic and analysis to make the best possible choices. Instinct and desire dictated the actions of lower animals rather than rationale and self-control. Evils such as poverty and slavery could only exist in a society where humanity exhibited animalistic qualities of cruelty and aggression.

With the success of Graham's lectures came a growing community of both devoted minions and frustrated critics. Detractors argued that Graham was antiscientific, a proud, vain, and demagogic speaker who offered exaggeration and blustery language rather than empirical proof.[81] To his followers, Graham was a prophet who gave practical advice for improved health, spirit, and intellect.

By the mid-1830s a distinct community was created by adherents to Graham's diet. Known as Grahamites, these individuals attempted to apply Graham's dietetic principles to everyday life. Many followers simply applied Graham's principles to their own kitchens, baking Graham bread, drinking cold water, and eating a vegetable diet, particularly in places like the South where few other Grahamites existed. Others—mainly urban and northeastern residents—crafted a Grahamite community through building and living in public institutions aimed at gaining converts and saving lost carnivores.[82] The boardinghouse, with its promises of room, board, and kinship, became the center of urban Grahamite living.

Asenath Nicholson—an abolitionist, writer, and former teacher—opened her first Graham boardinghouse in New York City at 118 Williams Street in 1835, following it up three years later with another home at 21 Beekman Street.[83] The so-called Temperance Boarding House offered Grahamites the basics of boardinghouse living—a place to sleep, three meals a day, and social interaction—with the added supplies necessary to live a Graham-endorsed life. A vegetable diet was offered; and breakfast, dinner, and supper were served in a communal dining area to encourage interaction among the faithful. Cold baths, hard mattresses, and Graham bread were mandated in order to encourage health, circulation, and proper digestion.[84]

Located in an area filled with reform organizations—the American Anti-Slavery Society's offices were down the block at 48 Beekman—Nicholson's temperance boardinghouse served as a meeting place for New

York's reform-minded citizens.[85] While dietetics may have been a central fixation of the home's residents, an all-encompassing attitude toward social reform prevailed. According to William Tyler, a professor of Latin and Greek at Amherst College and a resident of the Graham House on William Street, "the Boarders in this establishment are not only Grahamites but Garrisonites—not only reformers in diet, but radicalists in Politics. Such a knot of Abolitionists I never before fell in with."[86]

Most important, the boardinghouse ensured interaction between Grahamites, who shared experiences, meals, and ideologies. Grahamites were no longer content to share their dietary theories solely in lecture halls. Reformers also desired to live in communities of like-minded individuals within the urban landscape. The boardinghouse provided inhabitants meatless fare and the opportunity to discuss the important issues of the day—dietetics, slavery, suffrage, and temperance.

Sylvester Graham himself was not directly involved in the day-to-day operations of the boardinghouses he inspired. As much as Graham was responsible for the spreading of early proto-vegetarianism, practitioners morphed the ideology into a variety of life experiences. As Nicholson noted, while Graham served as an inspiration, his lectures and writings were merely "a starting point to be enlarged and improved as practice might suggest."[87] Graham's dietary principles served as the backbone for boardinghouse life; how these ideals were enacted depended on a variety of local forces including geography, economics, and demographics. Despite this disconnect, during the 1830s and 1840s proto-vegetarians were largely labeled Grahamites, by themselves and others, because of Graham's prominent public persona.

But why the need for Grahamite boardinghouses in cities rather than the private practice of a Grahamite lifestyle? Urban areas, stricken with perceived vice and degradation, were seen as both morally and physically dangerous by reformers. New York City, with its commercial sex districts and visible brothels, was seen as particularly threatening to young, middle-class men living on their own, renting rooms throughout the city.[88] One publication remarked on the Beekman Street home's demographics, finding it "truly surprising to see how many temporary sojourners in the city, from different parts of the country, take lodgings at the Graham House, in order to be accommodated with the plain mode of living they practise at home."[89]

Nicholson recognized the existence of these threats, believing that a Graham lifestyle provided moral clarity to her boarders and encouraged positive dietary habits by creating a small community of Grahamite practitioners.

Noting that "flesh-eating produces a moral obtuseness and irritableness of spirit," Nicholson offered Graham bread, fresh vegetables, and cold baths in order to produce a "firmness of nerve, and clearness of intellect" to better prepare her residents for the dangers of city life.[90] The proof of the diet's success, Nicholson pointed out, was in the level of health of the houses' residents, who exhibited "not a shadow of cholera . . . and the prevailing influenza, which has taken the lives of many." With a proper, natural diet and a little exercise and fresh air, boardinghouse residents were able to overcome any illnesses that might appear.[91]

All boardinghouses had house rules prescribing meal times, visitor policies, and cost.[92] Nicholson's Grahamite home was guided by a litany of regulations, thirteen principles of the natural life inspired by Graham and his lectures. Visitors agreed to abide by these rules in order to remain in good standing as residents of the boardinghouse. Democratic principles allowed for some amendment of the regulations, relying on boarder votes to change prescribed dinner and supper times.[93] Feather mattresses were banned, as Graham lectured that soft beds diminished "physiological powers."[94] Exercise was mandated for residents, either a thirty-to-sixty-minute walk or a slow horse ride, though guidelines encouraged residents to avoid "all violence and excess" in their efforts. Lastly, during a time when regular bathing was rare, residents were required to take a daily sponge bath and at least one full bath per week.[95]

Similar rules prevailed at Boston's first Grahamite boardinghouse, though without the flexibility of democratic decision making for meal times. The home opened at 23 Brattle Street near Harvard Square in April 1837.[96] The Boston Grahamite home was run by David Cambell, an abolitionist who in 1840 spread the gospel of Graham to reform-minded students at Oberlin College in Ohio. Students embraced the lifestyle, and the college briefly banned meat from all of its dining halls.[97] Boston's Grahamite boardinghouse purportedly drew a mixed crowd as well, ranging from "the most laborious to the most sedentary," and from the permanent to the "transient or occasional." The home reported housing between twenty and thirty permanent boarders at a time, consistently throughout the year. Advocates for the Boston house emphasized that it sought to draw healthy, vigorous individuals already acclimated to the Graham diet, rather than "invalids" who were "pale and sickly." Homes that drew unhealthy boarders had another name, one that Grahamites wanted to avoid being connected with: hospitals.[98] Boston's Grahamite boardinghouse was also utilized as a meeting place for dietary and social reformers.[99]

Animal flesh was barred from the New York Grahamite home, as were other poisons such as caffeine and alcohol. Toasted, stale Graham bread brewed with water was offered to those who craved a cup of morning coffee.[100] The simple meals furnished centered on vegetables and whole grains. Breakfast consisted of the omnipresent Graham bread, along with a variety of fresh fruits, including apples, peaches, cherries, and strawberries.

Interestingly, eggs *were* allowed at the breakfast table, and were even considered an important component of Grahamite diets, despite being animal-based. Eggs were not directly connected to death or suffering. As a result, Grahamites found them to be acceptable for consumption. Dinner—served in the afternoon and the largest meal of the day—consisted primarily of hominy, rice, porridge, and a variety of seasonal vegetables including beets, potatoes, carrots, turnips, and squash. Supper was a simpler, lighter meal and included Graham bread, milk, oatmeal, hominy, barley gruel, or mashed cornmeal.[101]

Grahamites represented a cross-section of moral and scientific reformers in the United States. The group's message eventually reached as far as the South and West, as evidenced by letters and articles that appeared in group's publication, the *Graham Journal of Health and Longevity*.[102] Grahamism, however, was most organized and popular in the Northeast, where Grahamite boardinghouses proliferated.

The houses drew a mix of urban middle-class reformers. Similar to abolitionists of the period, Grahamites were primarily skilled artisans or trade workers, including housewrights, piano makers, grocers, merchants, bookbinders, and cabinetmakers.[103] These were individuals with respectable occupations, and the boardinghouses provided structure and moral guidance. Residents were often interested in the total reform ideology associated with Grahamism. The boardinghouse on Beekman Street, for example, housed at various times such well-known New York reformers as *New York Tribune* editor Horace Greeley, pacifist Henry Clarke Wright, abolitionists Lewis Tappan and Theodore Weld, and future president of the American Anti-Slavery Society Arthur Tappan. Transcendentalist author Ralph Waldo Emerson—though not a Grahamite—did visit once to dine with Greeley and utopian socialist Albert Brisbane in March 1842.[104]

So not all reformers who entered the homes were Grahamites or longer-term residents. Visitors frequently arrived to discuss reform issues while dining based on the principles of the boardinghouse. These short-term guests illustrate the larger connections between Grahamism and other social reform movements. The Grahamite boardinghouse at 63 Barclay Street in

Manhattan—opened in 1840 by abolitionist Roswell Goss—was visited by a variety of reformers and even housed William Lloyd Garrison during his trip to New York in the summer of 1846.[105] Garrison himself had a high opinion of Graham, once stating, "I admire his firmness, his courage, and his manifest desire to bless mankind." While Garrison said that "comparatively few have been found disposed to adopt [Graham's] dietetic theory, in all its minutiae," he also believed that "tens of thousands of persons have been happily affected by his lectures and writings, and saved from the direful effects of a vitiated appetite."[106] In the fall of 1851, influential African American Christian religious leader Daniel Payne visited Nicholson's boardinghouse, where he met with Theodore Weld and Lewis Tappan to discuss the antislavery movement. Payne described Asenath Nicholson as "a devout Christian, in deep sympathy with every movement leading to the amelioration of the condition of the colored people and to the uplifting of humanity in general."[107]

The Graham house on Barclay Street in New York advertised itself as perfect for "gentlemen visiting New York, either transiently or for a considerable time who have no partiality for an atmosphere reeking with the fumes of alcohol and tobacco." The home was "near the centre of business, and within a few minutes' walk of all the Steamboat Landings," suggesting that the owners sought to draw members of New York's trade class. The home was described as "spacious, and commodious," promising potential boarders that the "fare, though vegetable," was "found acceptable and embracing every variety desired by the undepraved appetite."[108] While the house was founded on the basis of temperate living, boarders were assured that a meatless lifestyle did not need to be bereft of flavor and enjoyment. Much like Asenath Nicholson, Goss wanted his boardinghouse to be a location of moral control and guidance for the young urban men tempted by the city's distractions.

Grahamite boardinghouses—like other urban boardinghouses—allowed residents to create a sense of home in the face of an unfamiliar, often chaotic urban environment. However, they had the added appeal of functioning based on the principles of Grahamism while connecting residents who had common interests in social reform. The boardinghouse—unlike private dwellings—connected living spaces to the growing market economy, a business arrangement in and of itself. This was only more pronounced in the case of the Grahamite homes, where proprietors not only provided meals, laundry, and domestic help but all of the qualities of a Grahamite lifestyle—the food, cold baths, and hard mattresses.[109]

Boardinghouses also had to walk a thin line between their Grahamism and a desire for respectability. The structure of the homes, bringing together single white-collar males and single working women, transient individuals and recently wed couples, raised the eyebrows of moral reformers who emphasized the necessity of the single-family home. Grahamism was often met with skepticism, including accusations of "wild fanaticism" and "knavery" that seduced individuals through "spiritual charlatanry."[110] To counter such attacks, Grahamite boardinghouses emphasized that a meat-free life created healthy, industrious residents who were productive, respectable members of society.

The Grahamite doctrine appealed to both men and women, reflecting Graham's methodology of lecturing to both sexes on the benefits of his dietary system. Women, in fact, were vital to the growth of the Grahamite ideology and movement. Part of Grahamism's popularity was the public nature of its appeal to women. This was also a primary reason why it met frequent protest.

During Graham's lecture tours of the Northeast, he often spoke in front of all-female audiences, what he advertised as "lectures to mothers." Graham's lectures often touched on taboo topics in public; even if he was condemning the immorality of masturbation, he was still speaking about it to large, all-female audiences. These lectures were often met by male protests and riots, accusing Graham of being a "mass seducer" of women, despite the distinctly antisexual nature of his screeds.

Women ignored these protests and continued to attend Graham's lectures, a means of asserting their independence and dedication to reform.[111] The nature of Graham's lectures and the audiences exposed masculine fears of women empowered by knowledge of their own bodies. Grahamite publications included testimonials from both women and men, and prominent female reformers such as Mary Gove Nichols, Abbey Kelly Foster, and Angelina Grimké advocated for the Grahamite lifestyle. Asenath Nicholson's Grahamite boardinghouses attracted both men and women—one of these homes, in fact, was populated by more women than men, according to the 1840 U. S. census.[112]

In a society where logistical or economic motives often guided individuals' dietary choices, Grahamites decided what to eat and what not to eat based strictly on ideological convictions, in the process diminishing the number of edible foods. A common narrative thread bound together the Grahamite lifestyle, helping the new group unite diverse experiences and recruit new practitioners. The success of Graham's lectures on cholera earned him a strong following of dedicated reformers who were convinced that his diet had saved their lives, particularly as cholera continued to be a seasonal threat.

Just as Graham claimed that the benefit of a vegetable diet was scientifically observable, his new followers attested to the natural life's ability to ward off disease. These stories—often similar to Graham's own account of his moral and physical ascension—presented common narratives of the evolution from darkness to light, all thanks to a meatless diet. They used language similar to that of the conversion narratives of born-again evangelicals swept up in the period's Second Great Awakening.[113] The difference was that the Grahamites' conversions occurred at the table, rather than at a revival meeting or church.

These narratives outlined a timeline of sickness, transformation, and finally conversion that led the individual to advocate for a Grahamite diet. Nicholas Van Heyniger, a promoter of Grahamism, explained: "For some time previous to my adopting your plan of living, my health was a good deal impaired; and I was afflicted with many bodily pains; and particularly troubled with impaired sight." Conversion stories connected a wide variety of physical maladies with meat consumption, while a meat-free diet was claimed to produce instantaneous improvements. Van Heyniger adopted a Graham diet and reported that his "bodily pains are gone, and my sight is perfectly restored, so that I can read all the evening without the least inconvenience."[114]

Asenath Nicholson presented her own conversion story, recounting that until age sixteen she consumed tea, coffee, meat, and alcohol to the extent that her "nerves became so completely unstrung that the sight of a book put me in an universal tremor."[115] After attending a Graham lecture Nicholson was overcome by an almost spiritual rapture. She wrote that she "heard and trembled: the torrent of truth poured upon me, effectually convinced my judgment, and made me a thorough convert." A regimen of fresh air, Graham bread, and vegetables cured Nicholson, making her "entirely exempt from pain or weakness." In the process, everything from her sleep to her singing voice improved. Nicholson believed her life was saved: "Nearly four years have passed, and not the slightest indisposition, except a trifling cold, has ever returned, to remind me I was mortal. Good bread, pure water, ripe fruit and vegetables are my meat and drink exclusively."[116]

Conversion narratives were often published in volumes of Graham's writings. In the closing pages of A *Defence of the Graham System of Living*, a series of testimonials from "respectable individuals" is offered, all following the pattern of the conversion narrative. Years of abuse and woe were followed by multiple visits to doctors who did little to alleviate their suffering. But the adoption of a Graham diet cured all ills. Lavinia Wright, a teacher in

New York's rough Bowery neighborhood, reported the end of "physical and mental lethargy" caused by "the injustice and cruelty of destroying animal existence" and "the injurious effects produced by the undue stimulation resulting from the use of animal food."[117]

Amos Pollard, a medical doctor, said that after living meatless for five years "my health is much better, and my strength far greater, than when I used a mixture of animal food." Pollard used his personal example to encourage the universal adoption of a vegetable diet to benefit all of mankind. William Goodell, an influential abolitionist, suffragist, and early temperance reformer, claimed a vegetable diet cured him from chronic diarrhea that no doctor ever alleviated. Goodell also said that his "wife is relieved from her headaches, my child from summer complaints, and all of us in a good degree, from nervous irritability."[118] An early conversion testimonial from December 13, 1834, came in the form of a letter that called for "a total abstinence from all artificial stimuli. . . . The general adoption of a vegetable diet would tend, in a remarkable degree to meliorate the condition of mankind, both physical and moral." Included in the group of thirty-one cosignatories was Horace Greeley, who that year met his wife Mary Chency while living in the Beekman Street Grahamite boardinghouse in New York City.[119]

While much changed about movement vegetarianism during the nineteenth and early twentieth centuries, one constant feature was the use of the conversion narrative in order to justify the diet. Conversion narratives simultaneously reached out for converts and created a sense of community among dietary reformers. The conversion narrative also reflected the dedication and self-righteousness felt by Grahamites, compelled to share their personal stories of change. Grahamites also faced external social forces that reinforced feelings of inferiority, forcing meat abstainers to justify their life choices in order to gain credibility and create self-confidence.

These competing forces of self-rectitude and external mockery pushed Grahamites to seek each other out, build communities, and formulate a common lifestyle around meat abstention. With boardinghouses in place in New York, Boston, and Philadelphia, Grahamites created supportive, localized communities.[120] It was the printed word, however, that expanded the community of Grahamites beyond the local and into a larger movement throughout the United States.

::::::

In April 1837, the first issue of the *Graham Journal of Health and Longevity* became available to the public.[121] The journal served as a catalyst for a significant shift in the development of proto-vegetarianism. The new journal promoted Sylvester Graham's diet as well as his writings, lecture tours, and other public appearances, helping to expand the diet's prominence and reputation. Graham regularly contributed to the journal, providing both new essays as well as excerpts from his previously published books and pamphlets. However, the journal—despite bearing the name of the movement's founder—was published independently of Sylvester Graham, who was not directly involved in its production. Thus while the *Graham Journal of Health and Longevity* helped further expose the masses to Sylvester Graham and his ideology, it also emphasized that the actions of individuals helped determine its success. The journal helped further develop a nationwide community that, for the time being, bore Graham's name. However, the journal relied on the work of other writers, editors, and reformers to accelerate the spread of meatless dietetics.

The publisher of the new journal was David Cambell, owner of the first Graham boardinghouse in Boston. The journal quickly spread its reach throughout the United States. During its first three months of publication, only thirty-eight local agents were listed as selling the *Graham Journal* in twelve states.[122] By October of the same year, 108 agents were selling the journal in fifteen states, as far west as St. Louis; south to Macon, Georgia; and throughout all of New England.[123] In 1839, its final year of publishing, New Jersey was added to this list of states, and the journal was sold by a total of 140 agents.[124]

The journal featured a wide variety of articles and followed a similar structure in each of its biweekly issues. It opened with a series of letters and endorsements, offering the familiar conversion narrative structure of redemption.[125] Nathaniel Perry of Boston, writing in the first issue, recollected that soon after marrying he "began to indulge in what is called by most people, good living," consisting of "roast and fried meats, of all kinds, and poultry with their rich gravies." Meat and alcohol led to a battle with rheumatism, constant headaches, canker sores, and tooth decay.

Perry hit bottom when a dyspeptic stomach left him unable to attend to his business dealings or even leave his house. After hearing Graham lecture in Boston, Perry "became interested in the principles he taught; and finally adopted them in diet and regimen." The results were nearly immediate, Perry reported, with all maladies gone within a month. He slept soundly, and at fifty years of age could attest to "good health," "the keenest relish for my food," and an "elastic, energetic, untiring" ability to labor.[126] Both lay Grahamites and professional medical doctors wrote testimonials, attempting to lend populist and professional credibility to the cause.

In each issue Sylvester Graham himself was represented by an article, often a summary, excerpt, or reworking of themes and arguments made in lectures and published works on the science of human life or bread making.[127] The journal also included articles focused on anatomy and the inner workings of the human body as proof of the benefits of a meatless diet. Charts, figures, and drawings frequently accompanied these articles, attempting to make scientific arguments accessible to the average reader.

In a series of articles appearing in the journal, William Beaumont—a famed U. S. army surgeon—wrote on his observations of human digestion. Beaumont's research was based on firsthand observation of Alexis St. Martin, a patient who had been accidentally shot in the stomach. This wound caused a fistula, an observable hole in St. Martin's stomach leading to the digestive track. Beaumont placed various foods on a string in order to observe how food stuffs were broken down, leading to the observation that stomach acids helped digest food into various nutrients.[128] Beaumont's experiments illustrated that vegetables were easily broken down by stomach acid, in contrast to various meat products, which were "partly digested," observable proof of Grahamites' claims that meat was difficult to break down into digestible matter.[129]

Issues also included recipes, further linking Grahamites through common gastronomy. The recipes expanded the Grahamite diet beyond cold water and Graham bread, teaching meatless epicures how to properly prepare vegetables, bake pies, and prepare grains.[130] By expanding the repertoire of meatless cookery, the Graham Journal ironically further shifted proto-vegetarianism away from Graham. The publication closed with an advertising section, offering information on where to buy the journal and find Grahamite boardinghouses, literature, and dietary products.[131]

Health advocates frequently wrote letters to the journal, though not always in support of meatless dietetics. One concerned reformer wrote with the desire to express a few "hasty remarks" regarding the journal's advocacy for a vegetable diet. Not all advocates of dietary reform were followers of Graham, he argued. While admitting that Graham's diet had beneficial effects, the writer said he would call "no man master" and was writing to the journal to "protest against the common notion that the efforts of the advocates of physiological reform are designed solely or mainly to bring about the disuse of animal food." The writer believed that "there are far worse articles of food in common use than healthy flesh-meat. . . . A man may be a pure vegetable liver, and yet his diet be far less favorable to health than a diet of animal food might be." The letter concluded with a call for further scientific study into the effects of all dietary practices, stating that "we do not aim at dietetic reform solely—we advocate physiological reform."[132] The anonymous writer raised an important question for those interested in dietary reform to consider: Should the movement focus on a dogmatic dedication to a meatless diet or advocate for scientific study to continually redefine the most beneficial diet?

The fate of the journal at the end of 1839 seems to have offered an answer to the lingering question over the aims of dietary reformers, indicating that total dietary reform had become preferable to Grahamism. After three years of weekly publication, the *Graham Journal of Health and Longevity* ceased production, with its last issue dated December 14, 1839. The journal had originally planned to release a fourth edition, promising potential subscribers seven free issues for the remainder of 1839 when opening a new account for the coming year.[133] This enticement to subscribe seems to indicate significant financial difficulty for Cambell and the journal.

In the October 12 issue, the journal announced a merger with the *Library of Health*, edited by William Alcott, second cousin of the young Louisa May Alcott.[134] The *Library of Health* began publishing in 1837, the same year as the *Graham Journal*, and offered similar articles focusing on physiology, temperance, and a natural diet, though without the shadow of a singular, dominant, and emblematic leader to define the movement. Alcott himself was a regular contributor to the *Graham Journal* and a passionate advocate for a vegetable diet. However, he was also an experienced medical doctor, symbolically indicating a shift in meatless dietetics toward part of total dietary reform rather than a goal unto itself. Given the synergies between the two journals and the apparent financial difficulties Cambell faced, the merger was unavoidable. The effort to detaching the meat-free diet from Graham's shadow had begun. In the process a new movement began to emerge, one indebted to Graham for its birth but dependent on separation to continue to grow.

::::::

In twenty short years, meat abstention had moved from the domain of a small, localized religious movement focused on spiritual ascension to a growing community throughout the United States attached to the scientific and moral reform principles of Sylvester Graham. Originally the realm of the Bible Christian Church, meatless dietary reform evolved into an all-encompassing ideology that sought to negotiate the challenges and tensions inherent in a rapidly modernizing industrial and urban environment.

However, both groups were interested in the total reform possibilities connected to abstaining from meat.

By the 1830s, Grahamism became the most recognized lifestyle attached to meat abstention in the United States, eliciting praise from its adherents and harsh criticism from its opponents. Dietary reformers opened Grahamite boardinghouses in urban areas to serve as moral guardians while creating a larger community of interconnected dietary reformers. The printed word, meanwhile, supported the continued growth of this new community, conjoining Grahamites from disparate geographic regions while providing a forum to offer scientific proof of the diet's success. The group's existence, however, would be relatively short-lived. But as Graham's failing health pushed him into quasi-retirement, his community of meat-abstaining followers did not disappear. Rather, they continued to grow and reinvent themselves.

CHAPTER TWO

Transitional Years

::

Some also go farther, and seem to suppose us pledged . . .
to sustain the views taught by Mr. Graham. Now let it be distinctly
understood, once for all, that in this work we have nothing to do,
either directly or indirectly, with Mr. G. or his doctrines.
—Library of Health, 1837

In a January 1841 editorial focusing on the United States' growing population of meat abstainers, the article's author reflected on the current state of meatless dietetics in the United States. The writer proclaimed that "if the public choose to call us . . . Grahamites . . . we care very little. . . . Those to whom we may have the happiness to do a little good . . . will not care to inquire whether we bow at the shrine of any leader, ancient or modern."[1] The article was featured in the physiological journal *Library of Health*, which by the turn of the 1840s had supplanted the *Graham Journal of Health and Longevity* as the main published voice of meatless dietetics. At the risk of alienating its newly acquired readership, *Library of Health* touted the notion of individuals' choices and scientific study, rather than the works of a single individual.

As 1840 began, American meatless dietary reform had grown from a small group of renegade church members in Philadelphia to a full-fledged, recognizable movement that spread across geographic boundaries, connected by the common bond of Sylvester Graham's teachings. But now that a visible community of meatless dietary reformers had formed, a question remained: How would this group continue to grow? Public lectures and the printed word had served proto-vegetarians well, yet these methods were also limited, since they emphasized the growth of group leaders' popularity while leaving practitioners around the country somewhat disconnected. Through the 1840s a variety of reformers experimented with the social and political reform possibilities connected to abstention from meat. While these reformers remained somewhat fractured through the decade, by its end a variety of groups began to coalesce and become a single movement.

During this transitional period, reformers further developed their principles, fusing the realms of health and science with dietary and social reform. In order to continue growing they needed a centralized voice to unify the spectrum of dietary reformers. With the *Graham Journal of Health and Longevity* ending publication in December 1839, William Alcott's *Library of Health* filled the void. Other attempts, including a utopian experiment at Fruitlands and the use of water cure, linked dietary choice directly with social reform, expanding the motivations for adherence to a meatless diet.

The process of disconnecting proto-vegetarianism from Grahamism began, ironically, during the height of Graham's popularity. The interest that Graham sparked in dietetics and personal scientific and health study led to the establishment of other, more broad-based organizations. The American Physiological Society (APS) was a Boston-based group founded in 1837. Practitioners of a Graham diet began the society by integrating a Grahamite lifestyle into a larger physiologically focused ideology. The APS's constitution reflected this desire, welcoming those interested in learning about the "influence of temperature, air, cleanliness, exercise, sleep, food, drink, medicine, &c., on human health and longevity."[2] The organization sought to democratize the study of health, making this knowledge accessible to "every citizen," since it was "the duty of every person, of good sense, to make [health] a subject of daily study."[3] Unaffiliated with any particular religious group or leader, the APS also moved meat abstention away from religious, doctrinal structures and placed dietary reform firmly within the realm of scientific study.

The APS sought to empower its members by diffusing "a knowledge of the laws of life, and of the means of promoting human health and longevity."[4] In this sense the APS's goals were similar to Graham's. However, through its organizational-based structure, the APS formed a body that emphasized the collective work of its membership rather than the deeds and words of a leader. The organization met on the first Wednesday of each month and held a larger annual gathering each May. All members in attendance at the annual meeting voted for organizational officers.[5]

The APS at its founding had 206 members; nearly 40 percent were women.[6] The group's membership grew to 251 by 1838, though the organization estimated that closer to 400 individuals (including the family members of APS members) followed its dietary recommendations.[7] The large presence of women in the APS, while challenging some existing social structures in terms of promoting scientific knowledge, also reflected predominant notions of food and family. Women were, after all, most often in charge of crafting family diets.[8] The APS thus also included a Ladies Physiological Society, which met separately from the larger group throughout the organization's three-year existence. The group organized public lectures and met regularly to discuss meatless living, building a small community of like-minded reformers who wrestled with the most practical ways to live a reform lifestyle.

Members of the APS lectured against the effects of flesh foods, which caused "the most horrid, blasphemous thoughts" among its consumers.[9] However, the APS was careful to not appear doctrinal in its beliefs, guided by scientific study rather than adherence to a preconceived philosophy. The organization urged members to pay "strict attention to the importance of air, temperature, clothing . . . and a thousand other things besides diet and drink." However, "as to imposing on the world any system, even the 'Graham System,' excellent as we believe that to be[,] . . . we have never intended it."[10] The APS and its members largely believed in the efficacy of Grahamism, but they also believed in the need to free meatless dietary reform from the shadow of Sylvester Graham.

William Alcott was one of the founding and leading members of the APS and lent credibility to the growth of the meatless cause. He began advocating for a vegetable diet by the early 1830s, the heyday of Grahamism. Unlike Graham, however, Alcott was a formally trained physician, graduating from Yale University in 1836.[11] He began publishing a series of treatises attacking such vices as alcohol, tobacco, and sexual intemperance.[12] Alcott's advocacy of a meatless diet gained mass exposure for the first time in a letter supporting the Graham system, which he published in the *Boston Medical and Surgical Journal* in May 1836.[13]

A war of words had broken out in the journal between Sylvester Graham and Thomas Lee, superintendent of the McLean Asylum in Charlestown, Massachusetts. Lee claimed that Grahamism was "destructive in its operation," a cause of insanity and "emasculation." Graham, charged Lee, was "an intolerable impostor." Further, Lee claimed, Graham believed that it would be better for a patient to starve to death rather than dine on flesh foods.[14] Graham, in response, defended himself and his dietary system, accusing Lee of being driven by "a morbidly excited imagination" and producing a "most dangerous article to be thrown before the public." Graham concluded that Lee was threatened by new ideas, part of a medical establishment apt to treat its patients with "flesh, wine and opium."[15]

A month later, William Alcott entered the fray. Writing to the journal in defense of the Graham system, Alcott emphasized his own credentials as a trained medical professional. Alcott claimed that doctors like Lee were driven by "prejudice" and "supposed facts." Medical doctors were usually reasonable and rational. When it came to the Graham system, however, established medicine was "exceedingly lame" in its observations. Alcott argued that millions of laborers worldwide—particularly in northern Europe—had subsisted on vegetable diets for years and did not go insane. The letter closed with Alcott's own conversion story, claiming to have "abstained suddenly, about six years ago, from animal food, and from all fermented, narcotic, and alcoholic drinks; and have confined myself, to this hour, to vegetable food and water." The results were immediately observable to himself and those around him, causing "great gain" in mind and body. Alcott ended his missive by asking the public at large to judge whether or not he—a medical doctor, after all—was in the throes of insanity.[16]

This debate illustrated a larger change for proto-vegetarianism as the movement began shifting. Graham and his followers were harsh critics of doctors and established medical science. However, in the late 1830s food reformers began emphasizing meatless fare's legitimacy based on the scientific principles of physiology. Proto-vegetarians during this period defined themselves by proclaiming their medical expertise rather than their perspectives as outsiders. Organizations such as the American Physiological Society used medical credentials to support their controversial calls for dietary reform.

The closing of the *Graham Journal of Health and Longevity* at the end of 1839 enabled Alcott's *Library of Health* to emerge as the new public voice of meat abstention in the United States. Although not an official voice of the APS, *Library of Health* frequently reported on its activities. Originally published in 1837, Alcott's journal was similar to the *Graham Journal* in structure. However, *Library of Health* touted its writers' credentials as medical experts, advocating a vegetable diet as one component of healthy living. The journal hoped to take advantage of Alcott's medical pedigree, assuring readers that "we began the following volume with the full intention of striking a heavy blow at quackery. . . . Quackery is not confined to the venders of nostrums, nor to any one class of citizens; it is rife everywhere." *Library of Health* sought to distance itself from the claims of pseudo-science and religious heresy that traditionally followed meat abstainers, arguing that dietary reform "is indeed nothing less than the application of Christianity to the physical condition and wants of man."[17]

THE

LIBRARY OF HEALTH,

AND

Teacher on the Human Constitution.

WM. A. ALCOTT, EDITOR.

VOL. III.

BOSTON:
GEORGE W. LIGHT, 1 CORNHILL.
1837.

Title page of William Alcott's Library
of Health (1837).

Library of Health featured medical experts in its defense of a meat-free diet, further differentiating itself from the Grahamites' more personal notion of medical care, a view that attacked mainstream medical practitioners. Amariah Bringham, superintendent of the Retreat for the Insane in Hartford, Connecticut, argued that flesh foods caused "an inflammatory fever of an unusual character for children" and that "infants who are accustomed to eat much animal food become robust, but at the same time passionate, violent and brutal."[18] Alcott noted the efforts of one medical doctor who opposed the use of emetics to induce vomiting. The doctor's opinion was reached through years of observation, viewing irritated, expanded stomachs that suffered from poor digestion for years afterward.[19]

Reuben Mussey, a medical doctor, dietary and health reformer, and future president of the American Medical Association, frequently contributed to the journal. Mussey was regarded for his work exposing the poisonous

VEGETABLE DIET:

AS SANCTIONED BY

MEDICAL MEN,

AND BY

EXPERIENCE IN ALL AGES.

BY

WILLIAM A. ALCOTT,

Author of the " Young Wife," the " House I Live in," &c. &c., and Editor of the "Library of Health," and the "Annals of Education."

―――――――

BOSTON:
MARSH, CAPEN & LYON.
1838.

Title page of William Alcott's
Vegetable Diet: As Sanctioned by
Medical Men *(1838). Courtesy of*
U.S. National Library of Medicine
Digital Repository Project.

nature of tobacco, which he claimed caused dizziness, stomach pain, and swollen feet.[20] Another medical expert reported that hot drinks and foods made individuals more apt to catch a cold because extreme temperatures acted as a stimulant on the body.[21] Alcott emphasized scientific credentials in appealing to the masses, subtitling a treatise on the merits of a vegetable diet "As Sanctioned by Medical Men."[22]

Library of Health warned against the perils of dietary intemperance in all its forms. Poisoned cheese was widely available in the marketplace; an article claimed that small amounts of arsenic were used to tenderize curds, an assertion similar to Graham's criticisms of the bread making industry.[23] Late, heavy suppers were described as being "prejudicial to health," leading to digestive problems and poor sleep.[24] Condiments and sweets were condemned, as were complex, diversified diets; simplicity was far more advantageous and less stimulating.[25] These criticisms were similar to Graham's but were expressed through the language of medical expertise. Through 1839, the journal dealt with dietary issues in a generalized manner, rather than advocating the specific advantages of a meatless diet.

The *Graham Journal*, in contrast, focused on dietetics as a vehicle *for* healthy living rather than as a product *of* a better lifestyle. At the center of the Grahamite journal was a structured reform regimen that hinged on avoiding meat. With the absorption of the *Graham Journal*, *Library of Health* shifted from a generalized physiological journal to one focused on meatless dietary reform. *Library of Health* supported the continued growth of a meatless, proto-vegetarian community, in the process pushing meat abstention further away from the sole terrain of Grahamites.

The new focus on meat abstention was quickly and readily apparent by 1840. The year's first issue advocated for the use of a vegetable diet for children. The article opened with a conversion story, relaying the life of "J. B.," a three-year-old boy afflicted with large scabs all over his face. With the adoption of a vegetable diet, the author wrote, "a great change was manifest in the appearance of the child," and the scabs "entirely disappeared." The long-term benefits of dietary change were even more impressive, as the child seemed "to have known nothing about sickness or pain" since adopting the meat-free diet. This development was all the more remarkable given that J. B. had been "living, for the last year, in a region of the West, where, for months, almost all others were sick and dying." The child enjoyed better teeth, smoother skin, and a general increase in mental capabilities.[26]

In another article, the author tackled the difficulties faced in challenging meat culture and the lack of thought average Americans gave to their dietary choices. The writer argued that the majority of the population believed "that flesh-meat is not only the kind of food on which they were intended principally to subsist, but . . . it is indispensably necessary to preserve their strength, and to enable them to perform their various avocations in life." In order to gain converts it was essential to impress on the public that a "vegetable diet . . . by its mild but nutritive qualities, keeps the circulation in the human system regular and cool." The legacy of the need to keep the humoral body in balance was clearly still apparent. When properly executed, a meatless diet prepared the body to "become an appropriate temple of the mind, and leads man to a more perfect mode of being."[27] Throughout 1840 the journal increased its coverage of dietary issues, even reprinting William Beaumont's digestive experiments that had appeared in the *Graham Journal of*

Health and Longevity.[28] *Library of Health* made the connection between dietary choice and scientific discovery explicit.

By the middle of 1840, *Library of Health* started featuring vegetable diet stories at the beginning of each issue, proof that the publication's conversion to a natural dietetic journal was complete. The first volume of the year featured an article titled "Nutritive Properties of Various Kinds of Food," where vegetables, grains, and fruits were presented as easily digestible and nutritious, whereas meat was difficult to assimilate into the bloodstream and thus of little dietary value. Of the fifty most nutritive food products listed, forty were vegetables, grains, or fruits.[29] By including flesh foods on the list—though farther down in the rankings—the journal hoped to illustrate its scientific accuracy and rigor, advocating for a vegetable diet through study and observation.

The same issue advocated for the use of vegetable foods to ensure productive work, relaying the story of a young laborer who gained mental and physical strength from his dietary change. With the new meatless diet, the article claimed, it was possible to work "on an average, twelve hours a day at hard labor." Physical labor had previously made the worker unable to "relish for close study" because his "mind would shrink from it." However, with the support of a meatless diet, the young man reported becoming "perfectly calm, my mind clear, and delighted with close study and patient thought." Dietary conversion made him not only a better worker but also a sharper, more complete citizen, a model of the republican self-made man.[30]

Library of Health began seeking to distance natural dietetics from its most renowned advocate as Sylvester Graham intensified his public crusade against the physical and moral threats of masturbation. As early as 1840, *Library of Health* reported on the activities of one dietary reformer who had "the fear of being called a Grahamite," which had become "a species of phobia . . . exceedingly prevalent" among reformers.[31]

Even on the issue of bread, an area where Graham was previously sacrosanct among proto-vegetarians, the journal distanced itself, saying that while "an excellent Manual on bread has been prepared by Mr. Graham[,] . . . much remains to be said, as we believe—and to purpose—on the same subject." The article's author advised readers to utilize "simple coarse bread" because it "acts best on the stomach and alimentary canal, especially if it must be received hot." This marked a departure from Graham's theory of bread making, which instructed that bread should sit for at least twenty-four hours before consumption.[32]

By 1841, Sylvester Graham, suffering from ill health and family hardships, had essentially retired from his demanding public speaking schedule. A southern subscriber wrote *Library of Health* for an update on Graham's health—the response provides insight into the distance from Graham of a new generation of proto-vegetarian reformers. The journal responded to the inquiry by saying that "Mr. Graham is better in health—fighting on, though not without a good deal of complaining." Positioning Graham as a martyr of hard work and difficult odds, the journal reported that "goaded, however, as he constantly is, almost to madness, it is not strange, perhaps, that he should complain. . . . Those who know his trials will not render him evil, but contrarywise, blessing."[33] The journal's response to the letter foreshadowed the controversy and difficulties faced by vegetarians on Graham's death a decade later.

With reformers pushing meat abstention away from the sole domain of Graham, opportunities opened for other movements to formulate. Fruit—often ignored by Grahamites in deference to vegetables and grains—was a particular focus of *Library of Health*. The journal advised readers on how to properly choose ripe fruit, emphasizing the need to leave it uncooked and in its natural state. Cooked fruits were attacked from a distinctly class-driven prism, enjoyed by "fashionable society," smothered in molasses and sugar. The wealthy, it was implied, were most out of touch with the natural state of the body, too distracted by material goods and the trappings of polite society.[34]

The collapse of the *Graham Journal* and the lessening of Graham's role in dietetic reform provided opportunities to redefine meatless living.[35] While William Alcott's *Library of Health* was the first step in this separation, another member of the Alcott clan challenged the established dynamics of the American meatless dietary reform community. Bronson Alcott may best be known as the father of Louisa May, but during the height of his intellectual activities he was an active member of both the transcendental and the dietary reform movements.

In 1843 Bronson Alcott led an experiment in utopian, communal, meatless living that expanded the possibilities of meatless dietary reform during a transitional period for proto-vegetarians. Unlike most previous reformers, Alcott looked outside the city as the perfect location to experiment with dietary reform. His Fruitlands community also took the important step of connecting meat abstention and dietary reform to a variety of sociopolitical ideals.

Bronson Alcott spent his teen years laboring in factories throughout New England. After a few years of selling books throughout the South, Alcott returned to New England to follow his preferred vocation of teaching. Years spent working and living in Boston and Philadelphia—along with his marriage to the reform-minded Abigail (Abba) May—had converted Alcott to a variety of radical reform causes, primarily Garrisonian abolitionism and education reform. In 1834 Alcott opened the Temple School in Boston, attempting to apply reform philosophies to education. Alcott's methods utilized self-analysis, questioning, and criticism rather than strict lecturing. The Temple School also rejected the methods of rote memorization and corporal punishment popular during the period.[36]

By 1836 Alcott was a member of the Transcendental Club and a close associate of Theodore Parker, Henry David Thoreau, and Ralph Waldo Emerson, the latter describing Alcott as "a wise man, simple, superior to display."[37] Throughout the early 1840s, Alcott served as a frequent contributor to the transcendental movement's journal The Dial. Writing in his column "Orphic Sayings," Alcott crafted a series of brief aphorisms, hoping to communicate the essence of the reform spirit. The mottos were met with disdain in some circles. The Knickerbocker magazine, for example, printed a satirical column titled "Gastric Sayings" that mocked Alcott's writings, while the Boston Post reported that the "Orphic Sayings" were "a train of fifteen railroad cars with one passenger."[38] Despite such derision, Alcott's dictums were short, digestible, yet complex snippets of philosophical musings on a variety of issues, including social reform, education, dietetics, and humanity's relationship with nature.[39]

While traveling through England in 1842, Alcott came in contact with Charles Lane and Henry C. Wright. The two educational reformers had recently opened an "Alcott School" just outside of London based on the Temple School's teaching methods. During this time Alcott, Lane, and Wright discussed the merits of utopian communalism and its relationship with dietetics. Alcott had converted to a Graham diet in 1835 but was interested in connecting further the political possibilities of meatless living and social reform. Lane and Alcott decided that the only way to enact principles of gender, labor, and racial equality was through a self-sufficient, agricultural lifestyle. The two formulated plans for a settlement in Massachusetts that would work to subvert a variety of tools of social oppression, including taxation, individual land-ownership, slave-produced goods, alcohol, money, and meat.[40]

The group hatched a plan for the development of Fruitlands, a utopian, socialist experiment in meatless living. Alcott described the community to Emerson as being "commenced by united individuals, who are desirous, under industrial and progressive education, with simplicity in diet, dress, lodging . . . to retain the means for the harmonic development of their physical, intellectual, and moral natures."[41] Lane purchased an eleven-acre farm in the Massachusetts countryside at Harvard, thirty miles northwest of Boston and twenty miles west of Concord, Alcott's previous home.

Alcott and Lane sought reform-minded followers for their new settlement, advertising in *The Dial* about the advantages of Fruitlands. The group promised that in the community "ordinary secular farming is not our object" but rather "purifying and edifying of the inmates." Diet would consist of "fruit, grain, pulse, herbs, flax, and other vegetable products," challenging Grahamite orthodoxy that avoided fruits and emphasized bread and cold water. Products such as tea, sugar, and molasses were banned since they were produced with slave labor. The Fruitlands ideals sprang from a belief in the power of personal choices and their communal benefits. Lane and Alcott believed that only through "personal reform" could larger social and political evils be eradicated.[42] Personal and localized reform had the dual benefits of creating a moral exemplum for others to follow while simultaneously implementing practical steps for change. Fruitlands' founders sought to build a model community based on these reform values, with the hope that others would emulate the settlement's way of life.

Unlike previous proto-vegetarians, the Fruitlands founders considered animal welfare central to dietary reform, and the community hoped "to supersede ultimately the labor of the plough and cattle, by the spade and the pruning-knife." Physical exertion would be equally matched with mental and spiritual gratification, as the settlement offered a "choice library . . . accessible to all who are desirous of perusing these records of piety and wisdom." According to its founders, the success of Fruitlands could be measured in its ability to provide "human freedom," away from the evils of slave labor and gender inequality. Residents at Fruitlands believed that dietary ignorance and intemperance contributed to social ills, either through acquiescence (by purchasing and consuming goods produced by oppression) or through the moral sickness caused by flesh foods.[43]

Life at Fruitlands began smoothly, as the forgiving summer months and bountiful supplies allowed residents to enjoy what Lane described as the "beautiful green landscape of fields and woods."[44] The group was small, including just eleven members besides Alcott, his wife, and children. Alcott and Lane initially worked the fields along with two local farmhands. Despite a shortage of farm labor, residents were pleased with the early results, thanks in large part to what Alcott described as "the most delightful weather you can conceive."[45]

The inhabitants dressed in tunics and pants made out of linen, part of the community's desire to avoid all animal products such as wool, as well as slave-produced materials like cotton. Animal labor was utilized initially to construct the community's buildings, a compromise begrudgingly made by Alcott out of pure necessity. The fields, however, were tilled only by humans, who avoided the use of manure as a fertilizer partly because it was animal-based but also because Alcott viewed it to be unsanitary and vulgar. Maize, potatoes, beans, melons, and squash were initially planted on the four-acre farm, with the hopes of abundant fruits and vegetables supplemented with rye, oats, and barley.[46]

Ralph Waldo Emerson visited the community in July 1843 and was impressed by the results. "The sun and the evening sky do not look calmer," he wrote, "than Alcott and his family at Fruitlands. They seem to have arrived at the fact—to have got rid of the show, and to be serene. . . . There is as much merit in beautiful manners as in hard work." Emerson, however, did offer a warning that proved prophetic: "I will not prejudge them successful. They look well in July; we will see them in December."[47]

Emerson's misgivings would eventually prove to be accurate, though the initial months in Fruitlands were somewhat encouraging. Early harvests provided sufficient food, while Lane taught the Alcott children reform principles in daily lectures that connected meat consumption with social ills. Short, lyrical adages reminded Louisa May and Anna Alcott that while a vegetable diet promised "sweet repose," animal foods were a "nightmare." Further, Lane explained in prose to the children, "without flesh diet, there could be no blood-shedding war."[48] Proto-vegetarians stretching as far back as the Bible Christians argued that meat—with its stimulating properties—caused individuals to be irrational and often violent. Lane and Alcott took this line of argumentation to its next step, believing that total abstention from meat could promote peaceful coexistence. Prominent reformers visited the settlement, including abolitionist Parker Pilsbury, who spoke to the children about the evils of slavery, and transcendentalist Theodore Parker, who would frequently stop at Fruitlands to meet with Lane and Alcott while walking home in the evening.[49]

A variety of factors led to the swift end of the experiment at Fruitlands. A lack of agricultural experience and resources among the residents guaranteed a weak long-term crop output; so did the amount of time spent in the library studying and reading. Lane and Alcott were more enchanted with philosophical discovery than the small matter of ensuring food for the coming winter season. Lane's jaunts to a nearby Shaker village along with

Alcott's long walks into cities to preach (including a hike to Providence, Rhode Island, in September at the precise time when crops were ready for harvest) did little to ensure the survival of Fruitlands.

By the end of the summer, despair already started to seep into the community. Abba Alcott's opinion of the settlement declined rapidly. She reported in June that her experience at Fruitlands was "all beautiful, the hills commanding one of the most expansive prospects in the country. . . . One is transported from his littleness, and the soul expands in such a region of sights and sounds." Just two months later, in August, she despondently wrote in her diary that "a woman may perform the most disinterested duties. She may 'die daily' in the cause of truth and righteousness. She lives neglected, and dies forgotten."[50] Abba's response reflected the multifaceted burdens falling onto her shoulders, including taking care of the children, providing meals for the whole settlement, and managing the fields while her husband was off lecturing.

Ideological differences, however, also helped hasten the end of the new Eden. Charles Lane—the owner of the land and a frequent financial benefactor of Bronson Alcott—had become infatuated with the Shaker lifestyle, advocating for similar principles of complete sexual abstinence and gender separation at Fruitlands. The Alcotts did not share Lane's enthusiasm for Shakerism. The philosophical split between Lane and the Alcotts, combined with the results of a harsh winter and weak crop harvest, ensured that the group would eventually abandon its experiment. By the start of January 1844, Lane and his son moved from Fruitlands to the adjacent Shaker Village. Just two weeks later on January 14, the Alcotts fled Fruitlands as well, soon after resettling at their old house in Concord.

One early scholar of the Fruitlands experiment noted that the ideological split between Lane and Alcott was a result of a direct conflict between Lane's utopian socialism and Alcott's individualism.[51] The split between the progenitors of the experiment, however, was not as black and white as it appeared. Questions concerning Alcott's individualism offer insight into the relationship between Fruitlands and proto-vegetarianism. While Charles Lane was a staunch meat abstainer, by the fall of 1843 he viewed control over sexuality as the key to social reform. In other words, Lane mirrored Graham's transition toward sexual reform over dietary reform. Alcott, in contrast, reflected the type of reform advocated in *Library of Health*, placing meat abstention as the catalyst for all other reform.

Alcott's Fruitlands experiment, however, placed political and social reform at the top of a growing list of the benefits of abstaining from meat, according to adherents. Alcott explained that he joined Fruitlands driven by a desire to "abstain from the fruits of oppression and blood," including meat and alcohol, creating "entire independence" from stimulants and their trappings.[52] Whereas previous proto-vegetarians denounced social ills such as slavery as being symptomatic of a corrupt society that would also venerate unhealthy flesh foods, Bronson Alcott pointed out that dietary intemperance could materially support the proliferation of social inequality. Through personal choices such as abstaining from meat, tea, sugar, and cotton, a concerned reformer could improve one's own health and morality while simultaneously protesting social injustice.

The style of reform practiced by proto-vegetarians in the 1840s was individualistic in the sense that it relied on personal choices for its success. The meat abstention advocated by reformers like Bronson and William Alcott and explained in the pages of *Library of Health*, however, was utopian in its goals of complete social and cultural reform. And though individualistic in its practices, proto-vegetarianism during this period was inherently collectivist in its attempts to build and foster a community of individuals practicing the same lifestyle choices. Reformers touted the power of individual choices as a way to create a better society. Proto-vegetarians also believed that their movement would only be a success if it the diet was practiced by a community of likeminded individuals. However, even if this was the founders' goal for Fruitlands, the experiment failed to live up to its lofty intentions in at least one fundamental aspect.

Louisa May Alcott would fictionalize the events at Fruitlands thirty years later in her "Transcendental Wild Oats" (1873). The book used pseudonyms for the community's residents. The serenely named Abel Lamb replaced Bronson Alcott, while Charles Lane became the far more menacing Timon Lion. The name changes reflected the general tone of Alcott's piece. Bronson Alcott is portrayed as a somewhat aloof idealist driven by pure motives, unwilling to stand up to the aggressive and domineering Lane.

In this sense, "Transcendental Wild Oats" reflected Louisa May's diary of events written while at Fruitlands, in which she revealed a deep dislike of Lane.[53] Alcott drew a further contrast between her father and Lane, describing Bronson Alcott in "Transcendental Wild Oats" as guided by the "devoutest faith in the high ideal," motivated by a desire to build a "Paradise, where Beauty, Virtue, Justice, and Love might live happily together."[54] She presented Lane, in contrast, as an uncompromising megalomaniac, driven by motives of "being, not doing."[55]

Louisa May Alcott's indictment of Lane as a thinker rather than a doer was accurate, though in many ways Bronson Alcott was guilty of the same offense at Fruitlands. Perhaps Alcott's presentation was clouded by loyalty to her father and based on her family's disappointment with Fruitlands. Lane—Louisa May's teacher while at the community—was more likely to remember as an autocrat. The recollections in "Transcendental Wild Oats" may be somewhat unreliable in the precision of their presentation of Bronson Alcott and Charles Lane. The account is, however, striking in its consideration of gender dynamics.

Abba Alcott—known as Sister Hope in the text—is accurately portrayed as having to bear the direct burden of Bronson Alcott's and Lane's ideological haughtiness. While Lane and Alcott occupied themselves by reading through the many volumes contained in the library and taking frequent trips away from the community to lecture, Abba was left to actually run the settlement. Sister Hope deals with "heavy washes," "the endless succession of batches of bread," and all of "the many tasks undone by the brethren, who were so busy discussing and defining great duties that they forgot to perform the small ones." In essence, Alcott points out, Abba replaced farm animals as the only "beast of burden" at Fruitlands.[56]

Given that the community was founded partly to alleviate the "servitudes of the dairy and the flesh pots" that reformers thought chained women to the kitchen, the reality of Fruitlands' gendered dynamics was a striking failure.[57] The founders of Fruitlands created their community as a means to create social harmony. However, a staunchly gendered division of labor existed between male thinkers and female workers.[58] At Fruitlands physical labor was the norm for adult women, while adult male lives centered on the purely mental. Although gender roles at Fruitlands differed from those in normative society, they were still inherently limited and fraught with inequality. As a result, Fruitlands betrayed the utopian ideology it set for itself in terms of utilizing diet and lifestyle as means to promote gender equality.

In "Transcendental Wild Oats," Louisa May Alcott writes that the community subsisted on a diet based on apples and cold water. The circumstances that led to Fruitlands' disbanding left Louisa May with sour memories of the experiment. Alcott recollected that her father and Charles Lane spent more time pontificating over the fate of farm animals than they did considering the well-being of the community's residents. In addition, Louisa May did not share her father's dedication to dietary reform, preferring meat as a child despite her father's warnings and eating meat as an adult.[59] While Alcott respected her father's high-minded dedication, she also witnessed the deleterious effects of his blind devotion to dietary reform on herself, her mother, and other family members while at Fruitlands. Alcott noted that while her father and Lane "said many wise things," they also "did many foolish ones." And while they "preached vegetarianism everywhere and resisted all temptations of the flesh," the dietary reformers at Fruitlands also spent much time "afflicting hospitable hostesses by denouncing their food and taking away their appetites, discussing the 'horrors of shambles.'"[60]

Alcott portrayed the dietary choices made by the residents of Fruitlands as driven by a desire to care for the world at large. Ultimately, however, dietary reform at Fruitlands ignored the most basic needs of those in the immediate community. Louisa May Alcott scathingly concluded that, "to live for one's principles, at all costs, is a dangerous speculation."[61]

Unlike Grahamites, who were most often young, single, urban men and women, the Fruitlands experiment was inhabited primarily by adults with children who counted on them for basic care, one component of which was food. Bronson Alcott imposed his dietary preferences on his family, allowing his ideology to interfere with his ability to best care for his children, while simultaneously burdening his wife with unending domestic responsibilities. For the children and Abba, a meatless diet was not a matter of self-denial, as they were given little voice in their dietary choices. Thus, as a reform principle, flesh-free living at Fruitlands—in addition to causing a significant amount of personal anguish—did little to alleviate many of the social ills that its founders sought to conquer.

Despite these difficulties, the role and symbolism of Fruitlands are considerable. While Fruitlands is conventionally labeled as an unmitigated disaster, the utopian experiment symbolized many of the challenges and contradictions at play among dietary reformers in the early 1840s. Fruitlands appeared at a moment when meatless reform was emerging from under the shadow of Sylvester Graham and Grahamism. Grahamites began to concentrate on perceived threats to sexual purity—and the larger threats implicit to the republic itself. By contrast, other proto-vegetarians expanded the scope and goals of meat-free living. The experiment at Fruitlands was one such attempt, guided by high-minded ideals but beset by logistical and ideological contradictions.

In addition, the settlement at Fruitlands expanded the larger political possibilities connected to dietary choice. While the American Physiological Society and William Alcott's *Library of Health* emphasized the moral and physical benefits of a meat-free diet, Bronson Alcott and Fruitlands connected dietary choice primarily to social and political reform. And while the settlement was filled with complications, contradictions, and social inequalities, the philosophy behind the experiment influenced the development of a strong political consciousness attached to meatless living in the years to come. Despite Fruitlands' ultimate failure, it planted the seeds for the further growth of a nationwide community of meat abstainers.

Other movements experimented with a meatless diet during this period of transition. Water cure (also known as hydrotherapy) connected a vegetable diet with the practice of water healing. Based on the teachings of Vincent Priessnitz, an Austrian naturopath, hydrotherapy caught on in the United States by 1845 with the establishment of the first water-cure institutions. Priessnitz himself, however, did not advocate for total meat abstention, instead advising his followers that a mixed diet of unsalted, spice-free meat and plain vegetables was most advantageous for health and an even temper.[62]

American water curists believed—much like Grahamites—that illness was a result of the body existing in unnatural states. Advocates believed that continuous dousing with water—internally and externally—along with wrapping in wet sheets for bed rest would lead the body to expel poisonous toxins caused by intemperance, immorality, and poor diet. Combining the teachings of Priessnitz and Graham, American water curists created a new and distinct health reform. In the United States, many water curists argued for the benefits of meat abstention. Mary Louise Shew and Joel Shew—founders of the first water-cure establishment in the United States—advised patients that "the best health of body and mind does not require the use of flesh meat at all." When "stimulants and flesh meat are avoided; immediately the health, strength and appetite improve." The Shews argued that "many kinds of vegetable, farinaceous food contain double the amount of nutriment, pound for pound, that average meat does."[63]

American hydrotherapists were influenced by and often themselves observed a Graham diet. But water cure during this period formed its own community of adherents, albeit one that also advocated for a meatless diet. While not all water-cure enthusiasts abstained from meat—perhaps a reflection of just how popular the treatment eventually became in mass culture—many of its practitioners believed that meat abstention was a key component to an overall healthy lifestyle.

In December 1845, Joel Shew began publishing his *Water-Cure Journal*. The journal's masthead neatly summarized the goals of water cure, exhorting its readers to "Wash and be Healed."[64] As early as the second issue of the journal, the benefits of a meatless diet were espoused with the story of a young woman who overcame lung disease thanks to a combination of water cure and a farinaceous diet. The journal pointed out that "the regulation of the diet had no small share of effect in her remarkable cure."[65] Though water curists were a distinct community, the use of Grahamite-style conversion narratives illustrates the continuing influence of Grahamism on dietary reform through the mid-1840s. Hydrotherapists emphasized the dual benefits of a vegetable diet, protecting individuals from the onset of disease and serving as an important component of treatment when they became ill.

The *Water-Cure Journal* offered a litany of examples of how hydrotherapy combined with a meatless diet cured a variety of ailments. An anonymous Boston woman reported suffering for years from the symptoms of red gravel, the discharge associated with the passing of kidney stones. Shortly after commencing regular cold baths and a "diet of fruit and vegetables" the woman passed "large quantities of red sand without pain." The water cure and dietary changes were successful; the woman overcame her illness and enjoyed good health thereafter.[66] In the case of a young man stricken with scrofula—a tuberculosis-caused infection on the neck—the journal stated that "diet has much to do in such cases." The *Water-Cure Journal* advised a gradual change in diet "until a strict vegetable and fruit regimen is observed," at which point daily water treatment should be administered.[67]

The journal advised readers on the benefits of farinaceous living and the nutritive value of whole grains. One article explained that "wheat, rye, corn, rice, buckwheat, potatoes, sage, tapioca, arrow-root . . . are in general more easy of digestion than animal food, and consequently cause a less expedition of the vital powers in the process of digestion."[68] Here the water curists exhibited both continuity and separation from Grahamism. The notion of overexertion of vital energy during digestion was a central theme in Graham's exhortations for simple bread and meat abstention. Yet Grahamites advised against a diversified diet, emphasizing instead the importance of simplicity and predictability. Hydropaths, in contrast, advocated for the strength -building properties and easy digestibility of a variety of fruits and vegetables.

By 1847, when *Library of Health* folded, the *Water-Cure Journal* was the most widely distributed publication advocating for meatless living in the United States. It began featuring articles on the benefits of a vegetable diet in its issues. By then, hydropaths had built twenty-one water-cure establishments in nine states, and by 1850 the journal claimed to have 25,000 subscribers.[69]

In September 1847, the journal presented the "Comparative Benefits of Vegetable and Animal Food," highlighting a series of testimonials from medical practitioners who had witnessed firsthand the advantages of dietary reform in promoting strength, mental clarity, and disease prevention.[70] William Alcott provided an article to the journal arguing in favor of a vegetable diet, using his own life as an example of the benefits of abstaining from meat. Alcott witnessed increased vigor along with the loss of his previously chronic rheumatism, attributing these changes to meatless living. These observable results led Alcott to faithfully remain a meat abstainer since making the shift in his late twenties.[71]

Groups such as the water curists and the physiologists expanded the ideology of meatless dietary reform. The efforts of these reformers suffused proto-vegetarianism with the connections between health, social, and political reform. Their movements remained fractured, however, inhibiting the creation of a unified, visible community of meat abstainers nationwide. Though proto-vegetarianism in its various incarnations had established itself in the hierarchy of American reform movements and distanced itself from a single demagogic leader, formalized organization was necessary if its ideals were to survive and grow. For inspiration dietary reformers looked abroad to England, where the increasing popularity of meatless dietetics led reformers to embrace a new term—*vegetarianism*.

::::::

By the middle of the nineteenth century, meatless dietary reform had grown to the point that varying movements competed for the attention of those interested in utilizing flesh-food abstention as a means for personal and political change. Water curists, physiologists, and Fruitlanders all saw their food choices as having the inherent power to transform themselves and society at large. As evidenced by the events at Fruitlands, however, even the seemingly best of intentions for social justice and reform were affected by prevailing social norms and attitudes.

Dietary reformers were still largely on society's fringes, viewed with equal parts skepticism, anger, and fear. While this may have made reformers uneasy in their relationship with mainstream society, it also ensured that individuals interested in advocating for meatless dietetics would seek each other out and eventually join forces. Bible Christians, Grahamites, physiologists, and water curists all proliferated during the 1830s, advocating for dietary reform based on the principles of fleshless foods. Transatlantic exchanges between American and British reformers developed the marketplace of ideas internationally and helped meatless reform continue to evolve.

The continuing growth of these various movements helped ensure that dietary reformers would rally under the singular banner of vegetarianism and the social and political power of food choices. The familiar faces of dietary reform—Sylvester Graham, William Alcott, and William Metcalfe—continued to be involved in the conjoining of a variety of movements working to champion meatless fare. However, with the establishment of a singular organization aimed at advocating for meat abstention, reformers in the United States adopted a new name and with it a new, more unified community.

CHAPTER THREE

The American Vegetarian Society

::

How many both feast and grow fat to excess
On the flesh and the blood of brutes?
Nay! Stain not your lips with such food, but come feed
Alone as man ought, upon fruits.
We've tasted your flesh-meats of yore, it is true,
But ne'er mean to taste them again
Because now resolved, and determined for us
No creature shall ever be slain.
—"A Vegetarian Song," 1852

"In England the advocates of dietetic reform, some time ago, instituted an association," reported William Metcalfe. The new organization interested Metcalfe because of its stated goal of spreading information about the "abstinence from the consumption of animal food." Metcalfe was further intrigued because the group organized with an interesting and novel name, gathering "under the appellation of 'The Vegetarian Society.'"[1]

The new association was "creating quite an excitement throughout the country," and Metcalfe wondered why a similar organization could not be founded in the United States. After all, he argued, America was "distinguished throughout the civilized world for the noble stand she first made against intemperance." "Shall she be less zealous," he wondered, "in opposing a system of diet, as detrimental to the health and happiness of humanity as intoxicating liquors?" Having "conversed with . . . friends who highly approve[d] of the proposal," Metcalfe predicted a similar development would come to the United States: "The good time is coming . . . for the elevation of man from the bondage of an unnatural, destructive and barbarous custom."[2]

News of developments among British dietary reformers began stirring up excitement among American meat abstainers in the late 1840s. The original proto-vegetarian group in the United States—the Bible Christians—while from England, was now comprised largely of American-born members. However, despite the demographic shift, they and other U. S. proto-vegetarians remained linked to their British counterparts, as dietary reformers sent each other literature, pamphlets, and books across the Atlantic.[3] Americans and British were equally inspired by the notion of forming a singular organization bringing together the variety of groups advocating a meatless diet, including Bible Christians, physiologists, social reformers, and water curists.

In addition, prominent American dietary reformers like Sylvester Graham, William Alcott, and Bronson Alcott lectured extensively to British audiences, and British vegetarians visited the United States and spoke to American crowds.[4] The Americans also frequently subscribed to British dietary reform publications like the *Truth-Tester*. This transatlantic exchange of ideas ultimately emboldened Americans to form their own association.[5]

The founding and development of the American Vegetarian Society (AVS) in 1850 finally brought American meatless dietary reformers together under a single banner. In the process, the group helped define the term *vegetarian* and built a movement that promoted not just a diet but a total reform lifestyle. Through the AVS, vegetarians aligned themselves with other reform movements of the time, in particular abolitionism, women's rights, and pacifism. These other interests sapped the energies of the AVS, however, and kept it from having a longer life. With the coming of the Civil War, American movement vegetarianism fractured as its adherents focused on ending the slave system in the United States.

The advances of British vegetarians largely inspired the formalized organization of American dietary reformers. The *Water-Cure Journal* made this connection explicit, reporting that "the movements of the vegetarian societies in England, during the past year" had "stirred up the friends of dietetic reform on this side of the Atlantic."[6] The plans for an American vegetarian convention were coming to fruition. In February 1850, the *Water-Cure Journal* noted the proposal "by a number of influential individuals . . . that there be called in the month of May next, an American Vegetarian Convention."[7]

In this climate of increasingly vigorous organization throughout U. S. reform movements (abolitionists, suffragists, and temperance supporters all now had their own associations), meat abstainers from around the nation gathered in New York City on May 15, 1850, for the first meeting of the American Vegetarian Society.[8] The convention, held in Clinton Hall at the corner of Astor Place and Eighth Street, drew the country's most visible and renowned advocates of a meatless diet, including Joel Shew, William Alcott, William Metcalfe, and Sylvester Graham. Among the attendees were Bible Christians, Grahamites, social reformers, and water curists. They met with the intention to build the first nationwide organization in the United States to connect reformers around the principle of abstention from meat. Before sitting down to a sumptuous banquet, attendees worked together to formulate an organizational structure and a set of principles to guide their movement.

The first day of the conference was marked by speeches, testimonials, and conversion stories describing the benefits of adopting a vegetable diet. This seems to indicate that in addition to dietary reformers, the convention drew the curious and unconverted. Letters from both lay reformers and medical doctors were read, attempting to present the full breadth of dietary experiences and show that this movement included not just popular health advocates (vulnerable to attack from the medical profession) but also trained physicians. Lectures included a mix of the old and the new. David Prince, a medical doctor from St. Louis, presented his own conversion story and was happy to report that he had "abstained almost entirely from the use of meat, eggs and fish for 14 years." Price stated that his health was "uniformly good," his appetite "greater than it is proper to satiate," and his "power of resisting heat and cold, and of enduring fatigue, very considerable." Reuben Mussey, known for his medical advice, presented a new argument for meat abstention, placing it strictly within the realm of economic thriftiness. "Animals, as food," he argued, "will be substituted by the food of vegetable productions, on account of its greater cheapness and abundance."[9]

These preliminary speeches laid the groundwork for dietary reform's best-known advocates. William Alcott rose to the lectern and stated that it had been nearly forty-one years since he had made use of any kind of "flesh-food," and his life was "altogether satisfactory." Alcott had been lucky enough to have "raised a family," including "both children and grandchildren who had never tasted flesh." A vegetable diet had ensured a long, healthy life, productive in works as well as progeny.

Dietary reformers were becoming emboldened and increasingly self-righteous in the justness of their cause. When a water curist from Lebanon Springs, New York, admitted in his remarks that he gave some patients flesh food in order to "keep up the animal heat," an unknown audience member wondered if "perhaps you give them too much cold water," to which the audience responded with hearty laughter.[10] Although water curists—who were concerned primarily with maintaining physiological balance and not all of whom practiced strict vegetarianism—were welcomed at the convention, the audience made it clear that no issue was more important than the abstention from meat.

The session culminated with a lay audience member, Jonathan Wright of Philadelphia, addressing the crowd about his family's experiences practicing a vegetable diet. The meeting sought to emphasize that while the endorsements of doctors proved the success of the diet, the real-life applicability of the lifestyle was just as important. The new, more conjoined vegetarian movement sought to bridge the populist dietetics of Grahamites with the physiological emphasis of William Alcott and other medical doctors. Wright said that he had not touched animal food for forty years and had raised eight children who never knew the taste of flesh. The benefits of "that merciful system of living" were extensive, providing "physical, moral and intellectual" success. Avoiding meat and other stimulants ensured that Wright "never had to pay a dollar, on his own personal account, for a doctor's bill."[11]

At this point a voice rose from the audience. Frail yet determined, Sylvester Graham asked Wright if he had ever lost any children in infancy. Wright responded that three of his children had indeed passed away in infancy as a result of what doctors diagnosed as the croup. Graham asked "whether the croup or the doctor killed them," to the delighted applause of the gathered masses. Even in poor health, Graham continued his lifelong assault on the medical establishment.[12]

The new organization agreed on a mission statement stating that it sought to "induce habits of abstinence from the flesh of Animals as food." Members would pursue this goal through the dissemination of information "by means of verbal discussions, tracts, essays and lectures, exhibiting the many advantages of a physical, intellectual and moral character, resulting from Vegetarian habits of diet."[13] With opening statements and formalities over, the convention got down to the business of building an organization by drafting fourteen principles to guide the new society.

The convention agreed that a vegetarian diet was the most natural and spiritually perfect one for humans. Meat was simply an indulgence allowed by the divine spirit because of humanity's fall from grace, its cruelty, and its passions. Eating meat only furthered humankind's moral failings. Total reform was only possible, the guidelines argued, through the practice of a meatless diet. In order to promote the benefits of meatless living, a centralized organization would be formed, with smaller, localized associations under the national umbrella.[14] William Alcott was elected president of this new society, with nine co–vice presidents serving yearly terms. Among the first group of vice presidents were Sylvester Graham and the leader of American hydropathy, Joel Shew.

Mirroring the nomenclature of British dietary reformers, the convention named the new organization the American Vegetarian Society, though not without objection. Philo Penfield (P. P.) Stewart, another of the newly appointed vice presidents as well as a cofounder of Oberlin College and a former Grahamite, objected to the use of the term *vegetarian*.[15] For Stewart the term was misleading; many members at the convention ate eggs and drank milk. Were these not animal products as well? Further, Stewart pointed out, the term was limiting, focusing the group's identity on diet rather than the larger reform connections possible. Stewart's objections notwithstanding, the term was adopted as part of the organization's name, reflecting the growth of the word in the American vernacular vocabulary.[16] However, *vegetarian* meant something different to American dietary reformers than it did to their British counterparts. Britain's Vegetarian Society utilized the term to designate individuals who subsisted on a strictly vegetable-based diet. Stewart's objection to the term as being inaccurate and potentially constraining was well reasoned; in order to make the term salient, American vegetarians had to redefine their lifestyle for larger audiences.

At the organization's first anniversary meeting—held just five months later in September 1850 at Philadelphia's Chinese Museum—this issue was explored further. An attendee explained that vegetarianism was "the art and science which teaches man to cull, dispose and modify, for food, those products of the vegetable kingdom only, which are best adapted to produce and sustain a sound mind and a sound body." Emphasizing that vegetarianism was not simply a dietary choice but rather an art and science allowed vegetarianism to be flexible enough to catalyze a variety of reforms rather than just serve as a goal unto itself. Subsisting on foods that "produce and sustain a sound mind and a sound body" also allowed flexibility in what vegetarians could eat; if scientific study showed that milk and eggs—which could be produced without causing death—were conducive to mental and physical development, vegetarians could justify their use.

The first anniversary meeting of the AVS expanded on these themes, mandating that attendees sign a pledge promising that they had "abstained from the Flesh of Animals as Food, for the space of One Month, and upwards" and would work "in promoting the knowledge of the advantages of a Vegetarian Diet."[17] Flesh foods were seen as the source of moral and physical illness among humans. Vegetarians considered "animal food such substances only as have been a component part of a living animal body." The harmful effects of meat were caused by its inorganic nature, its sitting and rotting in the stomach rather than passing quickly through the digestive system. Products such as milk, cheese, and eggs, though derived from animals, did not cause death or extreme suffering and thus were deemed both safe and ethical for vegetarians to consume.[18]

The adoption of the term *vegetarian* spread quickly among the public at large, particularly in the medical field. Robley Dunglison—a founding faculty member of the University of Virginia and at one time Thomas Jefferson's personal physician—defined *vegetarianism* in his 1851 *Dictionary of Medical Science* as "a modern term, employed to designate the view that man . . . ought to subsist on the direct productions of the vegetable kingdom and totally abstain from flesh and blood."[19] This definition—emphasizing the avoidance of flesh and blood—matched vegetarians' sense of their movement and its allowance of limited use of animal products such as milk, cheese, and eggs, while avoiding animal flesh and meat. In addition, Dunglison's description of vegetarianism—reflecting the movement's own self-classification—made clear that the group believed in the naturalness of a meatless diet, while deemphasizing the notion of mere choice.

At the group's first anniversary meeting, a monthly journal was proposed. Four months later, in January 1851, the AVS began producing the *American Vegetarian and Health Journal*. The new publication served two purposes: it kept vegetarians informed of developments in the movement and reached out to potential converts. In the second issue, the journal addressed the question "vegetarianism—what is it?" "The answer to this oft repeated interrogation is plain and simple," the journal argued. Since "man is a physical, intellectual and moral being . . . by understanding rightly his own nature, . . . he should . . . totally abstain from the flesh and blood of the animal creation." Whereas British vegetarians emphasized dietary choice in the definition of their movement, American vegetarians stressed its all-encompassing naturalness. Vegetarianism was "not merely theoretical and speculative," the article argued, but rather was "sustained by the teachings of Comparative Anatomy, the doctrines of Human Physiology, the testimony of Analytical Chemistry, and the truths of Sacred and Profane History."[20] The vegetarian diet was not an abnormal dietary choice that individuals imposed on themselves; it was humanity's natural state.

The article further explained the totality of the burgeoning vegetarian movement, noting that "vegetarianism is connected with a grand set of social and moral reformations, not aiming at the elevation of a few merely, but securing the amelioration of the common lot of the human family." Vegetarianism was an all-encompassing reform ideology, including "kindness and humanity to the lower animals," "harmony with the great Temperance reformation," and "intimate association with the vital progress of every Reformation of the age."[21] Dietary reformers dating back to the Bible Christians had connected meat abstention to larger social reform, through the spiritual, mental, and moral cleanliness provided by a vegetable diet. The AVS, however, created and codified a new movement that presented vegetarianism as an "'Archimedian Lever' by which to move the world." Vegetarians viewed their diet as being the catalyst for all social change.[22]

The organization's first anniversary meeting in Philadelphia made this notion explicit, linking vegetarianism to both pacifism and abolitionism. Antebellum pacifism largely focused on the belief that the use of force by governments was inherently sinful.[23] As a result, pacifists utilized a variety of methods aimed squarely at governmental power, often refusing to vote or otherwise become intertwined with a political system they viewed as corrupt and prone to violence. Vegetarian pacifists, in contrast, focused on the effects of the collective actions of humanity. Social ills were only possible through intemperate diets that aroused violent urges. Therefore a collective turn toward vegetarianism—even more than a shift in political systems—held the power to change society's willingness to spill the blood of fellow humans. Vegetarians viewed communal dietary choices as having more transformative power than even the collective policies of the federal government.

Vegetarians argued that only a cruel society seduced by animal flesh could wage war, arguing that to ensure peaceful coexistence among humans "we must do away with the brutal custom of slaughtering animals."[24] Just three years removed from the Mexican American War and in the middle of a growing sectional crisis, vegetarians were tackling an issue of particular pertinence. For social reformers, the dual threats of internal strife and the spreading slave system were intertwined. The Compromise of 1850 temporarily quelled the threat of sectional warfare but left social questions and contradictions unanswered.[25] Vegetarians—staunchly abolitionist and generally concerned with the issue of violence—combined these issues in their arguments for a meat-free diet as a dietary choice that could solve the larger problems facing the republic.

In his address to the meeting, William Alcott argued that "abstinence from flesh [lay] at the basis of" abolitionism. "There is no slavery in this world," he continued, "like the slavery of a man to his appetite. . . . Let man but abstain from the use of flesh and fish, and the slavery of one man to another cannot long exist." While this simile may seem somewhat flippant—the mental, emotional, and physical effects of plantation slavery were, of course, more harmful than those of a steak—it shows how central vegetarians believed dietary reform to be. Only in a society where individuals were blind to the disastrous effects of poor diet on themselves could they be blind to the catastrophic effects of slavery on others.[26] Intemperate diet clouded the individual's ability to make morally appropriate decisions, causing aggression, anger, and irrationality. Food choices, the AVS argued, had inherent and important political power. Vegetarians were explicit in the unity of their reform goals, pointing out that "the true philanthropist seeks a medical reform, a temperance reform, the breaking of the fetters that bind humanity in degradation and servitude, and a reform in legislation."[27]

By the fall of 1850 Sylvester Graham must have barely recognized the movement that he was so influential in founding. No longer obsessed with stale bread and cold water, vegetarians had formed a national organization aimed at producing complete social reform through dietary choice. Graham did not even attend the society's first anniversary meeting in September— poor health had left the once omnipresent public figure virtually bedridden.

Vegetarians now expanded their palates beyond Graham bread and attempted to maximize the flavorful benefits of a meatless diet. The meeting's banquet ignored the simplicity in dining advocated in the past in favor of a banquet room "very tastefully decorated with heavy festoons of evergreen, flowers and fruit." Above an elongated table where the society's leadership sat, a large banner displayed the Genesis exhortation, "Behold I have given you every Herb bearing seed, and every tree in the which is the Fruit of a tree yielding seed; to you it shall be for meat."

The banquet included thirty different varieties of cooked foods, not including preserves. The first course consisted of savory dishes including baked potatoes and a variety of breads. The second course included a variety of fruit pies, custards, and puddings, dishes previously frowned on as too sweet and stimulating. Dessert was a variety of fruits and nuts. According to the *American Vegetarian and Health Journal*, this "rich and luxurious dinner" proved that "the vegetable kingdom affords 'plenty to eat, without any meat.'"[28] Vegetarians had begun seeking to entice new followers by appealing to their taste buds.

The group's second anniversary event expanded on the previous year's extravagance. Philadelphia's Chinese Museum was decorated with the finest fresh flowers and cruciferous fauna available, inspiring attendees to enjoy "A

Feast of Reason, and A Flow of Soul."[29] Vegetarians had made great strides, organizing a national advocacy society and creating a tight-knit community that emphasized each individual's duty to observe an ethical, healthy lifestyle. Still, vegetarianism was in its infancy and much confusion and misinformation surrounded the movement. Members of the AVS wanted to set the record straight. William Alcott told the audience that he wished "everybody to understand that we are something more than grass eaters." A vegetarian diet could be far more complex, embracing "the rich grains God has given us, in so great a variety."[30]

The banquet at the second annual meeting again reflected the growing culinary diversity of vegetarianism. The first course consisted of a variety of vegetable pies, fritters, and omelets. The use of eggs by the AVS at its banquet illustrates their general acceptance among the vegetarian faithful. The second course consisted of sweet rice, custards, cheesecakes, fruit pies, watermelon, peaches, and grapes. While vegetarians had moved far from their simple original fare, the vestiges of the past were still apparent: the only beverage available was pure ice water.[31]

The changing vegetarian diet also revealed itself in movement vegetarianism's national publication. The *American Vegetarian and Health Journal* advised on particularly nutritious and appetizing fruits, vegetables, and grains, while also providing recipes on how to prepare meatless dishes. In "Vegetarian Dietary," the journal provided a list of common vegetarian dishes, emphasizing their health advantages, quality of taste, and ease of preparation. For breakfast, the journal advised vegetarians to prepare wheat and Indian griddlecakes, served with rice gruel and stewed apples. Recommendations for dinner included potatoes, parsnips, squash, and green corn. Apples, grapes, rice pudding, and custard pie were presented as acceptable dessert options. Vegetarians, once skeptical of the effects of fruits and sweets on body constitution, were now advocating for dessert as part of a complete meal. The journal advised that supper be light to ensure proper digestion before sleep, and that it consist of dishes such as milk toast, cracked-wheat mush, baked potatoes, baked apples, stewed figs, and blancmange for dessert.[32]

The journal further supported the diversification of the vegetarian diet through recipe columns that provided step-by-step instructions on how to prepare dishes in the most nutritive and effective means possible. A March 1852 article highlighted the many ways that rice could be utilized as a component of all meals, including as a compliment to a main dish or in a sweet pudding.[33] The journal's "Domestic Economy" column provided a variety of recipes for such diverse foods as a tapioca omelet, a baked bread omelet, a potato pie, plum pudding, and brown gravy, all offered as alternatives to the boiled vegetables that had frequently dominated vegetarian meals.[34] In the process, the journal helped foster the building of a movement vegetarian community, encouraging vegetarians to share recipes with each other, while providing tips on how to create a socially and economically conscious kitchen.

While the journal provided culinary advice, its contents focused on the reform possibilities connected to a vegetarian lifestyle. Exploiting fears of industrial life's disconnection from and danger to personal health, the AVS promoted vegetarianism as a means to ensure the quality of life of one's family and oneself. The journal touted the peace of mind provided by vegetarianism. Meat was diseased, processed to the point of disaster. Attempts to fatten animals before slaughtering had caused "almost all the meats in our markets" to be "stricken with one disease after another."[35] A vegetarian diet, the journal argued, helped lessen the impact of the increasing disconnect between consumer and producer, as "a man could sit at such a table without wondering whether the food he was eating was not tainted with disease."[36] Motivated to take greater control of their lives, vegetarians offered a complex critique of the negative health consequences associated with the antebellum rise of industrial capitalism and distant markets.

Vegetarianism was also presented as an effective means to strengthen one's personal finances and increase economic equity in society at large. Writing in the Water-Cure Journal in 1853, a vegetarian advocate explained in great detail how the meat industry burdened the American economy. Commenting on the Kentucky hog industry specifically, the author argued that a vegetarian lifestyle would unburden Kentucky farmers, who wasted both money and resources in processing livestock, as well as consumers. Vegetarianism would also allow Kentuckians to use corn as a dietary staple. Further, "were there no hogs, even with the present failure in quantity, there would be a large surplus for bread, the price would be greatly reduced, and the staff of life within the reach of all, however poor."[37]

The author of the article pointed out that the high price of meat had already converted some Kentuckians to the vegetarian lifestyle out of necessity. People "submit in silence to such oppressive advances in the price of animal food as must necessarily force half the community into Vegetarianism," the author observed. "Roasting beef is from 21 to 28 cents a point, and steaks from 22 to 27 cents"; vegetables were both cheaper and more abundant. A vegetarian diet was empowering, moving individuals away from an economic system that the AVS described as "despotic" and "tyrannical." The economic arguments made by movement vegetarians sought to empower individuals as informed consumers, spreading awareness of the power of personal decisions.[38]

Publication of the *American Vegetarian and Health Journal* furthered the development of a unified American vegetarian movement, spreading the group's message and reporting on its activities. The journal urged vegetarians around the United States to live by the credo, "Take not away the life thou cans't not give, for all things have an equal right to live," and to live freely at that.[39] The journal emphasized this motto and its applicability to a variety of reform movements.

Writing in April 1851, J. H. Hanaford—a teacher and writer of popular women's advice manuals—connected vegetarianism directly to women's rights. Spending arduous hours working in the kitchen was demeaning to women, particularly the indignity of having to prepare diseased, rotting, decomposing meat. Hanaford believed that "woman has, or ought to have a far more ennobling round of duties and pleasures, than to become the drudge of society, the slave of man." Emphasizing idealized notions of female purity and serenity, Hanaford argued that the preparation of "the ceaseless odor of surloins, steams and hams" ought to be replaced by trips "in the beautiful fields of nature, to inhale the sweet fragrance of myriads of flowers, to breath the pure air of rural retreats, and to feast on the wonders and beauty of the broad page of creation."[40]

Anne Denton—an active suffragist and member of the AVS—argued that meat stunted social growth. Since food fueled blood, and blood connected body and spirit, it was impossible for "the soul to expand, or the heart to enlarge" if "every avenue is clogged by flesh—while every truth must pass through the grains and blood of mangled animals." Denton placed the onus on women to take control over their own bodies, as women were only empowered through "studying and obeying the laws of nature; and lastly, by taking possession of them."

Women had a moral imperative to take control of their own (and by implied extension their children's) ethical and physical destinies. To vegetarians like Denton, ignoring the ethical implications of a carnivorous diet was evidence of a lessening of female serenity. Denton pleaded that "woman should be something more than Fashion's doll, or a cooking machine." Cooking meat violated natural laws and demeaned women, who were "naturally refined and beautiful in spirit" but were "degraded to the work of cooking mangled flesh for vitiated appetites." Vegetarianism was a key component for women seeking to raise themselves above the degradation of household enslavement and a means to fight the perceived waning of female purity.[41]

The diet was also prescribed as a means to improve family health. Facing a rise in the number of marketed cures and treatments—the success of which varied considerably—the AVS cast vegetarianism as a means of preventative health care to be managed by the women of the household. One member of the organization argued that it was "the duty of parents especially to understand what food is best adapted to promote a sound and vigorous constitution in their children . . . and prevent the large proportion of infant mortality which now takes place in this country."[42]

The journal showed its interest in women's rights by offering advertising space for rights conventions around the United States.[43] Vegetarianism, adherents believed, was a catalyst for total reform, in which women's rights were central. As such, the AVS sought active participation from all of its members, male and female. Advertisements for AVS meetings noted that "ladies are expected to participate in dinner, toasts, and speeches."[44] Despite these obvious inclinations toward women's rights, however, the connection was somewhat compromised; throughout its history the AVS's board of directors was exclusively male.

Despite their lack of executive roles, women continued to play a central role in the development of American movement vegetarianism. Mary Gove Nichols, a novelist and prominent water curist, lectured extensively to women in Boston, Philadelphia, and Providence about the value of a vegetarian lifestyle as a means to control one's own health. Gove Nichols argued that physical strength and good health were essential to the process of ensuring social and political equality with men.

Having survived an abusive first marriage, Nichols understood firsthand the connection between physical and political empowerment, and the need for women to avoid being intimidated by men's stature in either domain. Through vegetarianism, Gove Nichols argued, women could strengthen themselves morally and physically, and thus prepare themselves for social and political equality.[45] Gove Nichols was an early advocate of Grahamism in the 1830s and continued her support of vegetarianism into the 1850s.[46] In addition, vegetarian meetings frequently drew prominent women's rights advocates such as physician Harriet K. Hunt and Emily Clark, who lectured on the connections between dietary and social reform.[47] Further, at public meetings the AVS called for improving "the sphere and rights of woman . . . her supreme right, the right to herself."[48]

AVS meetings and publications touted the scientific and moral advantages of vegetarianism while prescribing dietary change as the route to social reform. As a result, vegetarianism was not merely an exercise in dietary reform. Vegetarianism was, rather, "a radical reform . . . laying, as it evidently does, the 'axe at the root of the tree.'"⁴⁹ As the central issue facing the Union at the time of the AVS's founding, the slave system drew the ire of American vegetarians. Beginning with the AVS, movement vegetarianism during the antebellum era became indelibly connected to the abolition movement. Human slavery could only exist in a society where violence was endemic, as reflected in dietary practices. In order to abolish the slave system in the United States, a larger shift in attitudes toward cruelty and violence was necessary. Abstaining from meat was one step in this process.

Slavery existed in a variety of forms in the United States, the AVS noted, ranging from the institutionalized, chattel form, to the enslavement of animals, to the slavery of uncontrolled personal desire. Only by shedding the connection to violence-based diets, the AVS argued, could Americans ultimately free the African slaves in the United States. American reliance on meat was a social crutch affecting all of the country's inhabitants.

The close relationship between vegetarianism and abolition was mutual: while vegetarian publications and festivals advocated for the abolitionist cause, The Liberator—William Lloyd Garrison's abolitionist periodical—supported the growth of vegetarianism. As early as 1849, The Liberator reported on the activities of Irish temperance advocate James Haughton, who reported that he was able to withstand an outbreak of cholera because of his vegetarian diet.⁵⁰

One abolitionist wrote in The Liberator on vegetarianism's connection to total political reform. W. S. George reported that "a rabid conservative" had been overheard to claim that he had never met a vegetarian who was not "radical on all subjects." George—taking this as a compliment—acknowledged that "this remark was doubtless correct." Individuals concerned with keeping their bodies healthy were inclined to "naturally embrace truth" on social issues such as slavery. In contrast, an individual whose "stomach is crammed with animal abominations" would have difficulty understanding high-minded moral and intellectual ideals. George concluded by claiming that if the American populace embraced a vegetarian diet, it "would be half-converted to Anti-Slavery, Peace, Temperance, Land Reform, Woman's Rights, etc., in a single year."⁵¹

The Liberator informed its readers on movement vegetarianism's activities. Reporting on the upcoming fourth anniversary of the AVS, The Liberator

Announcement of the fourth annual meeting of the American Vegetarian Society on August 24, 1853. From The Liberator, August 5, 1853.

announced that the meeting should appeal to all "friends of human progress every where."[52] The publication also reported on a vegetarian banquet prepared for the Whole World's Temperance Convention held in New York in September 1853. Vegetarians at the convention were announcing their support for total reform, though also proclaiming their presence among a wide range of reform movements. The Liberator reported that 300 attendees dined on a vegetarian feast and listened to speeches delivered by a wide range of concerned reformers, including Horace Greeley, Harriet K. Hunt, Mary Gove Nichols, and Matilda Gage.[53]

Vegetarians claimed that abstention from meat not only provided moral clarity and physical health but also developed intellectual independence from the conventions of a cruel and unjust society. In one article, The Liberator outlined abolitionism's relationship with vegetarianism and other social reforms, arguing that "an 'abolitionist' is also an infidel, an agrarian[,] . . . a woman's-rights-man[,] . . . a water-curer, a vegetarian, a fourierite, and an opponent of tobacco and capital punishment."[54] Having a national organization paid dividends for vegetarians. The appearance of the AVS turned the movement into a more unified and defined community recognized among the growing number of U. S. antebellum reform movements.

Vegetarians had reached a key point in their development. Their newly centralized movement provided a certain level of uniformity among meat abstainers, united by a new term. A nationwide community of vegetarians was now in place and recognized by the general public. Vegetarians placed their diet at the center of a total reform ideology and lifestyle, believing the benefits of a vegetable diet to extend beyond the palate and into the political. Banquets and conventions received coverage in the mainstream media, and while the lifestyle was frequently mocked in some circles, America's reformist class embraced vegetarianism.[55] However, in September 1851 the American community of vegetarians faced a significant challenge to their movement's legitimacy.

The death of Sylvester Graham at age fifty-seven—despite his increasing distance from the movement—called into question the effectiveness of a vegetarian lifestyle. Graham had been in semiretirement from public life for years, though he periodically attended meetings of the American Vegetarian Society. While his name was still associated with American vegetarianism, Graham's actual participation in the crafting of movement vegetarianism was minimal. To the world outside of the growing community of American vegetarians, however, Graham remained indelibly linked to the concept of meat abstention. For example, an article critical of vegetarians written months after the founding of the AVS continued to use the term *Grahamite* interchangeably with the more prevalent and popular descriptor *vegetarian*.[56]

Nonvegetarians pointed to Graham's continuous poor health and eventually to his death as proof of the failings of dietary reform. Vegetarians looked for answers, trying to understand and explain his relatively early demise. The AVS's treatment of Graham's death and the controversy surrounding it in the *American Vegetarian and Health Journal* reveal the challenges facing vegetarians at the time and the current movement's attempt to differentiate itself from its predecessors.

The October 1851 issue of the journal announced Graham's passing but relegated the news to its back pages. Anticipating criticism, the journal assured readers that it was not vegetarianism that led to Graham's death but rather improper medical care. The article claimed that four days before he passed away, Graham gave the article writer an account of his care, in order to "understand that he had no mortal disease upon him, but thought he might die on account of not being able to carry out what he considered a philosophical course of treatment." The author stated that hard scientific fact supported this assertion; a post mortem examination showed that "the immediate cause of his decease to be the use, in his extreme state of exhaustion, of Congress water and the warm bath."[57]

The author claimed that Graham was given a hot bath to help induce sleep, under the poor advice of his physician. It is not a surprise that vegetarians would blame medical doctors for Graham's death, given that the group often found itself targeted by mainstream medicine. But the journal went further and argued that Graham himself was partially to blame for his demise. The journal foreshadowed its future treatment of Graham, stating that while he "was gifted with talents and genius of a high order," he was also "not exempt from imperfections and frailties." Without mentioning specific faults, the journal separated the vegetarian movement further from its Grahamite roots. This was not the end of the controversy but rather just the beginning.[58]

The November 1851 issue of the journal featured a letter from a concerned vegetarian speculating on the cause of Graham's death. Asserting that Graham must have made "some great error in his mode of life" or had a "very defective constitution" in order to have died so young while living a vegetarian diet, the letter writer insisted that "the world ought to be made acquainted with the facts in the case, or it will have an injurious effect on the minds of many reflecting but not fully informed men."[59] The publication promised a response in the next issue, written by someone who was present at Graham's deathbed.

In the December 1851 issue, Russell Trall—a medical doctor, naturopath, and vegetarian—recounted his witnessing of Sylvester Graham's death. The trend that began two issues previous continued; the journal simultaneously blamed both Graham and his medical doctor. However, unlike in previous issues, Trall offered a scathing attack on the totality of Graham's life, placing particular emphasis on the reformer's purported shortcomings.

Trall attempted to protect the reputation of vegetarianism, pointing out that Graham was fifty-nine, rather than fifty as was reported in some newspapers, and had only adopted a vegetable diet at forty.[60] The article insisted that Graham had "by inheritance, a feeble constitution," and while mental temperament helped fuel his work ethic, it also made him prone to nervous disorders. "Always over-worked," Graham had a strenuous travel schedule during his working years that had "hastened his death." Worst of all, Trall insisted, Graham "was not sustained in his supposed office of reforming the world, by that cooperation which might have been expected in the domestic relation." Trall could not testify whether or not "Mr. G. died in the true faith of the Gospel," but he did note that Graham had strayed from a strictly vegetarian diet at times.

Graham and his wife were both implicated—but they were not alone. The true culprit in Graham's ultimate demise was flesh foods. Trall reported that Graham was prescribed meat in order to increase blood circulation; in fact, his doctor threatened to stop treating Graham if he denied this request. According to Trall, Sylvester Graham immediately regretted the decision to accede to the doctor's demands. Trall assured readers that as Graham died he "fully and verily believed in the theory of vegetable diet as explained in his works" and that his last words were a proclamation that impending death was "the consequences of over-distension of the stomach, from eating too much and too great a variety."[61] In his article, Trall deftly crafted a narrative that protected vegetarianism by simultaneously blaming Graham's personal faults and the nefarious effects of flesh foods.

William Alcott fed more fuel to the fire surrounding Graham's death. The implications of Graham's death must have lingered for movement vegetarians, as Alcott's article on the subject was written nearly a year later, in September 1852. Alcott ignored the role of medical doctors completely in his account, focusing instead on Graham's physiological and emotional flaws. Although he and Graham were colleagues and associates for more than a decade, Alcott did not let that connection soften his scathing critique. Alcott wrote that Graham was perpetually stricken by "over-anxiety, irritability and fretfulness." While Trall attributed these characteristics to Graham's intense work schedule, Alcott claimed that Graham's nervousness resulted from "undue anxiety or worrying," to which "many good men are addicted, [and] which is quite as destructive to health, if not to happiness, as those occasional outbursts, which are usually considered as the most criminal."

Alcott argued that Graham's worrying was a particularly prominent malady, both "the consequence of ill health, as well as the cause of it." Graham's "excessive mental labors . . . coupled with neglect of exercise . . . rendered him irritable and fretful, and the more he fretted and worried, the worse the state of his nervous system." If Graham were "to sit down at home and . . . obey the laws of his own being . . . everybody would be pleased." Unfortunately the work of a crusader led to mental and physical exhaustion: "Though he may gain more proselytes . . . no allowance will be made for the circumstance of his premature death."[62]

The accuracy of Trall's and Alcott's accounts is questionable given their interest in protecting vegetarianism from its critics and considering the dramatic nature of the reports. Newspaper obituaries add little to the story; none speculated as to Graham's cause of death.[63] The full truth surrounding it is not as important as how vegetarians decided to represent the demise of one of their movement's progenitors. During a time when vegetarians actively worked to establish their own, distinct movement connecting social and dietary reform, the shadow of Sylvester Graham continued to loom large even as the reformer slipped into retirement. Vegetarians eagerly distanced themselves from Graham, while fully aware of the dangers of calling his works into doubt.

Vegetarians sought an opportunity to question the practices of mainstream diet and medicine while simultaneously asserting their own ideology as distinct from Grahamism. As a result, vegetarians crafted a narrative in response to Graham's death that both illustrated the dangers of meat consumption and emphasized the importance of individuals' responsibility in adhering to a vegetarian diet. While casting Graham as a martyr for his hard work—which contributed to his ill health—vegetarians also questioned Graham's constitution and dedication to the path of righteousness. Vegetarians managed to illustrate the dangers of intemperance and highlight the need for constant dedication to the cause, even resorting to besmirching one of their movement's founders as a means to warn followers of the perils of meat consumed in any amount. If someone as dedicated to health reform as Sylvester Graham could fall victim to temptation and a poor constitution, vegetarians argued, the threat existed for everyone. Always on guard against mockery by the medical establishment and normative society, the AVS hoped to preemptively discredit such attacks in its coverage of Graham's death. Dietary reformers were skeptical of the outside world and its flaws; Trall even speculated that Graham was fed meat as part of a conspiracy by carnivores to discredit vegetarianism.[64]

As the AVS itself described it, the society's third annual meeting, held once again at New York's Clinton Hall, was "not attended by so many persons as . . . the two previous meetings." There was therefore no elaborate banquet; instead the whole event "was purely intellectual." The *American Vegetarian and Health Journal* reassured readers that, despite the smaller turnout, "there was no lack of zeal and perseverance in the good cause of Vegetarianism."[65]

In September 1853, the AVS held its fourth annual meeting in the more modest confines of the Bible Christian Church in Philadelphia, a sign that financial constraints made a large-scale event difficult. At the meeting Henry S. Clubb, a leader of the British Vegetarian Society, reported on activities in Great Britain, calling for increased cooperation between the two groups.[66] Clubb would soon become a vital figure in the American vegetarian community by attempting to put into practice the principles of political reform through dietary choice.

Motivated by financial necessity, the AVS began relying heavily on a newly expanded relationship with British vegetarians. In June 1854, the *American Vegetarian and Health Journal* began featuring content provided by the British organization, including an address by British Vegetarian Society president James Simpson calling for increased cooperation between British and American vegetarians.

Despite the AVS's efforts to serve as a central voice for American vegetarians, the organization faced significant challenges, including decreasing membership. Members of the AVS were aware of the society's shortcomings; at its annual meeting in 1854, the organization debated the merits of its very existence, ultimately deciding to continue activities. While the meeting drew 150 attendees—the average number for an AVS convention—the difficulties that the organization faced reached beyond its core group of dedicated vegetarians. The AVS was losing money, and the number of subscribers to the *American Vegetarian and Health Journal* was diminishing.[67] As a result, the AVS decided that it was time to discontinue the journal, printing its final issue in October 1854.[68] In its place subscribers would receive copies of the *Water-Cure Journal* for the rest of the year.

Despite the decline of the AVS, vegetarians did not disappear from the spectrum of reform movements. As the sectional crises descended toward bloodshed, movement vegetarians decried that their admonitions had been ignored and that the rifle had replaced the ploughshare. The "mad passions and misguided counsels of men have prevailed, for the moment," warned the *Water-Cure Journal*, proclaiming the coming war "fratricidal." Vegetarians had long been largely pacifistic, viewing war as the culmination of humanity's violence and ignorance.

Movement vegetarians, however, also believed in the war's potential to effect seismic social change by ending slavery. Civil war would unfortunately lead to "loss of life, the riven hearts, the desolated homes, the ravaged fields and the ruined cities." But many vegetarians also believed that conflict was the only way that the "political atmosphere can be cleansed, our institutions regenerated, and our people brought to a realizing sense of the unexamined privileges and prosperity they have so long enjoyed." War had the potential to ensure that "the land of the free and the home of the brave, will now . . . be adjusted and settled permanently and forever."[69] Vegetarians looked for an opportunity to channel their ideology into practical works.

Despite the AVS's dwindling numbers, vegetarians maintained their dedication to the cause as it became entangled with the larger issues of the time. Henry S. Clubb of the British Vegetarian Society emigrated to the United States in 1853 and immediately became active in the vegetarian movement and abolitionism. Clubb had become a strident opponent of the slave system during his years writing for the New York Tribune, working under the tutelage of fellow abolitionist and one-time vegetarian Horace Greeley. Writing for the Tribune, Clubb furthered his antislavery education, producing a "History of Kansas" for the New York Tribune Almanac in 1854 that described abolitionist activities in the region.[70]

Born in Colchester, England, and raised in the Swedenborgian Church, Clubb was exposed to meatless living during his formative years and maintained the practice throughout his life. As a young man, Clubb was drawn to a variety of reform causes, leaving his job as a postal clerk in 1842 to live at London's Alcott House—a utopian home based on the reform ideals of the American Bronson Alcott.[71] After Alcott House closed in 1844, Clubb became involved with London's growing vegetarian community, serving as the secretary to James Simpson, the first president of the Vegetarian Society. By 1849, Clubb was named editor of the Vegetarian Messenger, the society's monthly newsletter. Clubb's relationship with Simpson eventually led to religious conversion, and he received his baptism in the Bible Christian Church in 1850. Three years later, Clubb emigrated to the United States, where he began serving as a shorthand reporter for the New York Tribune.

Clubb advocated for abolition in his columns, attempting to humanize slaves by describing in great detail the harsh conditions and mistreatment that characterized plantation life. In the fall of 1854, Clubb became an active member of the AVS, speaking at the organization's annual meeting, a practice he would continue for subsequent years. Clubb saw further possibilities in vegetarianism beyond just participation in the organization. In 1855, Clubb, like Bronson Alcott, of whom he had been a disciple, led vegetarians out of the city and into the country. This time the struggle against slavery was central to the group's purpose: vegetarianism was the vehicle, but abolition was the goal.

With Congress's passage of the Kansas-Nebraska Act in 1854, the new territories' status as free or slave states was left to be determined by popular vote of their residents. As a result of the new legislation, the Kansas territory became contested ground between proslavery forces, primarily from Missouri, and abolitionist activists, largely from the East Coast. Each group descended on Kansas in the hope of shaping its demographics and determining its future status as a state. Hostility and violence between the two groups was inevitable as the central unresolved issue facing the United States unwound on a micro level in Kansas, foreshadowing the coming Civil War.[72]

Henry Clubb and a large group of devoted followers attempted to further the causes of both vegetarianism and abolitionism when they founded the Kansas Vegetarian Settlement Company in 1855. Clubb had witnessed first-hand the federal implications on the debate surrounding Kansas, having served as a congressional reporter for the *Washington Union* newspaper in 1853. Clubb first outlined his plans for the emigration company in the *Illustrated Vegetarian Almanac of 1855*, exhorting "vegetarians who are desirous of promoting freedom in Kansas" to emigrate as part of an effort to "promote the growth of fruits, vegetables and grain."[73] While the experiment was not officially linked to the AVS, the experiment was discussed and promoted at AVS meetings and written about in vegetarian publications. The colony also included many members of the society.

A group of more than fifty interested vegetarians attended a planning meeting for the settlement in New York City on May 6, 1855. The organization was formed as a joint-stock company, with each member of the settlement purchasing five-dollar shares payable in either money or promised labor. Kansas absorbed a number of settlements based on the principles of abolition in the years leading to statehood, including socialists, free thinkers, and antislavery advocates funded by the New England Emigrant Aid Company.[74] The vegetarian settlement shared the goals of the Emigrant Aid Company: to further the cause of abolition *and* make a profit for its investors. However, unlike the aid company's colonies, the vegetarian settlement raised funds among its members rather than from private investors.

Residents were expected to be philosophically, physically, and economically invested in the settlement's success. The colony's hierarchy consisted of active members of the American vegetarian movement, and it elected members of the AVS to its governing board. Charles DeWolfe, a Philadelphia lawyer and temperance advocate was elected as the group's president. John McLauren, a water-cure physician from New York City, became the company's treasurer and "pioneer," in charge of scouting the exact location of the settlement. Henry S. Clubb was named the group's secretary, responsible for arranging logistical details.[75] Forty-seven interested individuals signed contracts at the meeting, agreeing to begin the process of moving to Kansas in the spring of 1856. Another sixty-one vegetarians wrote to the meeting pledging their intent to join the settlement company, bringing the total number of potential settlers to 108.[76]

The group drafted a constitution for the company, which noted that "the practice of [a] vegetarian diet is best adapted to the development of the highest and noblest principles of human nature." The settlement's primary goal, however, was "to promote the enactment of good and righteous laws in that territory, to uphold freedom, and to oppose slavery and oppression in every form."[77] The settlement was an attempt to put the social and political values of movement vegetarianism into direct action. The colony was planned both to serve as living proof of vegetarianism's health advantages and to advance abolition in the territory. An application process and rigorous review of candidates was conducted to ensure that members of the settlement company abhorred slaveholding and were of reputable moral character.

At the end of the screening process, the group consisted of fifty families and had raised nearly $75,000. By February 1856, the amount invested in the colony grew to $133,000.[78] Colonists were required to sign an oath promising to abstain from intoxicating liquors, tobacco, and animal flesh as a precondition of residency. Further, members pledged to "promote social, moral, and political freedom; to maintain the observance of all good and righteous laws" in order to ensure Kansas's entrance into the Union as a free state.[79] Whereas vegetarians—with the exception of Bronson Alcott—had previously built their own smaller communities within mainstream society, the emigration company was an attempt to "establish . . . a home where the slaughter of animals for food shall be prohibited, and where the principle of vegetarian diet can be fairly and fully tested, as to more fully demonstrate its advantages."[80] By the mid-1850s abolition had become the main social concern of movement vegetarians, and the one issue that led the group into taking direct, tangible actions.

The settlement was organized via the octagon plan first described by publisher and phrenologist Orson Fowler. Phrenology—despite its future connections with scientific racism—shared qualities with early vegetarianism. Each sought to understand the human body through supposed physiological evidence. Phrenologists examined skull shape and size, while vegetarians often examined dental, alimentary, and digestive processes in order to argue for their cause. In addition, both movements utilized methodologies outside the mainstream of medical practice and emphasized comprehension of root causes to understand behavior—either the skull or one's appetite.[81] Fowler himself was an active vegetarian and member of the AVS, and Clinton Hall—the headquarters of Fowler's publishing house—served as the site of the first and third annual meetings of the AVS.[82]

In A Home for All, Fowler advocated for octagonal design as being more efficient and cost-effective. When compared to rectangular homes, octagonal houses offered one-fifth more space. An octagonal home also provided health advantages, allowing for larger windows to invite a greater amount of natural sunlight into the home. A cupola tower above roof level topped off the house, providing further sunlight and ventilation.[83] The new design won some popular favor in the United States from the 1840s through the 1870s—particularly among homeowners interested in expressing their aesthetic individuality. The resources and materials needed to realize Fowler's designs, however, often proved costly. Yet the philosophy driving the design of the octagon plan was ahead of its time. As one architect has noted, "Fowler predates Louis Sullivan and Adolf Loos in his argument for purposeful form."[84]

Clubb was directly influenced by Fowler's theories on octagon design; the two had a close working relationship, and many of Clubb's writings were printed by Fowler and Wells, the publishing firm that Orson Fowler co-owned. At the heart of the octagon village plan was an emphasis on communal living, with all dwellings facing the same, shared central octagon. Collective living enabled inhabitants to "excel in the arts of domestic and social life, and in the elevating influences of mental and moral cultivation." The community's design was aimed at promoting productive, ethical living. Isolated, private communities, according to one colony resident, were feared because they caused people to "become indifferent to the refinements of civilized society, and sometimes sink into barbarism."[85] Communal living would promote collective responsibility, cultural development, and shared investment.

The octagon-shaped settlement was a four-square-mile plot of land divided into eight segments of 102 acres each; in essence, an octagon was superimposed on a square tract of land. Each plot faced a 208-square-acre central octagon that housed a common area—a park, library, church, school, agricultural college, or meetinghouse. Tuition for the agricultural college was to be paid to the settlement at large through labor. While individuals each owned their private lots, members of the settlement trust shared equal stakes in the communal, central octagon.

The joint-stock company articulated a series of specific benefits of the octagon style of settlement in its attempts to attract investors. The octagon plan offered the dual advantages of agricultural and communal life, as "every settler would live in a village, and at the same time be in the best possible situation on his farm—between pasture land in front, and arable land in the rear of his dwelling." The communal atmosphere ensured that "every settler would enjoy the mutual aid and protection of the other settlers," a quality—it was implied—lacking in both big cities and conventional western settlements.

Farm life provided practical educational opportunities for children, as well as "plenty of space for playgrounds, and pure air" that was not available in big cities. The settlement plan emphasized agricultural development but also "intellectual advantages," aimed at avoiding "the dullness and monotony, often incident to country life." The company may have been driven by ideological dedication, but it is also had a financial bottom line. Organizers promised potential settlers that the construction of an interdependent village would maximize investors' profits.[86]

The Kansas colony was planned to consist of four octagonal villages, with the hope of creating a sixteen-square-mile settlement. Extra land that fell outside the octagon shape was to be used for wood or grassland.[87] However, the octagon plan was essentially an attempt to build a small city.[88] While Clubb was bringing vegetarians back to the country, his octagon plan of settlement aimed to eventually produce a utopian, urban community. Given the largely cosmopolitan composition of the settlement's founders and citizens, the city-centric plans for Kansas are not surprising. Vegetarians were already familiar with community living in urban boardinghouses. The octagon plan offered residents the best of both worlds—a private home inside of a communal land mass. This undoubtedly appealed to vegetarians, who were the living incarnation of the competing forces of urban sophistication and rural romanticism.

By the winter of 1856, plans for the vegetarian settlement company had come to fruition, with a plot of land agreed on near the banks of the Neosho River in southeastern Kansas.[89] The group's activities attracted coverage in the mainstream press, eliciting a combination of bemusement and praise. The *Chicago Daily Tribune* mocked the group's ability to survive in the West, connecting meat consumption with American rugged individualism. The *Tribune* noted that "a diet of turnips and other garden sass" would not support the rigors of pioneer life. The article argued that Kansas had enough of an influx of eastern reformers, "philosophers, fiddlers, phrenologists, vegetarians, &c. already." What the territory needed to truly thrive was "beef-eating men . . . of thaws and sinews, who have blood to spare and the pluck to put themselves in places where loss of it might happen."[90] The message was clear—meat produced strength, vitality, and masculine men of action. Vegetables created fragile individuals more apt to discuss than to accomplish.

Eastern newspapers, in contrast, encouraged the enterprise. Brooklyn's *Circular* reported on the location's "abundance of water ten months in the year" and the "timber, coal, limestone" sources that abounded. Dedicated to the causes of vegetarianism and abolitionism, the group was strengthened by a "union among the members not usually enjoyed by new settlements . . . earnest reformers in every department of social progress."[91] The *New York Tribune* reported that "the location selected . . . combines all the advantages of mild climate, fertile land, water-power, limestone, coal, wood, pure springs, rolling prairie, and beautiful scenery. . . . It comprises some of the best land in the Territory."[92] Fowler's *Water-Cure Journal* praised the land for the "remarkable purity of the water" and for its "excellent timber," present "in much greater quantities" than in other Kansas locations.[93]

In March 1856, the first group of vegetarian settlers headed west to begin construction of the new settlement. The pioneer residents would build the central octagon building to welcome the new members as well as a sawmill and gristmill. In contrast to Bronson Alcott's attempt at a vegetarian utopia, the Kansas settlers understood the basic needs of sustenance and economic development. Clubb promised settlers a paradise as well as a fully constructed settlement. Early residents—perhaps with lower expectations since they arrived with the task of actually building the colony—were encouraged by what they witnessed. John Milton Hadley, one of the first arrivals, wrote after viewing the land for the first time that the region was "Paradise . . . taking all and comparing with other places of the habitable globe—this is as nearly the equal of Palestine as any."[94]

Hadley reported positively on the settlement's place among abolitionists in the region, reflecting that "the contest for free principles here is strong and well it may be—considering the manner in which the rights of the citizens were outraged at last election." Kansas was "in every respect . . . better suited to vegetarians" due to its climate, vegetation, and influx of eastern reformers. Hadley presciently recognized that "a struggle will be required to make Kansas a free state. It will call for firmness of the best kind. Or for more substantial free state men."[95]

Despite Clubb's paradisiacal promises and language, subsequent waves of immigrants were immediately disappointed when they arrived at the settlement. A difficult trip westward was compounded by the fact that very little had been built or accomplished by the time larger groups of settlers arrived. Miriam Davis Colt provided the most complete first-person account of the Kansas vegetarian settlement, publishing her memoirs six years later in 1862. Colt explained that both economic and social interests led her to join the settlement; she noted that the location of the settlement was in the middle of the path of the newly proposed Transcontinental Railroad, suggesting that the region would experience an economic boom. In addition, she believed that a move west would have "advantages to families of having their children educated away from the ordinary incentives to vice, vicious

*Title page of Miriam Davis Colt's
Went to Kansas (1862).*

company, vicious habits of eating and drinking, and other contaminations of old cities."[96]

The trip out to Kansas was difficult, particularly given that the convoy consisted of "plain eaters," who had to "pick here and there to get plain food." Supplies were limited as the group left the East Coast with only one box of soda crackers, some flour, corn meal, sugar, rice, and dried apples. The trip westward was broken into four parts. From the East Coast vegetarians had to travel to St. Louis, utilizing a combination of regional railroads and horse-drawn wagons. At St. Louis, residents boarded a steamship and headed south to Batesville, Missouri.

Settlers then continued their voyage on foot, traveling from Batesville to Kansas's Fort Scott, a military garrison built in 1841 to quell Native American resistance in the West. Fort Scott remained connected to the vegetarian settlement throughout its existence, providing protection and supplies to its residents. From Fort Scott the group completed its voyage on foot to the vegetarian settlement on the banks of the Neosho River in eastern Kansas. A trip from New York City—the easternmost departure point for residents—covered more than 1,200 miles.[97]

When they arrived in June 1856, the settlers' disillusionment was immediate. Colt said that on entering the colony the group realized that "no mills [had] been built; that the directors, after receiving our money to build mills, [had] not fulfilled the trust reposed in them, and that in consequence, some families [had] already left that settlement."[98] Watson Stewart—a resident from Indiana—noticed when he arrived that "these intelligent, but too confiding families have come from the North, East, South and West, to make pleasant homes; and now are determined to turn right-about, and start again on a journey, some know not where."[99]

There was no library, agricultural college, or even octagon-shaped dwelling. Just one new home was constructed, a basic log cabin with a dirt floor where the Colt family lived. Henry S. Clubb—the mastermind behind the settlement—lived in an abandoned Osage wigwam, a reminder of the changes wrought by continued Euro-American expansion into the West. The remaining residents lived in cloth-covered shacks.[100] Residents nonetheless subsisted off of a diverse diet of wild peas and beans, beds of onions, boiled greens, Johnny cakes, pumpkins, squash, melons, cucumbers, and potatoes.[101]

At the start of fall, the colony was on the brink of starvation and rife with sickness. Colt viewed the experiment as a "calamity . . . pent up in the black clouds" and wished only for her family's lives to be spared.[102] By October, with reports of violence between proslavery border ruffians and free-state abolitionists, many residents began fleeing the colony in advance of the coming harsh winter. The so-called boundless springs of water had dried up, and the settlement's riverside location ensured constant mosquito attacks and the corresponding diseases. The sprawling octagonal settlement that was promised offered only two ovens, one plow, no sawmill, no gristmill, and no octagons for its more than 100 residents. The dreams of utopia were shattered by the harsh realities of western agricultural life.

The group of vegetarians, however, did not disappear immediately. Some residents abandoned the lofty goals of the octagon plan but chose to stay on the land with local elections forthcoming. The remaining vegetarians continued their community, intent on adapting their methodologies for the difficult conditions. Villagers enjoyed close relations with a nearby tribe of Osage and, as documented by Watson Stewart, "often had them with us at dinner, or other meals, and many times some of them would remain with us over night." The new relationship between the settlers and Osage opened up trade opportunities for remaining residents and also exposed vegetarians to new agricultural and architectural methods that the group put into practice in its community.[103]

Perhaps the kinship between the settlers and the Native Americans can be explained by prevailing Osage folklore regarding the group's origins. The tradition holds that two competing tribes—one vegetarian and agricultural, and the other meat-eating and hunting—merged in the early eighteenth century after establishing trade relations and formed the Osage nation. While the Osage no longer adhered to a meat-free diet by the time they came in contact with the vegetarians, the tradition and memory of the Tshishu, or "peace people," were still strong in the group's collective consciousness.[104]

Despite the settlement's relatively short lifespan, its role in the development of vegetarianism in the antebellum era was significant. The colony aimed to remain connected to the larger nationwide vegetarian movement, through promotion by the AVS and Orson Fowler's *Water-Cure Journal*. Further, the group was conceptualized by established members of the American vegetarian community, intent on taking action to utilize dietary reform as a means to encourage abolition.

The settlement company was also an economic venture, albeit one that failed miserably. The experiment allowed for private ownership of individual tracts of land while also encouraging communal equality through ownership of the central octagon and the company itself. The group left its mark in the eventual state of Kansas, where the area surrounding the banks of the Neosho River is still known as Vegetarian Creek.[105] And while the octagon plan did not succeed in establishing a long-lasting vegetarian city in Kansas, it helped promote octagonal design in the public consciousness, and the architectural style remained popular in home design through the 1870s. Further, while the AVS was diminishing in its membership, dedicated vegetarians illustrated that the movement would not shrink into oblivion.

The residents of the Kansas Vegetarian Settlement were part of the free labor system advocated by the newly formed Republican Party in the 1850s. Whether driven by moral outrage or pure economic motives, free laborers viewed slavery as destructive to the republic and doomed to failure. Vegetarians themselves were driven by both of these goals, moving to Kansas to subvert the further spread of the slave system into the West, while at the same time investing their own economic resources in the venture. The coming of this new national force raised the profile of reform in the public's consciousness, and vegetarians were among the groups embraced.

Driven by an interplay between the competing forces of social philanthropy and economic self-interest, the colony was a cross-section of a new burgeoning American economy, including not only farmers and laborers but also merchants, printers, and physicians.[106] In addition, the settlement was geographically diverse. While the majority of residents were from the Northeast, the group also included members from the American South, Midwest, West, and even Canada.[107]

Most important, in regards to abolitionism, vegetarian residents of the settlement became involved in the dramatic events unfolding in the Kansas territory, which had implications for the larger national debate over slavery. Samuel Stewart—a stonecutter by trade and brother of fellow resident Watson—was elected as a member of the Kansas territorial legislature and served as a delegate to the Free State convention held in Grasshopper Falls in 1857.[108] Stewart later enlisted in Kansas's Tenth Infantry Regiment in February 1863, serving for more than a year before being killed in combat in August 1864.[109]

John Milton Hadley—one of the colony's original settlers—enlisted in Kansas's Eighth Infantry Regiment in October 1861. Hadley served for four years and was promoted numerous times along the way. By the time Hadley left the military, he held the rank of full major in Kansas's Ninth Cavalry Regiment. Hadley was honorably discharged after being wounded in a skirmish with Confederate troops at De Valls Bluff in Arkansas in July 1865.[110] Vegetarians from the Kansas settlement were volunteering to serve in fighting forces. Apparently some vegetarians saw no contradiction between their violence-free diets and fighting for the principles of abolitionism.

James H. Holmes—described by William Lloyd Garrison as "a modest, unassuming man, but full of enthusiasm and indomitable perseverance in the cause of impartial freedom"—was one vegetarian who saw no conflict between his dietary choices and the use of violence against slave interests.[111] Holmes was drawn to the Kansas settlement because of his abolitionism and training in the agricultural sciences. The young vegetarian left the colony in the summer of 1856 at the age of nineteen in order to take command of a regiment of free-state Iowans intent on attacking slavery supporters in Kansas.

In August 1857, Holmes joined forces with John Brown to defend free-state settlements in Osawatomie from advancing bands of proslavery forces from Missouri. In the months that followed, Holmes continued to lead raids against slavery supporters in the territory.[112] Far from seeing a contradiction between his vegetarianism and violent abolitionism, Holmes joined the

Union army soon after the start of the war. While the vegetarian settlement brought Holmes to Kansas, his dedication to the cause of abolition (also one of the goals of the settlement) outweighed vegetarianism's connections with pacifism. Holmes's connections with radical Republicans led President Abraham Lincoln to appoint him territorial secretary to New Mexico in July 1861.[113]

For Henry S. Clubb, the issue of warfare was more problematic. Soon after leaving the settlement, Clubb began publishing a Republican newspaper in Grand Haven, Michigan, long a stronghold of Democratic politics. Clubb remained active in Republican politics in the years leading to the war, serving as a delegate to the party's national convention in Chicago in 1860. In June 1862, Clubb enlisted in the United States Volunteers Quartermaster's Department of Infantry Regiment and was immediately given the rank of captain. Clubb, however, had long been steeped in an intellectual and spiritual tradition of pacifism, first through his practice of Swedenborgianism and later through his conversion into the Bible Christian Church. The vegetarian leader served for four years as a quartermaster, arming and supplying fellow soldiers, even being wounded during the Second Battle of Corinth in Mississippi in October 1862.[114] Clubb was spared further harm because the bullet fortuitously struck a purse filled with money and letters from his wife positioned in his lapel pocket. Among the documents that were shredded to pieces were Clubb's naturalization papers.[115]

Clubb served repeatedly on the frontlines and was present at the Battle of Vicksburg, where he was in charge of transporting troops during the siege. But Clubb's service during the war was remarkable for reasons other than his dedication to the Union. Clubb refused to carry a weapon, unwilling to compromise his personal abhorrence of violence.[116] In his role as a quartermaster, however, Clubb provided material and strategic support to soldiers marching out to the battlefield to kill. The war pushed Clubb to further compromise his ethics; he even ate meat out of necessity during his service years when no other provisions were available.[117]

Whereas Grahamites and movement vegetarians led by the AVS despised violence in all forms and even viewed meat-eating as a cause of aggression, the events of the period led a new group of vegetarians to compromise their pacifistic and even at times their dietary views. Some, like Stewart and Holmes, had no problems taking up arms. Others, like Clubb, were stuck in a position of internal conflict. Clubb also was torn away from his wife, Anne, who was pregnant. How did Clubb negotiate the contradictions between wartime violence and his personal vegetarianism and pacifism?

The letters Clubb wrote to his wife during the war offer insight into this issue. The subject of diet appeared in the first letters Clubb wrote after enlisting. In August 1862, he told Anne he "enjoyed excellent health since I left home" but craved some of the healthy culinary comforts of Michigan. Clubb asked Anne, who was scheduled to come visit Mississippi at some point in the fall, to be sure to bring along fruit. He did not "know anything that would be so serviceable to bring with you when you come as a few bushels of dried blackberries" because of their health-giving properties and ease of transport.[118] Even though Clubb was preoccupied with the business of war, his heart and mind were not entirely disconnected from his ideologically driven food needs.

On the issue of warfare, Clubb's letters depict a soldier conflicted between the cause he joined and his personal pacifism. Clubb's first three months in the army were largely spent moving throughout Mississippi, sleeping primarily in boardinghouses and hotels. Not coincidentally, during this time Clubb reported positively on his experiences, going as far as to say he liked his position "very well."[119] Once Clubb witnessed the horrors of the battlefield, however, his opinion quickly soured. As early as September 13, Clubb reported on his plan to limit his exposure to the harsh southern sun, hoping to "keep as cool as possible," preferring instead to have his clerks give direct instructions to soldiers in the field. Clubb told his wife that if he was not allowed this indulgence, he was "willing to resign." After all, Clubb explained, somewhat ironically given his post, "a man is not required to kill himself in the Government service."[120]

A week later, Clubb wrote to Anne following a battle between Union and Confederate forces in Iuka, Iowa. The scene on the frontlines must have affected him deeply; he reported that Union forces lost between 400 and 500 soldiers. Even though he was just a quartermaster and "in the rear of the train," Clubb witnessed the death of a young Southern soldier. Clubb received a letter from his brother-in-law James soon after leaving the field, sharing the news that Anne had given birth to twins. Clubb, having just watched the end of life, must have been struck by the poignancy of simultaneously learning of the start of two others: he wrote to Anne that he wanted to name one of the twins Iuka.[121] In a letter written nine days later, Clubb re-created the scene: "I saw a great many wounded and dead men, and saw scenes which I never wish to see again. It seems hard that our men, who are innocent, have to suffer so much, but such is war, and we must have patience until it is over."[122] Clubb, though often shocked by the violence he witnessed, and dissatisfied with his position and the rampant corruption that he observed, remained in his role for another two years before receiving his honorable discharge.[123]

Vegetarianism and its predecessors had for decades been linked indelibly to efforts to end slavery. In this sense, the active involvement of vegetarians in both Kansas and the Union army was a logical outgrowth of a movement that saw the end of slavery as one of its most important goals. However, vegetarians also practiced violence-free diets in order to be more peaceful individuals. The term *vegetarianism*—as defined by the AVS itself—referred to a diet free of flesh products produced by violence and suffering. Vegetarians believed in and preached the notion that dietary change could eventually lead to the end of the slave system. However, by the 1860s the slave system remained entrenched in the South. With the outbreak of the Civil War, vegetarians saw an opportunity to purge the United States of the blight of slavery.

This involvement illustrates a stark transition in the vegetarian movement. Vegetarians who joined the Union army and fought for the cause of abolition in Kansas subordinated their dedication to pacifism to what they believed was a greater good. In essence, the larger issues facing the Union made vegetarianism a secondary consideration for many dietary reformers. In the process, vegetarianism as a movement changed.

The experiment in Kansas lasted only about two years in total, yet in many ways it symbolizes the variety of challenges that the coming Civil War posed for the vegetarian community. Vegetarians were just as concerned with Americans' dietary practices as they were with the major social and political issues of the time, frequently linking them together. Vegetarians hoped that "the darkest of the twenty-four hours is just before the break of day" and that "vegetarianism may . . . break forth upon us with all the brightness of the morning sun."[124] During the years leading up to the Civil War, vegetarianism merged with national causes, helping the movement gain national prominence but also causing it to lose some of its ideological connection to the past.

:::::::

In 1857, the AVS fully integrated with the older, more established Vegetarian Society of England, and each organization's bylaws provided honorary membership for vegetarians in foreign countries. While this organizational shift was at first symbolic of an ongoing transatlantic exchange between vegetarians, it set the stage for the two organizations to conjoin. Comembership ensured that the *Vegetarian Messenger*, the monthly publication of the British Vegetarian Society, became the de facto publication of the AVS, which had ceased publication of its own journal in October 1854. American vegetarians received free subscriptions to the *Vegetarian Messenger*, and the journal began including regular coverage of activities in the United States. At the same time, the *Water-Cure Journal* continued reporting occasionally on vegetarian activities in the United States.[125]

As events in Kansas illustrated, movement vegetarians were becoming actively involved in the widespread social changes taking place in the United States. Abolition—long seen as one of the primary goals of vegetarianism—was seen as so important that vegetarians became more actively involved in efforts to end slavery, even to the point of compromising vegetarian principles. The Civil War with its extreme violence and opportunity for social and political transformation ensured that vegetarianism would become intertwined with and ultimately overwhelmed by national issues.

Further shifts within movement vegetarianism would affect the trajectory of the AVS. In March 1859, the death of William Alcott left the AVS without another of its founders and most notable proponents. The *New York Times* remembered Alcott as a "well-known physiological writer and lecturer" as well as a "prolific contributor to periodical literature" who "devoted his energies to the establishment of vegetarianism."[126] The *Chicago Tribune*, often a fierce critic of vegetarianism, reported on Alcott's death by noting that he was "one of the main pillars of the vegetarian cause in the United States."[127]

William Metcalfe—founder of the Bible Christian Church in the United States—took over the presidency of the AVS in the fall of 1859. At the age of seventy-two, Metcalfe was an exemplum of the benefits of vegetarianism, having led a long, healthy, and happy life. Dietary reformers had come full circle, looking to the past hoping for a continuing future. Society meetings and banquets were subsequently held at the Bible Christian Church in Philadelphia, though the group continued to include vegetarians from a variety of backgrounds. While the connection between American and British movement vegetarians created an internationalized movement, the relationship also presented difficulties.

With the British Vegetarian Society facing financial hardships, free memberships and newsletter subscriptions were no longer available to American vegetarians by 1860. As a result, many American vegetarians decided to join the British society in order to continue receiving the *Vegetarian Messenger*. American vegetarians wanted to subscribe to a journal dedicated specifically to the practice of vegetarianism rather than receive publications like the *Water-Cure Journal* that included spotty reporting on the movement.

The transatlantic exchange between American and British vegetarians during the 1830s and 1840s, which helped create the AVS in 1850, also led to the American organization's later decline. Membership numbers in the AVS continued to drop, and in 1862 the AVS dissolved following its twelfth annual meeting.[128] American vegetarians would be without a national organization for more than twenty years.

While in one sense the end of the AVS marked a loss for American movement vegetarianism, it also illustrated how much the community had grown. During an incredibly tumultuous period, vegetarianism remained. American vegetarians felt such a strong kinship and community with their British counterparts that they preferred to join the foreign organization rather than subscribe to a journal not centered on their movement. This overriding desire for community was, in many ways, a direct response to the attacks that vegetarians faced from mainstream culture.

CHAPTER FOUR

Vegetarianism and Its Discontents

::

Avoid most religiously all Vegetarians, whose long absence from mutton, necessarily works them into a ravenous state. —"A Vegetarian Cannibal," The Lantern, September 4, 1852

"He was the strictest Vegetarian of the community, and the most intolerant of the flesh-eating barbarians of the outer world," claimed *New York Tribune* reporter Thomas Butler Gunn. "He never used the words meat, beef, pork, or mutton; employing in lieu of them such denunciatory terms as dead flesh, cow's corpse, butchered hog, and the like." Such was the description of one dedicated vegetarian in Gunn's 1857 narrative of life in a vegetarian boardinghouse. Gunn's work, *The Physiology of the New York Boarding-House*, was filled with descriptions of visits to a variety of homes, including a boardinghouse filled with medical students, one populated by Irish immigrants, and one run by spiritualists. Gunn's purported visit to the vegetarian boardinghouse was one component of his larger satirical look at New York boardinghouse culture in the late 1850s.

Gunn mocked and demeaned the health and philosophy of the vegetarian home's residents. He presented boarders as physically frail, first evidenced by a corresponding illustration on the chapter's initial page. The drawing depicted a pair of vegetarians as a walking squash and a weak-looking carrot with protruding eyes and an expression of shock and dismay. Gunn described the vegetarian home's owner as dour-looking, "always dressed in black," wearing "scanty frocks, black cotton stockings, and thick shoes." There was at least one positive attribute to the woman. "Happily for society in general," Gunn wrote, "she had no children."

Gunn attempted to indicate that the flaws of a vegetable diet were so strong that they manifested themselves in the boarders' physical appearance. He described a male resident of the house as "a tall, spare man, with a large nose, light watery eyes and but little hair, though he wore a straggling hay-colored beard." Gunn mocked the man's wife as "a little rigid woman, without eye-brows," who resembled "an elderly frog laboring under the combined miseries of a severe stomach-ache and the conviction that he was going insane and had better commit suicide."[1] A middle-aged male resident was marked by a "colorless countenance" and resembled a "dropsical turnip, with two raisins stuck in it."

Gunn described vegetarians as faddists who had previously aligned themselves with a variety of religious and political groups. The home's proprietor spent his life searching for "new things" and was fascinated with a variety of ideals, all for short periods of time. Gunn wrote that the owner had "shower-bathed his soul with Unitarianism, frozen it up tight in Transcendentalism[,] . . . besmoked it in Swedenborgianism[,] . . . let it putrify in Mormonism, flayed it with Shaking-Quakerism . . . and dug it up with Spiritualism." He mockingly labeled a female resident as a "keen politician" of the "Whole-Ticket-Died-in-the-Wool-Anti-Union-Pro-Amalgamation-Anti-States-Rights-and-No-Backing-Out Stripe," inclined toward hypocrisy and inconsistency. Another resident of the home was so peculiar in his dietary habits that he even ate the rinds of melons and pineapples, digestive challenges notwithstanding.[2]

Most worrisome to Gunn were the physical and intellectual effects of the diet, that he observed causing "a strong disinclination to do any thing; an unnatural meekness of disposition; a tendency to boils; and a generally-sublimated and windy estimation of our own importance and destiny." Gunn concluded that vegetarians had "a sort of tranquil dissatisfaction with the world in general, and a desire to set it to rights through the medium of writing letters." Vegetarianism was marked by intellectual timidity, faddism, and pretentiousness. Gunn focused on what he viewed as inherent personality flaws as proof that vegetarianism was worthy of scorn. Liberation, however, was mercifully at hand for Gunn and his colleague; they fled the boardinghouse in the middle of the night for a moonlight picnic of ham sandwiches and champagne by the Hudson River.[3]

These claims about vegetarians would have been familiar to readers in the middle of the nineteenth century, vegetarian and nonvegetarian alike. In fact, attacks such as Gunn's on vegetarians were frequent during the early years of movement vegetarianism.

Critics of vegetarianism throughout the mid-nineteenth century focused primarily on vegetarians' purported physical, emotional, and mental frailty. During this period of growth for movement vegetarianism, the community was defined for the collective American cultural consciousness by both adherents and detractors alike. As a result, it is important to consider vegetarianism's critics. In some instances, objections to vegetarianism were driven by strongly held American culinary preferences. Other protests were expressed through the perspective of medical and scientific expertise. At times, the debate surrounding vegetarianism was even infused with the larger political debates of the period.

Examining the nature of attacks on vegetarians helps us understand how and why movement vegetarianism in the mid-nineteenth century was seen as culturally, socially, and politically undesirable to large swaths of mainstream society. Ad hominem attacks against vegetarians were frequently tinged with cruelty, vitriol, and contempt. However, the negative portrayals also had the unintended consequence of spreading awareness of vegetarianism among both supporters and critics, during a period of significant social and cultural tensions. Attacks on vegetarians persisted even following the dissolution of the American Vegetarian Society (AVS). Individuals attempted to keep the movement alive despite the simultaneous challenges of the loss of vegetarianism's national organization and continued intense public mockery.

Thanks to the activities of the AVS, vegetarians had become a visible part of the 1850s reform landscape. The group even found itself in the middle of the debate surrounding a presidential election. The radical and threatening nature of vegetarianism and its relationship with national social reform was unwittingly expressed in a political cartoon from the famed publishing firm of Currier and Ives. The cartoon offers insight into popular fears produced by both vegetarians and the newly formed, reform-minded Republican Party. The drawing also provides an accurate summary of popular images of movement vegetarians in the mid-1850s.

A caricature referencing the first Republican presidential candidate, John C. Fremont, presents a series of reformers attempting to have their particular reform principle noted and acted on by the new party. Included in this group are representatives of well-known reform movements, including a women's suffragist, a socialist, an abolitionist, a free lover, and a Catholic (Fremont was accused by some Democrats of being a closet Catholic).[4] Fremont responds to the requests by promising each of the representatives what they desire, if he is elected.

To the far left stands a frail and weakened vegetarian, advocating for the passage of a law banning the consumption of flesh, tobacco, and alcohol. Vegetarians, of course, did not seek any legislation regarding meat production in the United States, seeing the issue as a choice that should be made based on moral conviction. In this sense the lithograph is misleading.

The Great Republican Reform Party, Calling on Their Candidate (*New York:* Currier & Ives, 1856). *Courtesy of the General Research and Reference Division, Schomburg Center for Research in Black Culture, The New York Public Library, Astor, Lenox, and Tilden Foundations.*

However, the presentation of a vegetarian in the debate surrounding the 1856 presidential election reflects the irrational fear many American meat-eaters felt as well as the exaggeration often used by vegetarianism's detractors. The vegetarian's place in this image also speaks to the movement's growth and recognized role in formulating a radical reform critique in the antebellum era.[5] Despite the public mockery, vegetarians were successful in having their movement and ideology recognized by society at large.

The 1850s social reform movement of which vegetarians were part came to prominence during a period with the potential for fundamental political and social change in the United States. The rise and success of the early Republican Party lay in its ability to bring together a variety of interest groups and regions under the banner of moral, social, and economic reform. The nascent party appealed to a wide variety of constituents including former Whigs, Northern Democrats, abolitionists, religious leaders, and business capitalists, united by a common adherence to the ideology of free labor.[6]

Under the umbrella of wide social change and upheaval, vegetarians offered a singular, catalytic cure for society's ills—a decidedly traditional, agrarian-based methodology to improve modern, urban life. Vegetarians, in the process, questioned and doubted many of the practices of mainstream society, from the most fundamental—the food an individual chose to eat—to the social and political. While ultimately such a utopian view of vegetarianism was overstated, the threat that vegetarianism posed to American norms lay in its questioning of more established culinary, racial, gendered, and economic ideals.

In emphasizing the power of the personal, vegetarians stressed self-analysis as a route toward individual empowerment. And in criticizing the flaws in modern life, movement vegetarians also took advantage of modernization and the urban landscape in order to spread awareness. Given vegetarians' dedication to social equity—particularly in the form of women's suffrage and abolition—and the perceived role of diet in such social changes, it is not surprising that they met such aggressive responses.

The popular press and other critics did not so much debate the merits or disadvantages of vegetarianism as ridicule vegetarians' supposed physical and mental weakness. The scathing nature of the attacks on vegetarians illustrates just how threatening vegetarians and their reformist ideology were to established cultural and social norms in antebellum America.

In a July 1850 article, the *Saturday Evening Post* questioned the healthfulness of a vegetarian diet, preferring to "go for beef-steaks and mutton-chops" in order to gain physical strength and mental force. Although the article seemed to sympathize with the vegetarian pursuit of self-control, since "it may be argued . . . that we want to make men peaceable now-a-days—not quarrelsome and warlike," it questioned vegetarianism in starkly xenophobic language, arguing that "we do not want to make them peaceable by making them weak and cowardly, like the Hindoos." As the United States became a world economic power, the *Saturday Evening Post* made it clear that fragile, overly calm individuals were destructive to the interests of the republic.[7] The *New York Herald* went further, calling the AVS's second anniversary event a "feast of (t)reason."[8]

In "Confessions of a Vegetarian" (reprinted in newspapers stretching from New York to Georgia and Ohio), vegetarians were mocked as peculiar in their personal habits. The article was written from the perspective of a fictional vegetarian who would not sit in "hair-bottomed chairs" because his "conscience was so tender that I could not sit down upon them without feeling a degree of horror." The piece presented vegetarians as animal-obsessed and opposing natural laws, willing to "be employed in the forests to prevent the wild beasts from gorging upon each other" and apt to go "into the deep to tame the sharks and cause the larger fishes to live upon seaweed instead of upon the small fry." The article closed with a call to arrest and punish all butchers for "wilful murder" and sentence them to a lifetime of solitary reflection in a forest, essentially living the life of a plant.[9]

Vegetarians, of course, did not advocate for any of the extreme measures satirized in this "confession." However, the group did understandably seem strange in a society where meat consumption was standard practice. And vegetarians surely ruffled feathers with their arguments based in notions of moral superiority. But rather than argue the merits of dietary reform based on scientific or medical arguments, the popular press relied on exaggeration and fear to discredit the very notion of vegetarianism.

The *Daily National Intelligencer* of Washington, DC, reported on the AVS's fourth anniversary meeting, describing the group as among "the oddities of the day." The article emphasized that economics rather than morality or politics should drive culinary choices, arguing that "our retreat from animal to vegetable subsistence would yield very little advantage" in terms of monetary savings. The writer described William Alcott's arguments in favor of vegetarianism—specifically, the potential spiritual and health benefits of dietary reform—as being based in "some curious facts."[10]

Famed American travel writer Bayard Taylor injected the issue of race into the discussion of vegetarianism. Taylor's account of his travels throughout Northern and Central Africa included a report on the vegetarian diets that he observed among Berbers and Sudanese villagers. Taylor claimed that the Africans he observed living on a vegetable diet were "as weak as children, when compared with an able-bodied European," a condition that the "lank" American vegetarian would have to explain in order to justify the diet. Taylor's implication was clear; vegetarians in the United States were no better than Africans and African American slaves, both continually presented as childish and simple in American popular consciousness and culture.[11]

The *Lowell (MA) Daily Citizen and News* injected the issue of sexuality into the debate. In "An Anti-vegetarian Virgin," the paper mockingly reported on a vegetarian who was "courting to a plucky lass" and proposed marriage. According to the article, the woman responded with harshness and doubt, exclaiming, "Oh . . . go along with you! Do you think I'm going to be flesh of your flesh, and you live on cabbages? No, indeed, I don't belong to the rabbit family."[12]

Similar themes found their way into American popular culture. In Herman Melville's short story "Bartelby the Scrivener," a vegetarian character is described as a man who "never eats a dinner, properly speaking. . . . He never eats even vegetables, he eats nothing but ginger-nuts."[13] Vegetarians were even mocked in song. "Oh! Wasn't She Fond of Her Greens!" was first published in 1860 by the New York firm H. De Marsan, with subsequent versions printed until 1869. There is no surviving record of the song's melody. However, the lyrics provide insight into the intersections between popular images of vegetarians and perceived gender roles.

The song recounts a romantic pursuit from the perspective of a man who seeks the affections of the young Jane Bell, who surpasses all other women in his eyes. Unfortunately, he learns that she is a vegetarian: "A vegetarian she'd been, for some years; / No animal's food would she eat; / How wonderful strange it appears, / That she could exist without meat!" The song describes the oddness of the couple's courtship, filled with picnics of garden sorrel (a green, leafy herb) and breakfasts of watercress.

The last verse exposes the complex interplay between images of vegetarians, gender, and sexual norms. The lyrics flash forward to note that the couple remains together. The last stanza reports that once married, the woman has been tamed and settled, no longer adhering to her vegetarianism: "Now, we are married, and settled in life. / The old gal behaves very kind; / And, when I go home of a night, / There plenty of greens I can find. / Since marriage, she's taken to meat. . . . / How wonderful strange it seems! / And sometimes, by the way of a treat, / She has a little fat meat with her greens."[14] Having been corralled by the singer, the wife—previously obstinate in her diet and, perhaps, chastity—was now apt to enjoy meat in all of its variety of forms. The popular press frequently linked meat consumption with virility in mocking male vegetarians. Similarly, as in the song, female vegetarians were presented as strange and curious, spirits to be tamed and controlled. The lyrics, as well as the larger debate surrounding vegetarianism at the time, were about far more than just greens.

Gendered attacks against vegetarians were thus applied to both women and men. Popularly presented as frail, weakened, and feminized, the male vegetarian in the United States was cast as sickly, sexually impotent, and nearly invalid. This image proliferated in a flash press that questioned the very notion of a vegetarian diet in an era of urban hypermasculinity. The sporting press, which promoted a brand of masculinity obsessed with urban amusements, flourished in New York. The young men who produced it reported on pastimes ranging from commercialized sex to sporting events. These papers were largely unified by themes of "libertine republicanism" that embraced hypersexualized, heterosexual white Anglo-Saxon Protestant males while degrading minorities, especially African Americans, homosexuals, Jews, and Catholics. Vegetarians also gained the derision of the flash press.[15]

Spirit of the Times focused on sporting events, the theater, and celebrity gossip.[16] Despite its entertainment focus, it gave vegetarians more attention than did any other flash paper. One article, for example, reported on a visit to a vegetarian boardinghouse and mocked its menu, visitors, and waiters as strange, pompous, and frail. The author claimed that all he could receive to eat as an entrée was a plate of grass. The newspaper described vegetarians as being "infantine" and "humbugs," wondering how vegetarians could really be interested in health preservation given the paucity of their diet.[17] The publication made the connection between diet and quirkiness explicit, describing vegetarians as "eccentric."[18]

Another article combined nutritional advice with observations from the nascent field of phrenology. The author claimed that a vegetarian diet had made Indian Hindus "weakly and degenerated," illustrated by their "exceedingly narrow" heads. In contrast, Northern Europeans, who "feed much upon animal food," were noted for their "wide cranium," designed for a more complex process of mastication. The article attempted to validate its analysis by arguing that vegetarians were made more vulnerable to disease by an innutritious diet that caused their urine to be filled with more sugar than uric acid.[19] Vegetarians and detractors alike attempted to project supposed medical and scientific expertise in arguing for the proper diet.

Spirit of the Times frequently mocked the haughtiness of vegetarians, particularly those who demeaned carnivores. In one purported exchange, a meat-eater asked why his dining partner was not partaking in a roast beef dinner. When the vegetarian revealed his dietary predilections, the carnivorous diner wondered aloud how meat could be injurious given his own stout physique, red cheeks, and healthy "composition." The vegetarian responded by stating that he preferred "dieting to die-eating."[20] Given vegetarians' moral opposition to flesh foods, the caricature was perhaps not far from a realistic portrayal of some of the more vocal vegetarians. However, in its emphasis on satire, *Spirit of the Times* concentrated on the arrogance of some vegetarians rather than considering any possible benefits of the diet.

The publication also provided "A New Song for Grahamites" in an article that mocked vegetarians' pompousness and religiosity. The song claimed that vegetarians believed that everyone was a sinner, doing nothing "but sin, at breakfast, tea, and dinner." Verses referenced biblical stories, mocking vegetarians' tendency to use (and abuse, according to critics) scriptural references to advocate for vegetarianism.

The song went further in its sardonic treatment of vegetarians, however, saying they saw danger in all foods, that "even in greens there is meat," and "there is danger in each course of sprouts, and poison in all that we eat." True vegetarians, according to the song, would "never trust salt on your knife," because "the sin may lay deep on your breast, that you're eating a bit of Lot's wife." Obsessive in their habits, a vegetarian would even worry about "the mites that we munch in a cheese" or "the myriads of animal life you drink in a drop of cold water." The song concluded by providing a new biblical rally-ing cry for the peculiar vegetarian, and a hope that they would whittle away, proclaiming that, "Not alone do we shun meat and wine," but instead "let us eat and drink nothing at all, that our days may be long in the land."[21]

Spirit of the Times emphasized vegetarians' physical frailty, even when they were not the focus of a report. One article describing a sickly old horse said it was "leaner than a Grahamite's shadow."[22] In an article reporting on a gourmet restaurant, vegetarians were described as physically lean and men-tally dull.[23] One article—in a significant understatement—confessed that the newspaper had "laughed once or twice at the Vegetarians." The author argued that since vegetarians were "precluded by their rules from anything exhilarating," the mocking coverage was beneficial to them, "wholesome in a double sense" because "it will afford them the excitement of a laugh while it cures them of their folly." Vegetarians claimed to see a "grand union between the market-garden and the moral and mental attributes." However, the article proclaimed, any individual obsessed with "one perpetual round of potatoes, beans and broccoli" could not "attain to any very high degree of intellectual culture."[24]

The publication also questioned vegetarians' politics and patriotism. Re-porting on a mock Fourth of July celebration by reformers in New England, *Spirit of the Times* noted the appearance of vegetarians "bearing a string of sausages stuffed with turnips and beets." Vegetarians were simultaneously labeled as "readers of quack advertisements" and "dissolvers of the Union," which suggested fears that reformers would drive a permanent wedge be-tween North and South. And while the article questioned the motives of the parade's participants, its recognition of the connection between vegetar-ians and other reform movements (the description noted the participation of midwives, "members of women's rights," and the "President and Direc-tors of the Underground Railroad") illustrates vegetarians' recognized role among the social reformers of the period.[25]

Attacks on vegetarians continued as the movement grew. Writing to Van-ity Fair magazine in the fall of 1860 under the pseudonym "Julia Befeeter," a Brooklyn woman complained about the perils of her current existence. Rather than focus on the deepening sectional crises that threatened the Union, the author of the letter launched an invective against a dietary civil war taking place in her own household. She claimed to be tormented by "inflictions heaped on my plate three times a day by my cabbage headed husband." As a result, "Befeeter" was writing to the magazine for advice on how best to deal with her husband's dietary choices. She reported that her husband had traveled to "that wretched Philadelphia" on what he claimed was a business trip. In fact, he had gone there to "attend The Eleventh Anniversary of the American Vegetarian Society," where his head was crammed "with nonsensical ideas about beans, and potatoes, and cold water."

The letter concluded with a warning about a vegetarian diet's potential destruction of conjugal union. "I will sue for a divorce from this garden bed and vegetable life," she exclaimed. The writer claimed to be physically weakened by her husband's "odious vegetarian diet," which was more "fit for an old cow, instead of the graceful but half starved."[26]

Vegetarians certainly noted the widespread mockery and often hostility. Reflecting on the challenges of a vegetarian lifestyle, one advocate observed that "men get angry and rave against Vegetarians as if they had committed some mortal offence. . . . A man cannot make a simple natural meal, without suffering a sort of martyrdom, from all the flesh eaters around him."[27] Angry reactions by carnivores strengthened the resolve of vegetarians, who believed that a meat-based diet fueled violent, aggressive behavior. Dedicated to addressing larger issues of social justice and equity, vegetarians sought to ignore their critics and challenge many of the fundamental political questions facing antebellum America.

At the core of the vegetarian movement was an unwavering moral principle that equated violence against animals with a cruel and aggressive society. For vegetarians, violence of any type generated and bred an uncontrolled society driven by lust, rage, and desire. Vegetarianism was a means to bring order and serenity to a society that could often seem chaotic and disorganized thanks to the dual forces of urbanization and industrialization. In the process of economic growth, family and community connections gradually faded, increasing feelings of powerlessness. Threatened by vast social change and observing a nationwide culture that struggled to provide answers for the important ethical issues of the time, vegetarians wondered aloud whether humankind was descending into brutish behavior, whether "the flesh of the beast, when eaten by man, is apt to produce in him beastly habits and animal desires."[28]

The invectives aimed at vegetarians came from many different directions. Medical doctors and other health advocates attacked vegetarianism as both philosophically flawed and unnatural. One detractor believed that vegetarianism was part of "the characteristic traits of our nation, to hold our conventions and anniversaries, and to indulge in the luxury of societies and associations for every conceivable object." The *Saturday Evening Post* argued that food was intended to create "physical strength and mental force," which were best provided by "beef-steaks and mutton-chops." Despite the article's lack of scientific evidence, the author exhorted readers to "build theories on facts" and "not disregard facts for the sake of mere theories."[29]

For these writers, while meat consumption was an unquestioned standard, vegetarianism could only be valuable if scientifically and medically proven. The illustrations accompanying such articles often depicted vegetarians as anthropomorphized vegetables, revealing the widespread fear that the loss of meat consumption would entail a loss of one's basic humanity.[30]

Vegetarians and movement vegetarianism were roundly criticized in the medical and scientific literature of the period. Reporting on the first meeting of the American Vegetarian Society, *Scientific American* focused on the pompousness of vegetarians, pointing out that the group's resolutions provided "fulfillment of that old saying, 'it's a grand thing to have a good conceit of ourselves.'" Vegetarians were stridently confident in the righteousness of their cause, and this inevitably irritated meat-eaters. Vegetarians, the *Scientific American* author argued, "must be a moral set of mortals in their own estimation," having "come to the conclusion that a vegetable diet will make our earth a Paradise again." The writer predicted that vegetarians "will yet try to prove that the forbidden fruit was nothing less than a beef-steak or mutton-chop."

Echoing a claim that first appeared in Philadelphia in response to the Bible Christians, the article accused vegetarians of "heresy" in their "disposition to make all scripture square with conceived opinions, instead of endeavoring to square opinions to scripture." This did not prevent *Scientific American* itself from joining the battle over dietary expertise, illustrating that its objections to movement vegetarianism were based more on personality than on doctrine. In the same article, the magazine prescribed a vegetable diet in tropical climates, a mixed diet in temperate zones, and a solely animal-based diet in arctic regions.[31]

Vegetarianism received its harshest criticism in mainstream medical literature. In August 1853 the *Boston Medical and Surgical Journal* compared the

"*The Vegetarians.*" From Vanity Fair, October 6, 1860.

effects of vegetarianism to those produced by a serious opium addiction.[32] Another medical journal referred to meat as being "held in almost universal esteem by all civilized people."[33] The implication was, of course, that vegetarians denied themselves a fundamental component of a prospering, modern society. The same journal referred to vegetarianism as a "theoretical diet," arguing that the movement was focused more on an idealistic philosophy than on an applicable way of life.[34] Another medical journal sarcastically reported that attendees at the second meeting of the American Vegetarian Society "parted, much wiser and purer, it is presumed, than when [they] assembled."[35]

A journal published by the Medical College of Georgia claimed that spermatorrhea—the accidental or excessive discharge of semen, a condition seen as particularly damaging during the mid-nineteenth century—could be caused by an exclusively vegetarian diet.[36] As was common in medical journals' coverage of vegetarianism, the author's observations were tied to secondary observations and an inherent bias against the diet rather than to scientific study. The article linked vegetarianism and spermatorrhea with America exceptionalism and racial classification. The author claimed that "the further south we go, the more do we find a vegetable diet supplanting the animal food of northern nations, and the more prominent a place does spermatorrhea assume in the catalogue of diseases." The disease and the vegetarian diet that supposedly contributed to its frequency were both classified as "degenerating to civilization."[37]

Another journal, the *Treasury of Medicine*, stated that a vegetarian diet "was not based on sound physiology." The article again relied on indirect observations to discredit vegetarianism. It advised readers that while a vegetarian diet created a peaceful temper in Hindus, it also was the diet adopted—out of necessity—by the Irish peasant, described as "barbarous" and prone to committing "acts of cruelty and murder as the most carnivorous animals could do." The article concluded its consideration of vegetarians with a warning: "But let the pregnant female . . . indulge this vegetarian crotchet, and most likely, she will do mischief to her own constitution, and either kill her baby, or else see it brought into the world a very small and punk sickly thing."[38]

A variety of other extreme physical maladies were associated with vegetarianism. One doctor warned that a "nonsense" vegetarian diet caused a woman to have an excessive amount of milk produced for nursing, causing her child to starve, while "she herself looked wretched."[39] Ohio's *Eclectic Medical Journal* blamed vegetarianism for an acute case of laryngitis in a man that the diet had made "feeble."[40] Another medical journal believed vegetarianism to be the cause of an increase in cases of the gout among patients, as it "becomes more promptly visceral, in proportion as the appropriate diet and necessary exercise have been neglected."[41] Vegetarianism was also blamed in medical literature for scurvy and phthisis (pulmonary tuberculosis).[42] Vegetarian doctors were referred to as an "absurdity," a group of "pretenders" who aimed to "deceive and gain the ear of an ever-listening public."[43] Another journal referred to vegetarian physicians as "pseudo-philanthropists," more concerned with the fate of animals than with their patients' physical and mental health.[44]

Mainstream publications and newspapers usually focused on the physical and mental frailty of vegetarians as a means to discredit the diet, ideology, and movement. Since popular publications were geared toward lay readers, there was logic in this method. However, it is telling that journals aimed at medical professionals presented similar, alarmist caricatures of movement vegetarianism and vegetarian dietetics. When covering vegetarianism, medical publications largely offered facile, sarcastic observations that often descended into personal attacks or scare tactics similar to those found in the popular press.

At the AVS's seventh anniversary meeting, movement vegetarians passed a resolution aimed at their critics. Just "because an idea is laughed at," the resolution read, "it is thereby not proven to be untrue. . . . Vegetarianism is entitled to no less consideration because Flesh Eaters laugh at it or sneer at it."[45]

The radicalism of a vegetarian diet can only be understood in the larger context of American culinary culture in the mid-nineteenth century, particularly the elements that meat abstention opposed. The fundamental dynamics of the food industry changed during this time as the United States shifted from a primarily agricultural and localized society to a more industrial and urbanized one. This shift also altered the way Americans got their food. Trade systems crossed state boundaries as individuals with surplus goods exchanged their wares with the assistance and under the direction of local grocers. Markets and cities grew, as did the physical distance between producer and consumer.[46] Convenience most often dictated family diets as food was stored longer in order to reduce its cost. Catharine Beecher, an influential antebellum cookbook author and dietary educator, even advised her readers on how to restore spoiled meat and tainted butter.[47]

American food culture of the early nineteenth century was deeply influenced by British culinary traditions, which placed meat at the center of the diet. Mary Randolph's *The Virginia House-Wife*, a cookbook published in 1824, divided the American diet into thirteen categories, seven of which were meat.[48] Reflecting on his dietary experiences in the United States in the early nineteenth century, the French philosopher C. F. Volney wrote that "if a prize were proposed for the scheme of a regimen most calculated to injure the stomach, the teeth, and the health in general, no better could be invented than that of the Americans." Volney described American breakfasts as including "cheese of the fattest kind, slices of salt or hung beef," while dinner was marked by "turnips and potatoes" that "swim in lard, butter or fat" along with "roasted beef" and "boiled pastes . . . the fattest are esteemed the most delicious."[49]

Americans consumed a variety of meats, ranging from steaks to pork and poultry to more specialized meats such as sausages and sweetbreads, particularly with the arrival of increased numbers of immigrants in the 1830s.[50] Writing while visiting the United States, Charles Dickens reflected that "breakfast would have been no breakfast unless the principal dish were a de-formed beef-steak . . . swimming in hot butter, and sprinkled with the very blackest of all possible pepper." Dinners consisted primarily of "salmon, shad, liver, potatoes, pickles, ham, chops, black puddings, and sausages."[51] With advances in commercial tin canning, Americans diets became more diverse, extravagant, and carnivorous.[52] One historian of meat culture has estimated that in the nineteenth century Americans were consuming ap-proximately 150 pounds of meat per capita annually.[53]

U. S. vegetarianism grew as a movement at the precise moment that red meat consumption and culture became a truly national phenomena. In the years before the Civil War, territorial acquisitions in the Southwest ensured the expansion of commercial cattle raising and the live cattle shipping in-dustry, leading directly to the success of slaughterhouses in New York and Chicago, which were able to process live cattle shipped via ferries.[54]

Throughout the nineteenth century, pork remained America's most prominent meat product, used in its various forms as dictated by social and economic hierarchy. Cincinnati became the center of the U. S. pork indus-try, processing nearly 400,000 hogs by the start of the Civil War and export-ing 70 million pounds of cured pork and bacon.[55] By the time movement vegetarianism coalesced and was recognized by the culture at large, it faced the challenge of questioning one of the most deeply held cultural and culi-nary practices in the United States.

With all of the criticism of movement vegetarianism in the popular, medical, and scientific press, some vegetarians sought a way to justify their existence and prove their worth in a society that associated strength, virility, and even social status with meat consumption. On August 27, 1860, three months before the election of Abraham Lincoln, four months ahead of the secession of South Carolina, and just eight months before the first shots of the Civil War, boatman D. U. Martin rowed from Boston for New York City to prove the physical benefits of vegetarianism.

Nicknamed the "Vegetarian Wherryman" by colleagues and the popu-lar press, Martin began his journey with the goal of proving the benefits of a vegetarian diet to supporters and detractors alike.[56] Previous move-ment vegetarians used the word, spoken or written, to counter the claims of antivegetarians. Martin attempted to prove vegetarianism's worth solely through physical exhibition. He also crafted a new methodology that future vegetarians would follow.

D. U. Martin was a known figure among Boston reformers even before his well-covered journey. A typical movement vegetarian with connections to a variety of reform movements, Martin was an active member of the Massachusetts Anti-Slavery Society, the abolitionist organization founded by William Lloyd Garrison in 1831.[57] He was a relatively recent convert to vegetarianism, having eschewed meat in 1857 after hearing a lecture by AVS vice president and noted allopath Russell Trall that stressed the diet's natural healing properties.

Martin believed that he had benefited greatly from vegetarianism in three short years. As a result, he sought to disprove critics who claimed that the lifestyle weakened adherents. While living in Boston in 1860, Martin decided to undertake an experimental physical challenge aimed at illustrating that vegetarianism could be utilized to build strength and success.[58] At the age of thirty-two, standing a lanky five feet, ten inches tall, Martin offered himself as physical, scientific proof of the effectiveness of vegetarianism.

Martin departed from Boston on August 21, arriving in New York City three days later. The wherryman rowed the entire distance, approximately 400 nautical miles for eighty straight hours, relying on a diet of fruits and vegetables.[59] Martin arrived "very much sunburt and fatigued" but otherwise in good spirits and health as he was welcomed by the gathered New York Vegetarian Society.

At the banquet Martin relayed his own conversion narrative, recalling that he was "first induced to try the system of vegetarian living" while "troubled with the dyspepsia." Thanks to a vegetarian diet he could "do more work than any man he ever had an occasion to hire." These results motivated Martin to "demonstrate what a person could endure, living wholly on vegetable food."[60]

Martin's long-distance rowing was covered by the mainstream press, and not just in New York and Boston. At the very moment that the South was inching toward secession, the exploits of the Vegetarian Wherryman were notable enough to garner attention below the Mason-Dixon line. The *Charleston (SC) Mercury* reported that Martin's popularity in New York was particularly impressive given that "a cat is absolutely fond of aquatic sports compared with your genuine Gothamite." The newspaper described Martin as having accomplished "stupendous exertions" guiding his "fifty pound skeleton wherry all the way from Boston." Most impressive was the fact that Martin "could have done this big feat on vegetables alone." Even in the South, where vegetarianism had made little headway, Martin was lauded as a role model for vegetarians and an athletic hero to all.[61]

The banquet that the New York Vegetarian Society held in Martin's honor was a "sumptuous repast, strictly on the vegetarian principles." It featured a wide variety of fruits, vegetables, and puddings, contrasting the Vegetarian Wherryman's favored rowing diet of whortleberries, apples, and watermelons.[62] New York was only a stopover, however. Martin refurbished his supplies after the banquet, grabbing a handful of fruit, a rubber coat, and a navigating chart for the next leg of his trip, northward to the state capital of Albany.

Newspapers reported daily on Martin's progress, underscoring the physical fitness and strength necessary to row great distances. The *New York Times* emphasized Martin's muscularity and physical prowess, utilizing quasi-sexual imagery, noting "the splendid style in which Mr. Martin handled the sculls. His easy, graceful motion, long steady stroke, and powerful pull elicited continued praise, and whortleberries were considered triumphant." Vegetarianism, the newspaper reported, ensured that "his health was much improved, his mind clear, his muscles hard, his strength increased."[63] Such descriptions departed sharply from previous images of male vegetarians that emphasized weakness, frailty, and prudery.

Most remarkable, both the reform and the mainstream press lionized Martin. *The Liberator* wrote with pride of Martin's attempt to "demonstrate what a person could endure, living wholly on vegetable food," reporting that the wherryman was "in the enjoyment of first-rate health."[64] Other papers linked Martin's physical prowess with his political ideology. Martin was described by the *New York Times* as a "practical philosopher" who was "affable as he was healthy" and "seemed rather more inclined to desire the election of Lincoln and Hamlin than of any other candidates who have a possibility of being chosen."[65] The *Chicago Tribune* labeled Martin's travels a "remarkable voyage" guided solely by the sound of the surf.[66] The *Boston Herald* glowingly reported that "the experiment made by the Champion Wherryman goes to show that he had performed an extraordinary muscular feat, of long duration, while subsisting upon a diet of fruit, almost exclusively."[67]

Martin departed New York City on August 31, circumnavigating Manhattan Island. After heading southward on the East River and around the Battery, Martin rowed north on the Hudson River all the way to Albany.[68] He arrived there five days later, on the evening of September 5, in what the *Boston Herald* reported as "good health and spirits."[69] Martin's original plan to row to New Orleans was cancelled because of extensive damage to his rowboat,[70] but his voyage had nonetheless been a resounding success: he had navigated from Boston to New York City to Albany without an ounce of flesh foods, and coverage in both the vegetarian and the mainstream press had linked vegetarianism for the first time with physical prowess.

In March 1861—seven months after his trek—the *Louisville Daily Journal* reported that Martin had survived an attack by a pack of wild dogs. The article emphasized Martin's rugged individualism, noting that he "had been in the habit of camping out very often, to convince himself of the truth or fallacy" of the popular claim that a meatless diet could not produce enough vitality to survive cold weather.[71] Martin's journey generated so much interest that his experiments with vegetarianism were still considered newsworthy after his voyage.

A month later it was reported that Martin had overcome a severe illness and fever. Newspapers attributed Martin's quick recuperation to his vegetarian diet, noting that after losing fourteen pounds to the illness he regained twenty "and was fully restored to health without a particle of medicine."[72] A year later the press reported that Martin sought to make his fortune by heading west. Martin utilized his vegetarian diet to prepare his body for the rigors of gold mining in California, adding fruits such as bananas and oranges to his meatless regimen.[73]

Martin's popularity occurred at the precise time when movement vegetarians began linking physical strength and personal success with vegetarianism to rebuff detractors' claims that the diet created weak individuals. The *American Phrenological Journal*—an occasional voice of movement vegetarian activities—responded to a report on the wherryman that protested against "all this muscle humbugger." In an article tellingly titled "Muscle-Mania," the journal sought "to enter our protest and erect some barrier against" the objections.

The article's author suggested that "a glance at the men of influence in America within the current century will show, we think, a majority of strong bodies along with strong minds." Muscular Northern men such as Martin, Stephen A. Douglas, Lewis Cass, and Charles Sumner were protectors of the Union, whereas Southern leaders such as Senator John C. Calhoun and future Confederate vice president Alexander Stephens were "light and fragile."[74] Martin's vegetarianism—a diet often described as fragile and anemic—had switched roles among the new enemies of the Union. With war on the horizon, men of strength, honor, and discipline were needed to quell the rebellious South. The muscular values expressed in the popular and reform press encouraged audiences to embrace the wherryman's experiment, and by extension vegetarianism. Martin's voyage marked the beginning of a shift in movement vegetarianism away from a focus on social reform and communalism and toward physical strength and individualism.

The Vegetarian Wherryman's brief and successful trip illustrated that movement vegetarianism sought to remain in the public eye even with the coming of the Civil War and the slow dissolution of the AVS. Vegetarianism was still seen largely as a personality quirk or oddity found at the fringes of society. However, the wherryman's travels showed that vegetarianism could be aligned with notions of masculinity and strength as routes toward individual success. Once the tumult of the war years ended, a new generation of vegetarian health reformers—many of whom were first drawn to the cause in the years surrounding Martin's trip—learned these lessons and in the process developed a new brand of vegetarianism that glorified the individual.

Martin's exploit became ingrained in movement vegetarianism's collective memory. Years later, it continued to be used as scientific proof that the diet created strong, successful individuals. E. B. Foote, a trained medical doctor and prominent vegetarian advocate, repeatedly referenced Martin's voyage as evidence of the benefits of vegetarianism in his writings of the 1880s, 1890s, and early twentieth century.[75] The lessons of Martin's trip—its creation of a new, stronger image of the vegetarian, as well as its embrace by society at large—resonated with the health reformers who would change the nature of movement vegetarianism during the Progressive Era.

Movement vegetarians did not experience the full benefits of the wherryman's exploits until after the Civil War, which only intensified critics' questioning of vegetarians' physical and moral mettle. The anxieties prompted by the Civil War raised deep questions regarding loyalty, strength, patriotism, and social reform. For vegetarians this meant a continuation of the harsh attacks the U. S. movement had experienced in its early history.

In a June 1864 editorial, the antiwar, anti-Lincoln, proreconciliation *New York Herald* claimed that rival newspaper editor Horace Greeley's "weakness for vegetarianism" led him to become a "pariah . . . socially, mentally and morally . . . below the miserable negroes he worships." Greeley's purported vegetarianism made him a better candidate for a stay in a mental institution, where he could enjoy a lifetime of cold baths and a snug-fitting straitjacket, than for a voice in politics.[76]

During the war years the *Herald*'s editorial pages repeatedly assaulted Greeley for his advocacy of war against the South and continually blamed him for the conflict's perpetuation. That the *Herald* would attack its rival is not surprising, but the nature of these attacks is striking. Rather than focusing on Greeley's supposed influence on the federal government, the *Herald* vilified his supposed dietary choices. The *Herald* contended that vegetarianism made Greeley morally and politically corrupt, inherently debased in his desires to end slavery and defeat the South.

Greeley had long been a target of derision among the opponents of re-form. Born to poor farmers in New Hampshire, he began his career as a newspaper editor in 1834, founding the *Weekly New Yorker*. A rising figure in the Whig Party, Greeley established the *New York Tribune* in 1841, popularly known as the "Great Moral Organ" for its advocacy of social reform. After a brief political career as a congressman from New York, Greeley became involved in the burgeoning Republican Party, with his newspaper serving as the party's unofficial national voice. Staunchly abolitionist, the *Tribune* warned its readers of the Southern slave owners' dangerous power.[77] Greeley flirted with a variety of reform social movements, ranging from spiritual-ism to Fourierism, and had a brief dalliance with vegetarianism. The *Tribune* even employed Karl Marx as its European correspondent in the early 1850s.[78]

Greeley was labeled "the king of the vegetarians" despite his somewhat loose connection to the group, having practiced a strict meat-free diet only briefly while living in a Grahamite boardinghouse in 1835. Although he was a member of both the American Vegetarian Society and the local New York Vegetarian Society during the 1850s, he personally preferred a well-cooked steak.[79] But according to the *Herald*, Greeley's vegetarianism, no matter how brief, made his political and military advice unreliable, fraudulent, and dangerous.

The attacks on Greeley ignited in July 1862, prompted by the defeat of Union forces in the Shenandoah Valley and the growing fear of a Confeder-ate attack on Washington, DC.[80] The *Herald* claimed that, "deliberately, and with malice[,] . . . that horrible monster Greeley . . . instigated this dreadful civil war for years past, and carefully nurtured and fostered the abolition sentiment, with which he hoped to poison and kill the republic." Greeley was motivated primarily by financial gain, the article argued, claiming that the *Tribune* had invested money in gun manufacturers with federal contracts to supply the Union army.[81] The *Herald*'s attacks on Greeley as someone will-ing to send other men to die for his vision of the Union rather than fight himself fit the existing narrative of vegetarians as physically fragile.

Greeley's duplicity and greed knew no boundaries, according to critics, who pointed to his advocacy for the censorship of newspapers critical of Lincoln. With a hint of irony, the article claimed that Greeley profited from a state contract that provided diseased beef to the New York state prison sys-tem.[82] Greeley's vegetarianism was connected to greed, cowardice, chicken hawking, and an insatiable bloodlust. While Greeley had no problem send-ing soldiers to the battlefield to die, "the smell of roast meat or the sight of gravy made him sick at his stomach. Like other calves and donkeys, he eschewed fleshy food. . . . His idea of paradise was a kitchen garden." The *Herald* depicted Greeley as a hypocrite transformed "from a vegetarian . . . into an ogre, eating human flesh—into a ghoul, feasting upon corpses. He riots in blood and spoils." Greeley's appetite would only be satiated with continued conflict: "This monster, ogre, ghoul, will soon feast his last upon Union blood and national spoils."[83]

The *Herald* continued its assault in August, reporting that Greeley had always been a "teetotaler and a vegetarian. . . . The effect of this regimen upon his temper has been to render it indescribably bad." Greeley's anger manifested itself in "howls" and "threats of vengeance" that resembled "an Indian war dance." The *Herald* reported that the *Tribune* had only one subscriber in the Union army. Soldiers refused to read the *Tribune* as a result of Greeley's advocacy for the enlistment of black soldiers as well as his criticisms of Union generals that led to "such terrible losses in killed and wounded . . . at Manassas and before Richmond."

The paper claimed that Union soldiers wrote to the *Herald* that Greeley "and the other abolitionists should be hung, and we kindly hinted that the general public was almost unanimously of the same opinion." The *Herald* thus framed abolitionists and vegetarians as elitists, philosophers out of touch with both the general public and Union fighting forces.[84]

The *Herald* associated Greeley's supposed vegetarianism with personal cowardice and weakness, in direct contrast to his warmongering. It used its coverage of the New York City draft riots of July 1863 to continue its attacks, reporting that on the first day of the riots, Greeley escaped harm by running into a restaurant and hiding inside a refrigerator. The article wryly noted that "if this be true, it is a singular instance of the power of fear; for poor Greeley is so rigid a vegetarian that no one would have thought him capable of getting into a meatbox, even to save his life." Greeley's cowardice further revealed itself as he fled for New Jersey.

In essence, the *Herald* was mocking the very idea of Greeley's philosophical dedication. Greeley's vegetarianism made him incapable of making clear decisions and left him too weak and craven to face the consequences of his actions. Given that a mob attempted to storm the *New York Tribune* headquarters on the first day of rioting, and set part of it aflame, hiding would not have been unwise. The claim was more bluster from the *Herald*, however; Greeley was actually at the *Tribune*'s office at the time the building was attacked.[85]

Although it mirrored the popular press's tradition of mocking vegetarians as intellectually and physically weak, the timing of the *Herald*'s assault on

Greeley is instructive. Even during the years of sectional strife, secession, and civil war, vegetarianism aroused the wrath of its detractors. The *Herald's* treatment of Greeley was similar to the popular mockery of vegetarians during the antebellum years, but it also illustrates the particular difficulties facing vegetarians during the war years. The urgent political and social issues of abolitionism and sectionalism trumped the importance of vegetarianism as a lifestyle change. Further, attacks on vegetarians as physically weak only intensified during a time of war.

Abolition—a central goal of movement vegetarianism during the 1850s and early 1860s—would eventually come to fruition with the war's conclusion. The importance of pacifism, a generally accepted component of movement vegetarianism tracing back to its eighteenth-century English roots, became somewhat obscured as vegetarians willingly took up arms in order to overthrow the slave system. Vegetarians were frequently mocked as mere philosophers during the early years of the AVS, and the criticism was largely well-founded. However, with vegetarians' attempts to settle the Kansas territory, with their taking up arms during the Civil War, and with the exhibition of vegetarian-fueled rowing excellence, movement vegetarianism was shifting toward a community of action as well as thought. The immediate impact of this shift was minimal, as vegetarians continued to be mocked and distrusted by society through the Civil War. However, in the years that followed, movement vegetarianism would continue to follow a path toward muscular individualism, advancing away from its social reform-minded past.

CHAPTER FIVE

Looks Like Meat,
Tastes Like Meat, Smells Like Meat

::

Protose . . . contains the same nutritive properties as meat, is more digestible, and is an absolutely pure product of the vegetable kingdom. —Advertisement for Protose, June 1900

Beginning in the 1880s, vegetarians around the United States eagerly examined their mail, anticipating receiving their new catalog from the Battle Creek Sanitarium Health Food Company. Health reformers were anxious to see what new meat substitutes were available from the country's center of healthy living. John Harvey (J. H.) Kellogg and his Battle Creek Sanitarium made their products available via mail order, promising foods that preserved "permanent good health" and restored consumers' "well being." The right food choices, vegetarians were told, ensured healthy, productive lives.

Thanks to the company's mail-order catalog it was possible to "have in your own home the same foods used in the Battle Creek System." Consumers were reassured that the foods were the product of extensive scientific experimentation in the San's kitchen, maximizing both flavor and nutrition. Vegetarians were also promised a variety of products that looked, smelled and tasted like meat. Vegetarian cuisine was changing, and with it came increasing acceptance of the movement in mainstream culture.[1]

With the introduction of meat substitutes—vegetarian products purported to have similar qualities as meat—movement vegetarianism shifted in the 1880s. Through the later years of the nineteenth century and into the twentieth, movement vegetarianism became intertwined with the marketing and proliferation of vegetarian products to both adherents of the movement and outside audiences. As a result, the movement pushed away from its politicized past and toward a more socially acceptable future driven by individual improvement through scientific cookery and product consumption. The roots of this shift for movement vegetarianism began in the immediate postbellum years.

At the start of the Civil War, movement vegetarianism remained primarily a northeastern phenomenon led and followed by New Englanders, New Yorkers, and Philadelphians. During these years vegetarianism aligned itself with a vital, constantly evolving reform spirit that infused itself in the urban centers of Yankee life. But the Civil War period threw vegetarianism into a period of flux, and the movement redefined itself in the face of the more pressing social issues of warfare and abolition. The years following the war were still marked by dramatic economic and social transformation. These same agents of change geographically and ideologically reoriented movement vegetarianism in the United States.

After the Civil War, many of the reformist notions that had established themselves in the East spread westward, following the trail of migrants motivated by the postwar industrial and economic boom that encouraged the continued expansion of U. S. territory. These eastern migrants were buoyed by the passage of the Homestead Act in 1862, promising land grants of 160 acres in exchange for the cultivation of "unused" land in the western territories. Indian removal policies of the 1840s and 1850s ensured that migrant farmers would meet little resistance in settling their newly granted land possessions. The arrival of the transcontinental railroad created economic boomtowns supported by an interconnected transportation system that linked the region with economic interests on the East Coast.[2]

As migrants spread into the Upper Midwest following the Civil War, so did the ideas, cultural norms, and practices that had proliferated in the Northeast.[3] Reformers had already spread into the Upper Midwest in the era leading to the Civil War; the postbellum years, however, were marked by increased migrations from the East. The population of Illinois grew from just over 850,000 in 1850 to more than 2.5 million in 1870. Indiana's increased from about 988,000 to more than 1.6 million during the same twenty-year period. In Michigan, where vegetarianism established a strong foothold, the population grew from just over 397,000 in 1850 to more than 1.1 million people in 1870.[4]

Vegetarianism followed this general western migratory pattern of cultural and ideological infusion. Some vegetarians, of course, already resided in the "old Northwest" and were connected to the activities of the American Vegetarian Society during the 1850s. In addition, the appearance of vegetarians in Kansas in the prewar years further spread vegetarian ideals and practices westward. Nonetheless, vegetarians largely depended on East Coast activities for a sense of community. In the years following reunion, the Midwest—and the city of Battle Creek, Michigan, in particular—became the new hub of American movement vegetarianism. Battle Creek and its famed Sanitarium became the central location of vegetarian living and community building, while also diffusing vegetarian culture, ideals, products, and living to all other regions.

The story of Battle Creek and its ascent to the summit of American vegetarianism is intertwined with its rapid industrial transformation. In just over sixty years, Battle Creek evolved from a small village, to a growing mill town, to a major industrial center. The area was originally inhabited by tribes of Potawatomi who first came into contact with eastern land speculators led by Colonel John H. Mullet in 1825. A violent altercation between four men, two settlers and two Natives, led the Euro-American expansionists to jokingly name the stream near where the incident occurred Battle Creek. Soon after, settlers arrived from upstate New York—including a large group of Quakers—drawn by the promise of significant economic opportunities.[5]

By the 1830s, the area was a thriving mill town, spurred by the completion of a millrace and the damming of the Kalamazoo River. The town, then known as Milton, continued to grow with the appearance of flour, grain, and saw mills by the start of the 1840s, exploiting the natural waterpower of the river and corresponding creek. The arrival of the Michigan Central Railroad in 1845 connected the area with the East Coast as well as with the growing metropolis of Detroit, ensuring that Battle Creek would become intimately tied to the region's industrial economy. The Nichols and Shepard Company—manufacturers of farm machinery, mill machines, and steam engines—opened in Battle Creek in 1852 and exemplified the town's growing importance in the Upper Midwest.[6]

Seventh-Day Adventists were among the large influx of residents into Battle Creek during this period. The group originated in the Millerite religious sect that gained popularity during the Second Great Awakening of the 1830s and 1840s. Millerites were followers of William Miller, a lay preacher from New York who predicted that the second coming of Christ would occur around 1843. Miller's popularity grew through the 1830s, and he became a nationwide phenomenon by 1840 with publications that reached audiences throughout the United States.

When Miller's prophecy failed, the Millerites fractured into three sects, each with its own interpretation of the coming of the messianic age. One of these groups, labeled the Adventists, formed on October 23, 1844, the day after the so-called Great Disappointment, the date when Millerites believed

Christ would appear. Through concentrated study of the Book of Daniel, and based on a vision claimed by a group member, the Adventists came to the conclusion that the prophesized date of October 22 for the second coming was based on a misunderstanding: the events described were actually heavenly in nature, not occurring on Earth among humanity. Starting in 1844, Christians would be judged by their worthiness for salvation.[7]

As the Adventists grew, they adopted a Sabbatarian worldview, strictly observing Saturday as the biblical day of rest. Ellen Harmon (eventually White) and her parents were among the followers of this nascent group. Harmon was born in Maine in November 1827, the daughter of farmers. When Harmon was twelve, her family began regularly attending the lectures of William Miller and became involved in the growing Millerite community. At the age of seventeen, a few months following the Great Disappointment, Harmon reported her first prophetic vision of the Adventist group ascending into the city of God. The sect quickly embraced Harmon's vision. Two years later Ellen married James White, a prominent Millerite leader, further connecting her to the growing religious community.[8]

Ellen White's message and popularity spread during the 1850s with the appearance of publications and revival meetings that described her visions and particular principles of Adventism. The Whites struggled, however, as Ellen's writing and preaching left little opportunity for stability given the transient nature of her responsibilities. A group of Adventists in Battle Creek offered to allay the Whites' difficulties, promising them a printing house if the couple moved to the growing city. With a guaranteed audience and a mechanism to spread her prophecies, Ellen and James White moved to Battle Creek in November 1855.[9]

The Adventist community in Battle Creek grew as Ellen White's prophecies found more and more converts. While praying with a group of Adventists in Otsego, Michigan, in June 1863, she claimed a vision that changed the course of Adventist history and in the process U. S. movement vegetarianism. White had been a heavy meat-eater all her life, yet this vision called on Adventists to abstain from animal flesh as well as tobacco and alcohol. White "saw that it was a sacred duty to attend to our health, and arouse others to their duty . . . to come out against intemperance . . . and then point them to God's great medicine. . . . The more perfect our health, the more perfect will be our labor."[10]

White envisioned Adventists utilizing natural remedies such as fresh air, sun, exercise, and pure water to prevent and cure disease. Two years later, on Christmas Day 1865, White had another vision, this time exhorting her to establish a health reform institute to care for the sick. This new institute was to be charged with teaching the advantages of healthy living and drugless medical care to the masses. By September 1866 that dream was realized with the opening of the Western Health Reform Institute in Battle Creek.[11]

Even if Ellen White was motivated by divine prophecy, her decision to open a health reform institute was certainly affected by immediate events in her life. White's husband, James, suffered a stroke in 1865 and recuperated at Our Home, a health reform hospital in Dansville, New York. Illustrating the influence of movement vegetarianism on the Whites, Our Home was run by James Caleb Jackson, a former active member of the American Vegetarian Society. The new Western Health Reform Institute opened by the Whites largely modeled itself on Jackson's Our Home, emphasizing natural cures including air, water, light, rest, exercise, and a vegetable diet. Under the leadership of Horatio S. Lay, whose medical training included work at Our Home, the Whites' institute became an increasingly popular destination.

In its early years, however, the hospital was essentially a glorified water-cure establishment. The hospital was growing at a rapid rate and by January 1867 had to turn away potential residents for lack of space.[12] White needed to expand the hospital but had limited resources and few Adventist medical professionals to call on. She finally turned to a member of the Battle Creek Adventist community who had attended a mainstream medical school on the East Coast and was looking to come home and put his expertise into action.

John Harvey (J. H.) Kellogg had long, deep connections with the Whites. He was the son of a prominent Adventist family from eastern Michigan that moved to Battle Creek in 1856 when J. H. was four in order to be closer to the center of Adventist activities. Economic motives also drew the family to Battle Creek; the Kelloggs built a broom factory, taking advantage of the area's geography and growth as an industrial center. J. H. began working in the printing shop of the *Adventist Review and Herald Press*, the national publication of the Seventh-Day Adventist movement. In this role he worked directly with Ellen and James White, ascending from the starting position of errand runner to that of printer's apprentice.

Kellogg's voracious appetite for reading about health reform and his work in the print shop impressed the Whites enough that they sponsored his medical education. Kellogg began his training at Russell Trall's Hygeio-therapeutic College in Florence Heights, New Jersey, in the fall of 1873. Trall, too, had a long involvement with movement vegetarianism, having served as a vice president of the American Vegetarian Society. He had been at

Sylvester Graham's deathbed and reported on the event for the AVS's newsletter. In the 1870s, Trall's college served as a training ground for young Adventists looking to enter the medical field and find a job at the Whites' newly opened institute. Movement vegetarianism, despite the dissolution of its national organization, remained directly connected to its immediate past. With its emphasis on natural cures, Trall's training school aligned ideologically with the practices of Adventism, even though it was not formally affiliated with the religion. While Kellogg's time at Trall's college was short, his studies there cemented his dedication to vegetarianism and nature cures.

Despite his interest in seemingly radical cures, and against the Whites' advice, Kellogg sought legitimacy from the established medical profession. In this sense, Kellogg represented a break from movement vegetarianism's past and its critique of mainstream medicine. Kellogg spent two years at the College of Medicine and Surgery at the University of Michigan, where he excelled in his studies as a surgeon. This skill later won Kellogg extensive mainstream professional acclaim.

Kellogg completed his medical education in 1875, receiving his MD from Bellevue Hospital Medical College in New York City, where he focused his studies on natural cures and a distinctly Adventist perspective on illness. These ideologies remained fairly consistent throughout Kellogg's professional career. Kellogg argued in his graduate thesis that diseases and illnesses were the body's way of warning the individual that a natural process had become disturbed. Pain was an indication that the patient was violating natural laws. The only way to alleviate suffering was by following the basic principles of natural, healthy living—fresh air, clean water, exercise, and a vegetarian diet.[13] Even during the early years of his medical career, Kellogg's interests created a tension that continued throughout his life: he pursued mainstream medical acceptance while simultaneously espousing often controversial medical views.

When he returned to Battle Creek in 1875, medical degree in hand, Kellogg was immediately hired as a staff doctor at the Western Health Reform Institute. He deepened the Whites' trust in him through a combination of faithful service and support for the hospital's growth. The Whites named him superintendent of the health institute in early 1876. He was just twenty-four. The institute, while popular, was still underdeveloped, short on staff and equipment. Kellogg and the Whites both wanted to turn it into a large, progressive healing institution. For Kellogg, this would provide the professional accolades and mainstream acceptance he desired. For the Whites, it would promote their beliefs and mission as Seventh-Day Adventists.[14]

The reputation of Kellogg and the Western Health Reform Institute grew simultaneously thanks to a general shift in the status of the American physician and the hospital after the Civil War. A growing middle class sought answers for the causes of physical illness from doctors who crafted reputations built on the dual qualities of authority and impartiality, a process that has become known as "professionalization." Belief in physicians' expertise brought order and rationalization to an often chaotic and unpredictable industrial postbellum society.[15] And his affiliation with the Adventist church notwithstanding, Kellogg directed the institute to treat patients regardless of religious practice or background. Kellogg's ascendance and appeal to mass audiences continued movement vegetarianism's larger turn toward a more scientific-based ideology, rather than the sharply religious focus of dietary reform's early years.[16]

The stage was set for the hospital to grow rapidly. A new generation of Adventists were graduating from reputable medical colleges on the East Coast, ensuring an accredited labor force. As luck would have it, at the same time that the Adventists sought to expand their medical institute, Ellen White had a new vision that called for building a large administrative and residential center. Kellogg's medical expertise and a growing staff of "men of ability, refinement, and sterling sense," according to James White, provided the conditions for the institute to expand.[17]

In 1878, the Medical and Surgical Sanitarium was constructed on the grounds previously occupied by the institute. Whereas the preceding management had emphasized water cure, the new organization offered what Kellogg described as "new methods, appliances, and apparatus . . . to create an institution which would show in practical operation all the resources of rational and physiologic medicine."[18] Kellogg aimed to prove that nature cures were not eccentric, outdated quackery but rather driven by medical expertise and study. The new institution was a means to demonstrate the effectiveness of natural methods, implemented and measured by the most modern equipment and facilities.

The sanitarium's effort to distance itself from its roots began with its new name. The term *sanitorium* had long referred to a health resort utilized to treat injured British soldiers. Kellogg changed "sanitorium" to "sanitarium," implying that the institute served as a locale of both recovery *and* learning.[19] The new building was renamed the Battle Creek Sanitarium, often referred to by residents and staff as "the San." The name change also reflected Battle Creek's general growth, perceived as a location of modernity, economic opportunity, and personal advancement. Emphasizing Battle Creek in the sanitarium's name linked the institution with the city's expanding reputation and population.

In 1880 the San established a nurses' training school to serve as a source of labor and a sign of the institution's expertise. In addition, a growing fleet of "scientifically trained physicians" was employed as full-time doctors to accommodate the needs of nearly 200 guests at a time. A cooking school opened in 1883, aimed at teaching the San's principles to both guests and interested epicures who wanted to apply Kellogg's principles to their home kitchens. Renovations doubled the San's capacity as well as its popularity.[20]

At the center of the growing sanitarium was what Kellogg came to label the "Battle Creek System," a method of treatment and preventative medicine that emphasized natural cures. Kellogg created this system to emphasize the San's legitimacy, basing it on "a knowledge of physiology, and an intelligent grasp of all the resources of modern medical science."[21] Medical practitioners trained in the latest scientific advancements would apply the San's natural treatments. The Battle Creek System reflected Kellogg's belief in natural cures administered through scientifically rational methods.

The sanitarium appealed to guests involved in the growing national industrial ethos and culture that emphasized technological advancement and efficiency. The San drew residents who benefited from this economic system, individuals with both the time and disposable income to afford a stay in Battle Creek. The San's ascendance also corresponded with the growth of the modern hospital, shifting from a benevolent organization aimed at comforting the poor to an institution where the wealthy and middle classes went to be cured.[22] The San was positioned at the intersection of these two social trends, with Kellogg ensuring residents that Battle Creek experts practiced the right type of medicine the proper way.

While the Battle Creek System treated a variety of medical ailments—in particular dyspepsia, consumption, and constipation—it was, at its heart, concerned with correcting the conditions that created chronic disease. Illness was caused by "erroneous habits of life" that caused normal, natural bodily functions to wear down. The appearance of observable symptoms was the body's cry for help. The sanitarium staff was trained to hear these cries and help change the lifestyle mistakes that were causing illness.

While a staff of professionals implemented the treatment program, the Battle Creek System simultaneously emphasized the responsibility of individuals. Personal choices both at the sanitarium and in the outside world affected the body's healing process; avoiding intemperance ensured a quick, full recovery. Weakness, manifested in overindulgence, drinking, and meat consumption, doomed residents to a cycle of self-destruction. Life outside of Battle Creek was described as particularly dangerous given mainstream culture's preoccupation with meat, tobacco, and alcohol. Guests at the sanitarium thus were not mere patients but rather were expected to be agents in their own recuperation, learning from Kellogg's legion of trained professionals how to avoid the physiological causes of disease and lead healthy lives.

Daily lectures and classes informed guests about the Battle Creek System and why it was effective. Kellogg reminded patients that it was "rare indeed to find a person dying a natural death," that poor diet, unscientific living, and intemperance caused constitutional diseases and chronic ill health.[23] Lectures advised guests on a wide range of subjects, including vegetarian dietetics, exercise, and proper dress.[24]

Kellogg's Battle Creek System was comprised of a variety of components, some of which were standard for all treatments while others were prescribed for particular ailments. As technology evolved, so did its applications; by the beginning of the twentieth century, the San was utilizing new technologies such as electrotherapy, as a means to stimulate muscle activity. The trained medical staff at the sanitarium was responsible for determining which combination of curatives produced the best results.

Water cure remained a popular treatment at the San, though Kellogg emphasized its modernized applications by labeling it "rational hydrotherapy." The San's version of hydrotherapy differentiated itself from the "crude" water cures of the previous generation by allowing for both cold and warm bathing.[25] In addition, rational hydrotherapy integrated water cure with a variety of physical rehabilitation methods, including massage and "medical gymnastics," an early incarnation of physical therapy. The method aimed to make water cure adaptable to each individual's particular needs. Rational hydrotherapy was associated with modernity and differentiated from the water cure of years past.

Massage was an important component of the Battle Creek System, utilized for a variety of ailments. Abdominal massage was utilized to cure constipation and dyspepsia, chest massage to improve circulation and metabolism, and Swedish massage to cure insomnia. "Swedish movement," also labeled "medical gymnastics," was also key to Kellogg's system. Guests were expected to utilize low impact gymnastics to build muscle and strength and better prepare the body to resist disease.[26] Even exposure to fresh air was renamed to have a scientific association. Kellogg's "out-of-door method" was prescribed for all residents in order to build lung capacity and naturally deter illness.

At the center of the Battle Creek System, for all sanitarium guests, was dietetics. Vegetarianism was a nonnegotiable component of the Battle Creek System, practiced by all guests, staff, and visitors while at the San. Flesh foods, according to Kellogg, overtaxed the digestive system and lacked the powerful nutrients abundantly available in the farinaceous kingdom. Kellogg lectured repeatedly that dyspepsia, constipation, and nervous disorders were all connected to dietary overindulgence.

Kellogg claimed that flesh foods "cut off forty or fifty years" from the average lifespan and that meat-eaters' lives were marked by dyspepsia and other stomach ailments. Meat was filled with "impurities," while a vegetarian diet was inherently natural and healthy. The limited nutrients that meat transferred were not from the animals themselves. Meat-eaters, Kellogg warned, ingested "the dead matter and waste matter of another animal," thereby receiving secondhand nutritional value affected by impurities and disease. Vegetarians instead took a pure diet, receiving nutrition directly from fruits and vegetables.[27] In contrast to antebellum popular images of vegetarians, Kellogg's new vegetarian was to be physically vigorous, healthy, and strong, able to succeed in a fast moving, modern world.[28] Fruits, vegetables, nuts, and grains were the natural food of humanity, and Kellogg believed he was helping individuals return to their natural state. Meat consumption was merely indicative of humanity's disconnection from its own awareness of healthy living.[29]

Kellogg reminded his followers that "good food and drink make good blood; and good blood is manufactured into healthy brains, and strong bones and muscles." Unhealthy food created deficient brains, bones, and muscles. The Battle Creek System emphasized that individuals were, indeed, what they eat. The almost "universal disregard of dietetic rules" made America "a nation of dyspeptics."[30] The proof of vegetarianism's success lay in anatomical analysis, comparative physiology, and experiential evidence. Kellogg frequently pointed toward scientific reports, journal articles, and laboratory experimentations in his arguments for vegetarianism. He used rhetorical devices to build credibility for the Battle Creek System and to claim his own medical expertise.

Kellogg rejected the popular opinion that meat was necessary to maintain human life. Since all animals subsist to some degree on a vegetable diet, Kellogg argued that meat contained no nutritional elements not found in the plant kingdom. Whereas vegetarian foods were invigorating, meat stimulated the body. Meat was infused with "venous blood" that was filled with uric acid, cholesterol, and other toxins. Further, meat was rife with impurities, since few animals were healthy at the time of slaughter. In lectures and writings, Kellogg proclaimed that tapeworm, trichinosis, and consumption were on the rise as a result of the sick state of animals prior to slaughtering.[31]

To facilitate vegetarian living, the San established an experimental kitchen in the summer of 1883 to produce appetizing and nutritious vegetarian meals for its guests. Both Kellogg and his wife, Ella, worked in this kitchen. Since the San's visitors used valuable vacation time to visit, the daily menu needed to appeal to both the mind and the palate to ensure that guests would continue flocking to Battle Creek. The experimental kitchen applied the principles of scientific study to cookery in order to craft what Kellogg believed to be the most nutritious and flavorful food products.

The San's kitchen was created at the same time that the domestic sciences began to be embraced throughout the United States by respectable, middle-class households. The new home economics movement found its voice in the pages of innumerable domestic advice journals that advocated the principles of home economics. These domestic sciences emphasized that women were the moral guardians of the household. One of women's domestic responsibilities was to provide healthy, fulfilling meals to husbands and children in order to best prepare them for the difficulties and threats of the modern world.

The rise of the domestic sciences ensured the legitimacy of Ella Kellogg's visible and active participation in the experimental kitchen. By the 1880s women had become the primary authors of cookbooks, frequently written by graduates of a rapidly expanding number of home economics and cooking schools. In this sense, the rise of the domestic sciences reflected a professionalization of female domestic roles. Working-class women attended schools such as the New York Cooking School (founded in 1876) or the Boston Cooking School (opened in 1879) to train to become domestic servants in upper-class households.

Conversely, middle-class women were trained in these scientific cooking processes through cookbooks and pamphlets such as Fannie Farmer's *Cooking-School Cook Book*. The propagation of these books help standardized the process of kitchen cookery. The rise of middle-class professional standards in the realm of cooking led to the embrace of other middle-class values expressed through cookery, particularly the notion of self-restraint. Notions of middle-class gentility helped professionalize a general objection to gluttony by emphasizing a system of precise measurements and systematic, scientific cookery.[32]

The San's experimental kitchen fit within this larger cultural sphere attempting to bring order, modernity, and scientific rationalization to both private and public kitchens in order to solve questions of nutrition. For example, Ellen Swallow Richards's Rumford Kitchen applied the study of chemistry to the culinary sciences in order to maximize nutritional value for feeding the hungry and destitute. Much like Kellogg's experimental kitchen, the Rumford Kitchen included a full collection of scientific laboratory equipment in order to maximize the healthy properties of food. While the Rumford Kitchen and the scientific cookery movement in general—labeled the "New Nutrition" by one food historian writing about the period—were originally conceived as a means to assist society's least fortunate, their principles eventually expanded to encompass the middle class. Members of the under classes often rejected the principles of this new cookery largely because it failed to accommodate the gustatory preferences of ethnic traditions other than those of Anglo-Americans.[33]

Dietary reformers found an audience among politicians and business leaders who funded scientific food research at U. S. universities, government agencies, and industrial laboratories. Like these advocates, Kellogg used cookbooks, marketing pamphlets, public lectures, and his experimental kitchen to introduce new foods and scientific cookery to the public.[34] The San's experimental kitchen and cookery school had the same goals as the new scientific cookery and drew residents steeped in the values of the late nineteenth century's growing middle class.

The changes at the San were effective, evidenced by the fact that the complex housed more than 800 guests at a time by 1886, quadruple the number of a decade earlier. By 1897 that number doubled again to nearly 1,600 residents at a time.[35] Guests were treated with a combination of physical exertion and relaxation, appealing to members of a growing leisure-seeking middle class that sought cures to a variety of maladies that purportedly inhibited their continued economic and social success. Visitors embraced vegetarianism, at least while they were vacationing at the San. To ensure that new guests would visit Battle Creek, previous residents would return, and the San's methods would gain wider popularity, Kellogg invented new food products.

In addition to serving a variety of fresh fruits and vegetables, the San's experimental kitchen expanded the repertoire and nature of vegetarian cuisine, illustrating that the San's vegetarianism was powered by the new scientific cookery. One of Kellogg's obsessions was finding products that could easily substitute for meat flavors. Many of the San's residents had never practiced a vegetarian diet until their stay in Battle Creek. For these guests, Kellogg attempted to appeal to the taste and masticatory sensations that flesh foods produced. Although philosophically dedicated to the cause of vegetarianism, he realized that the diet needed to further diversify if it was going to be embraced by larger audiences. Kellogg thus introduced cereals, nuts, and so-called meat substitutes to the San's menu and eventually to wider audiences.

Kellogg began his experiments with cereals (whose use he recommended at both breakfast and dinner) in the late 1870s, crafting a mixture of well-baked grains and oats. A strikingly similar product was first developed and sold in 1863 by James Caleb Jackson, the owner of the Our Home health reform hospital after which the San was modeled. Jackson's cereal—called *granula*—was a mixture of Graham flour, water, and grains and was rolled out into a sheet of dough, baked in a brick oven and broken into small bits. Granula was sold through the Our Home Granula Company, which also marketed a coffee substitute, made of bran and molasses, called Somo. The dryness of the cereal made it difficult to eat and inconvenient to prepare. In addition, granula needed to rehydrate with milk in order to be edible, a process that took a minimum of twenty minutes, though many let the cereal soak in the icebox overnight. In an increasingly fast-paced world, the time it took for granula to rehydrate made it an undesirable breakfast option.[36]

In 1877 J. H. Kellogg developed his own version of granula, made of ground pieces of zwieback—hard, sweetened bread—and a variety of grains. To avoid legal problems when he sold the product outside of the San, Kellogg changed the name to "granola." He told San residents that it was among the most natural and easily digestible foods.[37] Even though Kellogg had softened his version of granola considerably, it was still difficult to chew, particularly for those with dental problems. As a result, Kellogg undertook the task of developing softer, more porous cereal products that would soak up milk instantaneously. During this time Kellogg invented a prototype for what would become corn flakes. The products invented in the San's experimental kitchen were served daily to the institute's residents. With Kellogg's emphasis on lifestyle change both inside and outside of the San, he was, in essence, attempting to create a market need for Battle Creek's health products year-round. The San's reputation continued to grow, intriguing consumers throughout the United States about the benefits of the Kellogg diet, even those who never traveled to Battle Creek.

In addition to cereals, Kellogg expanded vegetarian diets with his emphasis on the use of nuts, advocating for their use through scientific principles.

Previous generations of vegetarians eschewed the use of nuts in daily diet, viewing them as difficult to digest and of little nutritional value. Kellogg, however, understood the advantages of using nuts as a nonflesh protein for vegetarians. Nuts were most advantageous as a meat alternative, according to Kellogg, because they served "as substitutes for harmful, disease-producing foods, and especially as food remedies of incalculable value in medical dietetics."

Kellogg claimed that nuts were "nearly equivalent in blood-making qualities to a pound and a quarter of beefsteak." Fresh nuts were healthier than flesh meat, containing "more than 50 per cent of a most assimilable fat" for energy and muscle production, the "best food for strength." Nuts restored the dyspeptic and convalescent and were "adapted to the athlete no less than to the delicate babe, to the sedentary and sickly no less than to the toiler with pick or sledge hammer."[38] In emphasizing the scientific properties of nuts, Kellogg was furthering his claims to dietary expertise as a means to lend credence to vegetarianism.

Kellogg's advocacy for nuts embodied a shift in the nature of vegetarianism prompted by activities of the San. Previous generations of vegetarians singularly assailed all of the qualities of flesh foods as physically, morally, and emotionally destructive. While Kellogg abhorred what he saw as the unhealthy properties of meat, he also broadened his appeal by accepting the standardization of meat-based diets for most Americans, even accepting that flesh foods had beneficial qualities.

Kellogg recognized that meat had muscle- and energy-building capabilities. Although he despised the sensory excess that meat placed on the digestive system, he understood that meat remained so popular because it tasted good. Nuts, he argued, had the flavor and muscle-building properties that made meat a part of the average American diet but without the health risks caused by tainted flesh. Kellogg's marketing popularized nuts as a meat alternative and dramatically changed public opinion. In July 1899, the *Chicago Tribune* credited vegetarians directly with the proliferation of the popularity of nuts for everyday use.[39]

Kellogg argued for vegetarianism because it was actually *more* effective than meat in building muscular, healthy bodies while offering a varied and complex flavor profile. Malted nuts, for example, were "equal in total nutritive value to three and a half pounds of the best beef or mutton." Kellogg positioned nuts as "the vegetable analogue of meat" but believed they were actually "a more perfect nutrient than meat, as they are capable of sustaining human life for an indefinite period."[40]

Nuts were utilized in a variety of forms, including as butter, a product first popularized at the San. Marketing of the San's nut products emphasized scientific principles to prove their value as products of dietary worth. Advertisements selling the San's nut butter via mail order argued that it was "free from the disease germs and bacteria of dairy butter." Nut butter was also more versatile, appealing to all palates, a "perfect food" that was "popular for receptions, picnics, and luncheons."[41] Kellogg's marketing efforts promoting nuts as a meat alternative made headway among both vegetarians and nonvegetarians—during this period, the edible portion of a nut was popularly referred to as the "meat."[42]

At the same time that the San promoted nuts, Kellogg developed the first products marketed specifically as vegetable-friendly meat substitutes with flesh-like qualities. The principles of scientific cookery played a central role in the development of these meat substitutes. In early 1896 Kellogg began a correspondence with Charles W. Dabney, assistant secretary of the Department of Agriculture. Kellogg's popularity had reached the notice of politicians and key decision makers. Dabney was a trained agricultural chemist and long-time advocate of continued rural development in industrial America, especially in the New South. In particular, Dabney sought ways to utilize scientific study and experimentation to manufacture food products that were cheap and abundant, fearing the consequences of the growing price of meat and the potential for disease to cause a shortage in the United States.

Dabney was impressed by Kellogg's reputation and sought assistance in developing "a scientifically prepared plant product affording all the essential nutrient qualities of beef or mutton[,] . . . a food product which might be safely employed as an alternative for meats."[43] Kellogg was also interested in crafting a meat alternative that appealed to consumers' ethics, economics, and taste, and immediately went to work to develop flesh substitutes in the experimental kitchen. Nine meat substitutes were invented and initially prepared for the San's guests. Soon after, these products were sold to the public at large. The first, Nuttose, was a mixture of ground nuts bound together by cereal grains. It was, as Ella Kellogg explained, "intended as a substitute for meat[,] . . . having nearly twice the nutritive value, while it furnishes the same elements and in a form . . . wholly free from the objectionable features of meat."[44] Soon after, Kellogg concocted Granose, a wheat-based biscuit that could be utilized as a faux-filet of beef. The marketing of meat substitutes emphasized their benefits based on scientific research and expertise.

Continuing to expand in size and popularity, the San was able to accommodate more than 2,000 residents at a time in the early years of the twentieth century.[45] Guests consumed a diet of meat substitutes and clamored for the products to be available in their lives at home. J. H. Kellogg was happy to oblige, organizing the Sanitas Nut Company with his brother Will Keith (W. K.) in 1898. The Sanitas Company marketed a variety of the San's products, including granola, zwiebacks, nuts, and nut butters to vegetarians and nonvegetarian consumers around the United States. By 1906, the company employed a total of forty-six workers.[46]

The products were available via mail order, an increasingly popular form of consumption that challenged the dry goods wholesaler's dominance by the end of the nineteenth century. Large mail-order companies like Montgomery Ward helped hasten an era of increasing consumer consumption, a trend that Kellogg's vegetarian business exploited.[47] In addition to mail order, numerous health food stores throughout the United States became authorized dealers of the San's products, furthering the availability of vegetarian products.[48]

Scholars have illustrated how product consumption has created constructed communities. In some instances these communities were built through an imposed model of hegemony. In other examples, individuals consumed products and culture to create and instill community pride.[49] For vegetarians, the creation of a community of consumers was more complicated. Vegetarians occupied a middling position between the two opposing forces of hegemony and resistance in their consumption of Battle Creek products. On the one hand, vegetarians' desire for meat substitutes was invented through creative marketing techniques that exploited individual desires for physical and social transformation. On the other hand, through the consumption of new meat substitutes, vegetarians actively expanded the nature of their community, produced pride in their movement, and altered their relationship with food.

Vegetarian consumers reflected this excitement in their descriptions of San food products. The testimonials functioned similar to the conversion narratives of earlier vegetarians. A businessman from St. Louis reflected that Battle Creek products "simply made a new man of me. . . . For three years since that time I have not had one sick day. I have been able to carry on my business with more vigor and far greater success than ever before."[50] A Battle Creek enthusiast from New York City reported enjoying the thrill of eating a meat substitute: "It tastes like all the naughty things, but has the advantage of being digestible and wholesome." Nuttose, the vegetarian claimed, had the taste and sensation of meat without the health and ethical implications.[51] Another consumer said that eating Battle Creek products was "one of the chief pleasures," and that writing in favor of these goods was "the first time in my life I had indorsed [sic] anything. . . . I thought the goods had earned everything I could say."[52]

The marketing of meat substitutes and other Sanitarium health foods reflected popular practices of brand promotion practiced by nonvegetarian food companies during the period. Goods began to be marketed nationwide, leading to the growth of such famed brand names as Heinz, the National Biscuit Company (later Nabisco), and Pillsbury. These national brands built loyalty through promises of quality control, as consumers began to trust marketing campaigns over the opinions of local retailers.[53] In these advertising campaigns new food products were frequently associated with the principles of scientific cookery and the practitioners of food experimentation, similar to Kellogg's work in the San's kitchen.[54] Catalogs, periodical advertisements, and cookbooks were all used to market meat substitutes as healthy, filling, and affordable cuisine, lending credence to the San's national brand.

With the onset of the San's health food business, products became available to both San guests and individuals who could not afford the trip but wanted to bring a little bit of Battle Creek into their household. Nuttose was marketed as having "gustatory and nutritive processes almost identical with those of choice meats." Protose, however, set the standard for meat substitutes at the turn of the twentieth century. A combination of wheat gluten, cereal, and peanut butter, Protose was sold in twelve-ounce or one-pound tin cans and marketed to consumers as "vegetable meat."[55] By 1914, Protose was widely available and consumed throughout the United States, with shipments of more than 144,000 pounds around the country, doubling from 1901.[56] Also in 1914, more than 33,000 pounds of Nuttolene (a vegetarian loaf made primarily of peanuts) were sold in the United States, along with another 6,000 pounds of Nuttose.[57] While the popularity of meat substitutes paled in comparison to overall meat production and consumption rates of the period (in 1912, American families consumed 145 pounds of meat, per capita), Kellogg's meat substitutes became increasingly available and well-known in the early years of the twentieth century.[58]

Protose was cheaper than canned meats, selling at thirty cents for a one-pound can in 1912, five cents less than a comparably sized can of meat, a fact emphasized in its advertising.[59] One industrious Washington, DC–based company attempted to capitalize on the growing trend started by the San and took its name to the seemingly contradictory yet logical conclusion. The Vegetarian Meat Company sold products across the United States, including nut-based meat substitutes, peanut butter, and peanut oil.[60]

Protose's success led Secretary Dabney to reflect that it was not only "widely known" but "manufactured and used in the leading civilized countries in the world."[61] Meat analogs were in sufficiently widespread use that in 1910 the Interstate Commerce Commission introduced a new classification item called "meat substitutes" to regulate the shipment of such products. Vegetable meats received the same classification as prepared, canned vegetables and not canned meats, as vegetable-meat proponents desired.[62]

The methods utilized to market Protose illustrate a significant shift in the nature of vegetarianism and stressed the principles of modern scientific cookery. Protose was described as "one of the latest and greatest triumphs of modern discovery . . . so closely resembling meat in appearance, flavor, and texture as almost to deceive an epicure." The "vegetable meat" resembled the composition of beef or mutton.[63] Consumers reported that Protose "looks and tastes a good deal like what we call beef loaf, or a loaf made from chopped or ground meat."[64] Protose was advised for all meals, as a substitute for breakfast meats and steaks and even for picnic sandwiches.[65]

Civil War hero and American Red Cross organizer Clara Barton provided a testimonial for Protose, noting that she was not "accustomed to subscribing my name to any manufactured product" but would "gladly do so in this instance." Barton described Sanitas products as being "choice, appetizing, wholesome foods, very pleasant to the palate and exceedingly rich in nutrients and sustaining properties."[66]

In language that surely would have turned the stomachs and spirits of Sylvester Graham, William Alcott, and other early movement vegetarian luminaries, the developers of Protose boasted that it "looks like meat, tastes like meat, smells like meat." Kellogg, however, had more varied motivations than did previous leaders of American movement vegetarianism. Financial considerations were as important to him as his firm belief in vegetarianism's health benefits. At the dawn of the twentieth century, the Battle Creek Sanitarium was a wild success. Although the institute—as an arm of the Adventist Church—was established as a nonprofit, charitable, religious organization, there was a large profit to be made in the building of the Battle Creek Sanitarium brand.[67] Kellogg carefully avoided combining his Sanitas work with the San, making his brother the health food company's president. Nonetheless, the Sanitas Company was sure to advertise that its products had been proven beneficial in their development and use at the San.

Protose

—the Tasty Meat Substitute

LOOKS, smells and tastes like meat and can be used in as many ways as meat, yet has none of its harmful toxic effects. Makes delicious roasts, stews, meat pies and entrees. Contains twice as much iron and nine times as much food lime as beefsteak. Rich in the vitamines so deficient in meats—and cheaper because there is no waste.

Nuttolene

—Has a Delicious Meat Flavor

A pure nut product of the consistency of cream cheese. Used with Protose, it lends a splendid variety to the balanced biologic diet.

NUTTOLENE CUTLET

One egg beaten, three tablespoons thin cream, pinch of salt, one cup ZO rolled fine, one-half pound Nuttolene. Slice Nuttolene in one-quarter inch slices, dip into the beaten egg and cream. Then roll in the ZO and place in an oiled pan. Put a small piece of butter on the top of each slice and bake in the oven until a rich brown.

Battle Creek Foods for Health

Ad for *Protose* and *Nuttolene* in Battle Creek Foods for Health (1920). *Courtesy of Recipe Pamphlets, Chef Louis Szathmáry Collection of Culinary Arts, University of Iowa, Iowa City.*

The promotion and marketing of these new vegetarian foods fit perfectly in a product-driven society that emphasized comforts, material extravagance, and the continuous consumption of new goods.[68] Visitors thronged to department stores and ordered products via mail-order catalogs, seeking validation and improvement through the latest and greatest products. Vegetarians experienced a similar product fascination during this period, visiting the San, purchasing meat substitutes, and seeking other health foods as vehicles to personal gratification and advancement. Simultaneously, vegetarians were crafting a new movement and with it a newfound pride and confidence.

The growth of the Sanitas Nut Food Company and its marketing of the San's meatless fare changed the nature of the vegetarian diet in the late nineteenth century. Just as important, this culinary shift informed an ideological change for movement vegetarianism. This shift continued through the early decades of the twentieth century. No longer reliant solely on fruits, vegetables, and grains, vegetarians added cereals, nuts, and meat substitutes to their growing list of preferred foods. In response to the growth of the San, the invention of meat alternatives and a general growth of American vegetarianism, vegetarian cookbooks proliferated in the literary market of the late nineteenth and early twentieth century, marketing the principles of scientific vegetarianism to enthusiastic middle-class consumers.

The explosion of vegetarian cookbooks illustrated important qualities of a new vegetarian movement. First, it reflected the growth of movement vegetarianism during this period, connected to Kellogg and the popularity of the San. Second, just as Kellogg found a way to commoditize vegetarianism through mail order, cookbook authors (some vegetarian, others not) sought to benefit monetarily by spreading vegetarian information and recipes. These individualized motivations notwithstanding, the growth of meatless cookbooks cultivated and connected a previously geographically disparate American vegetarian community.

Some of these cookbooks came from a logical source: Ella Kellogg. J. H.'s wife and accomplice in the experimental kitchen began publishing a series of cookbooks that spread awareness of Sanitas products while also instructing home cooks on how to best prepare unfamiliar dishes efficiently while maximizing nutritional value. Her first cookbook, appropriately titled *Science in the Kitchen*, aimed to promote the San's vegetarian regimen. The book touted the science behind vegetarianism, the "observation, research, and experience." Reflecting the ordered, rationalized working ethos of the time, Ella Kellogg vowed that this new cookery would "bring order from out the confusion . . . which surrounds the average cook, by the elucidation of the principles which govern the operations of the kitchen."[69]

Science in the Kitchen offered practical tips on the chemical properties of food, the use of kitchen equipment, cooking techniques, and the negative effects of unhealthy diets. Nutritious food was necessary, but so were proper techniques to render "good food material more digestible." In a time of vast technological advancement, the Kelloggs' new cookery emphasized science and machinery's ability to optimize food's health potential, ideals that also produced new foods in the San's experimental kitchen. Recipes promoted the use of fresh vegetables, fruits, nuts, and cereals for a well-balanced, healthy diet.

Ella Kellogg continued her work on the subject, writing a more detailed cookbook four years later. In *Every-Day Dishes and Every-Day Work* (1897), she illustrated how a vegetarian diet could be seamlessly integrated into home life, underlining the practical applications of scientifically rational cooking at home. She chose the book's recipes for their economic, nutritional, and culinary value. Included were "substantial dishes suited upon the everyday bill of fare in the average home." In the book's introduction, she pointed out that many of the recipes were created in the San's experimental kitchen, enjoyed by guests and scientifically proven to be nutritious.[70] The cookbook was part of the Kelloggs' attempt at bringing the San's methods into general practice in private homes. The San's products—as sold by the recently renamed Battle Creek Sanitarium Health Food Company—were positioned as essential components of a healthy, happy lifestyle at home.

The cookbook noted the nutritional value of all food products as a means to show the benefits of fruits and vegetables over meat. A section on how to prepare the meat substitutes created at the San instructed vegetarian cooks on the best methods concocted in the experimental kitchen. Granola was advised as a breakfast dish but could also be utilized as a substitute for bread crumbs in a dish of scalloped vegetables. Granose was advantageous because it was assimilated into the body "with the smallest amount of labor on the part of the digestive organs." In addition, it could be used to cure ailments ranging from indigestion to chronic constipation. Granose was even versatile enough to be used in puddings, breads, and biscuits.[71]

Crystal wheat—a concentrated wheat grain that required rehydration—when combined and baked with tomatoes, lentils, peanut butter, and sage made a sumptuous vegetable roast. Wheat gluten—an insoluble form of starchless wheat flour dough—was particularly useful for infants as gruel, or it could be combined with stewed tomatoes as a savory, warm dinner.[72] Nuttose—the original meat substitute—could "be prepared and served in the same manner as the various forms of flesh food." When diced with potatoes, Nuttose made a hearty stew. The cutlets could even be sliced thinly and used as a meat substitute on a sandwich. The San's products were marketed as being as flexible as they were tasty, with nutritional value proven by experimental study.

In *Healthful Cookery*, published in 1904, Ella expanded on the number of meat substitutes as well as their health properties and uses. Flesh had dietary value, she conceded, primarily in the fat and protein elements that it supplied. However, since meat was morally objectionable and frequently tainted with disease, vegetable substitutions for flesh foods were necessary to replace "these important food elements." Nuts, rice, and legumes were valuable in any complete diet. But there was also a need for products that were easily digestible and could approximate the taste of meat. Protose was "the perfect substitute for flesh food," with more nutritional value than beef or mutton. The "vegetable meat" could be broiled with tomatoes, the same way one would cook a beefsteak. When cooked in a high-temperature oven covered in tin, a Protose steak was produced. Combined with nuts, eggs, and wheat flour, Protose could be manipulated into a mock hamburger steak. For more elaborate dinners, it was even possible to mix lentils with granola, walnuts, and gluten and enjoy a "vegetable turkey."[73]

As the San's products continued to grow in popularity, vegetarian cookbooks highlighting meat substitutes and spreading the gospel of scientific cookery—but not aligned with the institute—began publishing recipes on how to best prepare mock meat. E. G. Fulton's 1904 cookbook *Substitutes for Flesh Foods* provided instruction on cooking dishes utilizing Protose, Nuttose, and other analogues. The author touted his "experience conducting vegetarian restaurants in several cities and making a study of the food question." The cookbook was based on "the commonly accepted definition of the term vegetarianism, which means to abstain from flesh food, but allows the use of eggs, milk, and its products." Recipes were proven to be nutritious by the author's knowledge of every law "governing every chemical change" in food.[74]

Fulton's cookbook provided instructions on how to braise Protose, mash it into a cutlet, bake it with macaroni, and include it in a jambalaya.[75] Vegetarianism, once reliant on the basic, bland preparation of a small variety of vegetables, was becoming far more appealing, even gourmet in its diversity. With the right preparation and creativity, Protose and other fake meats could be manipulated to replicate the taste, flavor, and consistency of beef, chicken, turkey, and even seafood.[76]

Other vegetarian cookbooks of the era emphasized the use of meat substitutes in scientific cookery. *Practical Vegetarian Cookery*, published in 1897, advised home cooks on how to prepare a variety of vegetarian meals, seeking "to demonstrate the nutritious and appetizing possibilities of vegetable foods." The author wrote that it was women's responsibility to understand the scientific properties of cooking and that "mothers will have no difficulty in finding . . . nutritious foods for the children if they will study the following pages." Meat substitutes were perfect for simple, everyday dining as well as elaborate, formal dinners for friends. The book advised home cooks to utilize breadcrumbs soaked in oil as a substitute for beef fat, nuts as a replacement for flesh foods, and nut butters to create rich gravies.[77]

Henrietta Latham Dwight—a California watercolor painter and advocate of vegetarianism—published a cookbook a year later to provide recipes for those who had adopted a "bloodless diet" and "are still asking how they can be nourished without flesh."[78] The Golden Age Cook-Book (1898) included recipes for a variety of meat substitutes, such as mock chicken (made of walnuts, breadcrumbs, eggs, and lemon juice), mock clam soup (marrowfat beans and cream), and mock beef (breadcrumbs, eggs, walnuts, and onion juice). The cookbook underlined its credentials in proving vegetarianism's worth by claiming that it had been "attested by many scientists" that meat-eating was "not necessary to the perfect health of man." The cookbook included testimonials from scientists advocating for the nutritional value of vegetarianism, as well as reference tables explaining the chemical and nutritional properties of nonflesh foods.[79]

Vegetarian food preparation was positioned as "a science as well as an art" in The Practical Naturopathic-Vegetarian Cook Book. Louise Lust—author of the cookbook and co-owner of the Health Food Bakery in New York City at 105th Street and Park Avenue—emphasized meat substitutes as both economical and healthful. Protose was quick, easy, and convenient to prepare and could accompany a variety of sauces and vegetables. However, unlike its predecessor—which advocated for vegetarianism as a means to emancipate women from the kitchen—the new vegetarianism glorified women's domestic responsibilities as a rational discipline to be mastered. Lust noted that "good housekeeping is the science of composing perfect cleanliness with economy and comfort" and that "the woman who has the aptitude as well as the fondness for cooking may make herself almost any kind of a success as a cook."[80]

The growth of the domestic sciences earned vegetarianism and faux meats recognition outside of the vegetarian movement. Meat substitutes were popular enough that one of the era's foremost authorities on cooking and the domestic sciences authored her own meat substitute cookbook. Sarah Tyson Rorer—known as Mrs. Rorer to her throngs of readers—authored more than seventy-five cookbooks and cooking manuals during her prolific working years. Mrs. Rorer ran a cooking school in Philadelphia for eighteen years and was the editor of Table Talk magazine, in addition to writing for other domestic, household publications. One of the most respected and admired voices of cookery at the turn of the twentieth century, she was at the center of the growing domestic sciences movement. Although Rorer was not a vegetarian, her writings promoted healthy lifestyles, and the continually growing vegetarian movement got her attention.[81]

Rorer's vegetarian domestic guide promised to illustrate how to cook three meatless meals a day without meat, using "vegetables with meat value.

Title page of Mrs. Rorer's Vegetable Cookery and Meat Substitutes (1909).

Vegetables to take the place of meat." *Mrs. Rorer's Vegetable Cookery and Meat Substitutes* argued that a practical vegetarian recipe book was necessary given society's overindulgence in flesh foods, which "left us as a reminder much sickness and sorrow." Whereas many other vegetarian cookbooks provided unappealing and taste-free dishes, Mrs. Rorer's aimed to provide creative, diverse, and flavorful vegetarian recipes. The book began with an introduction classifying vegetables into three scientifically observable nutritional categories: muscle-making vegetables (including legumes and nuts), energy producers (such as rice, potatoes, and cereals), fat producers (nuts, olives, and oils), and intestine cleaners (green, "succulent" vegetables).[82]

The cookbook included an entire chapter on items to be used "in the place of meat." Sausages could be made with farina, pecans, and breadcrumbs. Lentils could be combined with breadcrumbs and peanuts to make a mock veal roast. Hominy grits mixed with nuts, eggs, onion, and parsley could be baked into a mock fish filet. Rorer's recipes offered complex flavors, introducing such "exotic" spices as red chilies, turmeric, curry powder, and paprika.[83] Vegetarian cuisine had grown significantly from its roots in bran bread and cold water. Rorer and other cookbook authors illustrated the full range of culinary options available to vegetarians, equally emphasizing taste and nutrition. Vegetarians' dietary choices did not have to be bland.[84]

The mainstream press, too, caught on to the rising popularity of meat substitutes and extolled their virtues as cheap, nutritious alternatives. The *Chicago Tribune*—a harsh critic of vegetarianism in previous generations—proclaimed in a June 1902 article that mock meats had solved the "meat problem." Kellogg was the "hardest and most persistent worker" that the article's author had ever met, a "living example of the superiority of a vegetarian over a meat diet." With the cost of meat "so high as to make it an expensive luxury even to the well-to-do-classes," the writer had come to prefer meat substitutes to actual flesh. These "temptingly prepared" foods were created by the "scientific investigations" of the San, utilizing rationalization to perfect nature's vegetable foods.[85]

The *Tribune* continued supporting mock meats in the early twentieth century, frequently advising readers how to prepare meatless recipes. Caroline Shaw Maddocks—known as Jane Eddington to her readers—was a syndicated *Tribune* columnist and dietician whose culinary advice appeared in newspapers throughout the United States.[86] Eddington advised the use of flavorful, wholesome, and thrifty home cooking in her columns, frequently providing both vegetarian and nonvegetarian readers with techniques and recipes for utilizing mock meats. Homemade vegetarian sausage could easily be made with dried lentils or beans combined with breadcrumbs, spices, and hardboiled eggs.[87] Eddington suggested eggplant as a suitable meat substitute, versatile in its possible uses.[88] In addition, macaroni, rice, and eggs could all serve as meat substitutes for those whose ethics or finances kept them from having a carnivorous diet.[89]

In October 1904, the *San Francisco Call* called vegetarianism a solution to a possible meat famine. One article reported that "vegetarianism . . . has of late received a great stimulus . . . establishing a new order of things on a more economical and truly more helpful basis." Meat substitutes including legumes, nuts, and faux-meat cutlets were not only cheaper but also more appealing than previous vegetarian fare.[90]

In the same year, the *Washington Times* reported glowingly on the meatless meals offered by Mary Foote-Henderson, wife of Senator John Brooks Henderson of Missouri, coauthor of the Thirteenth Amendment to the U. S. Constitution, which abolished slavery. When entertaining Washington's political elite, Foote-Henderson served a vegetarian banquet filled with a variety of meat substitutes. The article noted that the fake chicken croquettes and mock fish cakes were "practiced so skillfully" that members of high society were unaware they were not eating meat.[91] The *New York Tribune* utilized the language of wealth and technological development to glorify meat substitutes, describing a faux fish made of hominy grits, ground peanuts, and eggs as a mark of "ingenuity" and vegetarian sausages as "first-class."[92] Vegetarianism, once decried as apocryphal and dangerous by mainstream society, was quickly becoming a plausible lifestyle choice touted for its ability to create healthy, prosperous, and successful individuals.

Culinary changes inspired by meat substitutes and scientific cookery increased the popular appeal of movement vegetarianism, with Kellogg as its most recognizable advocate through the early years of the twentieth century. Simultaneously, Kellogg was also an active member of and frequent lecturer to the Vegetarian Society of America (VSA), movement vegetarianism's national organization, founded in 1886.[93]

The newly popular movement vegetarianism had departed significantly from its more politicized roots. From its founding through the 1860s, American movement vegetarianism was aligned with radical social criticism of the status quo. Working- and middle-class reformers led the movement and hoped to overthrow institutions that oppressed a variety of groups, including African Americans, women, and the poor. Vegetarians during this period ate simple and basically prepared meals of fruits, vegetables, and grains in their most rudimentary forms. With the popularity of the San and J. H. Kellogg's particular brand of scientific rational vegetarianism, however, the movement shifted in ideology, demographics, and culinary methods. The changes in social and culinary culture among vegetarians were intertwined and reflect the larger changes in the intellectual underpinnings of the movement. Vegetarianism through the Civil War emphasized the diet as a method to reform social injustice and focused on the benefits to American society at large. In contrast, the vegetarianism initiated by the San was almost singularly focused on the physical and medical benefits for the individual.

By the turn of the twentieth century, the San was drawing large numbers of visitors looking for cures to a variety of illnesses. Ailments such as dyspepsia, consumption, and constipation inhibited individuals' ability to advance socially, professionally, and economically. The San drew both wealthy and middle-class residents, people who could afford to pay for the residency and take the necessary time off from work. The San's best-known visitors over the years included Mary Todd Lincoln, William Howard Taft, Amelia

Earhart, John D. Rockefeller Jr., Henry Ford, Alfred Dupont, Thomas Edison, William Jennings Bryan, and George Bernard Shaw.

More important, however, were the droves of guests whose names are not necessarily familiar to history, all of whom participated in the growth of a new form of movement vegetarianism aimed at producing individual social advancement. In 1911, the San welcomed 5,035 patients, each of whom paid on average twelve dollars per visit.[94] For the growing American middle class, vacations became more accessible and affordable in the postbellum years thanks to the expansion of the railroad and the emergence of travel agencies. A stay at the San was a reasonably priced option for a middle-class traveler, competing with the similarly affordable nonvegetarian spas, health resorts, and camping trips that were popular at the time.[95]

A demographic analysis of the San's patients in its 1912 annual report illustrates that its visitors were representative of the new American socioeconomic system developing during the Progressive Era. The majority of the San's visitors were married couples, and many of these couples were older and enjoyed a certain economic and social stability: the largest single age group of visitors was between forty-six and fifty, nearly one-ninth of the total.[96] By expanding the range of ages it is possible to gain a better understanding of the representative nature of the San's guests. More than one-fifth of the patients were between the ages of twenty-one and thirty-five, younger, socially and economically mobile couples swept up in a consumerist environment that celebrated the physical and economic health of the individual. Men and women were nearly equally represented at the San, reflecting the fact that the majority of residents were married couples. The residents were also geographically diverse in their origins. In 1911, patients came from forty-five different states, plus Washington, DC.[97]

The occupations most frequently held by the San's patients were components of an expanding corporate office environment that grew significantly in urban areas in the late nineteenth and early twentieth century. The new corporate order not only ensured the rise of elite, wealthy business magnates but also gave birth to a rapidly expanding middle class of white-collar managers, clerks, and salespersons who helped drive a highly rationalized, scientifically managed corporate culture.[98] The professional lives of such individuals rewarded efficiency and structure, two qualities promised by the Battle Creek System and its scientifically constructed vegetarian diet. And while many of the visitors to Battle Creek did not adopt a vegetarian diet after returning to their homes, the developments at the San nonetheless helped reshape the direction of movement vegetarianism. Vegetarianism, as devised in the San's experimental kitchen, promised adherents increased productivity through personal health.

Though farmers were listed as the number one job category, accounting for 240 of the San's residents in 1911, the vast majority of patients held urban, middle-class, white-collar business-oriented positions. While lawyers and doctors were well represented, the ten most numerous positions also included clerks, bankers, merchants, traveling salesmen, manufacturers, and real estate brokers. Reflecting the new movement vegetarianism's place in a society, which emphasized stark, traditional gender roles, more than half of female residents were listed under the category of housewife, accompanying their white-collar husbands to Battle Creek.[99]

The San's guests were participants in a new vegetarian economy that expanded beyond visits to Battle Creek.[100] A new generation of vegetarians bought Kellogg's products through mail order and at health food stores throughout the United States, following recipes outlined in a variety of cookbooks that promoted meat substitutes. The Sanitarium brand expanded across the country, supported by Kellogg's books and publications, lecture tours, Battle Creek branded sanitariums, and the opening of Battle Creek Sanitarium health food stores. Vegetarianism, as a result, was changing rapidly. By 1904 twenty-one sanitariums in twenty-one states were "conducted under the same general management as the Sanitarium at Battle Creek." In addition, the Battle Creek method was adopted around the world, in sanitariums in Guadalajara, Mexico; Kobe, Japan; Basel, Switzerland; New South Wales, Australia; and Calcutta, India.[101]

Other branches of movement vegetarianism venerated Kellogg, his products, and his system. In 1904, a gathering of vegetarian organizations from around the world meeting in St. Louis congratulated Kellogg's "band of zealous workers, who are carrying the gospel of pure food to the uttermost parts of the earth."[102] *Vegetarian Magazine*, the official publication of the Vegetarian Society of American, regularly touted the benefits of Kellogg's regimen and vegetarian products.[103] Kellogg himself was deeply involved in the meetings, exhibitions, and publications of the VSA.[104] As Kellogg became further involved with movement vegetarianism, he also began to separate from the Adventist church.

At the dawn of the twentieth century, the San could accommodate more than 1,500 patients at a time. Guests clamored for Dr. Kellogg's care, hoping for fresh air, exercise, and Protose cutlets. The physical expansion of the San led its founders, the Whites, to question Kellogg's intentions. While the San was growing and a financial success, Adventist leaders saw the institute becoming too extravagant, a far cry from the principles under which it was created. As a split between Kellogg and his patrons neared, another crisis occurred: on February 18, 1902, the San's main building and hospital burned to the ground under mysterious circumstances. Just over a year later, the San was reconstructed with new, fireproof buildings that could accommodate 1,000 patients and a staff of several hundred. Four years later in 1907, Kellogg separated himself from the Whites and the Adventist church, keeping control over the Battle Creek Sanitarium and the Battle Creek Sanitarium Food Company's factory.

Further changes took place inside Kellogg's health empire. In 1906, his younger brother W. K. left the San after twenty-six years of employment. While working at the San, W. K. dealt primarily with business-related issues, administration, and correspondence with guests. But he was far more interested in making money via mail order. A bitter split occurred between the two brothers over the marketing of a newly developed breakfast cereal that would come to be known as Corn Flakes. W. K. wanted to add sugar in order to make the cereal desirable to the masses, while J. H. wanted to keep it a health food, free of sweeteners.

In 1906 W. K. left the San and started his own breakfast cereal company, laying the foundation for the iconic Kellogg Company that by 1930 had become a breakfast product behemoth. The split between the two brothers illustrated inherent tensions and contradictions that faced the vegetarian movement in the early years of the twentieth century. Thanks to the dedicated efforts of J. H. Kellogg, vegetarianism became a commercial success. As vegetarianism came to thrive in a growing consumerist culture, the movement became disconnected from its politicized roots. J. H. Kellogg attempted to keep some of his ideological purity, insisting that his products remain healthy. But for movement vegetarianism, a lifestyle once largely mocked, the process of being accepted by normative culture had begun.

Larger social forces and tensions that endorsed personal health reform for the benefit and triumph of the individual influenced movement vegetarianism. In a society that valued social, economic, and personal advancement, Kellogg's brand of vegetarianism offered product consumption as a path to self-improvement. Overwhelming social pressures to succeed and advance as individuals had dual implications for American movement vegetarianism. On the one hand, the new vegetarianism introduced the lifestyle to droves of individuals previously disinclined to change their diet. On the other hand, the new influx of believers moved the goals of vegetarianism away from its previous communal concerns. One scholar of the Progressive

Era has characterized the development of "clean living movements" as following a cycle of moral persuasion, coercion, criticism, and eventual complacency.[105] Vegetarianism during the early Progressive Era emphasized persuasion through visits to the San and the marketing and consumption of vegetarian products. Coercion was the next step.

A new form of movement vegetarianism became so focused on the gospel of individualism that it aligned itself with prevailing racial ideologies of the day. As early as 1897, Kellogg began writing and lecturing on the threats to American racial purity. In a tract written that year, Kellogg theorized that a group's resistance to disease could best measure "racial vigor" and predict long-term prospects for health and success. Kellogg argued that meat was ineffective in providing nutritional value and caused individuals to succumb "to the onslaught of . . . disease germs." Vegetables, in contrast, helped create a "sound stomach" and ensured resistance to such diseases as cholera, consumption, and yellow fever.[106]

Kellogg's attachment to the growing eugenics movement eventually shifted from advice to action. In 1914, he became a leader of the newly formed Race Betterment Foundation, advocating for eugenics to purify humanity of crime, intemperance, disability, and psychosis. He assailed public hygiene projects aimed at helping the impoverished and enfeebled as perpetuating weakness in the general population and thus further denigrating humanity.[107] At the foundation's first meeting Kellogg called for the establishment of a "new human race" unencumbered by the pitfalls of flesh-based diets, alcohol, and drug abuse. Untainted, vegetarian food would help create pure, productive individuals.[108]

The most effective way to avoid the continuation of negative physical, intellectual, and emotional traits, Kellogg argued, was to "prevent their multiplication" through legislation.[109] Kellogg prompted the Race Betterment Foundation to create a eugenics registry that would collect hereditary information from families classified as eugenically fit or unfit.[110] Other proponents embraced Kellogg's linking of vegetarianism with eugenics. Medical doctors Benjamin Grant Jefferis and James Lawrence Nichols both proposed the benefits of vegetarianism in building an unpolluted race.[111] The two ideologies converged further as *Vegetarian Magazine* advertised for subscribers in the *American Journal of Eugenics*.[112] Just sixty years after the height of its radical reformist ideology, movement vegetarianism's greatest advocate and most recognizable public figure was working to legislate mass sterilization programs for members of society he deemed unworthy of procreation because of mental deficiency or feeblemindedness.[113] Michigan—thanks in large part to Kellogg's advocacy—would pass sterilization laws in 1913 and 1923. While the numbers were at first small, by 1928 Michigan sterilized an average of 200 people per year.[114] The 1923 sterilization law targeted supposed "idiots, imbeciles, and feebleminded." A 1929 addendum to the law added "insane and epileptic persons" and "moral degenerates, and sexual perverts likely to become a menace to society or wards of the state."[115] This was a far cry from the ideologies that movement vegetarianism had linked with in the past.

:::::::

In the years following the Civil War, movement vegetarianism moved far from its radical, politically oriented roots. Many of the issues that vegetarians fought for in the antebellum era—an end to the enslavement and persecution of African Americans and the disenfranchisement of women, as well as a more just economic system—remained urgent in American society during Reconstruction and the early years of the Progressive Era. These concerns were of little consequence, however, to a new generation of movement vegetarians almost singularly focused on the benefits of dietary reform for themselves rather than society at large. John Harvey Kellogg's Battle Creek Sanitarium stood at the center of these changes, part of a rapidly expanding vegetarian ethos of production and consumerism that found its voice through the principles of scientific cookery.

A new generation of vegetarians venerated the benefits of meat substitutes purported to have higher nutritional value than meat, as proven by scientific, experimental study. These new products had tastes and consistencies similar to those of flesh foods. By utilizing mock meats, vegetarians actually set meat as being the standard diet, one to be emulated though scientifically altered. Although they still disapproved of meat consumption, vegetarians accepted that flesh foods had positive attributes, particularly in terms of flavor and protein.

Mock meats were marketed as having all of the taste advantages of meat with added nutritional value. Since products such as Protose and Nuttose were viewed as being "vegetable meats," vegetarians believed it was possible to morph nonflesh foods into something even better than their natural state—with health- and protein-building properties superior to meat's. Meat substitutes were positioned as beneficial to vegetarians and nonvegetarians alike; the use of mock meats was viewed as a means to achieve recognition. Vegetarians utilized cookbooks, lectures, and marketing materials to appeal to the middle class, connecting meat substitutes to notions of economic and social advancement.

Vegetarians were changing their own movement and with it the very basic identity of vegetarian foods. Meat substitutes created an accommodationist perspective toward meat, reflecting a far less politicized form of vegetarianism than had existed in the antebellum era. Earlier generations of vegetarians viewed social and economic developments with skepticism; the new, modern vegetarian movement embraced the competitive society that venerated individual success and performance.

The progenitors of the American vegetarian movement assailed meat and the corrupt, violent society they believed it helped produce. This worldview enabled vegetarians to join ideological alliances with abolitionists, women's suffragists, and temperance reformers. The new generation of vegetarians—led by the ethos of J. H. Kellogg and the Battle Creek Sanitarium—sought to integrate themselves into a consumption-driven society that celebrated the financially successful individual fueled by foods created through scientific study. The new vegetarians visited the San in order to cure a variety of illnesses that inhibited physical and economic health. When not visiting the San, these vegetarians became consumers of a growing health food industry that brought Battle Creek into homes throughout the United States.

Healthy bodies ensured productive bodies and minds; vegetarian consumers dined on Protose and other meat substitutes with the promise of enjoying an experience that approximated the desirable components of carnivorous living. These new, more mainstream qualities of movement vegetarianism appealed to larger audiences, as evidenced by the popularity of the San and its products as well as the interest in vegetarianism exhibited by the mainstream press. Advocates claimed that eating a vegetarian diet heavy in faux-meat products best prepared individuals for social and economic advancement. Purchasing these products helped move vegetarians away from reform concerned with the external, social effects of diet to a fascination with the possibilities of personal empowerment through consumption. A new vegetarian movement was being created, one far more tolerable to mainstream society. In the process vegetarians morphed into consumers, looking to purchase health, happiness, and individual triumph in a tin can.

CHAPTER SIX

Would You Like to Be a Successful Vegetarian?

::

Vegetarianism is the ethical corollary of evolution.
It is simply the expansion of ethics to suit the biological revelations
of Charles Darwin. —J. Howard Moore, Why I Am a Vegetarian

Although American vegetarianism shifted significantly with the development of Kellogg's Battle Creek Sanitarium, the movement was not wholly disconnected from its past. The new movement vegetarianism of the late nineteenth century attracted adherents thanks to a growing vegetarian population whose members transformed their diet to maximize strength, energy, and productivity. Henry S. Clubb, by then a veteran of American movement vegetarianism, monitored these developments with great interest.

Except for the brief time during his service in the Union army when he ate meat out of necessity, Clubb's dedication to vegetarianism never waned. Following the war, Clubb moved to Grand Haven, Michigan, where in 1869 he founded the *Grand Haven Herald*, the area's first Republican daily. He also became involved in local politics, serving as a Republican state senator from 1873 until 1874, as well as secretary to the state's constitutional convention of 1873.[1] Soon after, however, Clubb reconnected with his past and moved back east. His decision pushed movement vegetarianism back on the path toward building a new, national organization. In the process, movement vegetarianism embraced a new ideology, that of the "successful vegetarian."

During Clubb's years in Michigan his vegetarianism was personalized, lacking a larger community to conjoin with in the immediate area.[2] Isolated from the East Coast–oriented Bible Christian Church of which he was once a member, Clubb attended Grand Haven's First Holland Dutch Reform Church.[3] Clubb, however, was exploring his life options. The possibilities ranged from entering a seminary in Kalamazoo to enrolling as a medical student at the newly christened Battle Creek Sanitarium and training school. He even maintained a brief correspondence with J. H. Kellogg.[4]

In Michigan, Clubb was beset by professional and financial difficulties. In the summer of 1876, he traveled to Philadelphia to report on Philadelphia's Centennial Exhibition, the first world's fair held in the United States. Clubb sought to reconnect with his past and spoke with Bible Christian attendees at the fair. The church's elders had organized an exhibit on the sect and were excited to see a member of the faithful returning to the church's hometown. The group immediately invited Clubb to conduct Sunday services.[5]

Clubb had always been an inspiring speaker; his years lecturing to the American Vegetarian Society (AVS) and his public appeals to potential colonists for the Kansas settlement had honed his oratorical skills. Apparently his talent had not waned during his years in Michigan. The Bible Christian congregation was so moved by Clubb's impassioned preaching that it offered him the full-time position of church pastor, the leader of the movement, early in 1877. Clubb was eager to reestablish an active connection with the Bible Christian and vegetarian communities, and soon after he accepted the church's offer. The decision would have significant implications for movement vegetarianism.

Since the dissolution of the AVS in 1862, movement vegetarianism had been without a national organization advocating for the principles of dietary reform and connecting a geographically disparate group. While the lack of a singular association did not mean that vegetarianism itself disappeared, it did create an opportunity for movement vegetarianism to be redefined. In the twenty-four years between organizations, movement vegetarianism shifted from a primarily communal reform movement to one focused more on the individual. The new, personalized vegetarianism resonated with larger audiences, causing it to grow and become more visible. This increasing popularity made the emergence of a national organization reflecting these new values inevitable. And Henry S. Clubb—given his work with movement vegetarianism's previous national organization—was the perfect candidate to lead the group back to a national association.

Clubb spent the early 1880s leading the Bible Christian Church in Philadelphia. Church members remained active vegetarians and proponents of the diet. Clubb served as the church's pastor and spent the early part of the decade largely disconnected from developments taking place in movement vegetarianism in such locations as Battle Creek. He did, however, see the opportunity to create a more unified, national vegetarian movement.[6]

Clubb had worked with both the British Vegetarian Society and the AVS and believed that local changes could spread nationally, as evidenced by the vegetarian antislavery experiment he had led in Kansas. Under his guidance, Philadelphia-based vegetarians established the Vegetarian Society of America (VSA) in June 1886. Despite sporadic rain, about 200 vegetarians gathered in bucolic Alnwick Grove, about eleven miles outside of Philadelphia, for a celebratory picnic that included fruits, vegetables, pie, lemonade, and chamber music provided by a pair of violinists and a harpist.

Following dinner, Clubb welcomed the gathered vegetarians and introduced J. Harvey Lovell, a prominent Philadelphia physician and vegetarian. Lovell expounded on the new ethos of vegetarianism, proclaiming that "vegetarianism promises . . . the elevation of humanity, the eradication of disease and the preservation of health, the accumulation and enjoyments of wealth, for longevity and comfortable old age." A vegetable diet guaranteed health, happiness, and a long, productive life. It was no coincidence that these were the same promises made by movement vegetarianism's other center of operations, the Battle Creek Sanitarium.

By 1886 vegetarians from the East Coast had already been visiting Battle Creek and purchasing the San's food products in stores and via mail order. Philadelphia vegetarians noticed the changes to movement vegetarianism that began in Battle Creek. The connections ran even deeper; at the VSA's first meeting, letters were read from supporters throughout the United States. The correspondents included Clubb's fellow vegetarian prophet, J. H. Kellogg.

Clubb was elected the new organization's chairman and director general, since he had the most organizational management experience. Eighteen vice presidents were named, each from different states, reflecting the association's goal of emphasizing local vegetarian activities under the umbrella of a national organization. Lovell served as the group's first treasurer. Robert J. Osborne, a recent British émigré to the United States and a Bible Christian, was elected the organization's first secretary. The group adopted a committee of seven (three women and four men) to prepare a plan of organization to be adopted at a forthcoming meeting in Philadelphia. At that gathering in November 1886, participants formally established the VSA, with the goal of building vegetarian communities and organizations throughout the United States.[7]

The VSA in its infancy remained a fairly local organization, serving the needs of Philadelphia's sizeable vegetarian population. Annual picnics, monthly meetings, and regular social gatherings in the homes of

Philadelphia's vegetarian class were held throughout the year. Meeting at Lovell's residence in March 1887, the group listened intently as a letter from William Penn Alcott, the son of early vegetarianism advocate William Alcott, was read aloud.

Alcott reported that he had traveled the world, from Greenland to Africa, without ingesting even a shred of flesh. Thanks to vegetarianism, Alcott said, he was able to work harder and more effectively than meat-eaters, never missing a day due to illness. Previous generations of vegetarians had utilized conversion stories to contrast experiences before and after meat abstention. By the end of the nineteenth century, however, some adherents such as Alcott were able to attest to the diet's ability to promote health, prosperity, and achievement throughout an entire lifetime. Alcott optimistically reported that he saw the future, and it "belongs to the Vegetarians."[8]

In its early years, the VSA worked to grow in Philadelphia. Soon, however, the group began to look outside the city and to attempt to build bridges across state boundaries. In April 1889, the VSA began publishing *Food, Home and Garden*, its monthly magazine of vegetarian news, ideology, and cookery. The publication began as an eight-page pamphlet but doubled in size to sixteen pages just a year later, in 1890. The VSA sought to capitalize on vegetarianism's growing reputation prompted by the popularity of the Battle Creek Sanitarium and its expanding catalog of products available throughout the United States.

At the same time that the new VSA was growing in Philadelphia, another sizable but localized vegetarian association began formulating in an area both logical and unexpected. Chicago had been the center of the U.S. meatpacking industry since the opening of the Union Stockyard in 1865. Meat packers such as Philip Armour built packing plants near the stockyards, innovating technologies to allow for year-round packing and ease of transport. By the dawn of the twentieth century, Chicago employed more than one-third of the nation's total packinghouse employees, processing 75,000 cattle, 80,000 sheep and 300,000 hogs per day.[9]

As the "hog butcher for the world," Chicago seemed a curious location for vegetarian activities.[10] However, the full environmental and social repercussions of the development of Packingtown help explain why Chicago developed a thriving vegetarian community. For those working in the meat packing industry, the Back of the Yards was filled with poverty and pollution. The environmental impact of the meatpacking district affected Chicagoans both in and around the area. According to novelist Upton Sinclair's famous description, the concentration of flesh and entrails smelled like the "craters of hell."[11] Those same odors were blown by the wind throughout the city, producing what one reporter described as a snake-like effect of "folds and unfolds. . . . Its waves lap over each other like the waves of the ocean."[12] Chicago's status as the meatpacking center of the United States impacted people throughout the city, both those working in the industry and those seemingly unconnected to it.

With these conditions in the background, Chicago's concerned vegetarians began organizing themselves in the fall of 1889. Carrica Le Favre—a well-known health lecturer, dress reformer, physical culture advocate, and child-rearing expert—organized the new society. Described by *Everyday Housekeeping* magazine as "one of the prominent vegetarians in the country," Le Favre eventually also led the creation of vegetarian societies in New York City and Boston.[13]

Le Favre's renown as a child expert resulted from her book *Mother's Help and Child's Best Friend* (1890), which sought to give mothers the skills needed to produce moral and industrious children. Le Favre wrote the book because she believed that "in woman's hands are the materials for the creation of great intellects, the molding of heads and hearts that should elevate mankind." Women's role in raising children was "the most praiseworthy and sacred" and in "the interest of the nation."[14] Previous generations of reform-minded vegetarians viewed the diet as a means to liberate women from long and arduous hours in the kitchen. The new movement vegetarianism emphasized women's roles in the kitchen, preparing healthy and nutritious foods to fuel the development of the next generation of productive Americans.

Le Favre believed that a turn to vegetarianism was necessary for the moral and physical well-being of mother and child alike. Children should be fed a strict diet of only milk and vegetables, argued Le Favre, in order to create strong constitutions to meet the moral and physical challenges of modern life and enjoy a lifetime of economic and social success. Le Favre utilized the language of modernity and advancement, labeling the human body an "internal machine" and "instrument" whose "successful development" required its "systematic working." Stimulants like meat acted as "brakes" on this development. Le Favre extolled the benefits of cereals—first popularized as important components of the vegetarian diet at Battle Creek—in building brain matter, while meat caused omnivores to lose mental and physical capabilities. Only through vegetarianism could mothers become "sweet tempered and orderly," qualities for their children to emulate.[15]

Le Favre began the Chicago Vegetarian Society (CVS) without knowing that the VSA existed.[16] This is not necessarily surprising; the VSA remained a local, Philadelphia organization through the 1880s, and *Food, Home and Garden* was then a small pamphlet whose circulation was limited to the Philadelphia vegetarian community.[17] Like many movement vegetarians before her, Le Favre offered a conversion narrative to explain her adoption of vegetarianism. However, the lesson of such conversion narratives was beginning to exceed the scope of the physical or moral.

Le Favre became a vegetarian after having suffered from "chronic diarrhea during my entire meat eating life." She claimed that she "grew rapidly so much worse that I only escaped death by entirely discarding flesh food." Le Favre reported that after she gave up meat she was soon "entirely free from my chronic diarrhea and those frightful headaches."[18] Le Favre's conversion story was clearly influenced by J. H. Kellogg's particular brand of vegetarian medical advice, frequently advising vegetarianism as a cure for both diarrhea and constipation. Further, both Le Favre and Kellogg described diarrhea as an affliction that inhibited one's ability to advance socially.[19]

The Chicago organization began modestly in size, if not in environment, as a group of twenty-nine members met in the parlor of Chicago's palatial Grand Pacific Hotel in the summer of 1889. Twenty-five of these original members were women. The chosen surroundings—a central gathering place of both wealthy travelers and Chicago's upper class—stood in a stark contrast to previous vegetarian meeting places such as the sparsely adorned boardinghouses.[20] The group approved a constitution that stated "its object shall be to adopt and promulgate a Vegetarian line of diet, and by so doing elevate and purify humanity." While anyone who eschewed a flesh diet could become an associate, in order to become full members, candidates needed to be recommended by two established members and elected by a two-thirds majority.

The society, based on its meeting place and membership requirements, was not seeking just any vegetarians. Members were hoping to attract vegetarians belonging to the upper economic and social classes. The middle- and upper-class composition of the Chicago organization mirrored that of Battle Creek's frequent visitors. Le Favre herself recognized this reality, publishing a long list of respectable members while acknowledging that she was leaving out those who were more financially unstable, were "on the ragged edge, and might object to having their names published as Vegetarians."

The names that Le Favre did share included prominent members of Chicago's social and economic upper class. Celia Wallace was a well-known Chicago philanthropist particularly interested in funding gymnasiums and other health-oriented institutions. She was purported to own the only black diamond necklace in the United States. Also included was Juliet A. Darling, owner of Chicago's posh Hotel Isabella.[21] Le Favre's work in making vegetarianism respectable did not go unnoticed; she was celebrated in one publication for her role in "introducing Vegetarianism to the notice of people of culture in the U.S.A."[22]

Despite the Chicago society's limited geographic reach, the group quickly gained the attention of the Philadelphia-based VSA, which was beginning to extend its national reach. By March 1890 the VSA and CVS were working together, and Le Favre was named the editor of *Food, Home and Garden's* home department. At first glance these changes seemed to represent a feminization of movement vegetarianism. In fact, careful analysis of the role of women in this organization reveals a gendered division of labor.

The magazine's home department included recipes as well as daily sample menus describing how to provide the most nutritious combinations of vegetarian foods. Women wrote to the department with tips on how to best prepare foods in a timely but tasty manner. The department also connected domestic bliss with consumerist economics, promoting a variety of vegetarian products in its pages.[23] The message in the pages of *Food, Home and Garden*—similar to that of the domestic sciences that supported the growth of the Battle Creek San—was clear; home expertise was the exclusive department of women. Men, in contrast, were given the task of lending scientific expertise to movement vegetarianism, writing on such issues as the medical benefits of meatless dietetics and the importance of athletics and physical culture. These gender roles were not only reflected in movement vegetarianism's official publication. Only two women were elected to the society's decision-making positions during its more than forty-year history. This reflected the new movement vegetarianism's emphasis on women serving as the moral and physical protectors of children and the home.

The newly refocused *Food, Home and Garden*—offering practical advice on vegetarianism and connecting itself to the domestic sciences—helped increase converts to the new movement vegetarianism. A year after the Chicago group and the VSA began their collaboration, a Chicago vegetarian reported that the movement was "gaining ground . . . especially in Chicago[,] which is rapidly becoming the metropolis of America, and one of the greatest cities in the world." Chicago alone was the home of 100 subscribers to *Food, Home and Garden* just a year after the two organizations began working together.[24]

Le Favre's time in Chicago, however, would soon come to a close. Interested in establishing vegetarian organizations throughout the United

States, thus realizing the VSA's goal of having a national organization supported by local associations, she moved to New York in June 1892 and helped establish the New York Vegetarian Society, becoming the organization's first president. The group's first meeting included lectures from numerous vegetarians, including the journalist and president of the Sociologic Society of America Imogene Fales and VSA president Henry S. Clubb.[25] Vegetarians' strategy of building smaller, municipal organizations reflected a Progressive Era spirit that saw local movements respond to the social turbulence created by an increasingly impersonal, disconnected urban world.[26]

With Le Favre busy establishing a new vegetarian society in New York City, the CVS continued to grow under new leadership. Elea Luboschez, a travel agent and naturalized American citizen from Russia, took over the presidency of the Chicago group in early 1892. Illustrating the new links between local organizations and the VSA, Luboschez served concurrently as the national society's organizing secretary.[27]

The CVS increased its activities and membership, holding regular meetings throughout the Chicago area. The *Tribune* reported positively on the group's accomplishments, describing vegetarianism as evidence of wise, personal economic planning.[28] In February 1892, the organization met at the Sherman House hotel in downtown Chicago. The meeting was "well attended," and the group discussed the possibility of opening a vegetarian restaurant. Although members decided that not enough capital was available yet to make a restaurant possible, they decided to revisit the issue in the future.[29]

The new movement vegetarianism was quickly growing, thanks to the simultaneous expansion of Kellogg's San, the municipal vegetarian societies, and the larger, national VSA. By the summer of 1892 regional vegetarian societies appeared as far west as Oregon, where the local branch of the VSA reported that it was "growing considerably," with "its meetings being well attended by members and others." The new group of Oregonian vegetarians was active enough that it began meeting biweekly in August of that year.[30] During its formative years, movement vegetarianism remained primarily a northeastern community of reformers. The new vegetarianism, commencing in Battle Creek but quickly spreading throughout the United States, had appeal regardless of geographic location.

By the 1890s Chicago was the fastest growing center of vegetarian activities in the United States. The vital local organization had significant influence on the activities of the VSA. Members of the Chicago group were involved in planning strategies for movement vegetarianism's central organization. Simultaneously, Chicago itself was becoming more visible on the national scene, a center of industry associated with American modernity, business, and arts. In the summer of 1893 these forces converged at the Columbian Exposition.

Vegetarians were eager to stake their claim as part of the "White City" and spread the gospel of vegetarian success. The World's Columbian Exposition of 1893 was originally intended to celebrate the 400th anniversary of Christopher Columbus's arrival in the Americas. The massive event turned into a celebration of the burgeoning U.S. role as a world power, exhibiting national pride while touting the country's material and technological advancements. At the forefront of the fair was the city of Chicago itself, a center of shipping and economic activities in the United States. Strong enough to have overcome a massive fire, the city was promoted by its boosters as exhibiting American steadfastness and exceptionalism.[31]

U.S. vegetarians had begun planning to contribute to the Columbian Exposition three years earlier, in the summer of 1890. Movement leaders recognized that vegetarians and other interested parties would visit the fair with a sense of curiosity and exploration. Members of the VSA said they also wanted to connect with the worldwide vegetarian community and would "doubtless have great pleasure in meeting and obtaining a better knowledge of" vegetarians from around the globe. The VSA hoped to "secure some home for the reception of our members" and to provide "proper food and other necessities." A vegetarian restaurant and hotel were proposed to feed and lodge interested visitors.[32]

While the vegetarian movement was growing in the United States, it was also expanding its reach throughout the world. A Vegetarian Federal Union was founded in London in 1889 by dissatisfied former members of the British Vegetarian Society to connect the international vegetarian community. The rebel vegetarians attempted to draw members to their new "Parliament of the Vegetarian movement" through a more global approach that would link vegetarians from around the world without infringing on the activities of local organizations.[33] The union was successful in connecting vegetarians at the Columbian Exposition, but the responsibility for organizing the details of vegetarians' participation at the fair was strictly the VSA's.

Early in 1891, Henry S. Clubb and other representatives of the VSA met with Charles C. Bonney, president of the World's Congress Auxiliary of the World's Columbian Exposition. The group began its discussion at the Grand Pacific Hotel, the lavish setting for the Chicago Vegetarian Society's first meeting four years earlier. The evening culminated with a reception in Bonney's honor at the home of a Chicago vegetarian.

While Bonney initially hesitated to guarantee vegetarians a spot in the World's Congress, he was soon convinced of the value of the group's proposal and promised vegetarians the time and resources to hold a vegetarian gathering as part of the fair's Temperance Congress. Clubb urged the Vegetarian Federal Union to hold its annual meeting at the world's fair, which the group enthusiastically agreed would be a great opportunity to connect vegetarians and spread greater awareness of the movement.[34]

Vegetarian organizations from around the globe descended on Chicago for what was billed as the World's Vegetarian Congress. More than 200 vegetarian delegates met at the newly opened Art Institute from June 8 to 10, 1893, what vegetarians believed to be the largest gathering of like-minded food reformers in history.[35] Vegetarians came from diverse locations including England, Germany, Switzerland, Australia, and India.

The vegetarian meeting was placed under the auspices of the exposition's Department of Temperance, which aimed to "facilitate conventions of existing Temperance Organizations . . . for the consideration of the Living Questions in this Department . . . by the most eminent living leaders in the work." Vegetarianism, once viewed as a threatening, radical social reform, was grouped with organizations that supported "increasing productive ability" and "prosperity and virtue throughout the world."[36] While this was a type of social reform, it reflected the new vegetarianism's emphasis on reform for the material benefit of the individual.

Vegetarians were formally welcomed to their meeting with a speech by Bonney. While noting Chicago's position as "the greatest meat market in the world," Bonney reminded the audience that "it is equally well known as the greatest grain market in the world." Further, Chicago was home to "one of the finest fruit markets in the world." Bonney wished vegetarians a "most successful and satisfactory proceedings," believing that the group would receive fair consideration and treatment given that the congress was meeting "in a city the freest in the world from the influence of prejudice and caste." The result was "an atmosphere of freedom from prejudice, and a willingness to inquire and learn, such as is not always found in the older centres of civilizations." Bonney emphasized the connections between Chicago, vegetarianism, and modernism, while also noting the "cosmopolitan character" of the audience he was addressing; members of the world's social and economic elite.[37] Chicago's place as a center of progress made it an ideal meeting place for the newly modernist vegetarian movement.

The first day of the congress featured nineteen speeches delivered throughout sessions in the morning, afternoon, and evening. William Acton, from the British delegation, opened the day's meeting by emphasizing vegetarianism's role as "an important factor" in "modern civilization" that assisted in the "promotion of true citizenship."[38] Vegetarianism was presented as "vital food" that created "right thought and right living."[39] M. L. Holbrook—a leading American dietary advocate—also connected vegetarianism with notions of cultural hierarchy. Holbrook explained that with the arrival of Columbus and the influx of Europeans into the Americas came a transition from the simple farming of Native Americans to complex agricultural techniques that could support large populations. The fact that American agriculture had grown so much, according to Holbrook, was proof of a cultural triumph, and further evidence of the need for expanded agricultural systems to support greater vegetarianism.[40]

In the afternoon session, Rachel Swain—a medical doctor and women's suffragist—claimed that a turn toward vegetarianism exhibited the qualities of a highly evolved individual. Flesh foods were a remnant of humanity's "savage" roots. Previous generations were "superstitious and ignorant," doing "little thinking for themselves," drifting into the injurious habit of eating meat. Swain noted that the time was ripe for a mass cultural turn toward vegetarianism given society's "advancement in science and cultivation" that led individuals toward a more rational and self-analyzed existence. Vegetarians were continuing a new intellectual tradition started in Battle Creek a decade earlier, arguing for their cause through scientific expertise and rationality. Swain also compared the Progressive Era growth of municipal services such as sewage systems and street cleaning to a growing spirit among individuals to reform their own unhealthy behaviors.[41]

Despite movement vegetarians' expressed notions of cultural superiority, the meeting was also the most ethnically and nationally diverse gathering of worldwide vegetarians to date. This reflected a new method for vegetarians, who built classifications based on dietary choice rather than race.[42] Although movement vegetarians, like advocates of racial sciences, used language that classified individuals into categories of civilized versus noncivilized and modern versus outdated, vegetarians also had a tricky intellectual balance to maintain. Many non-European and non–North American groups around the world practiced a vegetarian diet. As a result, the stringent racial classifications of the period would not suffice to explain the benefits of vegetarianism. Movement vegetarians recapitulated racial classifications and the values attached to these groups to distinguish culturally advanced, modern vegetarians from antiquated, savage nonvegetarians.[43]

This method of classification created opportunities for a varied group of vegetarian advocates to speak at the Chicago meeting. Reformers from around the world made their presence felt, including an address on the curative properties of vegetarianism by a medical doctor from Belfast, Ireland. The evening session featured a presentation by Sidhn and Lala Jinda Ram, Punjabi Hindus who explained vegetarianism from a theological perspective. While the Columbian Exposition, particularly on the fairgrounds, exhibited images of explicit racism, the events at the World's Vegetarian Congress encouraged a certain level of cultural and ethnic diversity.[44]

Vegetarians closed the day's proceedings with a reception in the Art Institute's ornately decorated Hall II. An extravagant feast was provided for the gathered vegetarians, who included renowned American movement vegetarians J. H. Kellogg and Juliet Severance, as well as other members of the VSA and vegetarian leaders from Great Britain and Germany.[45] But the banquet and initial papers were just the preliminary gathering for the determined group; two more days of lectures, meetings, speeches, and proclamations allowed vegetarians to stake their claim as a modern movement worthy of attention.

On the morning of June 9, the World's Vegetarian Congress gathered for a marathon session of forty-four papers exhorting the benefits of a meatless diet.[46] During the morning session speakers continued connecting vegetarianism with modernity and high culture. A vegetarian diet was equated with "rational selection," called the "basis of all reform," and celebrated as an indication of humanity's progress from savagery to civility.[47] Arnold F. Hills, a delegate from London, made the connection between vegetarianism and modern advancement explicit. Hills compared the human digestive system to the functioning of a steam engine, explaining that, "as in the boiler, so in the body—when once the limit of vital accumulation has been reached, the process of spontaneous ebullition has begun." Vegetarianism produced vigorous spirits, Hills argued, creating the "great workers of the world" who "have begun their task, not in sorry, but in gladness, because the spirit moved in them to do great things."[48]

Father Louis Paroli, a Catholic priest from New Orleans, noted the connection between vegetarianism and economic success, believing that the former caused "great commerce and universal business" and created strong and "well looking people." In contrast, meat-eaters were "feeble" and "feverish as soon as they get a little overworked."[49] Arguments made at the Congress redirected the negative physical and mental characteristics affixed

THE VEGETARIAN DELEGATES TO THE WORLD'S FAIR.

Rev. P. W. Alcott.   (*From a Photograph taken at Chicago, June 1893.*)

Mrs. Alcott.   Elea Turaschez.   Mrs. LeFavre. J. Franks. Miss Yates, Mrs. Axon.   Dr. J. G. Stair.
London.

E. Dixon,   Rev. H. S. Clubb, Rev. Jas. Clark, W. E. A. Axon, E. Clark,   T. Hanson,
Cambridge.   Philadelphia.   Manchester.   Manchester. Manchester.   London.

"The Vegetarian Delegates to the World's Fair," Chicago, 1893. From C. W. Forward, Fifty Years of Food Reform: A History of the Vegetarian Movement in England (1898).

to vegetarians by the popular press through the 1860s. Speakers attempted to associate weakness with meat-eaters rather than with vegetarians. Dietary reformers used the world's fair as an opportunity to state vegetarianism's case through socially acceptable arguments of modernity and success.

Attendance at the afternoon session was, according to the *Tribune*, "even larger than that of the morning," though accounts noted that all sessions were "largely attended."[50] Vegetarianism was equated with modern progress and proclaimed "the food of the future" by one presenter. Charles W. Forward continued the meeting's emphasis on the connections between vegetarianism and civility, framing food choices as part of the battle between modernity and savagery. Forward denounced carnivorous diets as "a relic of barbarous times" because of their cost and cruelty. With a nod to the electric spectacle that wowed visitors at the "White City," Forward noted that conventional thought led "many a would-be philosopher" to declare coal gas as the answer to artificial lighting needs. Now, however, "everyone is looking to electricity as the most satisfactory solution of the problem of turning night into the semblance of day."[51] Forward's metaphor was clear; just as scientific knowledge and the modern world brought forth electrical light, they also led to a vegetarian diet.[52] The ethos of the fair was mixing with a new philosophy of scientifically rational movement vegetarianism.

While the World's Vegetarian Congress positioned itself as part of a new, evolving movement, it still recognized its historical connections. William Alcott's son, the Reverend William Penn Alcott, addressed the audience, following in the footsteps of his pioneering father. However, despite the younger Alcott's long-standing connection to American vegetarianism (William Alcott raised all his children from birth on a vegetarian diet), his speech focused on themes distinct to the new vegetarianism.

In his speech titled "Vegetarianism and Progress," Alcott described food reform as "the most important work we can assign ourselves." He connected dietary choices with evolutionary theory, juxtaposing humanity's power of reason with the "protozoa of simplest type," who were "all stomach within," multiplying through the assimilation of proteins. Humanity, with its advanced skills of reason and critical thinking, was meant to have a discerning palate. Alcott described individual productivity as driven strictly by diet, arguing that, "our activity and usefulness in every sphere are very directly dependent on, and conditioned by, habits of eating." Vegetarianism was the only way to guarantee healthy, productive bodies, minds, and spirits best suited for social and economic success.[53]

The evening session began with a patriotic twist, with the singing of the "Battle Hymn of the Republic." The session was presided over by movement vegetarianism's industrious business leader, J. H. Kellogg. The superintendent from the Battle Creek San followed one of his preferred lines of argumentation, explaining the benefits of vegetarianism from a medical perspective. In his speech, Kellogg argued that the vegetarian diet could strengthen all patients preparing for and recovering from surgery.

The late day lectures primarily focused on vegetarianism's connection to health and physical development. One delegate waxed poetic on the "aesthetics of vegetarianism," preferring the diet because "it is certainly favorable to the beauty of health and refinement." The lecturer noted that meat-eaters "miss good looks for want of the refinement and freshness which I think a vegetarian life would give them." Vegetarianism created a "peculiar sweetness of skin and breath," helping practitioners to avoid wrinkles and the signs of aging. Most important, the diet had social cachet, because it was never offensive to a dining partner or onlooker.[54]

Carrica Le Favre touched on similar themes in the evening's culminating paper, which focused on dietary contributions to physical beauty. Le Favre argued that "our bodies are literally built up of the food we eat, and the kind and quality of the food determines the possible use of the body." Flesh foods were "shoddy material" that produced bodies of which many "may well be ashamed and conceal beneath a conventional cloak of broadcloth." Repeating the common, central theme of the congress, Le Favre labeled vegetarianism as "civilized," practiced by "refined" men and women. In contrast, Le Favre condemned physical imperfections, proclaiming that, "there is nothing so discouraging to look upon as an ugly, sickly body." Physical imperfections implied personal frailty, qualities least apt to help one prosper in life.[55]

In addition to the speeches and festivities, attendees passed a series of resolutions aimed at expressing a general consensus. The principles adopted reflected many of the themes present in modern movement American vegetarianism by the 1890s, despite the congress's international composition. The congress glorified the civic reform spirit of the growing "city beautiful" movement that expressed itself at the Columbian Exposition. One resolution proclaimed that "the parks of this country, both municipal and national, merits [sic] the highest commendation," projecting both an appreciation for civic greenery and the government's role in supporting it. The congress did not call for the legislative banning of meat, but it did advocate for laws regulating the shipment of cattle to slaughterhouses. The congress agreed on one resolution that codified the event's repeated themes of culture and civilization. Meat promoted "a low standard of morality and conscience," delegates agreed, and thus should be avoided by people of "enlightenment."

The congress labeled the killing of animals for sport a "wanton cruelty," though it did not outline specific steps to take in order to ban sport hunting. Delegates further agreed that "social purity" was only possible through uncontaminated food and drink. Another resolution promoted J. H. Kellogg's scientific rationale, arguing that the healthful properties of vegetarianism were acquired directly, provided by the "products of the earth, air and water." Lastly, attendees at the World's Vegetarian Congress called on local and national legislatures to encourage and fund the development of fruit cultivation. The resolutions passed were indicative of a Progressive Era civic reform spirit that connected reformers with direct, political action, rather than solely concentrating on the power of personal dietary choices.[56]

Nonvegetarians likewise deemed the congress successful. Organizers of the Columbian Exposition described the vegetarian meeting as having "attracted special attention." In addition, designated fair historian Hubert Howe Bancroft declared the World's Vegetarian Congress "worth the hearing" because "nearly one half of mankind are vegetarians either through choice or necessity."[57]

Vegetarians had multiple aims at the Columbian Exposition. The congress itself connected vegetarians from around the world, with lectures and dinners allowing food reformers to feel a sense of community. In addition, vegetarians exhibited, reaching out to like-minded reformers and meat-eaters alike, publicly claiming that the movement deserved recognition among the great ideas of progress, culture, and modernity.

A vegetarian annex was constructed inside the Liberal Arts Division building, which also housed exhibits from the fields of education, engineering, hygiene, religion, public works, architecture, music, and drama.[58] Since the Vegetarian Federal Union was based in England, the booth was placed near other English exhibits, located between London's Royal Microscopical Society and a coffee importer based in Bradford.[59] While the World's Vegetarian Congress was aimed specifically at vegetarians (though some nonvegetarians attended), the vegetarian annex was the group's attempt to spread its message to average fairgoers.

Vegetarians celebrated the symbolism of their exhibit opening on July 4. On "this great day of Independence," announced one publication, "Vegetarianism proclaims freedom from the slavery of Drunkenness and Disease." A large blue and gold silk banner demarcated the space as the domain of the Vegetarian Federal Union, welcoming visitors to learn about meatless living. The exhibit was decorated with artwork glorifying the farinaceous kingdom, including "lovely pictures of golden corn, beautiful peaches, melons, grapes, apples and other tempting fruits."[60] Centered under the organization's name was a sign proclaiming the healing properties of vegetarianism, simply promising, in all capital letters, "HEALTH."

A painting of a young, cherubic child and his mother was juxtaposed with an oil painting of a tiger's head in order to illustrate the differences between humanity's flat teeth meant for fruits and vegetables, and the sharp, pointy, carnivorous teeth of the wild beast. An arrangement of flowers, fruits, grains, and nuts was placed on a table at the center of the exhibit, surrounded by a bounty of literature on the vegetarian cause available for visitors to read at the annex or take home for further study. Interested parties could read about topics including vegetarianism as "the Final Solution of the Drink Question," as "The Most Nourishment at the Least Cost," and as a preventative cure for "Rheumatism, Rickets and Consumption." The

Vegetarian annex at the Columbian Exposition, Chicago, 1893. From C. W. Forward, Fifty Years of Food Reform: A History of the Vegetarian Movement in England (1898).

lifestyle was equated with healthy, productive bodies and minds, best prepared to conquer the modern world.[61]

Speeches were also presented at the vegetarians' exhibit, including one geographically aware orator who noted that "vegetarians were looking forward to the day when . . . they would stand on the shores of Lake Michigan gazing at the ruins of the deserted stock yards." Another speaker hypothesized that the push to make Indian corn the national symbol of the United States resulted in part from the visibility of vegetarians in the United States. The speaker bellowed that it was not possible for "lovely and refined women" to select something as loathsome and debasing as a beefsteak or pork chop as their national symbol.[62] While vegetarians did not achieve their original goal of creating a vegetarian restaurant at the fair, they did host a series of receptions in the Pennsylvania State Building, where visitors were introduced to vegetarian cuisine.[63]

The Columbian Exposition was associated with modernity, progress, culture, civilization, and advancement. The fair glorified technological growth, with an illuminated "White City" that displayed the power and ascendance of electric lighting. By extension, the exhibitors and congresses represented at the exposition were tacitly endorsed as expressing the same qualities of importance and innovation. Leaders of the World's Vegetarian Congress were aware of these associations, and the event was marked by speeches, displays, and literature that touted these themes. Conveniently enough, these ideals also matched those touted by movement vegetarians by the 1890s. Vegetarianism, with its new focus on health, scientific rationalism, physical strength, and modernity was being embraced by growing audiences, whether they practiced the lifestyle or not.

The *Chicago Tribune* reflected on the success of the growing vegetarian movement, noting that while vegetarian ideals had existed since "the days of Pythagoras," the community remained largely "alone and isolated." The group had changed, according to the *Tribune*, which proclaimed that "vegetarians have grown to such numbers as to demand a hearing in the World's Congresses."[64] Vegetarians themselves described the congress as "one of the most successful and important events in the Vegetarian movement."[65] The congress was "successful beyond any previous gathering of the kind"; at its sessions "attendance was good, the interest deep and continuous, and the papers were, on the whole, of the highest value and importance."[66]

The exposition further cemented American vegetarians' confidence in their growing cause by witnessing a globalization of movement vegetarianism. Delegates from diverse locations connected in Chicago under the banner of vegetarianism and progress. Vegetarians from the United States mingled with cohorts from Switzerland, Germany, and India, illustrating that the movement knew few geographical and political boundaries. Vegetarians from a variety of ethnic, religious, and national backgrounds gathered in one central location and expounded on the diverse social and health benefits of vegetarianism. Vegetarians mixed the language of American triumphalism with that of economic development to place the movement among the great social changes of the modern world. The Columbian Exposition marked the ascendance of the United States onto the world scene; vegetarians for the first time were visibly included in the celebration.

The success of the vegetarian presence at the Columbian Exposition emboldened American dietary reformers, particularly in Chicago. Participants noted the potential transformative effect of the fair, hoping that the World's Vegetarian Congress would "form the starting point for an earnest and active forward movement, and lead to a wide diffusion of Vegetarianism alike in the Old and in the New world."[67] While vegetarianism may not have reached these lofty goals, the movement continued to expand. In August

1893, Chicago vegetarians hosted a reception for the visiting Henry S. Clubb at the home of a member of the Chicago VSA. At this meeting the organization elected a new commissioner, Francis G. Kemp, a health reformer and physical education advocate who made the establishment of a vegetarian restaurant in Chicago the group's top priority.

Soon after his election to head the vegetarian society, Kemp wrote a letter to the *Daily Inter Ocean*—a favored newspaper of Chicago's Republican upper class—describing the state of vegetarianism in the city.[68] Kemp assured readers that the VSA was "unsectarian in character," noting that "the aim of the society is to induce habits of abstinence from the flesh of animals (fish, flesh, and fowl) as food, and promote the use of fruits, pulse, cereals, and other products of the vegetable world." As a sign of the movement's growth, he pointed to the VSA's magazine *Food, Home and Garden*: previously an eight-page pamphlet circulated among Philadelphia's vegetarian community, it had grown to a twenty-four-page publication with a monthly circulation of 4,500 subscribers. Kemp concluded with the hope that Chicago vegetarians would open a restaurant and "make a practical demonstration of vegetarianism."[69]

Whereas movement vegetarianism through the 1870s was connected primarily to middle-class reform, the new, modern ethos of success also appealed to segments of the urban upper class. Movement vegetarianism, of course, continued to appeal to middle-class reformers. But with the financial support of Chicago's wealthy, philanthropic class, movement vegetarianism would take Kemp's advice to heart and venture toward building public institutions to spread the appeal of vegetarianism. The same demographic mix of upper- and middle-class reformers who visited J. H. Kellogg's Sanitarium also supported the growth of regional vegetarian societies and contributed to the activities of the VSA.

The inclusion of members of the upper class in movement vegetarianism provided the material resources that the community needed to grow and expand its activities. With the necessary capital, movement vegetarianism and its national organization, the VSA, were able to venture further into the realm of commercialization. From wealthy philanthropists, vegetarians simultaneously obtained social legitimacy and promoted organizational growth. The synthesis of the middle and upper classes also showed adherents that through vegetarianism they, too, could move into the highest ranks of social acceptance.

Vegetarianism was transforming into what one proponent described as "a 'becoming' diet," fashionable, appealing, and inoffensive to fellow diners.[70]

Vegetarian meetings, events, and businesses encouraged the mixing of upper- and middle-class reformers. The bloodless nature of vegetarian foods and the simple manner in which they could be eaten provided social cachet, and vegetarianism was acceptable in even the most genteel social circles.

Activities at the exposition helped create a new popular image of the vegetarian, in both the movement and some mainstream circles. Unlike the weakened figure of previous generations, the new vegetarian was associated with physical fitness, strength, and impeccable health. With a strong body created by vegetable foods, the vegetarian of the late nineteenth and early twentieth century was physically able to offset the perceived weakening effects of advanced American industrial society. With growing fears of the physical weakening of individuals after the corporate revolution of the late nineteenth century, vegetarians offered their diet as a singular cure-all to produce strong, robust, healthy individuals who had the vigor to succeed, images of civilized manliness.[71]

Inherent in the idea of the successful vegetarian was that of the unsuccessful one. The first generation of movement vegetarians had touted the diet as a means to create greater economic equity through the affordability of vegetable foods. The new generation of movement vegetarianism led by the VSA and including members of the mobile middle and upper classes had little concern for the working and lower classes, groups populated largely by recent immigrant workers by the turn of the twentieth century. Through 1910, the VSA's magazine, for example, did not include any articles on the economic benefits of vegetarianism for the lower classes. The one mention occurred in April 1900, a short paragraph noting that one Philadelphia mission was providing vegetarian meals to "working men" to spread "the wisdom of living vegetarian and sober lives." Neither did the magazine speak out against poverty or economic injustice, two favored issues of the first generation of movement vegetarians.[72]

How can this shift in focus among movement vegetarians be explained? Middle-class dietary reformers in the late nineteenth century relied on members of the upper class for the capital to begin vegetarian organizations, restaurants, and businesses, further interlinking the movement with an economic system that had created vast economic and social stratification by the early 1890s.[73] This was a far cry from early movement vegetarianism, which had preached the diet as a means to create greater economic equity. The new demographics of its membership, however, paid dividends for movement vegetarianism's public image, as the popular press praised the diet and its adherents during this period. Vegetarians understood that in order to grow and gain favor from wider audiences their movement would have to embrace notions of muscular civility and promote the diet as a means to social and economic advancement. This shift made vegetarianism more popular and commercially successful.

Vegetarian establishments sprouted up throughout Chicago, corresponding to the growth of the VSA, the events at the Columbian Exposition, and the inclusion of the upper classes in movement vegetarianism. In April 1894, a small vegetarian club was opened at 5800 Jackson Avenue in Uptown, a resort locale for Chicago's downtown upper class.[74] The club was one of four simultaneously functioning subdivisions of the VSA appearing in Chicago at the same time.[75] Alice Harsch, the owner of a vegetarian club at Sixty-Third Street in the Englewood neighborhood, learned to cook vegetarian meals while visiting the World's Vegetarian Congress and began promoting the establishment as a vegetarian hotel during the exposition. Boarding cost one dollar per day, though the price rose to two dollars for those interested in having vegetarian meals provided. The house held twenty-five vegetarian boarders at a time and remained a popular destination throughout the exposition, successful enough that Harsch decided to continue operating as a vegetarian club after the fair closed, offering boarding and three meals a day.[76] It was the first fully vegetarian establishment in Chicago.

The vegetarian clubs all received their products from a recently opened Vegetarian Supply House located on the South Side at Cottage Grove Avenue and Thirty-Eighth Street.[77] The *Chicago Tribune* reported that one club had aims beyond the merely culinary, since its "purpose is quite as much to bring about social relations between the students of opposite sexes as to taboo the use of flesh as food. . . . In a word, the Vegetarian club is a device for the mutual advantage of bashful youth and maidens."[78] While the *Tribune* was reporting with a tone of moral self-righteousness, it did indicate an important continuing development for vegetarians. As the group grew and became more visible, vegetarians sought each other out for a sense of community and common identity, sometimes even for romance.

Chicago had quickly become recognized as a center of movement vegetarian activities in the United States, culminating with the relocation of VSA's publication *Food, Home and Garden* from Philadelphia to Chicago in 1900.[79] Vegetarians continued to pursue the goal of opening a vegetarian restaurant, hoping to raise at least $1,000 in capital to begin the venture. The new connection between vegetarianism and commercialism was at the forefront of the plans for a restaurant, as the group planned to open its doors "in the business part of the city."[80]

In the fall of 1895, the *Tribune* estimated that around 6,000 vegetarians lived in Chicago.[81] The Department of Health of the City of Chicago in the same year reported the total population of the city at 1.6 million people. Based on the *Tribune's* estimation—which is difficult to prove or disprove—vegetarians would have comprised 0.4 percent of Chicagoans, a small share but one comparable to that of other niche reform organizations. As a comparison, Chicago's Woman's City Club—a collection of reformers and settlement-house workers that organized to increase women's participation in civic life—was comprised of only 1,200 members in its founding year, 1910.[82] Other tangential statistics point to vegetarianism gaining attention during these years. In 1905, *Publisher's Weekly* began listing a separate heading of "vegetarian" to track books published specifically on that subject.[83]

This newfound visibility and confidence had profound advantages for movement vegetarianism both inside and outside the community. In December 1895, Chicago hosted the inaugural banquet of the Chicago branch of the VSA with a twelve-course dinner at the majestic Great Northern Hotel, designed by Daniel Burnham.[84] Round tables with flowing fern centerpieces were surrounded by the tall, cruciferous palm trees placed in each corner of the ornately designed ballroom. Attendees dined on a menu that included lentil soup and vegetable turkey, a J. H. Kellogg–esque concoction of grains, nuts, and beans.

The meeting was presided over by legal scholar, civil libertarian, and University of Chicago lecturer William Addison Blakely, who read letters of support from suffragist and temperance advocate Francis Willard, as well as newspaper editor Murat Halstead.[85] In attendance was the famed lawyer and on-and-off vegetarian Clarence Darrow, who compared his opinion of dietary reform to his feelings on the labor movement, noting that his "attitude towards vegetarianism is that attitude which the Civic Federation holds toward reform—theoretically all right."[86] Darrow was referring to the National Civic Federation (NCF), a body of business and labor leaders that aimed to avoid conflict and resolve labor disputes through moderated reform. The NCF's positions were notably mainstream and nonconfrontational with respect to big business, so Darrow's comparison with modern vegetarianism was, perhaps unwittingly, quite accurate.

At this gathering, vegetarians utilized the language of success, strength, and social mobility, arguing that their diet was "best fitted to forward the mental, moral and physical advancement of mankind."[87] The developments in the new movement vegetarianism seemed to increase popular acceptance of vegetarianism. The same year that the Chicago VSA held its inaugural meeting, the *Tribune* exhorted the advantages of vegetarianism, going so far as to describe Henry S. Clubb as "strong and robust," "an ardent apostle of the cause he represents" at the advanced age of seventy.[88]

Chicago's vegetarian organizations continued to grow and hold numerous outings and meetings. The group was active throughout the city, with members residing as far south as Cottage Grove Avenue and as far north as the posh North Shore, home to Chicago's elite.[89] By the summer of 1897 the Chicago VSA's West Side branch attracted approximately 300 members at its monthly meeting.[90] Meanwhile, the national VSA was becoming recognized as an authority on vegetarianism, a development on which the organization capitalized commercially. As early as February 1897, *Food, Home and Garden* began marketing a "Vegetarian Society Mill" that ground out a variety of vegetarian victuals.[91]

Sales of the mill reflected the new dietary choices of vegetarians, including the nuts, legumes, and meat substitutes advocated by J. H. Kellogg. In addition, the marketing of products such as the mill exhibited the values affixed to the new movement vegetarianism. The society mill looked remarkably like a metallic meat grinder, furthering the association begun in the Battle Creek Sanitarium's experimental kitchen of vegetarian dishes as meat analogs. Just as products like Protose and Nuttose could approximate the taste and touch of flesh foods, the VSA's mill could break down nonmeat products and allow consumers to reconstitute the grinds into meat substitutes. A raised cup stood at the center of the mill where vegetarians would place nuts, beans, and vegetables to be ground down, thanks to a simple gear system driven by a hand crank.[92]

The Vegetarian Society Mill promised a "supply of good, clean, wholesome food . . . at very moderate cost." The mill not only ground wheat into flour, but it also was "equally adapted to the grinding of nuts which cannot be said of other grist and coffee mills" that would "choke up" given nuts' oily properties. According to advertisements, the modern, ingenious design of the mill ensured that the entire wheat kernel, including the bran, was ground so fine that the result was even superior to Graham flour.[93] The mill was described as versatile, able to make simple flour out of lentils, peas, and wheat, while also being proficient at grinding nuts into a paste, allowing users to bake mock meat croquettes. The mill was popular enough that a year later the VSA was marketing its "Improved Vegetarian Society Mill," a lighter mill that was easier to crank.[94]

The VSA argued for its product's effectiveness by providing testimonials from vegetarians whose lives had improved after purchasing the mill. The product testimonials were similar in tone, style, and structure to the vegetarian conversion narratives of previous generations, explaining how a shift in practice created instant life improvement. However, these new conversion stories emphasized not only the vegetarian diet but also the machine that made the diet easier to practice. One satisfied customer reported that thanks to the mill the members of his family "have no medicine . . . and no use for a Doctor."[95] The Reverend Elmer F. Krause from Leechburg, Pennsylvania, explained that his mill was "in constant use" and that he "could not do without it." The minister reported he continually found "new possibilities in the mill," such as producing a peanut butter ground "to perfection."[96]

Mrs. N. E. Arnold of Dayton, Florida, prized her mill because she could roast, salt, and grind peanuts "into paste which no meat-eater can tell from meat by look or taste." Utilizing the language of vigor that was increasingly attached to vegetarians, another consumer noted that the mill was "strong and durable," concluding that he was "well pleased with it."[97] The mill had even cured the bowel troubles that one former Confederate soldier "contracted in the army . . . during our unpleasantness between the North and South." The product had "many profitable uses," not the least of which was the reconciliation of this Alabaman's stomach and appetite.[98]

The Vegetarian Society Mill was just the first of a spectrum of products marketed to vegetarians in the pages of the VSA's publications. In addition to books and pamphlets—long sold to vegetarians—the VSA also produced and advertised everything from vegetarian soap to coffee substitutes, nut cheese, and fruit butters.[99] Vegetarianism had become a growing commercial enterprise, profitable for business owners and helpful for advocates seeking a sense of belonging and legitimacy. The society sold ad space to a variety of health food entrepreneurs, including the Battle Creek Sanitarium Health Food Company.[100] Just as J. H. Kellogg and the Battle Creek Sanitarium began marketing and selling meat substitutes, the VSA also marketed products—its own and those sold by others—to a new generation of vegetarians willing to spend money on products that promised to improve their lives.

In October 1899 the VSA's national magazine was renamed *Vegetarian Magazine*, directly preceding the magazine's move from Philadelphia to Chicago.[101] The new publication placed an emphasis on advertising vegetarian products, providing space for a wide variety of items including Protose, Wahl's Concentrated Pea Soup, Shredded Wheat Biscuits, and Ko-nut, a butter made from coconut oil.[102] The magazine's first issue included six full pages of advertisements, nearly one-fifth of the entire publication.

The move from Philadelphia to Chicago and the rebranding as *Vegetarian Magazine* at the turn of the twentieth century was a measureable, material success for the VSA, reflecting Chicago's emergence as the center of American movement vegetarianism. In 1900, its first year of publishing in Chicago, *Vegetarian Magazine* had 3,750 subscribers.[103] Just over a decade later, in 1911, the publication was reported to have more than 15,000 subscribers. The magazine reached its zenith of popularity two years later in 1913 with nearly 16,000 subscribers.[104] This growth reflected the general expansion of movement vegetarianism, as well as the increased commercial success of vegetarian businesses and industry. Mail order served the new movement vegetarianism well, particularly for adherents dispersed throughout the United States. In urban centers, vegetarian businesses began to proliferate.

New York opened the nation's first vegetarian restaurant on February 5, 1895, the very literally named Vegetarian Restaurant Number 1 on West Twenty-Third Street between Seventh and Eighth Avenues. The restaurant's menu left little doubt as to its goals, reminding diners of an axiom from Ovid's *Metamorphoses*: "Take not away the life we cannot give; For all things have an equal right to live."[105] An illustration of a young boy dressed in red, feeding rose petals to a young woman lying in a field, adorned the menu, reminding vegetarians of the natural bliss the diet produced. Local New York VSA members and representatives from the national organization, including Henry S. Clubb, were welcomed with bowls of fruit soup and bean entrees. Clubb welcomed diners with a speech marking the momentous occasion, calling for similar restaurants to be opened throughout the United States.[106]

Chicago's vegetarians met their goal of opening a restaurant in the middle of a busy business district five years later. The city's first vegetarian restaurant, the Pure Food Lunch Room, opened in 1900 at 176 East Madison Street, in the middle of Chicago's central business district known as "the Loop."[107] The Pure Food Lunch Room promised customers a "clean, airy" restaurant with "good ventilation" and "appetizing food." The restaurant also emphasized its affordable prices, convenient lunch counters, and quick service that provided instant, nutritious lunches to workers in a growing Chicago office culture that emphasized efficiency.

The opening of the restaurant marked the beginning of the establishment of a flood of vegetarian businesses in Chicago, most located in the city's commercial and business districts. A Vegetarian Publishing Company opened at 84 Madison Street, two blocks north of the Art Institute. The organization printed *The Vegetarian* but also vegetarian cookbooks and literature. The publishing company housed a printing press and storefront that also served as a vegetarian book and grocery store.[108] The Vegetarian Company also had administrative offices in the McVickers Theatre Building at 82 Madison Street, an Adler and Sullivan–designed entertainment palace surrounded by a shell of offices.[109] The Ionia vegetarian restaurant had two locations, one at 187 Dearborn Street and the other at 276 Clark Street, both in the Loop. Diners could also visit the Vegetarian Good Health Restaurant, located in the posh Gold Coast, appealing to Chicago's upper-class vegetarians.[110] A variety of vegetarian establishments were located near the University of Chicago, including a vegetarian dining club at 5622 Ellis Avenue and the Hygiea Dining Room at 5759 Drexel Avenue.[111] The locations of vegetarian businesses in Chicago reflected the new movement's attachment to notions of economic respectability and advancement. The businesses also gave vegetarians public locales in the city's landscape, further fomenting a notion of community.

The Mortimer Pure Food Company in the Loop was such a popular vegetarian restaurant by 1906 that it employed a staff of fifty.[112] The restaurant symbolically represented the intersection between vegetarianism and commercialism in Chicago. Alonzo (A. H. A.) Mortimer, a naturalized Canadian immigrant and local business leader, owned the restaurant and also helped manage the Illinois Athletic Club.[113] The restaurant was comanaged by Rufus Fisher Chapin, secretary and treasurer of the International Association of Rotary Clubs.[114] The restaurant's claim of serving pure food projected an image of quality and wholesomeness to its customers. It was no coincidence that the restaurant opened its doors soon after the passage of the Pure Food and Drug Act, the first legislation to provide federal inspection of meat products. By using the words "Pure Food" in its name, the restaurant made the point that vegetable-based products were inherently healthier and more trustworthy than the diseased and contaminated meats packed in the Back of the Yards.

Vegetarian grocery stores served a similar function as restaurants as sources of sustenance and locations for communal gathering. Benold's Pure Food Store on North Avenue near Lincoln Park specialized in unfermented wheat bread, illustrating that while the vegetarian movement had moved far away from its Grahamite roots, practitioners still wanted healthy, pure bread.[115] One enthusiast described Benold's wheat bread as being "more nourishing than meat" and a cure for stomach aches and constipation. Just as important, the writer noted the bread's social cachet, pointing out that "Mr. Benold's Bread finds its way into the homes of scores of Chicago's most prominent families."[116] In addition to its wheat bread, Benold's also carried a "full line of reform foods" including nuts, peanut butter, honey, and fruit preserves. The store also sold vegetarian literature, in order to "set your thoughts into successful action" and ensure "a sound, vigorous and active body." All of Benold's products could be shipped throughout the United States, in quantities up to 100 pounds.[117]

Berhalter's Health Food Store and Bakery in Old Town provided shoppers with products that were "in accordance with Vegetarian Dietetics," guaranteeing "progress in physical health." The store sold a wide range of goods, including gluten flour, olives, raisins, figs, and olive oil by the quart. The store utilized the language of advancement in its advertisements, noting that it carried "such a fine variety of foods that it enables vegetarians to select suitable supplies to carry on a vegetarian life successfully." The proprietors also had enough experience that they could "supply all the knowledge necessary to begin a vegetarian diet successfully." Berhalter's also shipped products throughout the United States. The shipping of vegetarian goods around the country by stores like Benold's and Berhalter's illustrated that vegetarians were increasingly connected as a community through product consumption.[118]

Although Chicago was the city that experienced the greatest proliferation in number of vegetarian businesses, it was hardly the only site of growth. According to a directory of vegetarian businesses published in a 1904 meatless cookbook, fifty-seven vegetarian restaurants could be found throughout the United States, either freestanding or inside vegetarian health resorts. This list was not comprehensive (Chicago's Pure Food Lunch Room, for example, was not included, although it was open in 1904). The directory identified vegetarian restaurants in such varied locations as San Francisco, Des Moines, Milwaukee, Colorado Springs, Salt Lake City, and Washington, DC.[119] Whatever the exact number of vegetarian restaurants in the early twentieth century, the lifestyle was clearly making itself known in urban areas.

While the new movement vegetarianism helped craft a community of vegetarians united through common consumerist practices, these practitioners were not the only individuals practicing vegetarianism in the United States. In fact, some groups sought to continue vegetarianism's historical tradition of connecting diet to political and social reform, and they competed over the meaning of vegetarianism in the late nineteenth and early twentieth century. Understanding alternative vegetarian perspectives and the choice by movement vegetarianism's central organization not

Advertisements in Vegetarian Magazine, November 1907.

to embrace them helps explain and illustrate the community's break from its more politicized past. One prominent group in particular, the Millennium Guild led by the decorative artist M. R. L. Sharpe, harkened back to the movement's roots, with an ideology focusing on social reform through vegetarianism.

Writing in the introduction to her *Golden Rule Cook Book*, Sharpe (eventually better known as M. R. L. Freshel) immediately made the connection between her vegetarianism and social reform known to her readership. Quoting Abraham Lincoln, she reminded readers to "let none falter who thinks he is right." Making the connection even more explicit, Sharpe went on to describe the "higher humanitarianism" created by "non-flesh-eating men and women."

Vegetarianism, Sharpe explained, "had come to mean one who abstains from animal flesh as food." She bemoaned the fact that vegetarianism had "unfortunately become intermingled with various dietetic theories." In comparison to the strictly dietetic new vegetarian, Sharpe argued that "the Vegetarian who is one because of his conscience . . . occupies a very different place in the world of ethics from one who is simply reframing from meat eating in an effort to cure bodily ills."[120] Vegetarianism, she believed, was a means to create social harmony, peace, and the empowerment of women. Sharpe's perspective drew a sharp line between the old and new movement vegetarians.

The cookbook's introduction expressed a variety of ethical motivations for a reform-based vegetarian lifestyle, including animal welfare, concern for the conditions of workers in the stockyards doing "revolting work," and the possibility of diseased, tainted meat. Two of these three concerns—excluding the notion of animal protection, prompted by a proliferation of animal welfare societies in the postbellum era—mirrored critiques levied by the first generation of movement vegetarians.[121] Sharpe's involvement in creating an alternative to movement vegetarianism in the early years of the twentieth century provided a strident critique of the established and growing vegetarian community.

Born in Chicago, Sharpe became a prominent member of the Boston-area upper class by the start of the twentieth century. She was formally educated in art and literature, with a deep appreciation of decorative arts. She was a well-known socialite, and the famed designer and artist Louis Comfort Tiffany decorated her elaborate home in Chestnut Hill, Massachusetts. Sharpe herself did not convert to a vegetarian diet until after the Columbian Exposition. However, her ideological influences sat decidedly outside the boundaries of movement vegetarianism at the time. She first considered the possibility of embracing a meat-free diet while discussing the ethics of diet with Buddhist leader Anagarika Dharmapala at the fair's World Parliament of Religions. Further influences came from other vegetarians from throughout Europe, including personal friends such as writer Count Leo Tolstoy, Frau Cosima Wagner (wife of composer Richard Wagner), and playwright George Bernard Shaw.[122]

Sharpe committed fully to a vegetarian diet in 1906 and published her cookbook a year later. Tellingly, The Golden Rule Cook Book provides no recipes or advice on how to prepare mock meats. During a time where J. H. Kellogg's meat substitutes were proliferating among vegetarians and gaining favor in mainstream circles, Sharpe's culinary advice included recognizing vegetables for their own inherent value. Although recipes such as nut croquettes appeared in the cookbook and were similar to dishes advised by meat substitute cookbooks of the period, Sharpe's desire for a more ethical, reform-oriented vegetarianism led her to avoid accepting the standardization of meat and instead to promote vegetables.

Sharpe argued that meat substitutes created vegetarians who were ignorant of the beneficial qualities of vegetables. She railed against vegetarians who frequented the "usual Vegetarian restaurant" because the diner had "little opportunity to know much about vegetables as food, the menu being . . . so crowded with various mixtures which are supposedly 'meat substitutes' that vegetables pure and simple find small place." Sharpe explicitly rejected mock meat recipes such as "Vegetarian Hamburg Steak" that "should repel rather than attract" because they brought to mind images of "scorched carcasses." The recipes in The Golden Rule Cook Book were far removed from the more basic preparations of the first generation of movement vegetarians. By referring to vegetables in their natural form rather than as meat analogues, however, Sharpe differentiated herself from the preferred, popular cuisine of early twentieth-century movement vegetarianism.[123]

Sharpe's cookbook was successful, being reprinted continuously until 1915. However, despite her success in spreading awareness of vegetarianism, she remained firmly on the fringes of movement vegetarianism. Sharpe received little consideration in the pages of Vegetarian Magazine, but the little coverage that did appear over the years is instructive. Sharpe's Golden Rule Cook Book advertised frequently in Vegetarian Magazine, illustrating that Sharpe at least attempted to reach out to those interested in movement vegetarianism.[124] In addition, Sharpe's cookbook received a positive review in August 1908, though the article was a reprint from a newspaper.[125] What is most notable about the magazine's coverage of Sharpe is that it includes no discussion of the reformist ideology that Sharpe attached to her vegetarianism. The reporting on Sharpe that did exist focused on the quality of the recipes and Sharpe's reputation as a home entertainer. The only other mention of Sharpe in *Vegetarian Magazine* was in a testimonial that she provided for the Millennium Food Company, a vegetarian business run out of Boston by her future husband, Curtis Freshel.[126]

After experimenting with vegetarianism for six years, Sharpe decided in 1912 to venture into the realm of organization. The Millennium Guild was an association of upper-class social reformers that sought to spread the ideals of pacifism, antivivisectionism, and vegetarianism. Sharpe's large estate was envisioned to serve as the central location for the group's vegetarian activities. Lectures, dinners, and organizational meetings were held at what one newspaper labeled "a vegetarian temple."[127]

Illustrating the group's connection to a more evangelical style of social reform, the guild was named after a prophesy of Isaiah predicting that one day humans and animals would live together in peace, and humanity would no longer know violence or cruelty. In contrast to modern movement vegetarianism, which presented vegetarian reform as a form of individualism, the Millennium Guild attached vegetarianism to external reform, including the welfare of animals and peaceful relations among humanity. As the group's mission statement explained, the Millennium Guild saw its vegetarianism as a catalyst for total reform. The guild existed "to promote by precept and example a just consideration of the rights of all races, human and subhuman."[128] At the center of the organization's goals was "to teach that foremost among the unnecessary evils of the world, and one which underlies most of the other evils, is the mutilation and slaughter of our fellow creatures for food and other selfish ends."[129]

There were similarities between the Millennium Guild and the Vegetarian Society of America. Similar to the VSA, Sharpe's organization sought to spread awareness through public events and exposure in the popular press. Further, Sharpe represented upper-class involvement in public vegetarian activities, similar to the visible role of wealthy VSA advocates like Carrica Le Favre. However, unlike movement vegetarianism's national organization—which focused on vegetarianism's connection to the reform of the individual—Sharpe's Millennium Guild preached vegetarianism as a means to reform society.

In addition to her social reform agenda, Sharpe attempted to connect a high-society image with vegetarianism. This goal was somewhat challenging given that the group's eschewing of any animal products included their use for clothing and shoes. As the *New York Times* explained, the organization was "devoted to spreading the principle of universal love" by avoiding the use of meat or clothing "produced by torture or death of a living thing." Rather than wool or leather, members of the Millennium Guild wore clothes of cotton and shoes made of cloth. In the same article, Sharpe echoed a perspective from the past, linking vegetarianism with social reform. As she put it, "a change of diet" could help "women . . . get their rights in this world."[130] Just as the first generation of movement vegetarians saw inherent communal political power in dietary choice, Sharpe's Millennium Guild touted the power of a meatless diet in creating wide social change.

During a time where movement vegetarianism and its emphasis on individualism received increasingly favorable coverage by the popular press, the more politically oriented Millennium Guild was frequently mocked in newspapers for its combination of vegetarianism and avoidance of animal-based clothing. The *Indianapolis Star* reported that the group "will use no article of food or clothing that has involved the death of any living animal." And while the guild members "eschew meat," the newspaper advised that it was more possible to be "saved by chewing it."[131] Another newspaper mocked the group's name and religious bent, writing that "we had all along been led to believe that the millennium had arrived in Boston a great while ago: but perhaps they intend to see that the rest of us get some of it."[132] One article (reprinted throughout the country during 1914 and 1915) reported on the group's existence, though it ignored the guild's human members and instead focused on the fact that the members owned a vegetarian terrier that preferred carrots and lentils to meat.[133]

One of the organization's most visible public activities was its annual vegetarian Thanksgiving dinner, held at the upscale Copley-Plaza Hotel in Boston. The dinners sought to lend credence to vegetarianism through a connection with high society, fashionable dress, and Boston's philanthropic class. Sharpe herself attempted to visually express the conjoining of high society and vegetarianism, frequently appearing in public wearing a fake fur coat. Through a public event celebrating an iconic American holiday, the Millennium Guild sought to project the compatibility of its style of vegetarianism with patriotism.

Sharpe's 1912 edition of *The Golden Rule Cook Book* included a suggested Thanksgiving menu. The aim was to provide guidance for "the arranging of a menu in such a way that it does not depart too far from the accustomed manner of serving food." The recommended meal was an elaborate affair with six courses. The menu included no meat substitutes by name. The main course nut loaf was presented as a vegetable dish rather than as a meat substitute. In addition, the menu did not list any of the popular meat analogues available for purchase at the time, reflecting Sharpe's rejection of their use, even when trying to imitate a traditional Thanksgiving menu.

The *Golden Rule*'s Thanksgiving meal included a first course of olives, celery, and a fresh mushroom cocktail. This was to be followed by cream of artichokes served with crackers and radishes. Asparagus cooked in Dutch butter was to be provided before the main course. And a nut loaf served with mashed potatoes, roasted sweet potatoes, cranberry sauce, and baked celery would approximate familiar Thanksgiving flavors. Dessert featured pumpkin pie, fresh fruit, and coffee, illustrating that even if Sharpe's Millennium Guild shared philosophical values with early movement vegetarianism, its cuisine departed significantly from its predecessor's limited flavors.[134] The menu also contrasted significantly with that of a Thanksgiving meal at the Battle Creek Sanitarium in 1912, which used Protose as a mock turkey.[135]

By 1913, the Millennium Guild reported 200 registered members.[136] The organization sought to link vegetarianism with its politicized past, even including William Lloyd Garrison Jr., the grandson of abolition's most prominent advocate, among its adherents.[137] Despite its growing size and socially prominent membership, however, the organization remained disconnected from the Vegetarian Society of America and movement vegetarianism. While the Millennium Guild preached vegetarianism as a lifestyle, its brand of external reformist vegetarianism was at odds with the individual social advancement that was the ethos of early twentieth-century movement vegetarianism.

The few times that movement vegetarianism recognized the contributions of Sharpe and her organization, it largely ignored the guild's antivivisectionism, pacifism, and advocacy of women's suffrage. In the early years of the twentieth century, vegetarianism was flexible enough that different groups could compete over the ideology, allowing some practitioners to focus on themselves and others to focus on the rest of humanity or even the rest of the animal kingdom. Movement vegetarianism could have allowed these multiple interpretations to exist together in one unified community defined solely by dietary choice, embracing the full spectrum of ideologies that could attach to meat abstention. Instead, movement vegetarianism focused its activities and publications on defining vegetarianism as a vehicle for personal, social, and economic success. As the years advanced the Millennium Guild remained largely disconnected from movement vegetarianism. It ultimately shifted its focus more toward vegetarianism as just one component of an animal rights–oriented ideology, rather than the reverse.[138]

Other, politicized reform movements of the time adhered to a vegetarian diet but were largely ignored by the movement. Suffragists such as Frances Willard, Lillian Stevens, May Wright Sewall, and Jessica Henderson practiced a vegetarian diet in the late nineteenth and early twentieth century, frequently framing the dietary debate between vegetarianism and meat in gendered language and qualities. Meat—associated with aggression and violence—was rejected by suffragists who viewed a flesh-based diet as incompatible with equality and social justice.[139]

Despite this embrace of vegetarianism among some suffragists and the historical connections between the two groups, movement vegetarianism at the beginning of the twentieth century remained largely disconnected from the debate over women's right to vote. The VSA's magazine rarely covered the suffrage movement, and when it occurred the nature was telling. In one of the few instances where the magazine took a stance in favor of the right to vote, the argument was made in terms of stark gender roles. The magazine argued that if a man could find the time in his busy work schedule to study political issues, a woman would also be able to "spare a few minutes each day from her dish-washing and baby-spanking labors" to become acquainted with political issues.[140] In other instances, the magazine noted the vegetarian diet of suffragists, though without reporting on or taking an editorial stance on the right to vote or equality.[141]

Vegetarians and suffragists were isolated enough from each other during this period that one suffragist-vegetarian wrote to *Vegetarian Magazine* decrying the lack of cooperation. The writer hearkened back to movement vegetarianism's past and linked vegetarianism with total reform. In the letter she also may have summarized the depoliticized status of movement vegetarianism by the twentieth century, asking, "Why do we make one reform topic a hobby and forget all others? Mercy, Prohibition, Vegetarianism, Woman's Suffrage and Peace would make Old Earth a paradise, and yet the majority advocate but one, if any, of these."[142]

In 1903, VSA president Henry S. Clubb published a pamphlet distributed by the Vegetarian Society of America's printing company titled *Thirty-Nine Reasons Why I Am a Vegetarian*. Clubb's explanation for his vegetarianism focused on both religious arguments (the traditional Bible Christian perspective that vegetarianism was the biblical diet) and personal health justifications. Notably, of the thirty-nine listed reasons, none was connected to other ideas of political reform.[143]

As the twentieth century progressed, VSA publications increasingly emphasized vegetarianism as a vehicle to economic and social advancement. The notion that a meatless diet created productive bodies also ensured the movement's continued commercialization. *Vegetarian Magazine* advertised itself by informing potential readers that to "Become a Vegetarian" meant to "grow stronger, healthier, happier, clearer-headed" and to "save money."[144] One Chicago-based vegetarian business made these connections even more explicit by marketing its products with the question, "Would You Like to Be a Successful Vegetarian?"[145] The question had a clear double meaning—noting the difficulties in practicing a meatless diet while also implying that vegetarianism produced financially and socially accomplished individuals.

By 1910, *Vegetarian Magazine* moved its publishing headquarters from Madison Street to the more visible Michigan Boulevard. It continued to house a bookstore into the second decade of the century.[146] Vegetarian restaurants and health food stores opened throughout the country, as far west as Seattle and Los Angeles, as well as throughout Chicago and New York City.[147] The VSA itself was already the longest lasting vegetarian society in the history of the United States and continued to thrive under the leadership of Henry S. Clubb.

Thanks to the establishment and growth of the VSA, vegetarian societies flourished throughout the United States by the dawn of the twentieth century. The new vegetarianism was a visible part of urban landscapes from coast-to-coast, not just in obvious locations like New York, Boston, and Philadelphia that had long-standing vegetarian traditions but also in Chicago, St. Louis, and Portland, Oregon, areas that previously had witnessed little vegetarian consciousness. The success of vegetarians' efforts at the Columbian Exposition propelled Chicago into a position of leadership in the U.S. vegetarian community. As a result, vegetarian publications, health food stores, restaurants, and organizations proliferated in the city, most located near Chicago's rapidly expanding centers of business. Vegetarianism was quickly embraced as a way to thrive in modern, competitive society, a route to personal health for improved productivity, strength, and vitality that would give vegetarians the strength to avoid the weakening effects of corporate life. Vegetarians staked their claim to a visible place in the meat capital of the United States, of all places. And while the city remained a meat bastion, vegetarians showed that there was also plenty of room for industrious, socially mobile plant eaters.

Vegetarians interested in connecting the diet to external social reform could involve themselves in organizations such as the Millennium Guild that followed in the footsteps of movement vegetarianism's original spirit of meat abstention as a means to social reform. Such attempts at a vegetarianism oriented around communal reform remained on the outskirts of movement vegetarianism, receiving little serious consideration in either the mainstream or the vegetarian press. Although different groups competed over the ideology of vegetarianism as the twentieth century began, it was clear which side of that competition the established vegetarian movement embraced.

CHAPTER SEVEN

Muscular Vegetarianism

::

Between flesh eating and rational vegetarianism, the flesh eaters do not begin to be in it when it comes to endurance. —Los Angeles Times, April 26, 1908

Writing in 1898 in his book documenting the history of worldwide vegetarianism in the nineteenth century, vegetarian and World's Vegetarian Congress speaker Charles Forward commented on the state of physical fitness in the vegetarian movement. "In the earlier days of Vegetarian propaganda," he wrote, "it was difficult to convince an audience of the possibility of any feats of physical strength or endurance being performed without the consumption of butcher's meat." There were two reasons for this, Forward explained. Athletes traditionally trained on a diet of mostly meat. In addition, "Vegetarian teachings were propagated mostly by men of intellectual mould, many of whom . . . not presenting the robust and plethoric condition which is looked upon by so many people as a sure sign of health." Forward believed it was necessary for vegetarians to spread news of vegetarians' physical strength and athletic accomplishments as proof of the diet's efficacy. In doing so, vegetarians could "meet objectors on their own grounds."[1]

American movement vegetarians soon embraced similar ideas. Writing in *Vegetarian Magazine* in February 1900, Henry S. Clubb, president of the Vegetarian Society of America (VSA), prophetically reported that "the various methods of health culture and . . . physical exercises calculated to promote and secure a sound mind in a sound body" would soon "be within our recognized sphere."[2] Soon after, physical culturists—individuals offering to train others on how to sculpt their bodies—began advertising in the VSA's magazine.[3]

Movement vegetarians were among a growing audience of Americans enamored with the possibilities of transforming themselves physically in order to survive the perceived weakening caused by America's expanding corporate culture.[4] For the physical culturists themselves, the lifestyle frequently proved profitable, allowing them to sell a variety of products, including exercise equipment and training manuals, that promised consumers both corporeal and social transformation. Although rooted in the antebellum years, American physical culture hit its peak of popularity during the Progressive Era. As this lifestyle evolved, movement vegetarianism became indelibly linked to physical culture and athletics.

Physical culture's widespread popularity began at the Columbian Exposition. The fair featured displays of strength and physical fitness, wowing visitors with muscularity, power, and the suggestion of a link between physical and social advancement. Famed boxing champion "Gentleman Jim" Corbett—fresh off of his knockout victory over John L. Sullivan the previous year—put his pugilistic expertise on display to the gathered crowds. Corbett was known for his measured, scientific approach to boxing, qualities similar to those the vegetarians meeting at the Art Institute emphasized in explaining their approach to dietary choices.[5]

Fairgoers paid a nominal fee to have their measurements taken and compared to the shapes documented as "normal" by Harvard physical education expert Dudley Sargent.[6] Revelers visiting Chicago because of the fair also flocked to gaze at the rippling, bulging muscles of the recently imported Prussian bodybuilder Eugen Sandow. Large audiences gathered at the Trocadero Theater on State Street, drawn by the promise of watching a "veritable Colossus of Rhodes" flex in classical Greek poses. Sandow—a living embodiment of strength, power, control, and seeming perfection—captivated spectators for three months, inspiring some audience members to sculpt their bodies as well.[7]

Physical culture (the linguistic precursor to the term physical education) referred to a general regimen of health, strength, and physical fitness, all tied to the development of individual morality. Gymnastics and calisthenics gained popularity initially in the United States during the 1850s and 1860s, but the movement to utilize athletics for physical health remained largely fractured and decentralized. In the 1880s the physical culture movement began the process of professionalization, and was introduced into the curriculum of colleges and universities.

The movement coalesced with the founding of the American Physical Education Association in 1895 and its monthly journal, the American Physical Education Review. Physical culture advocates represented a wide spectrum of Progressive Era reform, supported by politicians, urban reformers, journalists, and the athletes themselves.[8] Exploring vegetarianism was a natural path for those interested in the connections between the strenuous life and the development of individual character. With movement vegetarianism gaining mainstream acceptance through its glorification of the individual, physical culture had inherent appeal to dietary reformers.

During the late nineteenth and early twentieth century, numerous body-builders, physical culturists, and professional and amateur athletes adhered to a vegetarian diet because they believed it would bring them greater athletic success. The lessons provided by these athletes were intended to serve as a model for average Americans, showing how to create healthy, strong bodies to survive the rigors of modern industrial society. Movement vegetarians utilized these individuals as living proof of vegetarianism's benefits.

These new muscular vegetarians cared little for the potential social or political benefits of dietary reform. Instead, muscular vegetarians advocated for the diet that most benefited themselves. Even though vegetarianism throughout much of the nineteenth century was associated with weakness, new vegetarian athletes and strongmen—largely separated from the social and political streams of vegetarianism—sought to illustrate that powerful, vital bodies and minds could be crafted by a meatless diet. Through publications, exercise equipment, and even restaurants, muscular vegetarians profited from the links between physical culture and dietary reform. Movement vegetarianism's organizations, advocates, and publications supported muscular vegetarians and athletes in order to build credibility for the diet among the general public.

Gymnasiums first became popular in the Midwest in the 1850s, appearing in cities like Cincinnati and St. Louis with large populations of German immigrants. Followers of the Turner movement—adherents to the athletic principles of German nationalist and physical educator Friedrich Ludwig Jahn—imported the turnverein ("gymnastics clubs") to the United States in the years following the failed 1848 German revolution. German immigrants utilized these clubs to acclimate to their new American surroundings; gymnasiums served simultaneously as social, political, and athletic clubs. As the years progressed, the turnverein movement shifted from a largely working-class phenomenon to one dominated by a growing German American middle class. By the late nineteenth century, the gymnasium had become a national craze and spread throughout the United States, appealing to a postbellum society that emphasized the development of the individual.[9]

Most prominent among the muscular advocates connecting vegetarianism with physical culture was Bernard Adolphus McFadden. The rise of McFadden (who would become popularly known as Bernarr Macfadden) reflected the larger connection between movement vegetarianism and the burgeoning physical culture movement in the United States in the late nineteenth and early twentieth century. McFadden had come to physical culture following a difficult childhood marked by a serious illness brought on by the "arm-to-arm" method of smallpox vaccination common in the 1870s.[10]

Emotional scarring only compounded the physical pains the young child faced. Three years after his father's death, Bernard's mother sent him to an orphanage in southern Missouri and placed her two daughters in the care of other relatives. At nine, Bernard was sent away from his birth mother and forced to perform manual labor at a small hotel in western Illinois. Between sweeping, doing laundry, shining shoes, and carrying guests' luggage, Bernard was perpetually ill and exhausted. During these years, he began to grow out of his weakened, delicate state—a process perhaps hastened by rigorous, constant farm work. Having scrounged up enough money to ensure safe transit, Bernard eventually made arrangements to move to St. Louis, where his uncle and grandmother lived.

He worked a variety of jobs after arriving in St. Louis, delivering groceries while also serving as a clerk at the general store where his uncle worked. But dissatisfaction led once again to physical ailments. Doctors and medicine offered no relief. He soon discovered a potential cure for his illnesses, however, noticing an advertisement exhorting the benefits of the exercise program at a local gymnasium. Unable to afford the gymnasium's fees, Bernard instead invested fifty cents in a pair of dumbbells. The decision pushed him down a path of physical fitness that would define his long life.[11]

Immediately he began a regimen of repeated, vigorous lifting of the dumbbells, each curl an attempt to undo years of ill health, fragility, and frailty. The newly developed strength gave Bernard a sense of control, something he had lacked while serving the whims of a variety of guardians. He also began experimenting with a vegetarian diet at this time, a temporary change that provided mixed results but did lead the young grappler to significantly reduce his overall meat consumption. While he was not converted to vegetarianism, he found that a decrease in meat and increase in vegetables gave him greater energy and stamina.[12]

In the fall of 1892, he began teaching gymnastics and coaching football at the Marmaduke Military Academy in Sweet Springs, Missouri, where he became known as "Professor B. A. McFadden" despite not having received a formal education. When he learned that a friend was demonstrating a new piece of exercise equipment at the Columbian Exposition, McFadden immediately left for Chicago, hoping that the "White City" would provide opportunities. He found that inspiration while watching Sandow, whose poses he imitated while walking the grounds of the fair.[13]

He was sufficiently encouraged by his experience in Chicago to head east to further his reinvention, arriving in New York City in early 1894 intent on putting into practice what he witnessed while observing Chicago's fascination with physical culture. He rented two rooms in a building at 24 East Twentieth Street, just east of Broadway.[14] A master marketer, he decided that his name sounded weak, common, and forgettable, so he changed his last name to the somewhat more distinct Macfadden and shifted his first name slightly to Bernarr. The more unusual name Bernarr sounded strong, like the roar of a lion. And thus, early in 1894, Bernarr Macfadden, physical culturist, was born, a product of marketing, imagination, and self-promotion.[15] After a successful tour of England in early 1897, Macfadden decided it was time to bring his physical culture quest to the masses in the form of a new popular magazine.[16]

Macfadden returned to the United States early in 1898 intent on succeeding where he had previously failed in getting his health tracts published for mass consumption. Macfadden rented an office on Gold Street in lower Manhattan and established the Physical Culture Publishing Company, home to the new magazine *Physical Culture*. The nascent publication proclaimed in large block letters on the cover, "Weakness Is a Crime," exhorting its readers, "Don't Be a Criminal." The declaration was sure to grab attention, but what did it mean? Macfadden explained in an editorial in the first issue that while weakness was criminal, readers "had no more excuse for being weak." Similar to J. H. Kellogg in his explanation for illness, Macfadden believed that disease was the body warning the individual of injurious practices and was "a result of the victim's own ignorance or carelessness." The goal of *Physical Culture* was to "preach the gospel of health, strength and the means of acquiring it" in order to produce "vigorous, pulsating health."[17] The message was clear: read this new magazine and apply its principles, and strength, power, and vitality would follow.

Macfadden's self-reinvention—glorified throughout the pages of *Physical Culture*—exemplified a "recovery of lost manhood," the crafting of the male body as a means to illustrate the ability to succeed in a competitive society through hard work and determination.[18] During the late Progressive Era bodybuilders like Macfadden and Sandow promoted a narrative of bodily conversion to prove their worth in a society fascinated with tales of self-improvement. These stories of physical transformation mirrored the life story of the period's most iconic political figure, Theodore Roosevelt, who overcame a childhood battle with sickness and frailty to transform into a national symbol of strength, adventurism, and bravery.[19] It is little surprise that early issues of *Physical Culture* frequently praised Roosevelt as an emblem of vigor and vital masculinity.[20]

The new publication appeared every other month, packed with articles on physical fitness and exercise. And while *Physical Culture* was obsessed with sculpting muscular, physically powerful, productive bodies, dietary choice was also a focus. The first issue of *Physical Culture* dealt with the importance of proper foods in the development of vitality and health. In early issues of the magazine, Macfadden did not advocate specifically for vegetarianism. The magazine's first issue, however, pointed out that meat was a highly stimulating food to be used in moderation if at all. A diet composed of wheat bread, fruits, vegetables, milk, and eggs was most beneficial, creating the greatest amount of strength while maximizing the body's capabilities.[21]

Although Macfadden was not a staunch ideological vegetarian, his role in promoting vegetarianism needs to be considered. Through the first two decades of the twentieth century, his magazine was the most widely read publication that included vegetarian information and articles.[22] In addition, Macfadden would eventually open and operate the first successful chain of vegetarian restaurants in the United States. By November 1899, the magazine already had 40,000 subscribers, far more than the VSA's *Vegetarian Magazine*. While the VSA's publication had a more dedicated reader base of staunch vegetarians, *Physical Culture* exposed far more people to the possible benefits of avoiding meat and promoted the connection between vegetarianism and physicality.

As early as 1901 Macfadden turned his attention specifically to the issue of diet. In introducing his book *Strength from Eating*, Macfadden explicitly connected physical fitness with economic vigor, explaining that strength was "like money. You can never secure enough." He emphasized the importance of physical strength for building social worth, explaining that strength was necessary "to accomplish anything of value of life."[23] He preached that while some "eat to live" and others "live to eat," in order to experience the "highest and most intense" life, individuals had to eat in order to stimulate "every nerve with surplus power."[24]

Macfadden provided information on all diets, giving advice on both vegetarian regimens and those that included meat. Much like Ella Kellogg did in her first cookbook, Macfadden explained how to utilize meat in the least injurious ways possible. He conceded that meat had positive qualities. In fact, he argued, individuals living on a mixed diet that included moderate amounts of meat, regular exercise, and periodic fasting to purge their systems could live long, healthy lives. He warned, however, that meat was "stimulating in character" and full of "impurities" that would spread throughout the body.[25]

The book included a chapter on vegetarianism that promised ideological moderation. Despite being "inclined to favor a vegetable diet," Macfadden assured readers that he was not fanatical in his adherence.[26] His vegetarianism, in fact, was inherently flexible, driven by the whims of his appetite. The body knew itself best, far better than any ideology or movement could. Individualism and knowledge of self trumped communal adherence. Macfadden did believe, however, that in most instances a meatless diet was most beneficial. While meat tended "to fill the blood with elements that cannot be rapidly eliminated by the depurating organs," a vegetarian diet provided "far greater endurance" and made "a better quality of muscle."[27] Macfadden, who experimented with a vegetarian diet with some success in the early 1890s as a wrestler, was advancing toward more explicit support for the lifestyle.

According to Macfadden, vegetarianism had a wide array of benefits, including a "better quality of blood," while also tempering the desire to overeat or abuse alcohol. A vegetable-based diet ensured lean, healthy-looking bodies exhibiting natural signs of vitality. But Macfadden warned that it was important for vegetarians to avoid the tendency to be poorly nourished by eating too much white bread and other foods that contained little nutritional value. When practiced wisely, vegetarianism was "unquestionably the natural diet of man," promising a long, healthy, and productive life.[28]

Macfadden assured readers that he was not an "extremist" in his dietary choices. He did believe, however, that a vegetarian diet had the potential to save "thousands of lives" and provided "energy and power to go on and on without fatigue."[29] And his magazine explicitly supported the diet's benefits. Writing in the November 1900 issue, one *Physical Culture* columnist repeated a traditional argument in favor of vegetarianism, pointing out that humans' teeth were flat, made to grind vegetables and grains rather than rip through meat and sinew. The author supported physiological evidence with a critique of the meat industry, pointing out that cattle were confined in small, diseased pens. Those eating the subsequent processed meat were liable to catch the same diseases that plagued the animals en route to slaughter.[30] Meat-eaters were labeled as "gluttonous," a quality in direct contrast to the crafted, muscular images presented throughout the magazine, the result of careful dietary planning and dedicated self-control.[31]

In 1901 Macfadden published his first book of recipes, the *Physical Culture Cookbook*. Knowledge of cooking, he wrote, had "as much importance as that of reading or writing" because incorrect cooking methods ensured constant trips to doctors to treat a variety of stomach ailments.[32] The goal of physical culture cookery was to enhance strength, beauty, and intelligence, building potent bodies with nutritious foods.

With a nod to vegetarianism's past, the cookbook provided three different recipes for Graham bread, including a sweetened version aimed at dyspeptics.[33] "Americans eat far too much meat," warned Macfadden, "and too little vegetable food." Vegetables had medicinal, healing qualities. Spinach could improve ailing kidneys, while asparagus helped cleanse the blood stream. Starchy vegetables such as potatoes helped the body produce heat, while legumes promoted muscle development.[34] Vegetables gave the body more nutritional elements than did meat and were best served when cooked slowly on low heat for long periods of time, Macfadden wrote.

By 1902 the role of vegetarianism in the pages of Macfadden's pilot publication changed noticeably, reflecting a new business venture that benefited from the significant growth of vegetarianism as a profit maker. That year, Macfadden expanded his commercial interests, opening his first Physical Culture vegetarian restaurant at the corner of Pearl Street and City Hall Place in lower Manhattan. Within two years the venture expanded, with two more restaurants opening in Manhattan, one in Brooklyn, two in Philadelphia, and one in Boston. By 1908 the geographic reach of the restaurants expanded even further with twenty Physical Culture restaurants, some as far west as Pittsburgh, Buffalo, and Chicago.[35]

Macfadden's affordable dining establishments appealed to both long time vegetarians and new converts. The restaurants were so popular in New York City that eight different locations operated simultaneously by 1911.[36] One observer noted that in one of the New York locations, "at noon, every one of its 200 seats is occupied."[37] Similar to other vegetarian restaurants of the time, Macfadden's Physical Culture restaurants were largely located near urban commercial centers.[38] Macfadden explained his motives for opening the restaurant, expressing his hope to prove "how cheaply and satisfactorily the human body can be nourished." The Physical Culture restaurants aimed to provide food that was simultaneously affordable, nourishing, and delicate in flavor.[39]

The restaurants were split into two levels: a basement that served basic meals at only one cent a serving, and an upstairs self-service café where more elaborate dishes cost five cents. The fare was simple and filling vegetarian

Patrons at New York's *Physical Culture restaurant. From "The One-Cent Meal Restaurant,"*
Physical Culture (May 1902).

foods—at such prices meat substitutes would have been cost prohibitive. Despite the straightforwardness of the fare, the food and cost were enticing enough that the first Physical Culture restaurant had to close temporarily after just two days because it sold out of food.[40]

Diners had a choice of cereals, soups, steamed vegetables, whole wheat bread, steamed wheat, beans, rice, hominy grits, eggs, stewed fruit, or a variety of sweet and savory puddings. One-cent meals offered few accoutrements (a bowl of plain steamed hominy, for example), while five-cent meals provided flavor enhancers such as sugar and butter.[41] Advertisements promised visitors an opportunity to enjoy "nature's diet," emphasizing in big, block letters the physical culturist's endorsement of the restaurant, proclaiming the restaurant to be Macfadden's eatery.[42] The name association worked, the restaurants were a financial success for the original 600 stockholders, paying a 100 percent dividend on investments in 1902.[43]

The chain of restaurants was supported by a new focus in *Physical Culture* on the benefits of vegetarian living. In February 1904, *Physical Culture* began a monthly feature titled "Fifty Valuable Meatless Recipes."[44] It provided simple vegetarian dishes along with meat analogues such as a roast made of lentils or faux stewed marrowfats made from green peas, lemon juice, and lemon zest.[45] A vegetarian diet was presented as a key component to success. A January 1904 article was illustrated by numerous photographs of vegetarian physical culturists whose forms refuted the notion that vegetarians had weak, flimsy bodies.[46]

The magazine emphasized vegetarianism's long-term benefits, highlighting the life of one vegetarian who at age 106 still swung an ax, planted seeds, gathered grains, and went for daily brisk walks. A diet of fruits, vegetables, whole wheat bread, milk, and eggs had sustained him for more than fifty years.[47] A vegetarian diet was so beneficial, the magazine reported, that it had allowed Lieutenant Robert Peary to explore the Arctic on a diet of only compressed pea soup and baked beans.[48]

Physical Culture relied on the advice of experts and professional athletes to illustrate the diet's advantages. The magazine also provided proof of vegetarianism's effectiveness through testimonials from readers, a method similar to the conversion narratives written by Grahamites during the antebellum era. Each issue of the magazine from October 1903 forward featured a section titled "The Virtues of Our Methods Proven" that highlighted letters written to the magazine by physical culturists. Frequently these letters included vegetarian testimonials. A. W. Wefel, a firefighter from Portland, Oregon, explained that he had long suffered from stomach, liver, heart, lung, kidney, and bowel problems. However, since he turned to vegetarianism and physical culture, he had gained nineteen pounds of solid muscle and freed himself from all illnesses. To prove his new strength and vigor, Wefel provided the magazine with a picture of himself flexing his biceps.[49]

The victory of vegetarians in a walking race proved that "flesh foods should therefore be avoided as much as possible," particularly by athletes in competitions requiring endurance. A vegetable-based diet guaranteed the energy reserve needed for victory. *Physical Culture* claimed that vegetarian foods—particularly whole grains, nuts, and vegetables—were muscle builders. The "sustaining power" of vegetarianism had been proven repeatedly by the success of vegetarian athletes in long-distance running and walking races.[50]

Vegetarianism provided long-lasting strength and vitality, argued Macfadden, in contrast to the short-term burst of energy provided by flesh foods. Macfadden believed that vegetarians, particularly those adhering to a raw diet, would dominate the future of athletics in "the civilized world." A vegetarian diet was easier to digest and provided greater nutritional energy,

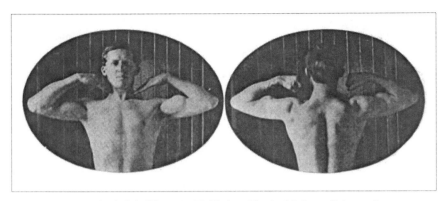

Vegetarian bodybuilder A. W. Wefel. From Physical Culture *(July 1909).*

helping support the rigors of athletic competition.[51] Macfadden—perhaps not coincidentally as his chain of restaurants continued to grow—continued his support of meatless dietetics, explaining that he had yet to meet an individual "who has not felt stronger and more energetic as the result" of a switch to a fleshless regimen.[52]

While Macfadden's perspective vis-à-vis vegetarianism in the pages of *Physical Culture* was constantly changing, other writers used the pages of *Physical Culture* to advocate for vegetarianism directly. In some instances, the worlds of physical culture and movement vegetarianism directly intersected. One article reporting on the activities of Henry S. Clubb noted the vegetarian leader's rugged appearance and "physical and mental youthfulness" at age eighty-two. The article's author promised readers similar results if they adhered to a vegetarian diet.[53] Another writer claimed that "in America . . . the finest, cleanest, most vigorous physical specimens of manhood and womanhood . . . are developed and sustained on a vegetable diet."[54]

Vegetarianism was connected directly with the "most brilliant minds" of both antiquity and the modern age. One article claimed that vegetarianism had produced vigorous, triumphant individuals throughout history. A vegetarian diet provided strength for the ancients, allowing Cyrus the Great to expand the Persian Empire, and it had given modern giants like Leo Tolstoy, Richard Wagner, and George Bernard Shaw the mental and physical tools to contribute to the betterment of the contemporary world.[55]

Physical Culture continued focusing its praise on the successes of vegetarian athletes. Max Unger, an amateur bodybuilder who eventually transformed into the well-known performer Lionel Strongfort, utilized his letter to the magazine to challenge Arthur Saxon, a famous strongman who performed in the Ringling Brothers Barnum and Bailey Circus.[56] Unger's declaration of greater strength was connected to a debate over diet. Saxon had claimed that he ate beef three times a day, believing meat to be fundamental to increase and preserve strength and muscle. The vegetarian Unger sought a test of strength against Saxon in order to prove the superiority of a meat-free diet. In this instance, the success of vegetarianism did not have an opportunity to be measured: Unger's challenge went unanswered.[57]

The lightweight boxing champion of England, "The Welsh Wizard" Fred Welsh, was also lauded because he quit smoking cigarettes, drinking coffee and tea, and eating meat. The article emphasized Welsh's speed, agility, and stamina, all provided by his vegetarian diet.[58] Another vegetarian boxer reported that a meatless diet had made him a better fighter, giving him quicker hands and feet as well as improved endurance.[59] A third young pugilist described his rapid and remarkable muscular development thanks to vegetarianism, and he provided a photograph as proof of his strength.[60]

An article reporting on the training habits of baseball stars described the vegetarian diet of "the grand old man of baseball," pitcher Cy Young. Though Young was the oldest player in the major leagues in 1910, his vegetarian diet, rigorous outdoor life, and relentless training regimen allowed him to be a "real marvel of the diamond" at forty-three years of age.[61] Amateurs also experienced the benefits of a vegetarian diet. A young vegetarian from Illinois was lauded for the "wonderful endurance" that led to his victory in a local swimming race.[62] Emphasizing athletic accomplishments made vegetarianism's connection to individual success explicit and showed the dominance of vegetarians over carnivores. Throughout the history of *Physical Culture*, however, very little attention was paid to the social benefits of vegetarianism.

Physical Culture marked the beginning of Macfadden's ascendance as a U. S. publishing magnate and popular culture icon. With the profits from *Physical Culture*, Macfadden expanded his company, starting with *True Story* in 1919, a magazine that featured salacious, confessional first-person narratives of real events provided by reader submissions. The magazine was an immediate, immense success, with more than 2 million readers per issue by 1926.[63] Macfadden's publishing empire continued to grow, including such varied titles as *True Detective*, *True Romance*, and *Ghost Stories*. It even branched out into the newspaper business with the popular tabloid the *New York Evening Graphic*. Briefly fascinated with Benito Mussolini and fascism, Macfadden ran for the Republican presidential nomination in 1936 and a Florida U. S. Senate seat in 1940. In 1951, he appeared as a celebrity "mystery guest" on the popular television program *What's My Line*.

Most important for the evolution of vegetarianism in the United States, Bernarr Macfadden and physical culture helped complete the transformation of movement vegetarians from politically radical social pariahs to a community bound by a common obsession with self and individual success. By moving away from their socially conscious roots, vegetarians gained social acceptance.

Macfadden, however, was not the only physical culturist to embrace vegetarianism. Gilman Low, a New York–based bodybuilder described as "a model of physical perfection," similarly advocated for the muscle-building properties of vegetarianism.[64] Low illustrated the power of vegetarianism in 1907, when he established a world record by reportedly hoisting 1.6 million pounds over a thirty-five-minute period.[65] *Vegetarian Magazine* celebrated Low's accomplishment, stating that an "event took place which should silence every carping critic of vegetarianism." The magazine directly linked Low's success with his adoption of a vegetarian diet during training, arguing that his feat proved "the superiority of a vegetarian diet from the standpoint of endurance and strength."[66]

Lionel Strongfort (aka Max Unger) was another well-known vegetarian physical culturist of the early twentieth century. Strongfort first became prominent thanks to his perfection of the "Human Bridge Act." Performing onstage in front of awestruck audiences, he supported the weight of a touring car filled with six passengers on a small metal platform, while the car crossed over a seesawing makeshift bridge. During this feat, Strongfort reportedly supported more than 7,000 pounds on his sculpted abdomen. By the early twentieth century, Strongfort built a successful mail-order training system that continued into the 1930s, advising adherents to subsist on a diet consisting of fruit, vegetables, grains, milk, and eggs.[67]

The correlation between vegetarianism and physical culture was strong enough that in 1911 one publication pointed to the increased number of vegetarian restaurants and physical culture exhibitions as proof of a general increase in Americans' enthusiasm for athletics.[68] Members of movement vegetarianism and health reformers alike were keen to prove vegetarianism's physical benefits. Health advocates used scientific studies to this end. In 1907, Irving Fisher—a Yale University economist and sometime vegetarian health advocate—attempted to comparatively measure the endurance of flesh-eaters and vegetarians.

Fisher's reputation as an economist grew posthumously, particularly among post-Keynesian economists. During his lifetime, however, his research interests extended beyond economics. Fisher had a personal interest in the subject of dietetics, having overcome a bout of tuberculosis in 1898 after a stay in a health sanitarium and adherence to a vegetarian diet.[69] His study, originally published in a medical journal, was also popularized in book form by the Battle Creek San's publishing company, illustrating the experiment's renown in movement vegetarian circles.

Fisher's study included forty-seven subjects split into three groups: the first were athletes who trained on a flesh-based diet, the second were vegetarian athletes, and the third—comprised of nurses and physicians from the Battle Creek San—were designated as sedentary vegetarians. Participants were asked to perform three tasks: deep knee bends, leg raises, and horizontal extension of their arms. The results of Fisher's test indicated that the vegetarians had significantly more stamina. Twenty-two of the thirty-two total vegetarians were able to keep their arms raised for fifteen minutes, and fifteen held for more than thirty minutes. Nine vegetarians lasted for an hour, and one managed to last for more than three hours. One young vegetarian, the six-year-old son of a San worker, was able to maintain the pose for forty-five minutes. Only two of the meat-eaters were able to last more than fifteen minutes.[70]

Consumers of flesh foods did not fare well in the other tests of endurance, either. Meat-eating athletes averaged 383 deep knee bends. Sedentary vegetarians, however, averaged 535. Vegetarian athletes dominated in this category, accomplishing an average of 933 deep knee bends per person, with the largest number being 1,225 bends. In the third test, vegetarian athletes were again victorious, though the results were much closer. Vegetarian athletes averaged 288 leg raises, in comparison to the 279 by carnivorous athletes and 74 by sedentary vegetarians.[71]

Fisher concluded his study by arguing that contrary to popular perception, a nonflesh diet low in protein was most conducive to building individual endurance. Why, he wondered, had this benefit of vegetarianism been traditionally ignored? Fisher's explanation reflected the larger changes that movement and muscular vegetarianism were undergoing at the time. First, Fisher contended, vegetarianism had previously been associated with "fanaticism[,] . . . which has done much to defeat its own ends." Rather than rely on such "unfortunate circumstances," Fisher believed that vegetarians would benefit from the "proper scientific attitude to study the question of meat-eating."[72] He emphasized the observable physical properties and advantages of vegetarianism over those of any other underlying philosophy or ideology.

Movement vegetarianism connected Fisher's experiment explicitly to the popularity of physical culture. *Vegetarian Magazine* reported numerous times on the results of Fisher's study. The magazine claimed that the "secret" to "becom[ing] a veritable Sandow . . . a giant in strength" was "don't eat any meat." The magazine argued that the tests of endurance were "simple but effective" and proved that "nonflesh eaters have far greater endurance than those accustomed to the ordinary American diet."[73] In another instance, the magazine labeled Fisher's test as a "demonstration of the superiority of the Vegetarian diet," which could only be doubted by "disseminators of misinformation." Since a scientist had conducted the experiment, personal bias could not be suspected.[74]

Fisher himself explained his study in the magazine, proclaiming, "In general it may be said that, whatever the explanation, there is strong evidence that a low proteid non-flesh, or nearly non-flesh dietary is conducive to endurance." Fisher partially linked vegetarians' success in the tests with their particular strength of character and fortitude. The "spirit" of the vegetarians, he wrote, was driven by the thought of competing against flesh-eaters and had provided the vegetarians with the extra motivation to succeed. The implication in his explanation was that vegetarians had both the extra physical stamina and the mental determination required for success in both athletics and general life.[75]

The movement vegetarian press was not alone in covering Fisher's study. The mainstream media—both daily newspapers and nonvegetarian health publications—also took notice. In March 1907, the *New York Times* reported that vegetarians were "the stronger" athletes. The article noted that vegetarians overcame the efforts of "some of Yale's most successful athletes," who were "obliged to admit their inferiority in strength" because of the results.[76] In another instance, the *Times* reported on a separate strength test conducted by Fisher. Whereas an "ordinary man of fair muscular equipment" could lift a weight "from 30 to 60 times without intermission," a vegetarian "lifted the weight 687 times, and showed no signs of exhaustion when he stopped."[77] The *Los Angeles Times* noted that Fisher's experiments proved that "between flesh eating and rational vegetarianism, the flesh eaters do not begin to be in it when it comes to endurance."[78]

The physical culture magazine *Health* described the result of Fisher's experiment as "somewhat surprising," because "it would appear . . . that the flesh-eating athletes got the worst of it all along the line. Not only were they outclassed, but greatly outclassed."[79] In another issue, *Health* assured readers that "these experiments . . . were really undertaken to discover the maximum of efficiency, without any idea of proving the superiority of vegetarianism or any other dietary system." When analyzed objectively, the study proved at the minimum that "the present individual use of meat is excessive, and should be reduced, in the interest of the general health."[80] For another publication, Fisher's investigations suggested that individuals should give up meat, because vegetarians "have much greater power of endurance."[81]

Movement vegetarians were clearly emboldened by the results of Fisher's experiments. Every issue of *Vegetarian Magazine* in 1907 either reported specifically on the study's results or mentioned the experiment in relation to another related subject.[82] The magazine claimed that the experiment added to the evidence that "has been shown over and over that athletes who are also Vegetarians are almost invariably superior to those who eat meat, in both strength and endurance."[83] The magazine itself did much to try to perpetuate this claim.

The Vegetarian Society of America and movement vegetarianism generally caught on to the growing association between vegetarianism and athletics and followed Henry S. Clubb's exhortations to illustrate the intersections. At the dawn of the twentieth century, *Vegetarian Magazine* began presenting the lifestyle as central to building strong, muscular, healthy bodies able to best advance in a competitive society. Movement vegetarianism's national organization lionized the athletic accomplishments of professional and amateur vegetarian athletes around the world, presenting victories as proof of the diet's advantages over meat-eating. Accomplishments in the athletic realm, the magazine noted, could translate to the physical health needed to succeed in both business and personal lives.

Articles in *The Vegetarian* implied that sporting accomplishments were empirical proof that vegetarianism was the most beneficial dietary choice. In an editorial in September 1900, a vegetarian cyclist argued that "athletes are beginning to realize that they can get better results from a vegetarian diet than from any other." There was another benefit of vegetarian athletics: building credibility for the movement. Since "athletic excellence is the acknowledged standard by which physical superiority is tested," vegetarians had to "demonstrate the truth of our teachings" through success in the athletic realm.[84] According to the magazine, another cyclist who had been a vegetarian for twelve years was able to bike forty-one miles during a December snowstorm because of the strength of endurance provided by her "choice of foods."[85]

Subsequent issues of The Vegetarian included similar features. The magazine reported on the victory of Germany's vegetarian competitive walker Carl Mann in a race from Berlin to Dresden (approximately 200 kilometers or 124 miles), noting that his winning time eclipsed the second-place finisher, a meat-eater, by nearly two hours. Of the international athletes who competed, only thirteen completed the event, and ten of these were vegetarians. Meat-eaters who completed the course finished seventh, eighth, and thirteenth.[86]

The Vegetarian also reported on the success of West Coast boxer William "Kid" Parker, who claimed that becoming a strict vegetarian had brought him multiple benefits. "I have gained a mental power and increased my physical endurance," he proclaimed. "I believe I am a better man in every way—physically, mentally and morally."[87] Another boxer was presented as "an argument for the anti-meat-eaters" because of his "ruggedness" created by a "strict vegetarian diet."[88] Given vegetarianism's traditional connections to pacifism and nonviolence, The Vegetarian's praise of boxers indicates a significant shift for the movement.

The magazine also reported on Canadian champion swimmer G. H. Corsan, who saw vegetarianism as fundamental to his success. Corsan believed that his vegetarian diet gave him greater speed and endurance than his meat-eating opponents. Corsan claimed that he required less sleep, slept better, and was physically and mentally stronger since eliminating meat from his regimen. The "right food in the right quantity" gave Corsan the physical tools to succeed.[89]

Vegetarianism also became associated with the often rough and violent sport of football. The Vegetarian noted the success of the 1907 University of Chicago football team, which trained on a strict vegetarian diet on the orders of its famous coach, Amos Alonzo Stagg.[90]

In 1892, Stagg was named the university's head football coach and director of the Department of Physical Culture, remaining in those posts until 1933. During those years Stagg changed college football, introducing such innovations as the tackling dummy, the huddle, the lateral pass, and even uniform numbers.[91] Stagg's ascension to the head coaching position and his role as a member of the university faculty as director of physical culture marked a significant step in college athletics' march toward professionalization, bringing college coaching new respectability. Emphasizing the morally transformative properties of sport, Stagg enforced proper decorum and respectable behavior among his roster, banning players from drinking, smoking, or using profanity.[92] Dietetics eventually also got Stagg's attention.

By 1907, Stagg had been a practicing vegetarian for two years and believed the diet had cured him of all physical ailments. He believed it could only improve his team's performance.[93] Stagg's ideological underpinnings and devotion to the cause of physical culture explain his motivation to train his team on a vegetarian diet. Physical culture and athletics were valuable, he believed, because they helped build individual character, discipline, and dedication. Vegetarianism had the potential to enhance these same qualities.

Stagg touted what one biographer referred to as a "gridiron gospel," the notion that football—when regulated by strict standards and regulations—helped develop morality through a life of muscular Christianity. He believed that vegetarianism would create superior dispositions in his players, resulting in better teamwork as well as faster and more agile athletes. Meat produced overly aggressive, violent players who resorted to injuring their opponents. In contrast, vegetarianism produced a "gentle and gentlemanly" squad that brought football the respectability Stagg desired.[94]

The mixture of athletic development with ethical uplift displayed stark similarities with the rapidly developing new movement vegetarianism of the early twentieth century. The trends in athletics and vegetarianism both emphasized physical health and improvement as vehicles to social ascension and respectability. In addition, both stressed the importance of individual advancement, achievable through personal dietary choices and actions. The connection also illustrates that movement vegetarianism—once viewed as threatening and dangerous—was associating itself with a new ethos that connected physicality and personal betterment. The VSA reported that a halfback could be made "strong and elastic with oatmeal porridge and cranberry sauce" in order to defeat "rude and coarse" meat-eating opponents. The organization wished the team success, because victory on the football field could help vegetarians become "vindicated" in their diet.[95]

The *Chicago Tribune* took notice of Stagg's training regimen, part of the paper's larger, growing interest in movement vegetarianism. The *Tribune* reported that the "blood red" rare roast beef that was usually the preferred meal of training football players was giving way to a vegetable diet. Vegetarianism not only helped Stagg's players increase their strength, weight, and agility, it also provided "quicker and more accurate thinking." The diet was vigorously supported by a variety of players, including starting halfback and team captain Leo De Tray, who had already converted to vegetarianism to cure his reoccurring indigestion.[96]

The *Tribune* equated the team's collective vegetarianism with the attributes necessary to succeed both on the gridiron and in life generally, including positive dispositions, strong teamwork, and poise. As vegetarians, the University of Chicago Maroons were faster and played the game with discipline and respectability, in contrast to their "beef-fed" opponents "with all their leg breaking and ear twisting savagery." The narrative of a more genteel style of football through vegetarianism fit perfectly in Stagg's efforts to promote the sport as a builder of moral character.[97]

The Maroons' vegetarianism gained enough notoriety that their supporters crafted a new rallying cry to chant during games: "Sweet potatoes, rutabagas, sauerkraut, squash! Run your legs off, Cap'n De Tray! Sure, our milk fed men, by gosh! Will lick 'em bad today!"[98] Writing in the *Tribune*, Walter Eckersall, a former star football player for the University of Chicago under Stagg, referred to the team simply as "the vegetarians." Despite Eckersall's personal preference for habits that Stagg viewed as immoral, like drinking and smoking, the former Maroon reported positively on the team's vegetarian-fed success during the 1907 season,[99] when the Maroons won four of their five games and were crowned the Western Conference champions.[100]

In a similar manner to its coverage of vegetarian athletes, *Vegetarian Magazine* highlighted the power, strength, and skill of vegetarian wild animals. *The Vegetarian* noted that the biggest members of the animal kingdom, such as the rhinoceros, elephant, camel, and horse, ate no meat. "If the largest, strongest, fleetest, tamest . . . of the living creatures subsist . . . on vegetation only," the magazine concluded, "surely then we have proof beyond question that the vegetarian diet excels a thousandfold the dead-flesh repast in its results to both man and beast."[101] Meat-eating was equated to violent wild animals like the tiger and hyena, "whose fangs and claws seem formed for the purpose of rending and tearing." Vegetarian humans were more like the "ox, the horse, the dromedary and the elephant . . . in every respect upon the upper plane of life."[102]

The magazine presented these vegetarians in the animal kingdom as irrefutable scientific, rational proof of the diet's effectiveness. One article noted that "many advance the argument that meat is necessary for hard-working men" to gain the strength of a lion. This was a mistaken analysis, the author argued, demonstrating "that viciousness, anger and animal passion are mistaken for courage, endurance and strength." It was far more advantageous to emulate the vegetarian elephant, who "can carry two or three lions on his back," or the horse or camel, whose endurance was renowned.[103]

Whether writing about bodybuilders, physical culturists, football players, boxers, or wild animals, movement vegetarianism's main voice promoted the notion that vegetarianism created powerful bodies of male muscularity. The marketing of these vegetarian athletes and strongmen reflected a conscious effort by vegetarians to invert the traditional image of the weakened vegetarian that had proliferated in the United States through the 1870s. The new vegetarian could utilize diet as a means to transform health, strength, and social status. With the correct vegetarian fuel, individuals were equipped to overcome the weakening effects of corporate culture that many feared feminized and emaciated male bodies. Whereas in past generations normative culture associated only meat with building strong, sturdy bodies and minds, during the first decade of the twentieth century, fruits, vegetables, grains, and meat substitutes also became the fuel of greatness. In the process, vegetarians themselves had gained a certain level of social renown.

:::::::

By the time the physical culture movement began playing an important role in its development, American movement vegetarianism, in its demographics and philosophy, barely resembled the first U. S. proto-vegetarians. Mainstream culture had already begun increasing its acceptance of vegetarianism, viewing it as a possible path to physical and mental perfection. Movement vegetarians in the early years of the twentieth century argued for their cause using notions of individualism and personal advancement. The physical culture movement, with its themes of strength, discipline, and personal transformation, fit naturally with the new movement vegetarianism.

Physical culturists like Bernarr Macfadden and Lionel Strongfort pushed this development even further, linking vegetarianism with the perfectly sculpted, productive body that used brute strength and power to conquer any obstacle and accomplish any goal. The publications of both physical culture and movement vegetarianism promised their readers that a fleshless diet combined with a dedication to physical exertion offered a guaranteed path to success. This argument appealed to vegetarians old and new, both those who already had helped shift the movement during the 1890s and those brought into the meatless fold by the appeal of physical culture and exercise.

At the very moment that a vegetarian diet became most embraced in American culture, the vegetarian movement was also most isolated from the reform principles on which it was originally founded. In movement vegetarianism, abstaining from meat had become aligned with concern for one's own physical and social condition. Being an inflexible, philosophically driven vegetarian, however, was equated with dogmatism, an objectionable radicalism that placed adherence to principle over intellectual flexibility and scientific rationalism. Movement vegetarians embraced these new perceptions as a means of gaining social acceptance, crafting their arguments via the language of the body rather than through the heart or mind.

The new modern vegetarianism argued for its cause based on principles of individualism; anyone could improve him- or herself through a vegetarian diet and dedicated physical fitness. The implication of this ethos was, of course, that those who did not follow these dictates were doomed to a life of sickness, nonproductivity, and ultimate personal failure—qualities that defined the modern social outcast. Early twentieth-century movement vegetarianism, comprised primarily of members of the middle and upper classes, strove to avoid such labels, advocating for its cause precisely because vegetarianism made its adherents industrious members of society. Movement vegetarianism was successful in shifting popular perceptions of the diet, illustrating that not only steaks and mutton but also fruits, vegetables, nuts, and grains could build beefy individuals of power, vitality, and strength. But what was the cost of this transformation?

Conclusion

::

There is naturally a desire to trace [vegetarianism's] origin and history. —Henry S. Clubb,
"History of Vegetarianism: Chapter 1," Vegetarian Magazine (October 1907)

The active years of the Vegetarian Society of America (VSA) helped shape the development of modern movement vegetarianism. While the group disconnected vegetarianism from its politically oriented past, it also ensured that the movement remained relevant in a rapidly changing world. With vegetarianism growing in the United States and the first generation of movement leaders all gone, the group became interested in understanding its collective past.

In March 1907, eighty-year-old VSA president Henry S. Clubb began writing a complete history of vegetarianism for *Vegetarian Magazine*. Clubb planned for the series to cover the movement from biblical times through the modern vegetarian societies and organizations that he had been personally involved in establishing. In addition to appearing in the magazine, the serialized history was available for purchase as a series of pamphlets. Although Clubb was writing about meat abstaining cultures throughout antiquity, his presentation and interpretation of the history of vegetarianism provides much insight into the state of the movement at the time he was writing.

In the introduction to the first installment of his history of vegetarianism, Clubb said he was motivated to write the series by the movement's growing popularity. Since vegetarianism had attained "the prominence of general acceptance," there was "naturally a desire to trace its origin and history."[1] In the first series of articles, Clubb repeatedly listed notable supposed vegetarians of antiquity, including Moses, John the Baptist, and Jesus. This was a method frequently utilized by the new movement vegetarians, listing prominent practitioners in order to gain credibility.

Themes associated with twentieth-century movement vegetarianism appeared throughout Clubb's history. Incredible feats of strength in the ancient world, including Daniel's victory in the lions' den, Samson's carrying off the gates of Gaza on his shoulders, Paul's immunity from a snake's poison, and the apostle John's resistance after being cast into a cauldron of boiling oil, were all credited to a vegetarian diet.[2] Other examples, according to Clubb, were observable throughout the ancient world. The prophet Daniel continued an active life until the age of eighty-eight because he was a vegetarian.[3] A vegetarian diet also helped the Essenes to live long lives and Saint Apollos to become an effective worker, Clubb argued.[4]

Clubb's history of vegetarianism was so detailed and ambitious that when it concluded at chapter 13, he had covered only through the years of early Christianity.[5] The series did not even approach his lofty goal of documenting the entirety of vegetarian history, as Clubb published the final chapter in December 1909, at which time his attention turned to caring for his ill wife.[6] The first attempt ever at writing a complete history of vegetarianism (its tenuous accuracy notwithstanding) ended well before the narrative reached the shores of the United States.

Given Clubb's emphasis on the value of strength and his success in documenting the ancient world, one wonders how he would have explained the earliest roots of the American vegetarian movement. Where would the original Bible Christian migrants to the United States, the Grahamites, the water curists, and other socially conscious members of the American Vegetarian Society fit in Clubb's narrative of American vegetarianism? Clubb was linked to at least two of these groups, the Bible Christians and the AVS, so it is possible that he would have accurately documented American movement vegetarianism's more political past. We must also consider, however, that by 1909 Clubb and the organization he led, the VSA, had spent more than thirty years distancing movement vegetarianism from its history. In an effort to emphasize the qualities of the new movement vegetarianism, would he have deemphasized antebellum vegetarianism's social reform–oriented past?

In the middle years of the 1910s, Clubb's health began to decline, and he slowly decreased his public activities. The long-time vegetarian passed away in 1921 at the age of ninety-four, having lived at least seventy-nine of those years as a vegetarian. Clubb's life surely was proof to followers of the longevity produced by a meatless lifestyle. He was remembered in the Philadelphia press as "a well-known figure . . . with his white, flowing beard and sturdy appearance, and always attributed his good health and long life to the vegetarian diet." Vegetarians paid homage to their long-time leader as "a veteran" of the cause "who retained to an advanced age enthusiasm and hopefulness and energy."[7]

At the time of Clubb's death, movement vegetarians had become defined by their common consumer practices and glorification of physical achievement rather than by their ideological dedication. The evolution of vegetarian cuisine reflected and even drove the societal shifts both within and toward vegetarian identity. Food shifted from plain, harsh wheat bread and cold water to flesh-like meat substitutes. With this change came a shift in vegetarians' perception of food as well as some nonvegetarians' views of the movement. This dietary evolution indicated and predicted future developments for a vegetarian and health food movement that had become a real moneymaker. In the 1910s, J. H. Kellogg remained at the center of the movement to capitalize on vegetarian consumption through the renamed Battle Creek Sanitarium Food Company.

Throughout his career as a vegetarian health advocate, Kellogg received both criticism and laurels from normative society. Objections to his work focused on the supposedly quirky, even strange faddism of his vegetarianism.[8] However, Kellogg was largely successful at navigating the tensions between being a natural curist and being a professionally accredited medical doctor. By the twentieth century, the methods of satirizing Kellogg shifted, reflecting his role in altering movement vegetarianism. A 1916 silent film starring Douglas Fairbanks, His Picture in the Papers, skewered Kellogg, though for reasons different from claims of faddism or quackery that proliferated in the late nineteenth century.

The film tells the story of Pete Prindle, the black sheep, meat-loving, alcohol-drinking son of a prominent vegetarian health food advocate. To ensure that audiences knew whom the father was based on, writers Anita Loos and John Emerson not so subtly named him Proteus Prindle, a play on the name of Kellogg's enduringly popular vegetable meat, Protose. The opening intertitle clearly expressed the film's moral: "Publicity at any price has become the predominant passion of the American People." As presented in the film, Kellogg was both a reason for and a symbol of this societal passion. The movie spoofed Kellogg's vegetarian fare, introducing products with such unappetizing names as Macerated Morsels, Perforated Peas, Toasted Tooties, and Desiccated Dumplings. It also noted how Kellogg successfully sold and transformed foods through marketing (rather than sell lentils, Prindle's Products shipped cans of Prindle's Life-Saving Lentils). More fundamentally, however, the film offered a parody and harsh critique of corporate America and movement vegetarianism's role in that culture.

In the film, Pete Prindle falls for Christine Cadwalader, the meat-eating daughter of a wealthy railroad magnate named Cassius Cadwalader, who "adores Prindle and lives on his products" and eats lunch daily at Bernarr Macfadden's vegetarian restaurant. However, in order to receive Cadwalader's permission to marry his daughter, Pete needs to own a half interest in his father's vegetarian food company. The film mocks the values of both Cadwalader and the elder Prindle, both more focused on fortune, fame, and prominence than love or familial warmth. Both fathers object to the possible engagement, Proteus Prindle angrily asking his son, "What have you ever done for Prindle's Products?!" Proteus initially denies his son's request for an interest in the company because of his meat-eating proclivities and lack of involvement in the Prindle's business empire.

However, Pete—knowing his father's true weakness, publicity—figures out a way to entice his father to relent. In exchange for a half-share in the company, Pete promises to get "his picture in the papers" in order to earn free publicity for Prindle's Products. Pete conceives of this plan after witnessing his father admiring an article in the so-called *Vegetarian Gazette* featuring his sisters, Pansy and Pearl.

Connecting Prindle's Products and vegetarianism with physical culture, Pete attempts a variety of athletic acts to gain publicity, including swimming to shore from a steamer and defeating a boxing champion. Pete proclaims that the strength he needed to accomplish these feats resulted from his lifelong consumption of Prindle's Products. Pete fails to get the press's attention, however, until he prevents a group of gangsters from derailing a train and kidnapping his would-be father-in-law. The film's intertitle sardonically observes, "Ain't he the REEL hero," as a montage of newspaper headlines offers exaggerated accounts of Pete's heroism, claiming that anywhere from 1,000 to 2,000 people were saved by his actions. Pete gets his picture in the papers, and as a result earns his half-interest in Prindle's Products and marries Christine. Ironically, he only receives the press's attention after performing a true act of selflessness, rather than a publicity stunt.[9]

Overwhelmed by the order and monotony of his low-rung corporate job working for Prindle's Products, Pete despises his professional life, preferring such authentic, masculine activities as drinking and sports. Proteus, in contrast, is obsessed with his public image, valuing business relations over those with his own family; he is only interested in his children to the extent that they can help build the Prindle's Products brand. In its portrait of father and son, *His Picture in the Papers* gave a harsh assessment of Kellogg's public persona.

The film provides an insightful look into the nature of movement vegetarianism in the early twentieth century while also criticizing many of its underlying ideological principles. On one hand, the film illustrates how movement vegetarians attempted to gain notoriety through acts of physical strength, as evidenced by Pete's swimming and boxing exploits. This reflected movement vegetarianism's emphasis on athletic accomplishments, both in the physical culture movement and in the pages of the VSA's publications. In addition, the film illustrated vegetarianism's established place in the American landscape by 1916, with well-known vegetarian restaurants and food products.

Even further, however, the film provides a distinctly ideological critique of what Kellogg and the new movement vegetarianism represented. While the film does make fun of the taste of Prindle's Products as well as their silly sounding names, the greater critique is of the publicity-obsessed Proteus. Whereas movement vegetarians in the nineteenth century were criticized for their rejection of mainstream social mores, by the twentieth century Kellogg was being satirized specifically because of his embrace of the normative cultural values of corporate America. As portrayed in the film, Kellogg's obsession with publicity and the selling of his products was inherently inauthentic, driven by an almost maniacal obsession with profit and attention rather than any ideological dedication.

The film's themes resonated with audiences and reviewers alike, and it was both a commercial and critical success. The film also helped launch Fairbanks into movie stardom.[10] *Variety* proclaimed that Fairbanks's performance "brings to mind that he is destined to be one of the greatest favorites with the film-seeking public."[11] The *Chicago Tribune* reported that "there's food for laughter" in "the deft and sparkling playet" starring Fairbanks that lampoons "the prevalence of the penchant for publicity and food fads."[12] The *Los Angeles Times* described *His Picture in the Papers* as "one of the most amusing film farces ever written."[13] Once marginalized because of its place on the fringes of society, movement vegetarianism had become far more acceptable in some circles of American culture. With its embrace of normative values, however, movement vegetarianism left itself open to criticism of its corporate associations.

By 1916, vegetarianism occupied a distinct middle ground between being a subcultural group and being a mainstream movement. The ideology had gained significant popularity in mainstream culture since its more politically radical years of the mid-nineteenth century. It was still rejected in many circles, however. At the height of vegetarianism's public acceptance in the early twentieth century, it was still a target for attacks, especially by mainstream medical practitioners.

The American Medical Association (AMA) and mainstream medicine were at the forefront of these attacks in the mid-1910s. Founded in the middle of the nineteenth century, the AMA by the early twentieth focused on the professionalization of medical colleges through licensing and inspection. As part of these attempts at professionalization, the AMA worked to discredit ideas and practices that its leaders deemed as fraudulent. The association opened its Propaganda Department in 1913 to investigate and expose movements it viewed as quackery. The department was an example of the medical field's response to the proliferation of personal health movements during the Progressive Era. It also was part of a conscious effort to proclaim mainstream medicine's sole expertise in the health field.[14]

Efforts to debunk vegetarianism appeared in the *Journal of the American Medical Association* (JAMA). In many instances, mainstream medicine's conclusions regarding vegetarianism at this time reflected an attempt to reprise the popular image of the vegetarian from the nineteenth century. For example, in 1918 JAMA published the results of a study that observed the effects of vegetarianism on the reproductive habits of albino rats. The report concluded that "the vegetarian diet produces sterility in both sexes" and "not only reduces the vitality, the growth and ability to reproduce, but also tends to the extermination of the race." Further, the study concluded, "the vegetarians were smaller, had less vigor, were less active, had rougher hair and a tendency to sore eyes, while the other groups were the reverse in these reports." The results evoked nineteenth-century images of the weakened, sexually impotent vegetarian and were in stark contrast with the public image of muscularity and physical health that vegetarians crafted at the time.[15]

In another AMA publication, vegetarians were compared to apes. Writing about dermatology, Martin F. Engman argued that "when man first became conscious that he was man, he was probably hanging from the limb of a tree with one foot, while he grasped a branch with another, and cracked nuts or ate fruit. He was a vegetarian."[16] One medical doctor broadly claimed that "it is a well known fact that peoples who live on a vegetarian diet are subject to cancer."[17]

Movement vegetarians had played a similar rhetorical game when arguing in favor of their diet. The accuracy of each side's argument is less important in understanding the nature of the debate than the similarity of the tactics utilized. Both vegetarians and medical critics attempted to claim expertise through scientific and medical study, while each also cherry-picked and highlighted studies that purportedly supported its perspective. Perhaps mainstream medicine and movement vegetarianism were not as different as they thought themselves to be at the time.

Vegetarianism struggled in the nineteenth and early twentieth century to define its relationship to society at large. Throughout most of the nineteenth century vegetarians distanced themselves from and fought against social norms and structures. By the start of the twentieth century vegetarians had become politically dislocated yet economically empowered in their relationship with consumer culture. By the 1920s vegetarianism stood firmly in between these two forces; distanced from its politicized past, gaining in reputation, yet kept somewhat at arm's length by mainstream society.

At the precise moment that vegetarianism's advocates presented the diet as creating superior stamina, the movement's organization began losing the momentum it had created beginning in the 1880s. Within months of Clubb's death in 1921 the VSA disbanded, illustrating just how reliant the group was on a centralized figure with a long connection to American dietary reform. The end of the organization also reflected vegetarianism's development into a more individualized movement by the 1920s. In the face of this shift a national organization became less vital.

The individual vegetarian societies that comprised the national organization continued to exist, though the closing of the VSA marked another transition for movement vegetarianism. At the time of the organization's dissolution it had become by far the longest lasting national vegetarian society in U. S. history. And the VSA's efforts to shift movement vegetarianism away from politics and toward greater mainstream acceptance greatly affected American vegetarianism's historical arc. As of 2012, the VSA was still the longest running national vegetarian organization in U. S. history.[18]

Vegetarianism, of course, did not disappear with the folding of the Vegetarian Society of America in 1921. While the dislocation of the vegetarian movement by the 1920s represented an end for organized, transcontinental American vegetarianism, the lifestyle—with more than 100 years of history in the United States—was established enough to continue to thrive independent of a centralized organization and national publication.

Vegetarianism's evolution from the early republic through the Progressive Era illustrates that ideological movements—even those rooted in the purest of motivations for humanity at large—are affected and changed by the society in which they function and interact, just as these movements in turn affect and alter society. Movement vegetarianism and its adherents had surely changed, as had many of society's perceptions of the movement. While movement vegetarianism gained recognition and popularity by breaking from its past, this success was tempered. Movement vegetarianism was ultimately unable to achieve the full mainstream acceptance that it so desperately sought. And yet, movement vegetarianism had its influence on American diet and culture. Vegetarians initially expanded the dialogue on dietary choice, linking meat abstention with social reform. Afterward, movement vegetarians altered the nature of American food culture, popularizing the use of nuts and introducing meat substitutes to both vegetarians and health-conscious carnivores alike.

A 1943 Gallup poll asked participants the question, "Many people in the United States are vegetarians, that is people who eat no fish, fowl or meat of any kind. Do you happen to be a vegetarian?" The poll's results showed just how much vegetarians had multiplied since the forty-one Bible Christian immigrants arrived in 1817. Gallup reported that between 2.5 and 3 million Americans in 1943 self-identified as vegetarians, around 2 percent of the country's total population.[19] While that was still a small fraction of American society, it also illustrated that movement vegetarianism had truly transformed into a recognizable and visible community.

Notes

INTRODUCTION

1. Debra Blake Weisenthal, "The Vegetarian Super Powers," *Vegetarian Times* 136 (December 1988): 25.

2. Paul Obis, "An Idea Whose Time Had Come," *Vegetarian Times* 160 (December 1990): 6.

3. A similar point is made in Spencer, *Vegetarianism*, x. For examples of publications illustrating historical amnesia of the movement, see Giehl, *Vegetarianism*; Mangels, Messina, and Messina, *The Dietitian's Guide to Vegetarian Diets*, 3; and Heather Gorn, "25 Years of Vegetarianism."

4. On Shakerism and vegetarianism, see Puskar-Pasewicz, "Kitchen Sisters and Disagreeable Boys."

5. Jon White, *Everyday Life of the North American Indian*, 107.

6. Alderfer, *The Ephrata Commune*, 66.

7. Brooke, *The Refiner's Fire*, 132; Bellesiles, *Revolutionary Outlaws*, 221.

8. Stuart, *The Bloodless Revolution*, 36.

9. Spencer, *Vegetarianism*, 239–40.

10. Ibid., 225.

11. Shelley, "Queen Mab."

12. Works on the history of the humoral body include Albala, *Eating Right in the Renaissance*; Arikha, *Passions and Tempers*; and Kupperman, "Fear of Hot Climates in the Anglo-American Colonial Experience."

13. Eden, *The Early American Table*.

14. Roosevelt, *The Strenuous Life*, 1–9, 16–21.

15. Vegetarianism fit this classification in the 1960s and 1970s. See Belasco, *Appetite for Change*.

16. "Unity of Reforms," AVHJ 3, no. 5 (May 1853): 24.

CHAPTER ONE

1. Maintenance Committee, Bible Christian Church, *History of the Philadelphia Bible Christian Church*, 8. This history includes a detailed listing of all the original adult migrants, numbered at twenty-two. The migrant church members traveled to the United States with nineteen children in tow. See also Scharf and Thompson, *History of Philadelphia*, 1404; and Clarke, *Memorials of the Clarke Family*, 24–25. Clarke placed the number at thirty-nine, but admits that his estimation is based on his memory, "so far as I can recollect."

2. Clarke, *Memorials of the Clarke Family*, 9.

3. For a summary of the intersections and differences between these two radical thinkers, see Hodson, *Language and Revolution*.

4. Maintenance Committee, Bible Christian Church, *History of the Philadelphia Bible-Christian Church*, 24.

5. Ibid.

6. Clarke, *Memorials of the Clarke Family*, 23. See also Archer, *Social Unrest and Popular Protest in England*.

7. Forward, *Fifty Years of Food Reform*, 13.

8. Clarke, *Memorials of the Clarke Family*, 25–30, 34.

9. Metcalfe, "History of the Bible-Christians," 125. Here Metcalfe is referencing Psalm 37:3. It does seem, however that the group was already somewhat splintered and aggravated; passage for the whole group of migrants was primarily paid for by five families. See Clarke, *Memorials of the Clarke Family*, 25.

10. Clarke, *Memorials of the Clarke Family*, 54; Scharf and Thompson, *History of Philadelphia*, 1404.

11. Clarke, *Memorials of the Clarke Family*, 35.

12. Warner, *The Urban Wilderness*, 70–74.

13. Hessinger, *Seduced, Abandoned, and Reborn*.

14. Metcalfe, "History of the Bible Christians," 125.

15. Nichols, *Religions of the World*, 115.

16. Bible Christian Church, North Third Street, *Constitution and By-Laws*.

17. Ibid.

18. "Review of Five Sermons," *Presbyterian Magazine* 1 (October 1821): 463–64.

19. Metcalfe also was the editor of this publication in 1820.

20. Metcalfe, *Bible Testimony*.

21. Ibid., 16.

22. Ibid., 35.

23. Ibid., 33.

24. Maintenance Committee, Bible Christian Church, *History of the Philadelphia Bible Christian Church*, 7–14. These membership records were copied directly from church ledgers.

25. Stuart, *The Bloodless Revolution*, 422–23.

26. Metcalfe, "Experience of the Bible-Christians," 73.

27. See Ouédragogo, "The Social Genesis of Western Vegetarianism," 163.

28. A reference to the Graham family and their life in Suffield can be found in "First Census of the United States, 1790," M637, RG 29, 12 rolls (National Archives and Records Administration, Washington, DC). For more on Graham's father, an important figure in local history, see Helen Carpenter, *The Rev. John Graham of Woodbury, Connecticut*.

29. Nissenbaum, "Sylvester Graham and Health Reform," 288–89.

30. Quoted in ibid.

31. For more on the omnipresence of alcohol in the early republic, see Lender, *Drinking in America*; and Rorabaugh, *The Alcoholic Republic*.

32. Balmer and Fitzimer, *The Presbyterians*, 165.

33. Gately, *Drink*, 257–62; Pegram, *Battling Demon Rum*, 19–32.

34. Young, *Bearing Witness against Sin*, 121.

35. The organization eventually changed its name to the Pennsylvania Temperance Society in 1832. For the first reference to the name change, see "Philadelphia Temperance Society Report," *Journal of Health* 4, no. 4 (1832): 123.

36. Osborn, "A Detestable Shrine," 105, 111–12.

37. Pennsylvania Society for Discouraging the Use of Ardent Spirits, *Report of a Committee Appointed by the Pennsylvania Society*.

38. Ibid., 12.

39. Graham, *Lectures on the Science of Human Life*, ii.

40. Maintenance Committee, Bible Christian Church, *History of the Philadelphia Bible Christian Church*, 40. Unfortunately these letters apparently have not survived.

41. Some works have overstated Graham's relationship with Metcalfe, referring to Graham as a Metcalfe protégé and even implying that Graham joined the Bible Christian Church. Graham was an ardent Presbyterian and never left his church. The Pennsylvania Temperance Society, in fact, was led by prominent Presbyterian leaders and was aligned with that denomination. It is, however, safe to say that Graham was greatly influenced and impressed by Metcalfe's writings on vegetable diets. The two worked together throughout the antebellum era, eventually founding the first vegetarian society in the United States (see chap. 3).

42. See Graham, *Lectures on the Science of Human Life*, 4.

43. Ibid., 2.

44. Ibid., 3.

45. See Lerner, *The Grimké Sisters from South Carolina*, 179.

46. Graham, *Lectures on the Science of Human Life*, 145.

47. Ibid., 136, 139.

48. Ibid., 137.

49. *New York Evening Post*, July 3, 1832.

50. For more on perceptions of cholera in 1832, see Rosenberg, *The Cholera Years*, 40–65.

51. For the more politicized reasons for Clay's call for a national prayer day, see Jortner, "Cholera, Christ, and Jackson."

52. Graham, *A Lecture on Epidemic Diseases Generally, and Particularly the Spasmodic Cholera*, 49.

53. Ibid., 33.

54. Ibid., 36.

55. Ibid., 77.

56. For information on choleric dehydration and its effects, see Mayo Clinic Staff, *Cholera: Symptoms*.

57. Graham, *A Defence of the Graham System of Living*, iii.

58. "Lecture on Epidemic Diseases," *Graham Journal of Health and Longevity* 3, no. 3 (February 2, 1839): 50.

59. See Susan Williams, *Food in the United States*, 18–20.

60. Ibid., 20; Gordon, *An Empire of Wealth*, 39–42.

61. Graham, *A Treatise on Bread and Bread-Making*, 92.

62. Ibid., 16–17.

63. Ibid., 16–17, 25.

64. "Wit and Sentiment," *Atkinson's Casket*, 431.

65. "The Art of Dining and Giving Dinners," *Spirit of the Times* 6, no. 8 (April 1836): 57.

66. HH, "Testimony in Favor of a Vegetable Diet, Letters to the Editor," *Boston Medical and Surgical Journal* 14, no. 14 (May 11, 1836): 223.

67. "Letters from Correspondents," *New York Review* 18, no. 11 (September 5, 1840): 84.

68. "Mr. Bell's Prize Dissertation and Mr. Graham's Strictures," *Boston Medical and Surgical Journal* 12 (1835): 379–81.

69. "A Chapter on Stale Bread—or the Grahamite Victim," *Morning Herald* 201 (January 19, 1838).

70. "The First Grahamite," *New England Review* 28 (July 13, 1839): 1.

71. "Dietetic Charlantanry," *New York Review* 4, no. 4 (October 14, 1837): 465.

72. "Bakers," in Edwin Williams, *New-York as It Is*, 226.

73. Nicholson, *Nature's Own Book*, 42. A follower of Graham wrote this recipe. However, its appearance does illustrate public awareness of the bread, as well as the fact that the recipe was starting to become diffused in print form.

74. "Household Department: Bread," *Minnesota Farmers' Institute Annual* (1835): 263.

75. Graham, *A Defence of the Graham System of Living*, 9–11.

76. Ibid., 18.

77. On urban amusements, see Gilfoyle, *City of Eros*, 29–41; and Cohen, *The Murder of Helen Jewett*, 230–47.

78. Quoted from a letter from Adams to Thomas Jefferson in Diggins, *John Adams*, 167.

79. On the self-made man and the tumultuous implications thereof, see Sandage, *Born Losers*; and Sellers, *The Market Revolution*, 11–32.

80. Graham, *A Defence of the Graham System of Living*, 114.

81. "Mr. Bell's Prize Dissertation."

82. The earliest mention of the term *Grahamite* can be found in 1833 in "Romance and Reality," *Portland Magazine: Devoted to Literature*, November 1, 1833, 33.

83. *Longworth's American Almanac*, 491. In addition to her reformist works in the United States, Nicholson traveled to Ireland from 1846 until 1848 as a Christian missionary, writing extensively documenting the destitution and famine that she witnessed. See Nicholson, *Annals of the Famine in Ireland* (1851).

84. Nicholson, *Nature's Own Book*, 15.

85. Also located nearby were the offices of the Temperance Union, the American Tract Society—an evangelical temperance group—and the New York Foreign Missionary Society. See Nicholson, *Annals of the Famine in Ireland* (1998), 9.

86. William S. Tyler to Edward Tyler, Amherst College, October 10, 1833, published in Le Duc, "Grahamites and Garrisonites." Tyler was the author of a history of Amherst College written in 1873. See Tyler, *History of Amherst College*. Amherst's website has detailed information about its nineteenth-century alumni, including Tyler. See http://www.amherst.edu/~rjyanco94/genealogy/acbiorecord/1830.html#tyler-ws. Tyler, however, was not one of Sylvester Graham's professors, as Graham left Amherst in 1823, four years before Tyler began teaching at the college.

87. Nicholson, *Nature's Own Book*, 1.

88. On commercialized sex in New York, see Gilfoyle, *City of Eros*, 29–35; on the young middle-class men living throughout New York City, see Cohen, *The Murder of Helen Jewett*, 230–47.

89. "The Graham Boarding House," *New England Farmer and Agricultural Journal* 11, no. 19 (November 21, 1832): 147.

90. Nicholson, *Nature's Own Book*, 28–29.

91. Ibid., 11.

92. For more on boardinghouse rules, see Gamber, *The Boardinghouse in Nineteenth-Century America*, 45.

93. Nicholson, *Nature's Own Book*, 14. Unanimous consent was necessary to change the established dinnertime of 1:00, while a three-fourths' majority could determine suppertime.

94. Graham, *Lectures on the Science of Human Life*, 626.

95. Nicholson, *Nature's Own Book*, 20–21. Regular bathing was commonplace among the upper classes that could afford indoor plumbing, but it was rare among the masses. See Hoy, *Chasing Dirt*, 12–15.

96. "Rules of a Graham House," *GJHL* 1, no. 6 (May 9, 1837): 47.

97. Fletcher, *A History of Oberlin College*, 1:323–30. See Walters, *American Reformers*, 153–54.

98. "History of a Graham Boarding House," *GJHL* 3, no. 25 (December 14, 1839): 398.

99. *GJHL* 3, no. 16 (August 3, 1839): 40.

100. Nicholson, *Nature's Own Book*, 48.

101. Ibid., 16–18.

102. Coleman, "Casting Bread on Troubled Waters"; "Acclimation in the West," *GJHL* 3, no. 7 (March 30, 1839): 113; "A Voice from the South," *LOH* 5 (1841): 294.

103. Nissenbaum, *Sex, Diet and Debility in Jacksonian America*, 144.

104. "Ralph Waldo Emerson to Lidian Emerson, March 1, 1842," in Cabot, *The Works of Ralph Waldo Emerson*, 489.

105. "Letter from William Lloyd Garrison to James Miller McKim," in Garrison, *The Letters of William Lloyd Garrison*, 3:337.

106. Garrison, *The Letters of William Lloyd Garrison*, 3:175.

107. Payne, *Recollections of Seventy Years*, 67.

108. "Boarding in New York," in A. E. Wright's *Boston, New York, Philadelphia & Baltimore, Commercial Directory*, 28.

109. On boardinghouses, see Gamber, *The Boardinghouse in Nineteenth-Century America*, 1–59; and Scherzer, *The Unbounded Community*, 97–110.

110. "Men of Sense," *The Hesperian* 3, no. 4 (September 1893): 293.

111. The dichotomy of Graham's exhortations against masturbation as a public spectacle is part of a movement that sprouted in the 1830s of reformers engaging in a dialogue about sex. On Graham in this movement, see Helen Horowitz, *Rereading Sex*, 94–99. On Grahamism as an empowering, female-centered movement, see Haynes, "Riotous Flesh," 32–39.

112. Year: 1840; Census Place: New York Ward 14, New York, New York; roll 307; page 413; image 837; Family History Library Film 0017197. The census lists just one male resident, along with four female residents between the ages of twenty and thirty.

113. Abzug, *Cosmos Crumbling*, 66–73; Cott, "Young Women in the Second Great Awakening in New England."

114. "Early Testimonials in Favor of the Graham System," *GJHL* 3, no. 3 (February 2, 1839): 45. While this was included in an issue of the Graham journal from 1839, the letter is originally dated from March 21, 1833, and connected to the cholera epidemic.

115. Nicholson, *Nature's Own Book*, 52.

116. Ibid., 52–56.

117. Graham, *A Defence of the Graham System of Living*, 196.

118. Nicholson, *Nature's Own Book*, 60.

119. Graham, *A Defence of the Graham System of Living*, 197–98. Greeley was not a lifelong vegetarian but was a follower of Graham's in the 1830s. The implications of his association with a vegetable diet will be considered in chapter 4. See Greeley, *Recollections of a Busy Life*, 103–4.

120. "Rules of a Graham House," *GJHL* 1, no. 6 (May 9, 1837): 47.

121. *GJHL* 1, no. 1 (April 4, 1837): 1.

122. "Local Agents for This Work," *GJHL* 1, no. 10 (June 6, 1837): 80. The states where the journal was available were Maine, Massachusetts, New Hampshire, Vermont, Connecticut, Rhode Island, New York, Ohio, Pennsylvania, Illinois, Indiana, and Missouri.

123. "Local Agents for the Journal," *GJHL* 1, no. 29 (October 1837): 232. The states where the journal was available were the original twelve plus Maryland, Georgia, and Michigan.

124. "Local Agents for the Journal," *GJHL* 3, no. 2 (January 19, 1839): 25.

125. See for example, "Letter from Dr. Reed," GJHL 1, no. 12 (June 20, 1837): 90; William Brown, "Testimony of Another Physician," GJHL 2, no. 12 (June 9, 1838): 138; "Extract of a Letter from a Subscriber," GJHL 3, no. 17 (August 17, 1839): 274.

126. Nathaniel Perry, "Letter to David Cambell, Corresponding Secretary of American Physiological Society," GJHL 1, no. 1 (April 4, 1837): 3.

127. See Sylvester Graham, "Public Bakers," GJHL 1, no. 5 (May 2, 1837): 38–39; "Dr. Lee vs. Graham System," GJHL 1, no. 1 (April 4, 1837): 7; "The Graham System: What Is It?" GJHL 1, nos. 2 and 3 (April 17, 1837): 17.

128. "Beaumont's Experiments on Digestion," GJHL 1, no. 1 (April 4, 1837): 6–7.

129. Ibid.; "Dr. Beaumont's Experiments and Observations on Digestion— Experiment 1, Experiment 2, Experiment 3," GJHL 1, no. 7 (May 16, 1837): 50; "Dr. Beaumont's Experiments and Observations on Digestion—Experiment 9, Experiment 10, Experiment 11, Experiment 12, Experiment 13, Experiment 14, Experiment 15, Experiment 16, Experiment 17, Experiment 18, Experiment 19, Experiment 20, Experiment 21, Experiment 22, Experiment 23," GJHL 1, no. 9 (May 30, 1837): 69–70.

130. See, for examples, "Receipts for Cooking," GJHL 1, no. 12 (June 20, 1837): 93; "Ruta Baga Pie," GJHL 3, no. 8 (April 13, 1838): 133; and "Pearl Barley as a Substitute for Rice," GJHL 3, no. 20 (September 28, 1839): 327.

131. "Valuable Works," GJHL 1, no. 11 (June 13, 1837); "Graham Boarding House," GJHL 2, no. 15 (July 21, 1838): 240; "Contents, Notices, &c.," GJHL 3, no. 19 (September 14, 1839): 312.

132. "A Word of Explanation," GJHL 3, no. 2 (January 19, 1839): 25–27.

133. "The Fourth Year of the Graham Journal," GJHL 3, no. 20 (September 28, 1839): 327.

134. "Arrangement for 1840," GJHL 3, no. 21 (October 12, 1839): 339.

CHAPTER TWO

1. "Thomsonianism or Grahamism," LOH 5, no. 1 (January 5, 1841): 69.

2. Constitution of the American Physiological Society, 14.

3. Ibid., 5.

4. Ibid., 14.

5. Ibid. 14–16.

6. Ibid., 17–19.

7. Second Annual Report of the American Physiological Society, 3–4.

8. Susan Williams, Food in the United States, 83.

9. Duncan, Evils of Violating the Laws of Health, 13–14.

10. Third Annual Report of the American Physiological Society, 6.

11. Walters and Portmess, Ethical Vegetarianism, 81.

12. William Alcott, The Use of Tobacco and The Young Man's Guide.

13. The Boston Medical and Surgical Journal would eventually become the New England Journal of Medicine in the twentieth century.

14. "Grahamism a Cause of Insanity," Boston Medical and Surgical Journal 14, no. 3 (February 24, 1836): 38. For biographical details on Lee, see Leonard Lee and Sarah Fiske Lee, comp., John Lee of Farmington, Hartford Co., Conn., and His Descendants, 2nd ed. (Meridien, CT: Republican-Record, 1897), 185–86.

15. Sylvester Graham, "Grahamism Not a Cause of Insanity," *Boston Medical and Surgical Journal* 14, no. 6 (March 16, 1836): 88, 93.

16. William Alcott, "The Graham System," *Boston Medical and Surgical Journal* 14, no. 13 (May 4, 1836): 199–201.

17. "Introduction," LOH 2 (1838): i–ii.

18. "Testimony of Dr. Bringham in Regard to Animal Food," LOH 4 (1840): 94.

19. "Poisonous Medicines," LOH 1, (1837): 18.

20. "Miscellany," LOH 1 (1837): 38.

21. "Cause of Colds," LOH 2 (1838): 25.

22. William Alcott, *Vegetable Diet*.

23. "Poisoned Cheese," LOH 2 (1838): 69.

24. "Late Suppers," LOH 2 (1838): 71.

25. "Animal Food for Laborers," LOH 2 (1838): 284; "Dietetic Reform," LOH 2 (1838): 119.

26. "Vegetable Diet for Children," LOH 4 (1840): 59–63.

27. "Animal and Vegetable Food," LOH 4 (1840): 220.

28. "Dr. Beaumont's Experiments," LOH 4 (1840): 125; "Fruits as Food," LOH 4 (1840): 292.

29. "Nutritive Properties of Various Kinds of Food," LOH 4 (1840): 59–63.

30. "Vegetable Food for Hard Labor," LOH 4 (1840): 28–29.

31. "Fruits as Food," 292.

32. "The Best Bread," LOH 5 (1841): 260.

33. "A Voice from the South," LOH 5 (1841): 294.

34. "Fruits as Food," 292; "Fruits for Adults," LOH 5 (1841): 224; "Manner of Using Fruit," LOH 5 (1841): 257. Grahamites previously attacked fruits as being difficult to digest and apt to be used as a stimulating dessert. See "Intemperance in Eating," GJHL 1, no. 5 (April 1837): 37.

35. By the late 1830s Graham himself shifted focus as well. Though he still remained a meat abstainer and dietetic reform advocate, the central issue for Graham during this time period was the danger of masturbation. For a discussion of Graham's antimasturbation crusade, see Helen Horowitz, *Rereading Sex*, 107–15.

36. Bickman, *Minding American Education*, 50–53.

37. Quoted in Sanborn and Harris, *A. Bronson Alcott*, 1:237.

38. "Gastric Sayings," *The Knickerbocker* 16, no. 5 (November 1840): 452; quoted in Emerson, *Heart of Emerson's Journals*, 175. An example of one of the Gastric Sayings from *The Knickerbocker* aimed at mocking Alcott: "The poles of potatoes are integrated; eggs globed and orbed: yet in the true cookery, flour is globed in the material, wine orbed in the transparent. The baker globes, the griddle orbs, all things. As magnet the steel, so the palate abstracts matter, which trembles to traverse the mouths of diversity, and rest in the bowels of unity. All cookery is of hunger: variety is her form, order her costume."

39. "Orphic Sayings," *The Dial* 1, no. 1 (1840): 351–61.

40. Sanborn and Harris, *A. Bronson Alcott*, 2:270.

41. "English Reformers," *The Dial* 3, no. 4 (1842): 238.

42. Quoted in Sears, *Bronson Alcott's Fruitlands*, 45.

43. Bronson Alcott, *Concord Days*, 181.

44. Harding and Bode, *The Correspondence of Henry David Thoreau*, 115.

45. Sears, *Bronson Alcott's Fruitlands*, 29.

46. Ibid., 25.

47. Emerson, *Journals of Ralph Waldo Emerson*, 421.

48. Louisa May wrote down these aphorisms in the diary that she kept while at Fruitlands. Only small fragments of the diary remained after the settlement disbanded, though they are the first documented evidence of her writings. Louisa May Alcott, *Louisa May Alcott: Her Life, Letters, and Journals*, 41.

49. Ibid., 36; Sears, *Bronson Alcott's Fruitlands*, 32.

50. Bronson Alcott, *The Journals of Bronson Alcott*, 155.

51. Shepard, *Pedlar's Progress*, 361.

52. Sears, *Bronson Alcott's Fruitlands*, 72.

53. Louisa May Alcott, *Louisa May Alcott: Her Life, Letters, and Journals*, 41; Matteson, *Eden's Outcasts*, 130.

54. Louisa May Alcott, "Transcendental Wild Oats," in Sears, *Bronson Alcott's Fruitlands*, 150.

55. Ibid., 155.

56. Ibid., 161, 163.

57. Sears, *Bronson Alcott's Fruitlands*, 48.

58. Cook, *Working Women, Literary Ladies*, 208.

59. Bronson Alcott even speculated that Louisa May's temper came from her preference for meat. See Saxton, *Louisa May Alcott*, 93.

60. Louisa May Alcott, "Transcendental Wild Oats," 166.

61. Ibid., 169.

62. Priessnitz, *The Cold Water Cure*, 47.

63. Shew and Shew, *Water-Cure for Ladies*, 63–64, 95.

64. *WCJ* 1, no. 1 (December 1, 1845): 1.

65. "Lung Disease," *WCJ* 1, no. 2 (December 15, 1845): 28.

66. "Case of Red Gravel," *WCJ* 1, no. 3 (January 1, 1846): 39.

67. "Letter from a Physician—Cases of Scrofula," *WCJ* 1, no. 1 (December 1, 1845): 11.

68. "Farinaceous Food," *WCJ* 1, no. 3 (January 1, 1846): 42.

69. Cayleff, *Wash and Be Healed*, 26.

70. "Comparative Benefits of Vegetable and Animal Food," *WCJ* 4, no. 3 (September 1, 1847): 1–28.

71. "Vegetable Diet—Experience of Dr. W. A. Alcott," *WCJ* 4, no. 4 (October 1847): 289.

CHAPTER THREE

1. "Physiological Conference," *Truth-Tester* 1 (1847): 121.

2. "Vegetarianism," *WCJ* 7, no. 4 (April 1, 1849): 116.

3. Maintenance Committee, Bible Christian Church, *History of the Philadelphia Bible Christian Church*, 43.

4. Ibid., 166.

5. "A Lecture to Young Men on Chastity," *Penny Satirist* 367 (April 27, 1844): 2; "Classified Ads," *Penny Satirist* 366 (April 20, 1844): 2.

6. "American Vegetarian Convention," *WCJ* 10, no. 1 (July 1850): 5.

7. "American Vegetarian Convention," *WCJ* 9, no. 2 (February 1850): 60.

8. Clinton Hall was the location of the famed Astor Place Opera House, where the year before a large riot fed by Anglophobia and class tensions had opposed partisans of the American actor Edwin Forrest and the British actor William Charles Macready, leaving at least twenty-five dead and more than 120 injured. The hall also served as a popular location for a variety of lectures and organizational meetings, and would eventually house the Mercantile Library. See Hemstreet, *Nooks & Corners of Old New York*, 169–70.

9. "Proceedings of the American Vegetarian Convention," *AVHJ* 1, no. 1 (November 1850): 1–2.

10. Ibid., 2–6.

11. Ibid., 6.

12. Ibid.; Maintenance Committee, Bible Christian Church, *History of the Philadelphia Bible Christian Church*, 171–76.

13. "Proceedings of the American Vegetarian Convention," 2.

14. For all fourteen resolutions, see ibid., 6.

15. For more on Stewart and his work at Oberlin, see Morgan, *A Worker and Workers' Friend*, 50–60. Stewart eventually became renowned for his designs of cast iron stoves.

16. "Proceedings of the American Vegetarian Convention," 7.

17. Ibid., 32.

18. "The Controversialist," *AVHJ* 1, no. 2 (February 1851): 46.

19. Dunglison, "Vegetarianism," 896. For more on Robley Dunglison and his relationship with Jefferson, see Burstein, *Jefferson's Secrets*, 19–29.

20. "Vegetarianism—What Is It?" *AVHJ* 1, no. 2 (February 1851): 37.

21. Ibid., 37.

22. "Anniversary of the American Vegetarian Society," *T. L. Nichols' Water-Cure Journal* 20, no. 1 (July 1855): 1.

23. Walters, *American Reformers*, 115.

24. "Proceedings of the American Vegetarian Convention," 25.

25. The Compromise of 1850 admitted California as a free state, New Mexico and Utah under the principle of popular sovereignty, and banned the slave trade in Washington, DC. It also adopted the Fugitive Slave Act. McPherson, *Battle Cry of Freedom*, 71–73.

26. "Proceedings of the American Vegetarian Convention," 25.

27. "Unity of Reforms," *AVHJ* 3, no. 5 (May 1853).

28. Ibid., 24.

29. "The Festival," *AVHJ* 1, no. 10 (October 1851): 176.

30. Ibid., 169.

31. Ibid., 176.

32. "Vegetarian Dietary," *AVHJ* 1, no. 12 (December 1851): 215.

33. "Receipts," *AVHJ* 2, no. 3 (March 1852): 46.

34. "Domestic Economy," *AVHJ* 1, no. 6 (June 1851): 129.

35. S. M. Hobbs, "Diseased Meat," *AVHJ* 1, no. 2 (February 1851): 45.

36. "American Vegetarian Society," T. L. Nichols' *Water-Cure Journal* 10, no. 4 (October 1850): 157.

37. "Dietetics," T. L. Nichols' *Water-Cure Journal* 16, no. 4 (October 1853): 83.

38. Ibid.

39. AVHJ 1, no. 3 (March 1851): 54.

40. J. H. Hanaford, "Women's Sphere," AVHJ 1, no. 6 (June 1851): 104.

41. Anne Denton, "The Soul's Medium," AVHJ 1, no. 11 (November 1851): 192; Denton, "The Rights of Woman," AVHJ 2, no. 12 (December 1852): 186–87.

42. "American Vegetarian Society," 157.

43. For example, see "A Woman's Rights Convention," AVHJ 2, no. 5 (May 1852): 79.

44. "Special Notices: Grand Meeting of American Vegetarian Society," *New York Daily Times*, August 31, 1852, 1.

45. Silver-Isenstadt, *Shameless*, 111–12.

46. "Exciting Week in New York," *The Liberator* 37 (September 16, 1853): 146.

47. Ibid.

48. "Fourth Annual Meeting of the American Vegetarian Society," AVHJ 3, no. 9 (September 1853): 162.

49. Ibid.

50. "Letter from James Haughton," *The Liberator* 19, no. 41 (October 12, 1849): 162.

51. W. S. George, "Reform in Diet," *The Liberator* 51 (December 23, 1853): 203.

52. "The Meeting—The Festival!," *The Liberator* 31 (August 5, 1853): 123.

53. "Exciting Week in New York," 146.

54. "Abolition and Secession," *The Liberator* 31 (November 22, 1861): 1.

55. See "Special Notices: Grand Meeting of American Vegetarian Society"; "The American Vegetarian Society Festival," *New York Daily Times*, September 11, 1852, 2.

56. "Items: Cozzening," *Spirit of the Times* 20, no. 16 (June 1850): 183.

57. Congress water was saline spring water from the Congress Springs in Saratoga, New York. It was popular for its supposed healing properties. See Fitch, *Mineral Waters of the United States and American Spas*, 53.

58. "Death of Sylvester Graham," AVHJ 1, no. 10 (October 1851): 188.

59. "Letter from Dr. Hayes," AVHJ 1, no. 11 (November 1851): 200.

60. As noted above, Graham was actually fifty-seven at the time of his death.

61. "Mr. Graham," AVHJ 1, no. 12 (December 1851): 216–17.

62. William Alcott, "Sylvester Graham," AVHJ 2, no. 9 (September 1852): 137–38.

63. "Recent Deaths," *New York Daily Times*, September 18, 1851, 2; "Summary," *New York Evangelist* 22, no. 38 (September 18, 1851): 151; "Sylvester Graham: The Father of Grahamites, and the Godfather of Graham Bread," *Home Journal* 41, no. 296 (October 11, 1851): 1.

64. AVHJ 2, no. 2 (March 1852): 41.

65. "Proceedings of the American Vegetarian Society," AVHJ 2, no. 10 (October 1852): 160.

66. "Fourth Annual Meeting of the American Vegetarian Society," AVHJ 3, no. 9 (September 1853): 174–78.

67. Maintenance Committee, Bible Christian Church, *History of the Philadelphia Bible Christian Church*, 171–76.

68. "Proceedings of the American Vegetarian Society and the Festival," *AVHJ* 4, no. 10 (October 1854): 189.

69. "A New Volume," *WCJ* 31, no. 6 (June 1861): 81.

70. "History of Kansas," in *Tribune Almanac and Political Register*, 19–30.

71. Maintenance Committee, Bible Christian Church, *History of the Philadelphia Bible Christian Church*, 70–72.

72. See Etcheson, *Bleeding Kansas*. Etcheson argues that Bleeding Kansas was, at its heart, a contestation between forces attempting to preserve liberties as each group perceived them.

73. Clubb, *The Illustrated Vegetarian Almanac of 1855*, 21.

74. Abbott, *Cotton and Capital*, 28–49; Lause, *Race and Radicalism*, 13–14.

75. Clubb, *The Maine Liquor Law*, 207; Octagon Settlement Company, *The Octagon Settlement Company*, i.

76. Octagon Settlement Company, *The Octagon Settlement Company*, 10.

77. Blackmar, *Kansas*, 842.

78. Octagon Settlement Company, *The Octagon Settlement Company*, 3.

79. Colt, *Went to Kansas*, 209.

80. "Vegetarian Settlement Company," in Dana, *The Great West*, 226.

81. Chinn, *Technology and the Logic of American Racism*, 49–50.

82. "A List of Works by Fowler and Wells," *WCJ* 17, no. 3 (March 1854): 61.

83. Fowler, *A Home for All*, 82–85, 126–30. Ninety-nine octagonal buildings are listed on the National Register of Historic Places. See National Park Service, "National Register Information System."

84. Holl, *Rural and Urban House Types in North America*, 26.

85. Colt, *Went to Kansas*, 281.

86. Octagon Settlement Company, *The Octagon Settlement Company*, 5–6; "Vegetarian Company Kanzas," *WCJ* 20, no. 1 (July 1855): 11.

87. Hickman, "The Vegetarian and Octagon Settlement Companies," 379; Reps, *The Making of Urban America*, 496; Octagon Settlement Company, *The Octagon Settlement Company*, 3–7.

88. See Reps, *The Making of Urban America*, 496.

89. The location is now the present-day town of Humboldt, about forty miles west of Fort Scott and 100 miles south of Kansas City.

90. "Not Wanted in Kansas," *Chicago Daily Tribune*, February 12, 1856, 2.

91. "A Vegetarian Colony," *Circular* 4, no. 48 (December 20, 1855): 191.

92. *New York Daily Tribune*, January 21, 1856.

93. "The Kansas Enterprise," *WCJ* 21, no. 3 (March 1856): 60.

94. Letter from John Milton Hadley to George Allen, April 25, 1855.

95. Ibid.

96. Colt, *Went to Kansas*, 14, 21.

97. Octagon Settlement Company, *The Octagon Settlement Company*, 7.

98. Colt, *Went to Kansas*, 49, 66, 76.

99. Stewart, "Memoirs of Watson Stewart."

100. Ibid.

101. Colt, *Went to Kansas*, 66.

102. Ibid., 71.

103. Stewart, "Memoirs of Watson Stewart," 392.

104. Blackmar, *Kansas*, 904; Lévi-Strauss, *The Savage Mind*, 69; Jon White, *Everyday Life of the North American Indian*, 107.

105. Grout, *Kansas Curiosities*, 101; Fitzgerald, *Ghost Towns of Kansas*, 132.

106. According to the settlement's founders, here is a list of the professions of the colony's residents: one accountant, two blacksmiths, one builder, two cabinetmakers, two carpenters, one colporteur, one cooper, eighteen farmers, one gardener, one barber, one ironworker, one journalist, one lecturer, one librarian, two lumbermen, two mechanics, four merchants, one millwright, one nurseryman, four physicians, three printers, one shoemaker, one stonecutter, one tailor, one tinsmith, three teachers, one weaver, and one woolen manufacturer. The list also noted two widows and two single women. Octagon Settlement Company, *The Octagon Settlement Company*, 10.

107. The geographic breakdown of residents is as follows: Fourteen families from New York, eight from Pennsylvania, five from Ohio, five from Ontario, three from New Jersey, three from Illinois, four from Indiana, three from Michigan, two from Tennessee, two from Wisconsin, two from Kentucky, two from Rhode Island, one from Maine, one from Massachusetts, and one from Iowa. Ibid., 8–9.

108. At this event, free staters decided to become involved in the contest for control of the soon to be formed state legislature. Blackmar, *Kansas*, 264–66; Stewart, "Memoirs of Watson Stewart"; Stampp, *America in 1857*, 259.

109. "Samuel Stewart," in *American Civil War Soldiers*; "Samuel J. Stewart," in *General Index to Pension Files*, T288.

110. "John Milton Hadley," in *U. S. Civil War Soldier Records and Profiles*.

111. "William Lloyd Garrison to Charles Sumner, February 26, 1861," in Garrison, *The Letters of William Lloyd Garrison*, 5:10.

112. Reynolds, *John Brown, Abolitionist*, 198; Oates, *To Purge This Land with Blood*, 165.

113. "Capt. James H. Holmes Dead," *New York Times*, November 23, 1907, 9; Colton, *The Civil War in the Western Territories*, 192; Tegeder, "Lincoln and the Territorial Patronage," 84; McGinnis and Smith, *Abraham Lincoln and the Western Territories*, 77–78.

114. "Henry Stephen Clubb," in *U. S. Civil War Soldier Records and Profiles*; "Henry Stephen Clubb," in *Official Records of the Union and Confederate Armies, 1861–1865*, 217.

115. "The Rev. Henry S. Clubb," *Vegetarian Messenger*, January 1896, 9; Henry S. Clubb to Anne Clubb, October 5, 1862, HSCP, box 1, folder 17.

116. Maintenance Committee, Bible Christian Church, *History of the Philadelphia Bible Christian Church*, 89.

117. "American Institute of Phrenology," *Phrenological Journal and Science of Health* 119, no. 1 (January 1906): 33; "A Vegetarian from Childhood: Rugged and Youthful at Eighty-Two," *PC* 23, no. 1 (January 1910): 108.

118. Henry S. Clubb to Anne Clubb, August 31, 1862, HSCP, box 1, folder 17.

119. Ibid.

120. Henry S. Clubb to Anne Clubb, September 13, 1862, HSCP, box 1, folder 17.

121. Clubb's letter made the parallel explicit: "The news reached me just as I was coming from witnessing the death scene of a Rebel that same day this celebrated battle

was fought, one of the most singular engagements of the war, and I want to name the boy after that place, Iuka. It was the first battle I witnessed and I think it is fitting that the first son have that name." The son was named Henry Iuka Clubb. Henry S. Clubb to Anne Clubb, September 21, 1862, box 1, folder 17.

122. Henry S. Clubb to Anne Clubb, September 30, 1862, HSCP box 1, folder 17.

123. Henry S. Clubb to Anne Clubb, August 24, 1863, HSCP box 1, folder 17. Writing to Anne from Vicksburg, Clubb explained that he was "too honest a man to be in the Quartermaster department" and that "none but a rogue will be assistant in this department."

124. W. A. A., "Prospects of Vegetarianism," WCJ 4, no. 81 (October 1856): 81.

125. For examples, see George W. Nichols, "Importance of Diet," WCJ 23, No. 3 (March 1857): 56; Emily M. Guthrie, "Vegetarian Life," WCJ 23, no. 5 (May 1857): 115; and Juliet H. Stillman, "Hints to Reformers," in WCJ 26, no. 6 (December 1858): 96.

126. "Obituary," New York Times, April 1, 1859, 4.

127. "Miscellaneous Items," Chicago Press and Tribune, September 27, 1859, 2.

128. Ibid.; "Annual Convention of the American Vegetarian Society," New York Times, September 25, 1861, 8; Maintenance Committee, Bible Christian Church, History of the Bible Christian Church, 176.

CHAPTER FOUR

1. Gunn, The Physiology of New York Boarding-Houses, 181–85.

2. Ibid., 181–83.

3. Ibid., 190–91.

4. On the anti-Fremont campaign conducted by slavery defenders, Know Nothings, and states' rights advocates, see McPherson, Battle Cry of Freedom, 155–57.

5. Currier and Maurer, The Great Republican Reform Party. For a digital version of the print, see http://digitalgallery.nypl.org/nypldigital/dgkeysearchdetail.cfm?trg=1&strucID=549585.

6. Foner, Free Soil, Free Labor, Free Men, 149, 309.

7. "The Vegetarians," Saturday Evening Post 24, no. 1510 (July 6, 1850): 2.

8. "The Great Bran Bread Festival," New York Herald, September 5, 1853, 1.

9. "Confessions of a Vegetarian," Savannah Daily Morning News 160, July 16, 1852, col. A; Ohio Observer 33, August 18, 1852, col. D, 130.

10. "Vegetarian Convention," Daily National Intelligencer, September 8, 1854, col. F.

11. Taylor, A Journey to Central Africa, 262. Taylor's report was reprinted in the popular press, see "The Food of Man," Scientific American 7, no. 39 (June 12, 1852): 306. It is interesting to note that in the latter, Taylor's quote reads, "That lank Sylvester Graham to explain." This is perhaps reflective of the still nascent status of the term vegetarian, newspaper editors believed their readers would recognize Graham's name more easily. On the popular image of the contented slave, see Fredrickson, The Black Image in the White Mind, 52.

12. "An Anti-vegetarian Virgin," Lowell Daily Citizen and News, January 9, 1857.

13. Melville, Piazza Tales and Other Prose Pieces, 34.

14. "Oh! Wasn't She Fond of Her Greens!"

15. Cohen, Gilfoyle, and Horowitz, *The Flash Press*, 55–72.

16. Ibid., 11.

17. "The Vegetarians," *Spirit of the Times* 18, no. 36 (October 28, 1848): 422.

18. "Littleness of the Great," *Spirit of the Times* 25, no. 31 (September 15, 1855): 364.

19. Edward J. Lanoe, "On Animal Physiology," *Spirit of the Times* 23, no. 38 (November 5, 1853): 453.

20. "Items: Cozzening," *Spirit of the Times* 20, no. 16 (June 8, 1850): 183.

21. "A New Song for Grahamites," *Spirit of the Times* 20, no, 14 (May 25, 1850): 158.

22. "A Good Horse Story," *Spirit of the Times* 18, no. 13 (May 20, 1848): 148.

23. "The Art of Dining and Giving Dinners," *Spirit of the Times* 6, no. 8 (April 9, 1836): 57.

24. "Punch and the Vegetarians," *Spirit of the Times* 21, no. 8 (April 12, 1851): 86.

25. "Fourth of July: Magnificently and Uniquely Celebrated by the People," *Spirit of the Times* 20, no. 22 (July 20, 1850): 257.

26. Julia Befeeter, "The Vegetarians," *Vanity Fair*, October 6, 1860, 172.

27. T. L. Nichols, "Letter from Dr. Nichols," *AVHJ* 1 (August 1851): 136.

28. "A Word with the 'A. V. S.,'" *Medical and Surgical Reporter* 4 (1860): 546.

29. "The Vegetarians" (*Saturday Evening Post*).

30. For examples of such illustrations, see Befeeter, "The Vegetarians"; and Gunn, *The Physiology of New York Boarding-Houses*, 180–81.

31. "A Vegetable Diet," *Scientific American* 5, no. 36 (May 25, 1850): 285.

32. "Case of an Opium-Eater and Vegetarian Becoming Bedridden," *Boston Medical and Surgical Journal* 49 (August 31, 1853): 108.

33. "Miscellaneous Memoranda," *Medical World: A Journal of Universal Medical Intelligence* 2 (1857): 446.

34. "Arctic Appetite," *Medical World: A Journal of Universal Medical Intelligence* 2 (1857): 535.

35. "American Vegetarian Society," *Boston Medical and Surgical Journal* 43 (October 23, 1851): 246.

36. On perceptions of spermatorrhea in the nineteenth century, see Darby, "Pathologizing Male Sexuality"; and Haller, "Bachelor's Disease." For the journal article with the observation regarding spermatorrhea and vegetarianism, see "Nature and Treatment of Spermatorrhea," *Southern Medical and Surgical Journal* 10, no. 9 (September 1854): 537.

37. "Nature and Treatment of Spermatorrhea," 537.

38. "Prevention of Disease," *Treasury of Medicine*, 1854, 59–60.

39. "Selected Papers," *Nashville Monthly Record of Medical and Physical Science* 1, no. 9 (May 1859): 550–51.

40. "Clinical Reports," *Eclectic Medical Journal* 1, no. 4 (April 1860): 240.

41. "Current Medical Literature," *Berkshire Medical Journal: Devoted to the Interests of Rational Medicine* 1, no. 10 (October 1861): 465.

42. Alan, *Medical Examinations for Life-Insurance*, 41; "Original Communications," *Medical Independent: A Monthly Review of Medicine and Surgery* 3, no. 4 (June 1857): 185.

43. "Correspondence," *Cincinnati Medical Observer* 1, no. 11 (November 1856): 505.

44. "Domestic Intelligence," *Medical News* 25, no. 289 (January 1867): 41.

45. "The American Vegetarian Society," *American Medical Journal* 1 (December 1856): 119.

46. See Dublin, "Women and Outwork in a Nineteenth-Century New England Town."

47. Beecher, *Miss Beecher's Domestic Receipt Book*, 30–31, 286.

48. Randolph, *The Virginia House-Wife*, iii–viii. The categories listed in the cookbook were soup, beef, veal, lamb, mutton, pork, fish, poultry, sauces, vegetables, pickling, cordials and dishes for lent.

49. "A Frenchman's Opinion," in *GJHL* (April 18, 1837): 22.

50. For a full account of the types of meats consumed in the United States, see Susan Williams, *Food in the United States*, 29–33; and Hooker, *Food and Drink in America*, 227.

51. Dickens, *American Notes for General Circulation*, 70, 167.

52. Volo and Volo, *The Antebellum Period*, 167–68.

53. Roger Horowitz, *Putting Meat on the American Table*, 1.

54. Ibid., 26–27.

55. Ibid., 46–47.

56. Less popular nicknames for Martin included the "Boston wherryman" and the "wherryberryman." This seems to illustrate the transcendence of the term *vegetarian* by 1860, as well as the importance of his lifestyle to Martin's experiment. For examples, see "Dietetic Reform," *Herald of Health and Water-Cure Journal* 1, no. 1 (January 1863): 18; and "The Wherryberryman off for Albany," *New York Times*, August 31, 1860, 8.

57. Martin is listed as a member in "Collections," *The Liberator* 27, no. 24 (June 12, 1857): 95; and "Collections," *The Liberator* 29, no. 23 (June 10, 1859): 91. The group included such important abolitionist leaders as Frederick Douglass, who served as president in 1847. See Franklin and Moss, *From Slavery to Freedom*, 196–200.

58. In the *Boston Directory of 1860*, Martin is listed as a currier living at a boardinghouse at 136 Pearl Street. Given the location of the home—near the docks where the Mystic and Charles Rivers meet, and with an outlet to Boston Harbor—it seems to imply that Martin was a professional boater. See *Boston Almanac for the Year 1860*, 264.

59. "The Vegetarian Wherryman," *The Liberator* 30, no. 36 (September 7, 1860): 144.

60. Ibid.

61. "Our New York Correspondence," *Charleston Mercury*, August 27, 1860, 1.

62. The whortleberry is a wild berry that is a close relative of both blueberries and huckleberries.

63. "The Wherryberryman off for Albany."

64. "The Vegetarian Wherryman" (*The Liberator*).

65. "The Wherryberryman off for Albany."

66. "A Remarkable Voyage," *Chicago Daily Tribune*, August 21, 1860, 3.

67. "Complimentary Supper to Martin, the Wherryman," *Boston Herald*, September 11, 1860, 2.

68. "The Vegetarian Wherryman" (*The Liberator*).

69. "The Vegetarian Wherryman," *Boston Herald*, August 31, 1860, 2; "Domestic Intelligence," *Harper's* (September 15, 1860): 582–83; "The Vegetarian Wherryman,"

New York Herald, September 6, 1860, 7. Even though the *New York Herald* often mocked vegetarians, and wrote dismissively about Martin, the paper also followed his exploits.

70. "Our New York Correspondence."

71. *Louisville Daily Journal*, March 13, 1861, 1.

72. "The Trials and Pleasures of Vegetarian Life," *Scioto Gazette* 4, March 19, 1861, col. F; *New Hampshire Statesman* 2079, April 6, 1861, col. E.

73. *Daily Evening Bulletin* 101, February 5, 1862, col. A; *Lowell (MA) Daily Citizen and News* 1752, January 15, 1862, col. E.

74. "Muscle-Mania," *American Phrenological Journal* 32, no. 6 (December 1860): 84.

75. Foote, *Plain Home Talk about the Human System*, 67; Foote, *Home Cyclopedia*, 66; Foote, *Dr. Foote's New Book on Health and Disease*, 66.

76. "A Shower Bath and Strait Jacket for Poor Greeley of the *Tribune*," *New York Herald*, February 17, 1863, 4.

77. Robert Williams, *Horace Greeley*, 29–54, 180–208.

78. Ibid., 66–70, 132–35.

79. Greeley's wife, Mary Cheney, remained a strict vegetarian for life and would not allow her husband to eat meat or drink coffee at home. However, Horace Greeley's vegetarianism was finite, ending after his dalliance with Grahamism. Greeley was a member of both the AVS and local New York Vegetarian Society and believed that "a strict vegetarian will live ten years longer than a habitual flesh-eater." However, despite his sympathy for the vegetarian cause, Greeley admitted that he ate meat, "when unspoiled by decay or bad cookery" believing it to be healthier than rotten fruits, hot bread or rancid vegetables. "Exciting Week in New York," 146; Greeley, *Recollections of a Busy Life*, 105.

80. McPherson, *Drawn with the Sword*, 133–34.

81. "Blood and Spoils—The Fruits of the *New York Tribune*," *New York Herald*, July 8, 1862, 4.

82. "The Corruption and Imbecility of the Party Press," *New York Herald*, June 27, 1864, 4.

83. Ibid.

84. "Greeley's One Subscriber in the Army," *New York Herald*, August 16, 1862, 4.

85. "Poor Greeley and the Recent Riots," *New York Herald*, August 3, 1863, 4; see also Bernstein, *The New York City Draft Riots*, 21–22.

CHAPTER FIVE

1. *Battle Creek Foods and Vegetarian Recipes*, 1–6.

2. Trachtenberg, *The Incorporation of America*, 20–31.

3. This notion is derived based on geographer Fred Kniffen's study of housing in the Midwest in the immediate postbellum era. Kniffen argues that the Northeast generated cultural ideas that spread into the Upper Midwest, while the Mid-Atlantic region served as the primary diffuser for new settlers into the Lower Midwest and upland South. See Kniffen, "Folk Housing," 560. This argument is further supported by reform publication subscription patterns that followed settlers into the Upper Midwest. See McCarley, "Orson S. Fowler and a Home for All."

4. *The Seventh Census of the United States*, 702, 756, 886; *Ninth Census*, 3.

5. *Battle Creek Centennial*, 40–42; Peirce, "The City of Battle Creek," 79–81.

6. Peirce, "The City of Battle Creek," 87–88.

7. Knight, *Millennial Fever and the End of the World*, 163–64.

8. Ellen White, *A Sketch of the Christian Experience*; Anderson, "Sectarianism and Organisation," 31.

9. Butler, "Prophecy, Gender, and Culture."

10. Quoted in Knight, *A Brief History of Seventh-Day Adventists*, 69.

11. Bull and Lockhart, *Seeking a Sanctuary*, 163–65.

12. Numbers, *Prophetess of Health*, 166.

13. Schwartz, *John Harvey Kellogg, M. D.*, 33–35.

14. Numbers, *Prophetess of Health*, 180–81.

15. Haller and Haller, *The Physician and Sexuality in Victorian America*.

16. Walters, *American Reformers*, 173.

17. James White, "Home Again," *Review and Herald* 49, May 24, 1877, 164.

18. John Harvey Kellogg, *The Battle Creek Sanitarium System*, 11.

19. The suffix -*arium* defines a location where something takes place, a more passive implication in line with the emphasis at "the San" on rest, relaxation, and fitness. Thus the term *sanitarium* was meant to invoke a place of health. In contrast, the suffix-*orium* refers to a place that performs an action, implying treatment over individual empowerment and responsibility.

20. John Harvey Kellogg, *The Battle Creek Sanitarium System*, 13.

21. Ibid., 15.

22. Vogel, *The Invention of the Modern Hospital*.

23. John Harvey Kellogg, "How to Live a Century," JHKP, Bentley Historical Library, University of Michigan, box 3, folder 4 (February 15, 1884): 1–2.

24. John Harvey Kellogg, "The Weather and Its Effects on Health," JHKP, box 3, folder 6 (November 12, 1891); John Harvey Kellogg, "How to Dress Hygienically," JHKP, box 3, folder 7 (January 14, 1892).

25. Ibid., 73.

26. John Harvey Kellogg, *The Battle Creek Sanitarium System*, 97–99.

27. John Harvey Kellogg, "How to Live a Century," 3–4, 9–10.

28. John Harvey Kellogg, "The Quality of Food," JHKP, box 3, folder 15 (July 26, 1897): 3.

29. John Harvey Kellogg, "The Natural Diet of Man," JHKP, box 3, folder 23 (April 16, 1900): 1–2.

30. John Harvey Kellogg, *Practical Manual of Health and Temperance*, 112.

31. Ibid., 36–37.

32. Leavitt, *From Catharine Beecher to Martha Stewart*, 15–18; Shapiro, *Perfection Salad*, 124–27, 135–37.

33. Levenstein, *Revolution at the Table*, esp. chaps. 5 and 6.

34. Hayden, *The Grand Domestic Revolution*, 151–62.

35. John Harvey Kellogg, *The Battle Creek Sanitarium System*, 13.

36. Smith, *Eating History*, 142.

37. John Harvey Kellogg, "The Natural Diet of Man," 1–2.

38. *Sanitas Nut Preparations and Specialties*, 2; "The Best Food for Strength," *Nut Cracker* 1, no. 1 (July 1900): 13.

39. "Nut Grows in Favor," *Chicago Daily Tribune*, July 20, 1899, 39.

40. "The Best Food for Strength," 7, 14.

41. "Sanitas Nut Butter," *Nut Cracker* 1, no. 1 (July 1900): 16.

42. Ibid. 14. For examples of the use of the term *nut meat* in nonvegetarian publications, see Farmer, *The Boston Cooking-School Cook Book*, 449; Frank Carpenter, *Foods and Their Uses*, 77; "The Food Value of Nuts," *Good Housekeeping* 37, no. 4 (October 1903): 360.

43. "Notes and Memoranda, Diet," JHKP, box 8, folder 5 (1896).

44. Ella Eaton Kellogg, *Every-Day Dishes and Every-Day Work*, 149.

45. John Harvey Kellogg, *The Battle Creek Sanitarium System*, 13.

46. Michigan Bureau of Labor and Industrial Statistics, *Annual Report of the Bureau of Labor and Industrial Statistics*, 63.

47. Friedman, *Birth of a Salesman*, 86–87.

48. Sanitarium food stores appear to have proliferated from coast to coast by 1908 and can be found in "Sanitariums" *Modern Medicine* 15, no. 1 (January 1906): 27; VM 11, no. 9 (February 1908): 32; "Health Foods": 104; *San Francisco-Oakland Directory*, 100, 434. The stores were not owned by Kellogg, but they were approved distributors of Battle Creek Sanitarium products.

49. See Lears, *Fables of Abundance*. Lears traces how advertisers shaped the urges of consumers, in a top-down model of hegemonic dominance. In contrast, Nan Enstad has illustrated how workingwomen utilized dime novels and fashion to build an identity of "working ladyhood." See Enstad, *Ladies of Labor, Girls of Adventure*.

50. "Healthful Living," Battle Creek, MI: Battle Creek Food Company, Battle Creek Food Company Papers, Bentley Library, University of Michigan, folder 1, 4.

51. *Sanitas Nut Preparations and Specialties*, 2, in SNFCA.

52. "A Physician's Opinion of Granose," *Modern Medicine and Bacteriological Review* 5 (March 1896): 73.

53. Koehn, *Brand New*, 98–99.

54. Shapiro, *Perfection Salad*, 182–83.

55. Cooper, *The New Cookery*, 307.

56. Herbert Lust, *United States Interstate Commerce Commission*, 154; Economic Research Service, U. S. Department of Agriculture, *Food Availability (per Capita) Data System*.

57. Herbert Lust, *United States Interstate Commerce Commission*, 154.

58. Roger Horowitz, *Putting Meat on the American Table*, 12.

59. Ibid.

60. "Vegetarian Meat Company," in *Boston City Directory*, 1910, 2792; *Washington D. C. City Directory*, 1911, 1426.

61. "Notes and Memoranda, Diet," JHKP, box 8, folder 5 (1906).

62. *Interstate Commerce Commission Reports: Decisions* 26, 612–13.

63. "Sanitas Nut Company," *Nut Cracker* 1, no. 1 (July 1900): 11, 18.

64. "Substitute for Beefsteak and Lean Meat in General," *Nut Cracker* 1, no. 4 (January 1901): 56.

65. *Literary Digest* 19, no. 15 (July 1, 1899): 26; "Advertisement 24," *Forum* 27 (August 1899): 10.

66. "Advertisement 36," *The Independent* 40, no. 2638 (June 29, 1899): 1720.

67. John Harvey Kellogg, *The Battle Creek Sanitarium System*, 28.

68. Leach, *Land of Desire*, xii.

69. In the cookbook, the kitchen is referred to as a "workshop," further illustrating its connections to rationalization. Ella Eaton Kellogg, *Science in the Kitchen*, 4–5. The emphasis on ordered efficiency reflected the rise of "scientific management," advocated most notably by business management consultant Frederick Winslow Taylor. On Taylorism, see Kanigel, *The One Best Way*; and Nelson, *Frederick W. Taylor and the Rise of Scientific Management*.

70. Ella Eaton Kellogg, *Every-Day Dishes and Every-Day Work*, 3.

71. Ibid., 140–43.

72. Of all the Kellogg meat substitutes, wheat gluten—often known as seitan—has remained most popular among vegetarians. Kellogg did not invent the dietary use of wheat gluten; it was long used in a variety of Asian cuisines. He was, however, the first to market it as a meat substitute in the United States, though in a granulated, dry form. For more on the modern use of seitan, see Nussinow, "Seitan."

73. Ella Eaton Kellogg, *Healthful Cookery*, 72–75, 84.

74. Fulton, *Substitutes for Flesh Foods*, 4, 9.

75. Ibid., 87–88.

76. For example, the cookbook claimed that a combination of milk, farina, tomatoes, eggs, Nuttolene, and eggplant would taste like salmon filets. Protose could be combined with Nuttolene, milk, potatoes, nuts, and eggs to make a mock chicken pie. Ibid., 67, 102.

77. Wachtmeister and Davis, *Practical Vegetarian Cookery*, vii, 160.

78. Latham Dwight studied under the famed California water colorist Christian Jorgensen, and her paintings focused on scenic California coastal life. McClelland and Last, *California Watercolors*; Roger Dunbier, *The Artists Bluebook*, http://www.askart.com/askart/artist.aspx?artist=124534.

79. Latham Dwight, *The Golden Age Cook-Book*, 5, 8–12, 45–46, 50.

80. Louise Lust, *The Practical Naturopathic-Vegetarian Cook Book*, 9, 13–14.

81. Haber, *From Hardtack to Home Fries*, 59.

82. Rorer, *Mrs. Rorer's Vegetable Cookery and Meat Substitutes*, i, iv, v.

83. Ibid., 18, 42–46, 66, 136.

84. For other examples, see Allen, *Mrs. Allen's Book of Meat Substitutes*; Christian, *250 Meatless Menus and Recipes*; and Sharpe, *The Golden Rule Cook Book*.

85. R. S. T., "The Solving of the Meat Problem," *Chicago Daily Tribune*, June 5, 1902, 7.

86. Leonard, *Woman's Who's Who of America*, 533.

87. Jane Eddington, "The World's Cooks," *Chicago Daily Tribune*, March 11, 1913, 13.

88. Jane Eddington, "Economical Housekeeping," *Chicago Daily Tribune*, August 20, 1910, 6.

89. Jane Eddington, "Vegetable Souffles," *Chicago Daily Tribune*, August 11, 1917, 10; "Beans Good Meat Substitute," *Chicago Daily Tribune*, November 13, 1917, 14; "Economical Housekeeping," *Chicago Daily Tribune*, July 27, 1911, 8; Jane Eddington, "The Tribune Cook Book," *Chicago Daily Tribune*, November 13, 1917, 14.

90. "If There Were a Meat Famine—What Then?," *San Francisco Call*, October 16, 1904, 23.

91. "Meat Forms No Part of These Washington Banquets," *Washington Times*, March 13, 1904, 3.

92. "Mock Meats for Vegetarians," *New York Tribune*, September 19, 1909, 18.

93. The full history of this organization will be explored in chapter 6.

94. The length of stay at the San varied depending on the illness being treated and the proscribed treatment plan. The price for a stay, therefore, was different for each patient, particularly depending on the treatment plan (those necessitating surgery, for example, paid more than those given a prescription of fresh air and rest). The San brought in $60,382 in accounts receivable in 1911. By dividing this number by the total number of residents, I arrived at the average cost of twelve dollars per person. *Annual Report of the Battle Creek Sanitarium and Hospital*, 31.

95. Aron, *Working at Play*, 148–50; Shaffer, *See America First*.

96. The San's annual report broke residents up into age groups of five-year intervals.

97. *Annual Report of the Battle Creek Sanitarium and Hospital*, 61.

98. Zunz, *Making America Corporate*.

99. *Annual Report of the Battle Creek Sanitarium and Hospital*, 62.

100. Ibid. The average stay at the San in 1911 was thirty-one days for men and forty-one days for women.

101. See "Directory," *Modern Medicine* 13, no. 1 (January 1904): 24.

102. "International Vegetarian Congress 1904," *Vegetarian Messenger* (February 1905).

103. See, for example, "Progress of the Movement," VM 11, no. 2 (July 1907): 19.

104. "Vegetarians at a Reception," *Chicago Daily Tribune*, June 8, 1893, 3; *Hygienic Review* 2 (October 1893).

105. Engs, *Clean Living Movements*, 5–7.

106. John Harvey Kellogg, *Are We a Dying Race?*, 1–6.

107. Schwartz, *John Harvey Kellogg, M. D.*, 208–11.

108. The connection went further; starting as early as November 1907, the *American Journal of Eugenics*, the "only publication in the English language devoted to the important subject of race culture," began advertising in VM, the national publication of the Vegetarian Society of America. See "The American Journal of Eugenics," VM 11, no. 7 (November 1907): 26.

109. Race Betterment Foundation, *Proceedings of the First National Conference on Race Betterment*, 431, 537.

110. Stern, *Eugenic Nation*, 53–54.

111. Jefferis and Nichols, *Search Lights on Health*, 459; Jefferis and Nichols, *Safe Counsel*, 459.

112. For example, "Vegetarian Magazine," *American Journal of Eugenics* 2, no. 1 (January 1908), 54. The advertisement continued running in the journal throughout its third volume in 1909.

113. John Harvey Kellogg, "We Are a Dying Race," *Medical Missionary* 19, no. 10 (November 1910): 315–19.

114. Hodges, "Dealing with Degeneracy," 185.

115. Ibid., 141.

CHAPTER SIX

1. Clubb, *Journal of the Constitutional Commission of Michigan*, 8.

2. Clubb left Michigan in the summer of 1876, the same year that John Harvey Kellogg took over as the superintendent of the Battle Creek Sanitarium, and before the San's significant expansion.

3. HSCP, box 2, folder 8. The folder includes a photo of Clubb standing in front of the First Holland Dutch Reform Church.

4. Clubb corresponded with a variety of therapeutic colleges and religious training schools during this time. See "Michigan Seminary to Henry S. Clubb," HSCP, box 1, folder 14; "J. H. Kellogg to Henry S. Clubb," January 24, 1877, HSCP, box 1, folder 14; Uriah Smith to Henry S. Clubb, 29 January 1877, HSCP, box 1, folder 14; "S. A. Reynolds to Henry S. Clubb," HSCP, box 1, folder 14.

5. "Church of Vegetarians," *New York Times*, October 13, 1895, 25.

6. Maintenance Committee, Bible Christian Church, *History of the Philadelphia Bible Christian Church*, 82.

7. "The Founding of the Vegetarian Society of America," *Dietetic Reformer and Vegetarian Messenger* (September 1886): 279–81; Maintenance Committee, Bible Christian Church, *History of the Philadelphia Bible Christian Church*, 176–78, 189.

8. *Vegetarian Messenger*, April 1889, 105.

9. Barrett, *Work and Community in the Jungle*, 18–19.

10. Sandburg, "Chicago," 3.

11. Sinclair, *The Jungle*, 335.

12. Quoted in Wade, *Chicago's Pride*, 133.

13. "A Vegetarian Banquet," *Everyday Housekeeping: A Magazine for Practical Housekeepers and Mothers* 1, no. 2 (May 1894): 88.

14. Le Favre, *Mother's Help and Child's Friend*, 5–6.

15. Ibid., 108, 112–13, 116, 123, 127.

16. "The Chicago Vegetarian Society," *Vegetarian Messenger* (January 1890): 4.

17. Through 1890, the publication did not even indicate the number of subscribers. See *N. W. Ayer & Son's American Newspaper Annual* (1890): 632.

18. "Why a Vegetarian?," *Phrenological Journal and Science of Health* 638, no. 2 (February 1892): 2.

19. The most succinct summary of Kellogg's thoughts on diarrhea can be found in John Harvey Kellogg, *The Stomach*, 185–88.

20. Sandoval-Strausz, *Hotel*, 161. A. K. Sandoval-Strausz points out that the Grand Pacific, despite being considered an iconic representation of Gilded Age architecture, was actually far more austere than most other hotels of the 1870s and 1880s.

21. "Chicago, U. S. A.," *Vegetarian Messenger*, January 1890, 23. See "Items," *Chicago Clinic* 11, no. 5 (May 1898): 122; and "A Necklace of Black Diamonds," *Jewelers' Circular and Horological Review* 37, no. 14 (November 2, 1898): 49; "Do Not Hurt," *FHG* 1, no. 1 (May 1896): 13. The group also included four Chicago medical doctors.

22. "Chicago, U. S. A.," *Vegetarian Messenger*, November 1891, 316.

23. "Home Department," FHG 3, no. 27 (April 1899): 59–61; "Home Department," FHG 4, no. 36 (1900): 12.

24. "A Letter from a Chicago Vegetarian," *Vegetarian Messenger*, March 1891, 96.

25. "The New York Vegetarian Society," *Phrenological Journal and Science of Health* 92, no. 6 (June 1892): 275.

26. Wiebe, *The Search for Order*.

27. "People Who Eat No Flesh," *Chicago Daily Tribune*, February 17, 1892, 1; "The Vegetarian Delegates to the Fair," *Hygienic Review* 2 (1893): 218; National Archives and Records Administration, *Images of Handwritten Letters and Application Forms for US Passports, 1795–1905*, vol. 768, roll M1372.

28. "Lived on Five Cents' Worth of Figs," *Chicago Daily Tribune*, February 7, 1892, 1.

29. "Announcements," *Daily Inter Ocean* 334 (February 21, 1892): col. C, 6; "Vegetarians at Work," *Daily Inter Ocean* 337 (February 24, 1892): col. C, 5.

30. "City News in Brief," *Morning Oregonian*, August 5, 1892, 5; "City News in Brief," *Morning Oregonian*, August 19, 1892, 5.

31. Muccigrosso, *Celebrating the New World*, 12–16.

32. "The American Vegetarian Society at the World's Fair," *Vegetarian Messenger*, July 1890, 194.

33. "The Vegetarian Federal Union," *Hygienic Review* 2 (1893): 432.

34. "Echoes of the Chicago Exhibition," *Vegetarian Messenger*, February 1894, 57–61.

35. "The International Vegetarian Congress," *The Vegetarian*, July 1, 1893; "The Fair Must Close," *Bismarck (ND) Daily Tribune*, June 10, 1893.

36. *The General Programme of the World's Congresses of 1893*.

37. "The Proceedings of the Congress of the Vegetarian Federal Union at Chicago, 1893," *Hygienic Review* 2 (1893): 237–38.

38. Ibid., 238–39.

39. "The Fair Must Close," *Bismarck (ND) Daily Tribune*, June 10, 1893.

40. M. L. Holbrook, "Vegetarianism and Agriculture," *Hygienic Review* 2 (1893): 258.

41. Rachel Swain, "The Evolution of Vegetarianism," *Hygienic Review* 2 (1893): 275–77.

42. Prevailing anthropological perspectives of the period divided humanity into three main racial categories: Caucasoid, Negroid, and Mongoloid. See Jacobson, *Whiteness of a Different Color*, 91, 109.

43. Gail Bederman illustrates how different groups, including middle-class white males, white women, and African Americans, defined notions of civilization to legitimize a variety of political positions ranging from white supremacy to opposition to racism. Vegetarians practiced a similar method in their definition of civilization as setting apart vegetarians and nonvegetarians. See Bederman, *Manliness and Civilization*.

44. Examples of works that have described the racist images and practices of the fair include Rydell, "The Chicago World's Columbian Exposition of 1893"; Baker, *From Savage to Negro*; and Hund, "Negative Societalisation," 72–74.

45. "Vegetarians at a Reception," *Chicago Daily Tribune*, June 8, 1893, 3.

46. "For the Vegetarian Congress," *Chicago Daily Tribune*, May 29, 1893, 9.

47. "Want Diet of Fruits and Plants," *Chicago Daily Tribune*, June 10, 1893, 3.

48. "Vegetarianism as Vital Food," *Hygienic Review* 2 (1893): 245.

49. Louis Paroli, "Rational Selection of Food," *Hygienic Review* 2 (1893): 335.

50. "Want Diet of Fruits and Plants."

51. Charles W. Forward, "Food of the Future," *Hygienic Review* 2 (1893): 355, 359.

52. For more on the "White City" and the social meanings of its elaborate display of electricity, see Platt, *The Electric City*, 62; and Nye, *Electrifying America*, 34–41.

53. W. P. Alcott, "Vegetarianism and Progress," *Hygienic Review* 2 (1893): 346–50.

54. Mrs. Rice, "The Aesthetics of Vegetarianism," *Hygienic Review* 2 (1893): 265–68.

55. Carrica Le Favre, "Health and Beauty," *Hygienic Review* 2 (1893): 480–83.

56. For the resolutions, see "The International Vegetarian Congress," *The Vegetarian*, July 1, 1893; and "Their Work Is Felt: Champions for Temperance Show Strength," *Daily Inter Ocean* 78 (June 10, 1893): col. D.

57. Higinbotham, *Report of the President to the Board of Directors of the World's Columbian Exposition*, 329; Bancroft, *The Book of the Fair*, 955.

58. Finn, *Official Guide to the World's Columbian Exposition*, 34.

59. Handy, *The Official Directory of the World's Columbian Exposition*, 412.

60. "The Vegetarian Annexe at the World's Fair," *The Vegetarian*, September 23, 1893. *The Vegetarian* was the official journal of the Vegetarian Federal Union. See also Forward, *Fifty Years of Food Reform*, 140–49.

61. Ibid.

62. Ibid. The push to adopt Indian corn as the national symbol of the United States was led by interior design pioneer Candace Wheeler, who designed the interior of the Women's Building at the Columbian Exposition. See Blanchard, *Oscar Wilde's America*, 58–60. Wheeler published a tract in defense of Indian corn as a symbol in 1893, arguing that "no other plant is typical of our greatness and prosperity as a nation." Wheeler, *Columbia's Emblem, Indian Corn*, iii.

63. "Methods of Charity," *Chicago Daily Tribune*, June 10, 1893, 3.

64. "Vegetarians Hold a Congress," *Chicago Daily Tribune*, June 4, 1893, 11.

65. "Chicago Congress Number," *Hygienic Review* 2 (1893): 164.

66. "International Vegetarian Congress, Chicago, June, 1893," *Vegetarian Messenger* 4, no. 7 (1893): 286.

67. Ibid.

68. Bates, *American Journalism from the Practical Side*, 113.

69. Francis G. Kemp, "Letter to the Editor: A Vegetarian Reception for Dr. Clubb," *Daily Inter Ocean* 154 (August 27, 1893); N. W. Ayer & Son's *American Newspaper Annual* (1893): 676.

70. Mrs. Rice, "The Aesthetics of Vegetarianism," *Hygienic Review* 2 (1893): 265–68.

71. On civilized manhood and the fears of the feminization of industrialization, see Bederman, *Manliness and Civilization*, esp. chap. 5; and Kasson, introduction to *Houdini, Tarzan, and the Perfect Man*.

72. This includes *Food, Home and Garden*, published from 1889 to 1899 and its eventual successor VM. The sole mention occurred in "Cheap Meals for Workmen," VM 4, no. 7 (April 1900): 8.

73. Trachtenberg, *The Incorporation of America*, 54–55.

74. Guy, *From Diversity to Unity*, 31–32.

75. "The Branch Societies," FHG 1, no. 5 (March 1897): 75. The 5800 block of Jackson Avenue is now known as Argyle Avenue.

76. "Vegetarian Boarding in Chicago," *Vegetarian Messenger* 4, no. 7 (1893): 270.

77. "Its Vegetarian Club on the Boom," *Chicago Daily Tribune*, April 11, 1894; "Four Apple Blossoms," *FHG* 1, no. 10 (August 1897): 158.

78. "Will Not Eat Meat," *Chicago Daily Tribune*, March 5, 1894, 11.

79. *N. W. Ayer & Son's American Newspaper Annual* (1900): 1032.

80. "They Eat No Meat: Chicago Is to Have in the Near Future a Vegetarian Restaurant," *Morning Oregonian* 11, no. 132 (June 8, 1895): 3.

81. "Vegetarian Society Meets," *Chicago Daily Tribune*, October 2, 1895, 3. It is difficult to ascertain how the *Tribune* came up with this number, and even more difficult to verify its accuracy. It is, however, important to note that vegetarianism was gaining enough attention to have its numbers estimated.

82. Flanagan, "Gender and Urban Political Reform."

83. *The American Catalog*, 1129.

84. For more on the construction of the hotel, see Condit, *The Chicago School of Architecture*, 101–3.

85. For a discussion of Blakely, see Paulsson, *The Social Anxieties of Progressive Reform*, 62–66.

86. For more on the NCF, its conservatism, and its connections with Theodore Roosevelt and reform, see Kolko, *Triumph of Conservatism*, 66, 77.

87. "No Meats in the Menu," *Chicago Daily Tribune*, December 29, 1895, 3.

88. "Apostle of Vegetarianism Arrives," *Chicago Daily Tribune*, August 28, 1895, 7.

89. "Cut Meat and Fish Dead," *Chicago Daily Tribune*, June 20, 1896, 5. The group held a picnic outside the home of a member of the society in Evanston that was attended by more than 100 people.

90. "Chicago Enthusiasm," *FHG* 1, no. 8 (June 1897): 117.

91. For the first mention of the mill, see *FHG* 1, no. 4 (February 1897): 54.

92. "Vegetarian Society Mill," *FHG* 1, no. 8 (June 1897): 129.

93. "Vegetarian Society Mill," *FHG* 1, no. 12 (October 1897): 176.

94. "New and Improved Vegetarian Society Mill," *FHG* 2, no. 14 (February 1898): 33.

95. "Butchering Day Never Comes," *FHG* 2, no. 15 (March 1898): 38.

96. "New and Improved Society Mill," *FHG* 2, no. 15 (March 1898): 49.

97. Ibid.

98. "Advertising in *Food, Home and Garden*," *FHG* 2, no. 22 (November 1898): 149.

99. *FHG* 2, no. 23 (December 1898): 182–84.

100. *FHG* 1, no. 4 (February 1897): 54.

101. VM previously was the name of a newsletter published by the Chicago VSA. *Food, Home and Garden*'s merger with VM further illustrates Chicago's status as a vegetarian hotbed. For a copy of a letter written by Henry S. Clubb explaining the merger, see Maintenance Committee, Bible Christian Church, *History of the Philadelphia Bible Christian Church*, 179.

102. TVOFC 5, no. 1 (October 15, 1900): 24, 28, 32.

103. *N. W. Ayer & Son's American Newspaper Annual* (1900): 1032.

104. *N. W. Ayer & Son's American Newspaper Annual* (1911): 15, 333; *N. W. Ayer & Son's American Newspaper Annual* (1913): 184. The precise subscription numbers were 15,333 in 1901 and 15,954 in 1911.

105. Ovid, *Metamorphoses*, 505.

106. "Vegetarians in Their Restaurant," *New York Times*, February 6, 1895, 3; "No Flesh, Fish or Fowl but Plenty of Cauliflower, French Peas, Watercresses and Pickles in New York's Vegetarian Restaurant," *North American*, February 15, 1895, 2.

107. This was about three blocks away from the Art Institute, which hosted the vegetarian meeting at the Columbian Exposition. "A New Pure Food Lunch Room," VM 4, no. 12 (September 1900): 17.

108. "Meatless Dishes," TVOFC 6, no. 3 (December 15, 1901): 63.

109. Condit, *The Chicago School of Architecture*, 40.

110. VM 14, no. 2 (October 1910): 69–71, 73; *Lakeside Classified Directory*, 1911, 1761.

111. *City Directory for Chicago*, 1897, 1462; *City Directory for Chicago*, 1905, 1087.

112. *Annual Report of the Factory Inspectors of Illinois* 13 (1906): 838.

113. "Alonzo H. Mortimer," Year: 1910; Census Place: Chicago Ward 7, Cook, Illinois; roll T624_247; page: 16A; enumeration district: 391; image: 472. Quick Reply, "A Rotary Roster Fifteen Years Ago," *Rotarian* 16, no. 2 (February 1920): 65; "New Move by Athletic Club," *Chicago Daily Tribune*, January 31, 1909, 6. Mortimer was involved in establishing a State Pure Food Association in Illinois in 1900. See "Few Pure Food Men Turn Out," *Chicago Daily Tribune*, June 2, 1900, 16.

114. Leonard and Marquis, *The Book of Chicagoans*, 2:131.

115. VM 13, no. 12 (August 1913): 65.

116. William A. Huckins, "The Real 'Staff of Life,'" in *Tomorrow Magazine*, April 1907, 57.

117. "The Sanitarium Pure Food Store and Bakery of Benold's Unfermented Whole Bread," in Lane, *Diagnosis from the Eye*, 164; VM 11, no. 7 (November 1907): 1.

118. VM 14, no. 3 (November 1910): 70. Berhalter's was still in business in 1930, receiving a patent for its invention of "Figrain," a coffee substitute. *Index of Trademarks Issued from the United States Patent Office*, 239.

119. Fulton, *Substitutes for Flesh Foods*, 251–52.

120. Sharpe, *The Golden Rule Cook Book*, 11–12.

121. Ibid., 14–25. For more on the proliferation of animal welfare advocacy in the post–Civil War era, see Pearson, *The Rights of the Defenseless*.

122. Sharpe, *Selections from Three Essays by Richard Wagner*, 29.

123. For the nut croquette recipes, see Sharpe, *The Golden Rule Cookbook*, 201–2. For the unflattering description of mock meats, see ibid., 12.

124. See, for example, VM 14, no. 3 (November 1910): 108.

125. Edward Clement, "An Appreciation of a Humanitarian Cook-Book," VM 11, no. 10 (August 1908): 17–18.

126. See the back cover of VM 14, no. 3 (November 1910).

127. "Vegetarian Temple for Boston," *Boston American* 1, February 1, 1914. Quoted in Iacobbo and Iacobbo, *Vegetarian America*, 147.

128. By "subhuman," the guild meant all other members of the animal kingdom.

129. "The Millennium Guild," in *The World Almanac and Book of Facts*, 1915, 290.

130. "Bar Products of Death: These Women Wear Cloth Gloves and Shoes and Eat No Meat," *New York Times*, June 2, 1913, 1.

131. "Men and Women," *Indianapolis Star*, June 17, 1912, 6.

132. "Topics of the Day," *Mansfield (OH) News*, November 22, 1912, 8.

133. "Terrier Is a Vegetarian," *Boynton (OK) Index*, January 29, 1915, 3.

134. Sharpe, *The Golden Rule Cook Book*, 303.

135. "Thanksgiving at the Sanitarium," *Battle Creek (MI) Idea* 5, no. 38 (December 5, 1912): 5.

136. "Wearing of Furs Barred by Guild," *Galveston (TX) Daily News*, March 2, 1913, 31.

137. "Millennium Guild Meeting," *Boston Daily Globe*, October 28, 1915, 18. Garrison's grandson himself was a prominent reformer involved in the women's suffrage movement.

138. The organization remained active in the animal rights movement in the United States into the 1980s. For more on the later development of the Millennium Guild, see Iacobbo and Iacobbo, *Vegetarian America*, 161–63, 170; and Singer, *Ethics into Action*, 61, 95.

139. Carol Adams, *The Sexual Politics of Meat*, 223–26.

140. "The Suffrage Question," VM 13, no. 3 (November 1909), 17.

141. See, for example, "Thanksgiving—1907," VM 11, no. 7 (November 1907): 3.

142. "Congratulations Mrs. Hayward," VM 10, no. 12 (April 1907): 16–17.

143. Clubb, *Thirty-Nine Reasons Why I Am a Vegetarian*.

144. "Become a Vegetarian," *Phrenological Journal and Science of Health* 124, no. 1 (January 1911): 42.

145. "Berhalter's Health Food Store and Bakery," TVOFC 14, no. 2 (October 1910): 90.

146. TVOFC 14, no. 2 (October 1910): 25.

147. A partial list of vegetarian restaurants in the United States in 1910 is available at "Vegetarian Restaurants and Homes," TVOFC 14, no. 2 (October 1910): 37; for more health food stores, see TVOFC 14, no. 3 (November 1910): 66, 68. The issue also reported on the opening of the first Jewish vegetarian restaurant, at 168 Henry Street on the Lower East Side of Manhattan. See TVOFC 14, no. 3 (November 1910): 99. Vegetarian restaurants in New York City will be considered in greater detail in chapter 7.

CHAPTER SEVEN

1. Forward, *Fifty Years of Food Reform*, 152. While Forward's subtitle suggests a focus on England, his book offers a fairly comprehensive history of vegetarianism throughout the United States and Europe.

2. "Our Aims," VM 4, no. 5 (February 1900): 13.

3. See, for example, "College of Physical Sciences," FHG 4, no. 36 (January 1900), 17.

4. See Bederman, *Manliness and Civilization*, esp. chap. 5; and Kasson, introduction to *Houdini, Tarzan, and the Perfect Man*.

5. Elliott Gorn, *The Manly Art*, 240–45; Isenberg, *John L. Sullivan and His America*, 300–312. For speeches at the congress emphasizing this theme, see Louis Paroli, "Rational Selection of Food," *Hygienic Review* 2 (1893): 335; Charles W. Forward, "Food of the Future," *Hygienic Review* 2 (1893): 355–59; and W. P. Alcott, "Vegetarianism and Progress," *Hygienic Review* 2 (1893): 346–50.

6. Kasson, *Houdini, Tarzan and the Perfect Man*, 81.

7. Ibid., 52–54; Chapman, *Sandow the Magnificent*, 60–64.

8. Porter, *Health, Civilization, and the State*, 303–5; Dyreson, "Regulating the Body and the Body Politic"; Schneirov, *The Dream of a New Social Order*, 137–39.

9. Barney, "Forty-Eighters and the Rise of the Turnervein Movement in America," 19–32; Riess, *City Games*, 23, 96–99.

10. Patients would place their arm on the scab of a smallpox patient's arm. The method was not only ineffective in preventing smallpox but also helped transfer other diseases to the recipient. Hopkins, *The Greatest Killer*, 85–88.

11. On McFadden's early life, see Ernst, *Weakness Is a Crime*, 1–16, Mark Adams, *Mr. America*, 74–76; and Hunt, *Body Love*, 1–17.

12. Wood, *Bernarr Macfadden*, 63, 66–70. The biography needs to be approached with a critical eye as Macfadden commissioned it. At times it reads as hagiography. Peeling through the romanticized language, however, it does offer a detailed summary of Macfadden's wrestling years.

13. Ibid., 17.

14. Ibid., 17–20; Adams, *Mr. America*, 36–38.

15. Ernst, *Weakness Is a Crime*, 18; Adams, *Mr. America*, 36–38.

16. On Sandow's exploits in England, see Kasson, *Houdini, Tarzan, and the Perfect Man*, 35–39; on Macfadden's tour of Great Britain, see Ernst, *Weakness Is a Crime*, 19–20, 38–40.

17. Bernarr Macfadden, "Weakness Is a Crime," *PC* 1, no. 1 (March 1899): 3.

18. The phrase is taken from Kasson, *Houdini, Tarzan, and the Perfect Man*, 30–31, and was originally applied to Sandow.

19. On Roosevelt's reinvention, see ibid., 31; and Bederman, *Manliness and Civilization*, 170–84.

20. George Ruskin Phoebus, "Theodore Roosevelt, Rough Rider and Athlete," *PC* 2, no. 2 (November 1899): 123; "Governor Roosevelt as a Wrestler," *PC* 3, no. 1 (April 1900): 36.

21. Bernarr Macfadden, "The Development of Energy, Vitality and Health," *PC* 1, no. 1 (March 1899): 7–8.

22. For the number of subscribers, see *PC* 2, no. 2 (November 1899): 241.

23. Macfadden, *Strength from Eating*, 7.

24. Ibid., ii.

25. Macfadden, *Strength from Eating*, 73–74.

26. Ibid., 76.

27. Ibid., 79.

28. Ibid., 80.

29. Bernarr Macfadden, "No Meat Diet," *PC* 2, no. 2 (November 1899): 189.

30. J. R. Blake, "The Food We Eat," *PC* 4, no. 2 (November 1900): 73–74.

31. John R. Stevenson, "Meat-Eating Folly," *PC* 4, no. 4 (January 1900): 173–74.

32. Macfadden, *Physical Culture Cookbook*, 3.

33. Ibid., 30–32.

34. Ibid., 47.

35. *PC*, October 1908, 7.

36. Lane, *Diagnosis from the Eye*, 160; "Vegetarian Restaurants and Homes," *VM* 14, no. 2 (October 1910): 37.

37. Lefèvre, A Scientific Investigation into Vegetarianism, 19.

38. PC, October 1908, 7.

39. Bernarr Macfadden, "The Editor's One-Cent-Meal Restaurant," PC 7, no. 1 (April 1902): 26.

40. "The One-Cent Meal Restaurant," PC 7, no. 2 (May 1902): 102.

41. Ibid., 102–4.

42. New York Times, February 15, 1910, 10; New York Times, February 17, 1910, 7; New York Times, August 26, 1910, 15.

43. "One-Cent Restaurant Making Money," PC 7, no. 6 (September 1902): 347.

44. Amelia M. Calkins, "Uncooked Foods," PC 11, no. 2 (February 1904): 131.

45. Albert Broadbent, "Fifty Valuable Meatless Recipes," PC 23, no. 3 (March 1910): 364.

46. "Vegetarian Physical Culturists," PC 11, no. 1 (January 1904): 25.

47. Grace H. Potter, "An Athlete at 106 Years of Age," PC 7, no. 6 (September 1902): 350–52.

48. W. E. Meehan, "Food and Drink of an Arctic Explorer," PC 9, no. 1 (January 1903): 13–14.

49. "The Virtues of Our Methods Proven," PC 22, no. 1 (July 1909): 84.

50. Otto Carque, "Meat Eaters vs. Vegetarians," PC 7, no. 6 (September 1902): 330–31.

51. Bernarr Macfadden, "Vegetarian Athletes," PC 7, no. 4 (July 1902): 228.

52. Bernarr Macfadden, "How the Meat Trust Was Scared," PC 8, no. 2 (November 1902): 121–22.

53. Henry G. Hedden, "A Vegetarian from Childhood," PC 23, no. 1 (January 1910): 107–8.

54. Guy Walter Sarvis, "Vegetarianism in Central Africa," PC 23, no. 2 (February 1910): 169.

55. George Howard Jackson, "The 'Cleverness' of Dr. Woods Hutchinson," PC 22, no. 3 (September 1909): 220–22.

56. Saxon had a famous encounter with Sandow in England in 1897 that ended in a somewhat disputed result. Saxon began billing himself as "The Man That Defeated Sandow," which led Sandow to file (and win) a lawsuit against Saxon for libel. See Chapman, Sandow the Magnificent, 105–8.

57. "Arthur Saxon Challenged to a Weight-Lifting Contest," PC 22, no. 1 (July 1909): 93–94; PC 22, no. 3 (October 1909): 340.

58. John R. Coryell, "Fred Welsh and How He Trains," PC 23, no. 5 (May 1910): 456–57.

59. "A Celebrated Society Athlete," PC 23, no. 3 (March 1910): 282.

60. "Young Boxer Gains Benefit from Our Literature," PC 23, no. 5 (May 1910): 430.

61. Sam Miller, "Tuning Up the Ball Players of the Big Leagues," PC 23, no. 5 (May 1910): 469.

62. "Marvelous Swimming Record," PC 9, no. 1 (January 1903): 21.

63. Ernst, Weakness Is a Crime, 75–77.

64. Eales, Healthology, 86.

65. Carrington, Vitality, Fasting and Nutrition, 382.

66. "Gilman Low's Great Feat," VM 11, no. 2 (June 1907): 3.

67. For more on Strongfort, see Caden-Corne, *Reconstructing the Body*, 166–67, 207–9. For a typical ad for Strongfort's mail-order system, see "When Your Stomach Goes on Strike," *Popular Science*, May 1920, 130.

68. "Physical Culture," in *The Americana Supplement*, 2:933.

69. "To Make Outdoor Sleeping Easy and Popular," *New York Times*, May 26, 1907, 4.

70. Fisher, "The Influence of Flesh Eating on Endurance." The study was also reprinted in pamphlet form. For the reference regarding the six-year-old vegetarian, see Fisher, *The Influence of Flesh Eating on Endurance*, 12.

71. Fisher, *The Influence of Flesh Eating on Endurance*, 6.

72. Ibid., 20.

73. "Vegetarians Win in Endurance Tests," VM 10, no. 12 (April 1907): 14–15.

74. "Vegetarianism Proves Again," VM 11, no. 1 (May 1907): 3–6.

75. Irving Fisher, "What the Recent Tests at Yale University Have Proven," VM 11, no. 1 (May 1907): 6–7.

76. "Vegetarians the Stronger," *New York Times*, March 22, 1907, 3.

77. "Dr. Chittenden on Vegetarianism," *New York Times*, November 13, 1908, 8.

78. Harry Brook, "Care of the Body—Suggestions for Preserving Health," *Los Angeles Times*, April 26, 1908, 29.

79. "Flesh Eaters Tested," *Health* 59, no. 6 (June 1909): 251.

80. "Vegetarianism versus Meat Diet," *Health* 57, no. 7 (July 1907): 423.

81. "Ought We Give Up Meat?," *The Independent* 62, no. 304 (March 28, 1907): 752.

82. VM 11, nos. 1–11 (May 1907–April 1908).

83. "Vegetarianism Proves Again."

84. "Vegetarian Congress at Paris: Athletics," VM 4, no. 12 (September 1900): 3.

85. "Girl Cyclist's Remarkable Endurance," TVOFC 10, no. 12 (July 1907): 5.

86. "Another Great Triumph for Vegetarianism," TVOFC 6, no. 9 (June 1902): 198–99.

87. "The Conversion of a Noted Pugilist," TVOFC 6, no. 7 (April 1902): 147.

88. "Vegetarian Diet Is Responsible, Says English Pug," TVOFC 11, no. 9 (June 1908): 24–25.

89. "What Must a Man Do to Be Strong?," TVOFC 6, no. 5 (February 1902): 99.

90. "Vegetarianism and Football," TVOFC 11, no. 6 (October 1907): 4; "Vegetarian Diet for the Chicago University Football Team," TVOFC 11, no. 6 (October 1907): 6.

91. Putney, *Muscular Christianity*, 60.

92. Lester, *Stagg's University*, 19; Watterson, *College Football*, 40–45; Putney, *Muscular Christianity*, 60–61.

93. "Kickers to Train on Squash," *Chicago Daily Tribune*, September 18, 1907, 11.

94. Ibid.

95. "Vegetarianism and Football," 5.

96. "Kickers to Train on Squash."

97. Lester, *Stagg's University*, 95–98.

98. "Kickers to Train on Squash."

99. Walter H. Eckersall, "Eckersall Discusses Early Football Practice," *Chicago Daily Tribune*, September 26, 1907, 7; Eckersall, "Outlook for the Eastern Elevens," *Chicago Daily Tribune*, September 27, 1907, 11; Eckersall, "Big Contests on Gridiron," *Chicago*

Daily Tribune, October 12, 1907, 10; Eckersall, "'Big' Games Begin in West and East," Chicago Daily Tribune, October 19, 1907, 12. On Eckersall and Stagg's complex and often contentious relationship, see Lester, Stagg's University, 55–62.

100. The Western Conference was the progenitor of the Big Ten Conference. Lester, Stagg's University, xx, 104.

101. "Size, Strength, Sweetness and Docility," TVOFC 5, no. 1 (October 15, 1900): 7.

102. "Why I Am a Vegetarian," TVOFC 5, no. 1 (October 15, 1900): 17.

103. J. George Heid, "Advantages of Vegetarian Diet from a Scientific Standpoint," TVOFC 6, no. 9 (April 15, 1902): 195–96.

CONCLUSION

1. Henry S. Clubb, "History of Vegetarianism: Chapter 1," VM 10, no. 11 (October 1907): 5–7.

2. Henry S. Clubb, "History of Vegetarianism: Chapter 13," VM 13, no. 3 (November 1909): 28.

3. Henry S. Clubb, "History of Vegetarianism: Chapter 8," VM 11, no. 6 (October 1907): 10.

4. Henry S. Clubb, "History of Vegetarianism: Chapter 5," VM 11, no. 3 (July 1907): 19; Clubb, "History of Vegetarianism: Chapter 9," VM 11, no. 7 (November 1907): 9–10.

5. Clubb, "History of Vegetarianism: Chapter 13," 26–30.

6. Clubb's wife, Anne, became ill to the point of immobility around this time, which probably explains his failure to finish the history. See Maintenance Committee, Bible Christian Church, History of the Philadelphia Bible Christian Church, 85–87.

7. Ibid., 89.

8. See, for example, "The Battle Creek Idea," Lancet-Clinic 103, no. 10 (March 1910): 270.

9. Loos and Emerson, His Picture in the Papers (silent film).

10. Basinger, Silent Stars, 106.

11. "His Picture in the Papers," Variety, February 4, 1916.

12. Kitty Kelly, "Flickerings from Film Land," Chicago Daily Tribune, February 1, 1916, 20.

13. "Fairbanks in Screen Farce," Los Angeles Times, February 13, 1916, 31.

14. Johnson, The Radical Middle Class, 212; Robins, Copeland's Cure, 121–23.

15. "Effects of Diet on Reproduction," Journal of the American Medical Association 70, no. 2 (June 1918): 2011.

16. Martin F. Engman, "Some Thoughts on Precedent," Archives of Dermatology and Syphilology 2 (1920): 276.

17. "What Causes Cancer?," National Provisioner 65, no. 7 (August 1921): 127.

18. This record will almost certainly be eclipsed, as the North American Vegetarian Society (NAVS), formed in 1974, will celebrate its fortieth year in 2014. See "About NAVS."

19. "Do You Happen to Be a Vegetarian?" Gallup Poll 302, Question 7a–b, September 14, 1943.

Bibliography

PRIMARY SOURCES

Archival Sources

American Medical Association, Department of Investigations, Chicago, Illinois
  Physical Culture Magazine Records
Arthur and Elizabeth Schlesinger Library, Radcliffe College, Cambridge, Massachusetts
  Culinary Collection
Bentley Historical Library, University of Michigan, Ann Arbor, Michigan
  Henry S. Clubb Papers
  John Harvey Kellogg Papers
  Sanitas Nut Food Company Papers
  Battle Creek Sanitarium Health Food Company Papers
Charles Deering Library, Northeastern University, Evanston, Illinois
  Physical Culture Magazine
Houghton Library, Harvard University, Cambridge, Massachusetts
  American Vegetarian and Health Journal
William L. Clements Library, University of Michigan, Ann Arbor, Michigan
  Janice B. Longone Culinary Archive

Digital Archives

"Henry Stephen Clubb." In *Official Records of the Union and Confederate Armies, 1861–1865*,
  roll 128, no. 130. Washington, DC: National Archives and Records Administration.
"Henry Stephen Clubb." In *U.S. Civil War Soldier Records and Profiles* (online database).
  Compiled by Historical Data Systems. Provo, UT: Ancestry.com Operations, 1999.
"John Milton Hadley." In *U.S. Civil War Soldier Records and Profiles* (online database).
  Compiled by Historical Data Systems. Provo, UT: Ancestry.com Operations, 2009.
"Samuel J. Stewart." In *American Civil War Soldiers* (online database). Compiled by
  Historical Data Systems. Provo, UT: Ancestry.com Operations, 1999.
"Samuel Stewart." In *General Index to Pension Files, 1861–1934*. Washington, DC: National
  Archives and Records Administration.

Censuses

First Census of the United States, 1790. National Archives and Records Administration, RG
  29, M637, 12 rolls.

Year: 1840; Census Place: Ward 14, New York, New York. Family History Library Film
    0017197, roll 307, page 413, image 837.
The Seventh Census of the United States, 1850. Washington, DC: Robert Armstrong, 1853.
Ninth Census: The Statistics of the Population of the United States. Washington, DC: U.S.
    Government Printing Office, 1872.

Published Works

A. E. Wright's Boston, New York, Philadelphia & Baltimore, Commercial Directory. New York: A.
    E. Wright, 1840.
Alan, Jonathan Adams. *Medical Examinations for Life-Insurance.* Chicago: Clarke, 1866.
Alcott, A. Bronson. *Concord Days.* Boston: Roberts Brothers, 1872.
————. *The Journals of Bronson Alcott.* Edited by Odell Shepard. Boston: Little, Brown,
    1938.
Alcott, Louisa May. *Louisa May Alcott: Her Life, Letters, and Journals.* Edited by Ednah Dow
    Cheney. Boston: Roberts Brothers, 1889.
Alcott, William. *The Use of Tobacco: Its Physical, Intellectual, and Moral Effects on the Human
    System.* New York: Fowler and Wells, 1836.
————. *Vegetable Diet: As Sanctioned by Medical Men, and by Experience in All Ages.* Boston:
    Marsh, Capen & Lyon, 1838.
————. *The Young Man's Guide.* Boston: Lilly, Wait, Colman, & Holden, 1833.
Allen, Ida C. Bailey. *Mrs. Allen's Book of Meat Substitutes.* Boston: Small, Maynard, 1918.
*The Americana Supplement: A Comprehensive Record of the Latest Knowledge and Progress of the
    World.* 2 vols. New York: Frederick Converse Beach, 1911.
The American Catalog. New York: Publisher's Weekly, 1900–1905.
Annual Report of the Battle Creek Sanitarium and Hospital. Battle Creek, MI: Sanitarium, 1912.
Bailey, Pearl L. *Domestic Science: Principles and Application.* St. Paul, MN: Webb, 1914.
Bancroft, Hubert Howe. *The Book of the Fair.* Chicago: Bancroft, 1893.
Bates, Charles Austin. *American Journalism from the Practical Side: What Leading Newspaper
    Publishers Say Concerning the Relations of Advertisers and Publishers and about the Way a Great
    Paper Should Be Made.* New York: Hughes, 1897.
Battle Creek Centennial, 1831–1931. Battle Creek, MI: Ellis, 1931.
Battle Creek Foods and Vegetarian Recipes. Battle Creek, MI: Battle Creek Food, 1920.
Battle Creek Sanitarium and Hospital. Battle Creek, MI: Sanitarium, 1912.
Beecher, Catherine Esther. *Miss Beecher's Domestic Receipt Book: Designed as a Supplement to
    Her Treatise on Domestic Economy.* New York: Harper & Brothers, 1846.
Blackmar, Frank W. *Kansas: A Cyclopedia of State History.* Vol. 2. Chicago: Standard, 1912.
Bible Christian Church, North Third Street. *Constitution and By-Laws.* Philadelphia, 1834.
Boston Almanac for the Year 1860. Boston: J. P. Jewett.
Boston City Directory, 1910. Boston: Sampson & Murdock, 1910.
Bradley, Alice. *Wheatless and Meatless Menus and Recipes.* Boston: Miss Farmer's School of
    Cookery, 1918.
Cabot, James Elliot, ed. *The Works of Ralph Waldo Emerson: A Memoir of Ralph Waldo
    Emerson.* 2 vols. Boston: Houghton, Mifflin, 1887.
Carpenter, Frank Oliver. *Foods and Their Uses.* New York: Charles Scribner's Sons, 1905.

Carrington, Hereward. *Vitality, Fasting and Nutrition*. New York: Rebman, 1908.

Christian, Eugene. *Meatless and Wheatless Menus*. New York: Alfred A. Knopf, 1917.

———. *250 Meatless Menus and Recipes to Meet the Requirements of People under the Varying Conditions of Age, Climate and Work*. New York: Mollie Griswold Christian, 1910.

City Directory for Chicago, 1897. Chicago: Chicago Directory, 1897.

City Directory for Chicago, 1905. Chicago: Chicago Directory, 1905.

Clarke, James. *Memorials of the Clarke Family: Formerly of the County of Northampton, in Great Britain: Their Immigration to Shelby County, Ind*. Indianapolis: Indianapolis Publishing and Printing House, 1845.

Clubb, Henry S. *Journal of the Constitutional Commission of Michigan*. Lansing, MI: W. S. George, 1873.

———. *The Maine Liquor Law: Its Origin, History, and Results*. New York: Fowler and Wells, 1856.

———. *Thirty-Nine Reasons Why I Am a Vegetarian*. Philadelphia: Vegetarian Society of America, 1903.

Clubb, Henry S., ed. *The Illustrated Vegetarian Almanac of 1855*. New York: Fowler and Wells, 1855.

Colt, Miriam Davis. *Went to Kansas; Being a Thrilling Account of an Ill-Fated Expedition to That Fairy Land, and Its Sad Results*. Watertown, NY: L. Ingalls, 1862.

Conklin, Hester Martha, and Pauline Dunwell Partridge. *Wheatless and Meatless Days*. New York: D. Appleton, 1918.

Constitution of the American Physiological Society. Boston: Marsh, Capen & Lyon, 1837.

Cooper, Lenna Frances. *The New Cookery: A Book of Recipes, Most of Which Are in Use at the Battle Creek Sanitarium*. Battle Creek, MI: Good Health, 1913.

Currier, Nathaniel, and Louis Maurer. *The Great Republican Reform Party, Calling on Their Candidate*. New York: Currier & Ives, 1856.

Dana, C. W. *The Great West, or the Garden of the World: Its History, Its Wealth, Its Natural Advantages, and Its Future*. Boston: Wentworth, 1856.

Dickens, Charles. *American Notes for General Circulation*. New York: Penguin, 2000.

Duncan, Rev. Abel G. *Evils of Violating the Laws of Health, and the Remedy: An Address Delivered before the American Physiological Society at Their Monthly Meeting, February 17, 1838*. Boston: Marsh, Capen & Lyon, 1838.

Dunglison, Robley. "Vegetarianism." In *Medical Lexicon: A Dictionary of Medical Science*. Philadelphia: Blanchard and Lea, 1851.

Eales, Irving James. *Healthology*. London: L. N. Fowler, 1907.

Emerson, Ralph Waldo. *Heart of Emerson's Journals*. New York: Houghton Mifflin, 1926.

———. *Journals of Ralph Waldo Emerson*. Edited by Edward Waldo Emerson and Waldo Emerson Forbes. Boston: Houghton Mifflin, 1911.

Farmer, Fanny Merritt. *The Boston Cooking-School Cook Book*. Boston: Little, Brown, 1896.

Finn, John Joseph. *Official Guide to the World's Columbian Exposition*. Chicago: Columbian Guide, 1893.

Fitch, William Edward. *Mineral Waters of the United States and American Spas*. Philadelphia: Lee and Febiger, 1927.

Foote, E. B. *Dr. Foote's New Book on Health and Disease*. New York: Murray Hill, 1903.

———. *Home Cyclopedia*. New York: Murray Hill, 1901.

————. *Plain Home Talk about the Human System.* San Francisco: H. H. Bancroft, 1870.

Forward, C. W. *Fifty Years of Food Reform: A History of the Vegetarian Movement in England.* London: Ideal Publishing Union, 1898.

Fowler, Orson Squire. *A Home for All; or, The Gravel Wall and Octagon Mode of Building.* New York: Fowler and Wells, 1854.

Fulton, Edward Guyles. *Substitutes for Flesh Foods; Vegetarian Cook Book.* Mountain View, CA: Pacific, 1904.

Garrison, William Lloyd. *The Letters of William Lloyd Garrison.* Vol. 3, *No Union with Slaveholders, 1841–1849.* Edited by Walter M. Merrill. Cambridge, MA: Harvard University Press, 1974.

————. *Letters of William Lloyd Garrison.* Vol. 5, *Let the Oppressed Go Free.* Edited by Walter M. Merrill. Cambridge, MA: Harvard University Press, 1979.

The General Programme of the World's Congresses of 1893. Chicago: World's Columbian Commission, 1893.

Graham, Sylvester. *A Defence of the Graham System of Living; or, Remarks on Diet and Regimen—Dedicated to the Rising Generation.* New York: W. Applegate, 1835.

————. *A Lecture on Epidemic Diseases Generally, and Particularly the Spasmodic Cholera: Delivered in the City of New York, March 1832, and Repeated June 1832, and in Albany, July 4, 1832, and in New York, June 1833: With an Appendix, Containing Several Testimonials, and a Review of Beaumont's Experiments on the Gastric Juice.* Boston: David Cambell, 1838.

————. *Lectures on the Science of Human Life.* Boston: Marsh, Capen, Lyon and Webb, 1849.

————. *A Treatise on Bread and Bread-Making.* Boston: Light and Stearns, 1837.

Greeley, Horace. *Recollections of a Busy Life.* New York: J. B. Ford, 1868.

Greer, Carlotta Cherryholmes. *A Text-Book of Cooking.* Boston: Allyn & Bacon, 1915.

Gunn, Thomas Butler. *The Physiology of New York Boarding-Houses.* New York: Mason Brothers, 1857.

Handy, Moses P., ed. *The Official Directory of the World's Columbian Exposition, May 1st to October 30th, 1893: A Reference Book of Exhibitors and Exhibits, and of the Officers and Members of the World's Columbian Commission.* Chicago: W. B. Conkey, 1893.

Harding, Walter, and Carl Bode, eds. *The Correspondence of Henry David Thoreau.* New York: New York University Press, 1958.

"Health Foods." In *Boyd's Directory of the District of Columbia.* Washington, DC: R. L. Polk, 1908, 104.

Hemstreet, Charles. *Nooks and Corners of Old New York.* New York: Charles Scribner's Sons, 1899.

Higinbotham, Harlow N. *Report of the President to the Board of Directors of the World's Columbian Exposition.* Chicago: Rand, McNally, 1898.

Hill, Lewis Webb. *Clinical Lectures on Infant Feeding.* Philadelphia: W. B. Saunders, 1917.

Howe, Edward E. *Vegetarian Cook Book.* New York: Squire, 1887.

Index of Trademarks Issued from the United States Patent Office. Vol. 930. Washington, DC: U.S. Patent Office, 1930.

Indiana Directory and Business Mirror for 1861. Indianapolis: Bowen, Steward, 1861.

Interstate Commerce Commission Reports: Decisions 26. Washington, DC: U.S. Government Printing Office, January 1913.

Jefferis, B. G., and J. L. Nichols. *Safe Counsel: The Science of Eugenics and Other Health Secrets.* Atlanta: J. L. Nichols, 1919.

———. *Search Lights on Health: Light on Dark Corners; A Complete Sexual Science and a Guide to Purity and Physical Manhood.* Atlanta: J. L. Nichols, 1904.

Kellogg, Ella Eaton. *Every-Day Dishes and Every-Day Work: A Collection of Choice Recipes for Preparing Foods, with Special Reference to Health.* Battle Creek, MI: Modern Medicine, 1897.

———. *Healthful Cookery: A Collection of Choice Recipes for Preparing Foods.* Battle Creek, MI: Modern Medicine, 1904.

———. *Science in the Kitchen.* Chicago: Modern Medicine, 1893.

Kellogg, John Harvey. *Are We a Dying Race?* Battle Creek, MI: Civic-Philanthropic Conference, 1897.

———. *The Battle Creek Sanitarium System: History, Organization, Method.* Battle Creek, MI: Gage, 1908.

———. *The Household Manual of Domestic Hygiene, Foods and Drinks, Common Diseases, Accidents and Emergencies, and Useful Hints and Recipes.* Battle Creek, MI: Office of the Health Reformer, 1875.

———. *The Natural Diet of Man.* Battle Creek, MI: Modern Medicine, 1919.

———. *Practical Manual of Health and Temperance: Embracing the Treatment of Common Diseases, Accidents and Emergencies, the Alcohol and Tobacco Habits, Useful Hints and Recipes.* Battle Creek, MI: Good Health, 1885.

———. *The Stomach: Its Disorders, and How to Cure Them.* Battle Creek, MI: Modern Medicine, 1896.

Kemble, Frances Anne. *Journal of a Residence on a Georgian Plantation in 1838–1839.* London: Longmans, 1863.

Lakeside Classified Directory, 1911. Chicago: Chicago Directory Company, 1911.

Lane, Henry Edward. *Diagnosis from the Eye.* Chicago: Kosmos, 1904.

Latham Dwight, Henrietta. *The Golden Age Cook-Book.* New York: Alliance, 1898.

Le Favre, Carrica. *Mother's Help and Child's Friend.* New York: Brentano's, 1890.

Lefèvre, Jules. *A Scientific Investigation into Vegetarianism.* London: John Bale, Sons & Danielsson, 1922.

Leonard, John William. *Woman's Who's Who of America: A Biographical Dictionary of Contemporary Women of the United States and Canada, 1914–1915.* New York: American Commonwealth, 1914.

Leonard, John W., and Albert Nelson Marquis. *The Book of Chicagoans: A Biographical Dictionary of Leading Living Men of the City of Chicago* 2 vols. Chicago: A. N. Marquis, 1911.

Longworth's American Almanac, New-York Register and City Directory for 1839. New York: Thomas Longworth, 1839.

Lust, Hubert Confield. *United States Interstate Commerce Commission, Supplemental Digest of Decisions under the Interstate Commerce Act.* Washington, DC: Traffic Law Book, 1914.

Lust, Louise. *The Practical Naturopathic-Vegetarian Cook Book: Cooked and Uncooked Foods.* New York: Benedict Lust, N.D., 1907.

Macfadden, Bernarr. *The Encyclopedia of Physical Culture.* Vol. 5. New York: Physical Culture, 1912.

————. *Marriage: A Lifelong Honeymoon; Life's Greatest Pleasures Secured by Observing the Highest Human Instincts*. New York: Physical Culture, 1903.

————. *Physical Culture Cookbook*. New York: Physical Culture, 1901.

————. *Strength from Eating*. New York: Physical Culture, 1901.

Melville, Herman. *Piazza Tales and Other Prose Pieces, 1839–1860*. Vol. 9, scholarly ed. Evanston, IL: Northwestern University Press, 1987.

Metcalfe, William. *Bible Testimony: On Abstinence from the Flesh of Animals as Food; Being an Address Delivered to the Bible Christian Church*. Philadelphia: J. Metcalfe, 1840

————. "Experience of the Bible-Christians." In Orson Squire Fowler, *Physiology, Animal and Mental: Applied to the Preservation and Restoration of Health of Body, and Power of Mind*. New York: Fowler and Wells, 1848, 72–73.

————. "History of the Bible-Christians." In *History of All the Religious Denominations in the United States*, edited by Israel Daniel Rupp. Harrisburg, PA: John Winebrenner, V.D.M., 1849.

————. *On Abstinence from the Flesh of Animals as Food; Being an Address Delivered to the Bible Christian Church*. Philadelphia: J. Metcalfe, 1840.

Michigan Bureau of Labor and Industrial Statistics. *Annual Report of the Bureau of Labor and Industrial Statistics*. Lansing, MI: Wynkoop Hallenbeck Crawford, 1906.

Moore, J. Howard. *Why I Am a Vegetarian: An Address Delivered before the Chicago Vegetarian Society*. Chicago: Purdy, 1895.

Mullendore, William Clinton. *History of the United States Food Administration*. Palo Alto, CA: Stanford University Press, 1941.

Nichols, Thomas Law. *Religions of the World*. Cincinnati: Valentine Nicholson, 1855.

Nicholson, Asenath. *Annals of the Famine in Ireland*. New York: E. French, 1851.

————. *Annals of the Famine in Ireland*. Edited by Maureen Murphy. Dublin: Lilliput, 1998.

————. *Nature's Own Book*. New York: Wilbur and Whipple, 1835.

Octagon Settlement Company. *The Octagon Settlement Company, Kanzas, Containing Full Information for Inquirers*. New York: Fowler and Wells, 1856.

"Oh! Wasn't She Fond of Her Greens!" Song score. New York: H. De Marsen, 1860.

Ovid. *Metamorphoses*. London: Wordsworth, 2001.

Owens, Francis Emugene. *Mrs. Owens' New Cook Book and Complete Household Manual*. Chicago: Owens, 1899.

Payne, Daniel Alexander. *Recollections of Seventy Years*. Nashville, TN: Publishing House of the A.M.E. Sunday School Union, 1888.

Pennsylvania Society for Discouraging the Use of Ardent Spirits. *Report of a Committee Appointed by the Pennsylvania Society, for Discouraging the Use of Ardent Spirits, to Examine and Report What Amendments Ought to Be Made in the Laws of the Said State, for the Suppression of Vice and Immorality, Particularly Those against Gaming*. Philadelphia: Atkinson and Alexander, 1828.

Pierce, Anne Lewis, and Harvey Washington Wiley. *1001 Tests of Foods, Beverages and Toilet Accessories: Good and Otherwise*. New York: Hearst's International Library, 1914.

Priessnitz, Vincent. *The Cold Water Cure: Its Principles, Theory, and Practice*. London: William Strange, 1842.

Race Betterment Foundation. *Proceedings of the First National Conference on Race Betterment*. Battle Creek, MI: Race Betterment Foundation, 1914.

Randolph, Mary. *The Virginia House-Wife*. Edited by Karen Hess. Columbia: University of South Carolina Press, 1984.

Roosevelt, Theodore. *The Strenuous Life: Essays and Addresses*. New York: Century, 1902.

Rorer, Sarah Tyson. *Mrs. Rorer's Vegetable Cookery and Meat Substitutes*. Philadelphia: Arnold, 1909.

Sandburg, Carl. "Chicago." In *Chicago Poems*. New York: Henry Holt, 1916.

San Francisco-Oakland Directory. San Francisco: Walter S. Fry, 1907.

Sanitas Nut Preparations and Specialties. Battle Creek, MI: Review and Herald, 1898.

Second Annual Report of the American Physiological Society. Boston: George W. Light, 1838.

Sharpe, Maud Russell Lorraine. *The Golden Rule Cook Book: Six Hundred Recipes for Meatless Dishes*. Boston: Little, Brown, 1910.

———. *Selections from Three Essays by Richard Wagner*. Rochester, NH: Record, 1933.

Shew, Mary Louise, and Joel Shew. *Water-Cure for Ladies: A Popular Work on the Health, Diet, and Regimen of Females and Children, and the Prevention and Cure of Diseases*. New York: Wiley and Putnam, 1844.

Sinclair, Upton. *The Autobiography of Upton Sinclair*. New York: Harcourt, Brace & World, 1962.

———. *The Fasting Cure*. New York: Mitchell Kennerley, 1911.

———. *The Jungle*. New York: Simon and Schuster, 2004.

Taylor, Bayard. *A Journey to Central Africa; or, Life and Landscapes from Egypt to the Negro Kingdoms of the White Nile*. New York: G. P. Putnam, 1854.

Third Annual Report of the American Physiological Society. Boston: George W. Light, 1838.

The Tribune Almanac and Political Register. New York: G. Dearborn, 1856.

Twentieth Century Club of Pittsburgh. *Twentieth Century Club War Time Cook Book*. Pittsburgh: Pierpont, Siviter, 1918.

Tyler, W. S. *History of Amherst College during Its First Half Century, 1821–1871*. Holyoke, MA: C. W. Bryan, 1873.

Wachtmeister, Countess Constance, and Kate Buffington Davis, eds. *Practical Vegetarian Cookery*. San Francisco: Mercury, 1897.

Washington D.C. City Directory, 1911. Washington, DC: R. L. Polk, 1911.

Wheeler, Candace. *Columbia's Emblem, Indian Corn: A Garland of Tributes in Prose and Verse*. Boston: Houghton Mifflin, 1893

White, Ellen G. *A Sketch of the Christian Experience and Views of Ellen G. White*. Saratoga Springs, NY: James White, 1851.

Williams, Edwin, ed. *New-York as It Is*. New York: J. Disturnell, 1834.

Newspapers and Journals

American Journal of Eugenics (1908)

American Medical Journal (1856)

American Phrenological Journal (1860)

American Vegetarian and Health Journal (1850–54)

Annual Report of the Factory Inspectors of Illinois (1906)

Archives of Dermatology and Syphilology (1920)

Atkinson's Casket (Philadelphia, 1832)

Battle Creek (MI) Idea (1912)

Berkshire Medical Journal: Devoted to the Interests of Rational Medicine (1861)

Bismarck (ND) Daily Tribune (1893)

Boston Daily Globe (1915)

Boston Herald (1860)

Boston Medical and Surgical Journal (1835–36, 1851, 1853)

Boynton (OK) Index (1915)

Charleston (SC) Mercury (1860)

Chicago Clinic (1898)

Chicago Daily Tribune (1856, 1859–60, 1892–96, 1899, 1902, 1907, 1909–11, 1913, 1916–18)

Cincinnati Medical Observer (1856)

Circular (1855)

Daily Evening Bulletin (Philadelphia, 1862)

Daily Inter Ocean (Chicago, 1892–93)

Daily Missouri Democrat (St. Louis, 1856)

The Dial (Boston, 1840, 1842)

Dietetic Reformer and Vegetarian Messenger (1886)

Eclectic Medical Journal (1860)

Everyday Housekeeping: A Magazine for Practical Housekeepers and Mothers (1894)

Food, Home and Garden (1896–1900)

Galveston (TX) Daily News (1913)

Good Housekeeping (1903)

Graham Journal of Health and Longevity (1837–39)

Harper's (1860)

Herald of Health and Journal of Physical Culture (1867)

Herald of Health and Water-Cure Journal (1863)

The Hesperian (1893)

Home Journal (1851)

Hygienic Review (1893)

Illustrated World (1916)

The Independent (Dearborn, MI, 1899)

Indianapolis Star (1912)

Jewelers' Circular and Horological Review (1898)

Journal of the American Medical Association (1918)

Journal of Health (1832, 1840–41)

The Knickerbocker (1860)

Library of Health (1838, 1840–41)

The Liberator (1853, 1857, 1859–60)

Literary Digest (1899)

Los Angeles Times (1908, 1916)

Louisville Daily Journal (1861)

Lowell (MA) Daily Citizen and News (1862)

Mansfield (OH) News (1912)

Medical and Surgical Reporter (Philadelphia, 1860)

Medical Independent: A Monthly Review of Medicine and Surgery (1857)

Medical Missionary (1910)

Medical News (1867)

Medical World: A Journal of Universal Medical Intelligence (1857)

Minnesota Farmers' Institute Annual (Minneapolis, 1835)

Modern Medicine (Battle Creek, MI, 1904, 1906)

Modern Medicine and Bacteriological Review (1896)

Morning Herald (New York, 1838)

Morning Oregonian (Portland, 1892, 1895)

Nashville Monthly Record of Medical and Physical Science (1859)

National Geographic Magazine (1915)

National Provisioner (1921)

New England Farmer and Agricultural Journal (1832)

New England Review (1839)

New Hampshire Statesman (1861)

New York Evangelist (1851)

New York Evening Post (1832)

New York Herald (1853, 1860, 1862–64)

New York Observer and Chronicle (1911)

New York Review (1837, 1840)

New York Times (1851–52, 1869–71, 1895, 1901, 1907, 1910, 1917–18)

New York Tribune (1862, 1909)

North American (1895)

Nut Cracker (Battle Creek, MI, 1900–1901)

N. W. Ayer & Son's American Newspaper Annual (Philadelphia, 1890, 1893, 1900, 1911, 1913)

Ohio Observer (Hudson, 1852)

The Outlook (1905)

Pennsylvania Inquirer and Daily Courier (1837)

Penny Satirist (London, 1844)

Phrenological Journal and Science of Health (1892, 1906, 1911)

Physical Culture (1899–1904, 1906, 1908–11, 1917)

Popular Science (1920)

Portland Magazine: Devoted to Literature (1833)

Presbyterian Magazine (1821)

Review and Herald (Battle Creek, MI, 1877)

Rotarian (1920)

San Francisco Call (1904)

Saturday Evening Post (1850)

Savannah Daily Morning News (1852)

Scientific American (1850)

Sciotto Gazette (1861)

Southern Medical and Surgical Journal (1854)

Spirit of the Times (1836, 1848, 1850, 1851, 1853, 1855)

T. L. Nichols' Water-Cure Journal (1850, 1853, 1855)

Tomorrow Magazine (1907)

Treasury of Medicine (1854)

Truth-Tester (London, 1847)

Vanity Fair (1860)

Variety (1916)

The Vegetarian (1893)

The Vegetarian and Our Fellow Creatures (Philadelphia, Chicago, 1900–1902, 1907, 1910, 1913)

Vegetarian Magazine

Vegetarian Messenger (London, 1886, 1889–91, 1894–96, 1905)

Vegetarian Times (1988, 1990)

Washington Times (1904)

Water-Cure Journal (1845–47, 1849–50, 1853, 1855, 1857–58, 1861)

Weal-Reaf (Boston, 1860)

SECONDARY SOURCES

Abbott, Richard H. Cotton and Capital: Boston Businessmen and Antislavery Reform, 1854–1868. Amherst: University of Massachusetts Press, 1991.

Abzug, Robert. Cosmos Crumbling: American Reform and the Religious Imagination. New York: Oxford University Press, 1994.

Adams, Carol J. The Sexual Politics of Meat: A Feminist-Vegetarian Critical Theory. New York: Continuum, 2010.

Adams, Mark. Mr. America. New York: Harper Collins, 2009.

Albala, Ken. Eating Right in the Renaissance. Berkeley: University of California Press, 2002.

Alderfer, E. G. The Ephrata Commune: An Early American Counterculture. Pittsburgh: University of Pittsburgh Press, 1985.

Anderson, Godfrey T. "Sectarianism and Organisation, 1846–1864." In Adventism in America: A History, edited by Gary Land. Berrien Springs, MI: Andrews University Press, 1998, 36–65.

Archer, John E. Social Unrest and Popular Protest in England, 1780–1840. Cambridge: Cambridge University Press, 2000.

Arikha, Noga. Passions and Tempers: A History of the Humours. New York: Ecco, 2007.

Aron, Cindy Sondik. Working at Play: A History of Vacations in the United States. New York: Oxford University Press, 2001.

Arthur, Anthony. Radical Innocent: Upton Sinclair. New York: Random House, 2006.

Baker, Lee D. From Savage to Negro: Anthropology and the Construction of Race, 1896–1954. Berkeley: University of California Press, 1998.

Balmer, Randall, and John R. Fitzimer. The Presbyterians. Westport, CT: Greenwood, 1993.

Barney, Robert Knight. "Forty-Eighters and the Rise of the Turnervein Movement in America." In Ethnicity and Sport in North American History and Culture, edited by George Eisen and David Kenneth Wiggins. Westport, CT: Praeger, 1994, 19–42.

Barrett, James R. Work and Community in the Jungle: Chicago's Packinghouse Workers, 1894–1922. Urbana: University of Illinois Press, 1987.

Basinger, Jeanine. Silent Stars. Hanover, NH: University Press of New England, 1999.

Bederman, Gail. A Cultural History of Gender and Race in the United States, 1880–1917. Chicago: University of Chicago Press, 1996.

Belasco, Warren. *Appetite for Change: How the Counterculture Took on the Food Industry.* Ithaca, NY: Cornell University Press.

Bellesiles, Michael A. *Revolutionary Outlaws: Ethan Allen and the Struggle for Independence on the Early American Frontier.* Charlottesville: University of Virginia Press, 1993.

Bernstein, Iver. *The New York City Draft Riots: Their Significance for American Society and Politics in the Age.* New York: Oxford University Press, 1991.

Bickman, Marty. *Minding American Education: Reclaiming the Tradition of Active Learning.* New York: Teachers College Press, 2003.

Blanchard, Mary Warner. *Oscar Wilde's America: Counterculture in the Gilded Age.* New Haven, CT: Yale University Press, 1998.

Braude, Ann. *Radical Spirits: Spiritualism and Women's Rights in Nineteenth-Century America.* Boston: Beacon, 1989.

Brooke, John L. *The Refiner's Fire: The Making of Mormon Cosmology, 1644–1844.* Cambridge: Cambridge University Press, 1996.

Bull, Malcolm, and Keith Lockhart. *Seeking a Sanctuary: Seventh-Day Adventism and the American Dream.* Bloomington: Indiana University Press, 2007.

Burstein, Andrew. *Jefferson's Secrets: Death and Desire at Monticello.* New York: Basic Books, 2006.

Butler, Jonathan M. "Prophecy, Gender, and Culture: Ellen Gould Harmon [White] and the Roots of Seventh-Day Adventism." *Religion and American Culture* 1, no. 1 (Winter 1991): 3–29.

Caden-Corne, Ana. *Reconstructing the Body: Classicism, Modernism, and the First World War.* New York: Oxford University Press, 2009.

Carpenter, Helen Graham. *The Rev. John Graham of Woodbury, Connecticut and His Descendants.* Chicago: Monastery Hill, 1942.

Cayleff, Susan. *Wash and Be Healed: The Water-Cure Movement and Women's Health.* Philadelphia: Temple University Press, 1991.

Chapman, David L. *Sandow the Magnificent: Eugen Sandow and the Beginnings of Bodybuilding.* Urbana: University of Illinois Press, 1994.

Charles, Ron. "War Is No Place for Saints." *Christian Science Monitor* 97, no. 66 (March 1, 2005): 15.

Chinn, Sarah E. *Technology and the Logic of American Racism: A Cultural History of the Body as Evidence.* London: Continuum, 2000.

Cohen, Patricia Cline. *The Murder of Helen Jewett.* New York: Vintage, 1998.

Cohen, Patricia Cline, Timothy J. Gilfoyle, and Helen Lefkowitz Horowitz. *The Flash Press: Sporting Male Weeklies in 1840s New York.* Chicago: University of Chicago Press, 2008.

Coleman, John P. "Casting Bread on Troubled Waters: Grahamism and the West." *Journal of American Culture* 9, no. 2 (February 1986): 1–8.

Colton, Ray Charles. *The Civil War in the Western Territories: Arizona, Colorado, New Mexico, and Utah.* Norman: University of Oklahoma Press, 1984.

Condit, Carl W. *The Chicago School of Architecture: A History of Commercial and Public Building in the Chicago Area, 1875–1925.* Chicago: University of Chicago Press, 1998.

Cook, Sylvia Jenkins. *Working Women, Literary Ladies: The Industrial Revolution and Female Aspiration.* New York: Oxford University Press, 2008.

Cott, Nancy F. "Young Women in the Second Great Awakening in New England." *Feminist Studies* 3, no. 1/2 (Autumn 1975): 15–29.

Darby, Robert. "Pathologizing Male Sexuality: Lallemand, Spermatorrhea, and the Rise of Circumcision." *Journal of the History of Medicine* 60 (2005): 283–319.

Deutsch, Ronald M. *The Nuts among the Berries*. New York: Ballantine, 1967.

Diggins, John P. *John Adams*. New York: Henry Holt, 2003.

Dublin, Thomas. "Women and Outwork in a Nineteenth-Century New England Town: Fitzwilliam, New Hampshire, 1830–1850." In *The Countryside in the Age of Capitalist Transformation: Essays in the Social History of Rural America*, edited by Steven Hahn and Jonathan Prude. Chapel Hill: University of North Carolina Press, 1985, 51–69.

Dyreson, Mark. "Regulating the Body and the Body Politic: American Sport, Bourgeois Culture, and the Language of Progress, 1880–1920." In *The New American Sport History: Recent Approaches and Perspectives*, edited by S. W. Pope. Urbana: University of Illinois Press, 1997, 121–44.

Eden, Trudy. *The Early American Table: Food and Society in the New World*. DeKalb: Northern Illinois University Press, 2008.

Engs, Ruth C. *Clean Living Movements: American Cycles of Health Reform*. Westport, CT: Greenwood, 2001.

Enstad, Nan. *Ladies of Labor, Girls of Adventure*. New York: Columbia University Press, 1999.

Ernst, Robert. *Weakness Is a Crime: The Life of Bernarr Macfadden*. Syracuse, NY: Syracuse University Press, 1991.

Etcheson, Nicole. *Bleeding Kansas: Contested Liberty in the Civil War Era*. Lawrence: University Press of Kansas, 2004.

Fisher, Irving. "The Influence of Flesh Eating on Endurance." *Yale Medical Journal* 13, no. 5 (1907): 205–21.

———. *The Influence of Flesh Eating on Endurance*. Battle Creek, MI: Modern Medicine, 1908.

Fitzgerald, Daniel. *Ghost Towns of Kansas: A Traveler's Guide*. Lawrence: University Press of Kansas, 1988.

Flanagan, Maureen. "Gender and Urban Political Reform: The City Club and the Woman's City Club of Chicago in the Progressive Era." *American Historical Review* (October 1990): 1032–50.

Fletcher, Robert Samuel. *A History of Oberlin College: From Its Foundation through the Civil War*. 2 vols. New York: Arno, 1971.

Foner, Eric. *Free Soil, Free Labor, Free Men: The Ideology of the Republican Party before the Civil War*. New York: Oxford University Press, 1969.

———. *Reconstruction: America's Unfinished Revolution, 1863–1877*. New York: Perennial Classics, 1988.

Franklin, John Hope, and Alfred A. Moss Jr. *From Slavery to Freedom: A History of African-Americans*. New York: Alfred A. Knopf, 2000.

Fredrickson, George M. *The Black Image in the White Mind*. Middletown, CT: Wesleyan University Press, 1987.

Friedman, Walter A. *Birth of a Salesman: The Transformation of Selling in America*. Cambridge, MA: Harvard University Press, 2004.

Gamber, Wendy. *The Boardinghouse in Nineteenth-Century America*. Baltimore: Johns Hopkins University Press, 2007.

Gately, Iain. *Drink: A Cultural History of Alcohol*. New York: Gotham, 2008.

Giehl, Dudley. *Vegetarianism: A Way of Life*. New York: Harper & Row, 1979.

Gilfoyle, Timothy. *City of Eros: New York City, Prostitution, and the Commercialization of Sex, 1790–1920*. New York: W. W. Norton, 1992.

Gordon, John Steele. *An Empire of Wealth: The Epic History of American Economic Power*. New York: Harper Collins, 2004.

Gorn, Elliott J. *The Manly Art: Bare-Knuckle Prize Fighting in America*. Ithaca, NY: Cornell University Press, 1989.

Gorn, Heather. "25 Years of Vegetarianism and a Look into the Future." *Vegetarian Journal* 26 no. 3 (2007): 6–13.

Grout, Pam. *Kansas Curiosities: Quirky Characters, Roadside Oddities and Other Offbeat Stuff*. Guilford, CT: Morris, 2007.

Guy, Roger. *From Diversity to Unity: Southern and Appalachian Migrants in Uptown Chicago*. Lanham, MD: Lexington, 2007.

Haber, Barbara. *From Hardtack to Home Fries: An Uncommon History of American Cooks and Meals*. New York: Free Press, 2002.

Haller, John S. "Bachelor's Disease: Etiology, Pathology, and Treatment of Spermatorrhea in the Nineteenth Century." *New York State Journal of Medicine*, August 15, 1973, 2076–82.

Haller John S., Jr., and Robin M. Haller. *The Physician and Sexuality in Victorian America*. New York: W. W. Norton, 1974.

Hayden, Dolores. *The Grand Domestic Revolution: A History of Feminist Designs for American Homes, Neighborhoods, and Cities*. Cambridge, MA: MIT Press, 1982.

Haynes, April. "Riotous Flesh: Gender, Physiology, and the Solitary Vice." PhD diss., University of California, Santa Barbara, 2009.

Hessinger, Rodney. *Seduced, Abandoned, and Reborn: Visions of Youth in Middle-Class America, 1780–1850*. Philadelphia: University of Pennsylvania Press, 2005.

Hickman, Russell. "The Vegetarian and Octagon Settlement Companies." *Kansas State Historical Society* 2, no. 4 (November 1933): 377–85.

Higham, John. *Strangers in the Land: Patterns of American Nativism, 1860–1925*. Piscataway, NJ: Rutgers University Press, 2002.

Hodges, Jeffrey. "Dealing with Degeneracy: Michigan Eugenics in Context." PhD diss., Michigan State University, 2001.

Hodson, Jane. *Language and Revolution in Burke, Wollstonecraft, Paine, and Godwin*. Hampshire, U.K.: Ashgate, 2007.

Holl, Steven. *Rural and Urban House Types in North America*. Princeton, NJ: Princeton Architectural, 1983.

Hooker, Richard J. *Food and Drink in America: A History*. Indianapolis: Bobbs-Merrill, 1981.

Hopkins, Donald R. *The Greatest Killer: Smallpox in History*. Chicago: University of Chicago Press, 2002.

Horowitz, Helen Lefkowitz. *Rereading Sex: Battles over Sexual Knowledge and Suppression in Nineteenth-Century America*. New York: Alfred A. Knopf, 2002.

Horowitz, Roger. *Putting Meat on the American Table: Taste, Technology, Transformation.* Baltimore: Johns Hopkins University Press, 2006.

Hoy, Suellen. *Chasing Dirt: The American Pursuit of Cleanliness.* New York: Oxford University Press, 1995.

Hund, Wulf D. "Negative Societalisation." In *Wages of Whiteness and Racist Symbolic Capital,* edited by Wulf D. Hund, Jeremy Krikler, and David R. Roediger. Piscataway, NJ: Transaction, 2011, 57–96.

Hunnicutt, Benjamin. *Kellogg's Six-Hour Day.* Philadelphia: Temple University Press, 1996.

Hunt, William R. *Body Love: The Amazing Career of Bernarr Macfadden.* Madison, WI: Popular, 1989.

Iacobbo, Karen, and Michael Iacobbo. *Vegetarian America: A History.* Westport, CT: Greenwood, 2004.

Inness, Sherrie A. *Secret Ingredients: Race, Gender, and Class at the Dinner Table.* New York: Macmillan, 2006.

Isenberg, Michael T. *John L. Sullivan and His America.* Urbana: University of Illinois Press, 1994.

Jacobson, Matthew Frye. *Whiteness of a Different Color: European Immigrants and the Alchemy of Race.* Cambridge, MA: Harvard University Press, 1999.

Johnson, Robert D. *The Radical Middle Class: Populist Democracy and the Question of Capitalism in Progressive Era Portland, Oregon.* Princeton, NJ: Princeton University Press, 2003.

Jortner, Adam. "Cholera, Christ, and Jackson: The Epidemic of 1832 and the Origins of Christian Politics in Antebellum America." *Journal of the Early Republic* 27, no. 2 (Summer 2007): 233–64.

Kanigel, Robert. *The One Best Way: Frederick Winslow Taylor and the Enigma of Efficiency.* Cambridge, MA: MIT Press, 2005.

Kasson, John F. *Houdini, Tarzan, and the Perfect Man: The White Male Body and the Challenge of Modernity in America.* New York: Hill and Wang, 2001.

Kennedy, David M. *Over Here: The First World War and American Society.* New York: Oxford University Press, 2004.

Kniffen, Fred. "Folk Housing: Key to Diffusion." *Annals of the Association of American Geographers* 55, no. 4 (December 1965): 549–77.

Knight, George R. *A Brief History of Seventh-Day Adventists.* Hagerstown, MD: Review and Herald, 2004.

———. *Millennial Fever and the End of the World.* Boise, ID: Pacific, 1993.

Koehn, Nancy Fowler. *Brand New: How Entrepreneurs Earned Consumers' Trust from Wedgwood to Dell.* Boston: Harvard Business School Publishing, 2001.

Kolko, Gabriel. *Triumph of Conservatism.* New York: Free Press, 1977.

Kupperman, Karen Ordahl. "Fear of Hot Climates in the Anglo-American Colonial Experience." *William and Mary Quarterly* 41, no. 2 (April 1984): 213–40.

Landau, Sarah Bradford, and Carl W. Condit. *Rise of the New York Skyscraper, 1865–1913.* New Haven, CT: Yale University Press, 1999.

Lause, Mark A. *Race and Radicalism in the Union Army.* Urbana: University of Illinois Press, 2009.

Leach, William. *Land of Desire: Merchants, Power, and the Rise of a New American Culture.* New York: Vintage, 1994.

Lears, T. J. Jackson. *Fables of Abundance: A Cultural History of Advertising in America.* New York: Basic Books, 1994.

Leavitt, Sarah Abigail. *From Catharine Beecher to Martha Stewart: A Cultural History of Domestic Advice.* Chapel Hill: University of North Carolina Press, 2002.

Le Duc, Thomas H. "Grahamites and Garrisonites." *Quarterly Journal of the New York State Historical Association* (1939): 189–91.

Lender, Mark Edward. *Drinking in America: A History.* New York: Free Press, 1987.

Lerner, Gerda. *The Grimké Sisters from South Carolina: Pioneer for Women's Rights and Abolition,* 2d ed. Chapel Hill: University of North Carolina Press, 2007.

Lester, Robin. *Stagg's University: The Rise, Decline, and Fall of Big-Time Football at Chicago.* Urbana: University of Illinois Press, 1999.

Levenstein, Harvey. *Revolution at the Table: The Transformation of the American Diet.* Berkeley: University of California Press, 2003.

Lévi-Strauss, Claude. *The Savage Mind.* Chicago: University of Chicago Press, 1966.

McCarley, Rebecca Lewin. "Orson S. Fowler and a Home for All: The Octagon House in the Midwest." *Perspectives in Vernacular Architecture* 12 (2005): 49–63.

Maintenance Committee, Bible Christian Church. *History of the Philadelphia Bible Christian Church for the First Century of Its Existence.* Philadelphia: J. B. Lippincott, 1922.

Mangels, Reed, Virginia Messina, and Mark Messina. *The Dietitian's Guide to Vegetarian Diets: Issues and Application.* Sudbury, MA: Jones and Bartlett Learning, 2004.

Matteson, John. *Eden's Outcasts: The Story of Louisa May Alcott and Her Father.* New York: W. W. Norton, 2007.

Maurer, Donna. *Vegetarianism: Movement or Moment?* Philadelphia: Temple University Press, 2002.

McClelland, Gordon T., and Jay T. Last. *California Watercolors, 1850–1970.* Santa Ana, CA: Hillcrest, 2002.

McGerr, Michael. *A Fierce Discontent: The Rise and Fall of the Progressive Movement in America, 1870–1920.* New York: Oxford University Press, 2005.

McGinnis, Ralph Y., and Calvin N. Smith. *Abraham Lincoln and the Western Territories.* Chicago: Nelson-Hall, 1994.

McPherson, James. *Battle Cry of Freedom: The Civil War Era.* New York: Oxford University Press, 2003.

———. *Drawn with the Sword: Reflections on the American Civil War.* New York: Oxford University Press, 1996.

McWilliams, James. *A Revolution in Eating: How the Quest for Food Shaped America.* New York: Columbia University Press, 2007.

Morgan, John. *A Worker and Workers' Friend: P. P. Stewart, a Life Sketch.* New York: John J. Reed, 1873.

Muccigrosso, Robert. *Celebrating the New World: Chicago's Columbian Exposition of 1893.* Chicago: Ivan R. Dee, 1993.

Nash, George H. *The Life of Herbert Hoover: Master of Emergencies, 1917–1918.* New York: W. W. Norton, 1996.

Neil, Marion Harris. *The Thrift Cook Book.* Philadelphia: David Mckay, 1919.

Nelson, Daniel. *Frederick W. Taylor and the Rise of Scientific Management.* Madison: University of Wisconsin Press, 1980.

Nissenbaum, Stephen. *Sex, Diet and Debility in Jacksonian America: Sylvester Graham and Health Reform.* Westport, CT: Greenwood, 1980.

———. "Sylvester Graham and Health Reform." In *A Place Called Paradise: Culture and Community in Northampton, Massachusetts.* Northampton, MA: Historic Northampton Museum and Education Center, 2004, 282–300.

Numbers, Ronald L. *Prophetess of Health: A Study of Ellen G. White.* Knoxville: University of Tennessee Press, 2008.

Nussinow, Jill. "Seitan—The Vegetarian Wheat Meat." *Vegetarian Journal* (March–April 1996): 6–10.

Nye, David E. *Electrifying America: Social Meanings of a New Technology.* Cambridge, MA: MIT Press, 1992.

Oates, Stephen B. *To Purge This Land with Blood: A Biography of John Brown.* Amherst: University of Massachusetts Press, 1984.

Osborn, Matthew Warner. "A Detestable Shrine: Alcohol Abuse in Antebellum Philadelphia." *Journal of the Early Republic* 29, no. 1 (Spring 2009): 101–32.

Ouédragogo, Arouna P. "The Social Genesis of Western Vegetarianism to 1859." In *Food, Power and Community: Essays in the History of Food and Drink,* edited by Robert Dare. Adelaide, Australia: Wakefield, 1999, 154–66.

Paulsson, Marin. *The Social Anxieties of Progressive Reform: Atlantic City, 1854–1920.* New York: New York University Press, 1996.

Pearson, Susan. *The Rights of the Defenseless: Protecting Animals and Children in Gilded Age America.* Chicago: University of Chicago Press, 2011.

Pegram, Thomas R. *Battling Demon Rum: The Struggle for a Dry America, 1800–1933.* Chicago: Ivan R. Dee, 1999.

Peirce, Henry B. "The City of Battle Creek." In *History of Calhoun County, Michigan.* Philadelphia: L. H. Everts, 1877, 79–94.

Platt, Harold L. *The Electric City: Energy and the Growth of the Chicago Area, 1880–1930.* Chicago: University of Chicago Press, 1991.

Porter, Dorothy. *Health, Civilization, and the State: A History of Public Health from Ancient to Modern Times.* London: Routledge, 1999.

Puskar-Pasewicz, Margaret. "'For the Good of the Whole': Vegetarianism in Nineteenth-Century America." PhD diss., Indiana University, 2004.

———. "Kitchen Sisters and Disagreeable Boys: Debates over Meatless Diets in Nineteenth Century Shaker Communities." In *Eating in Eden: Food in American Utopias,* edited by Etta Madden and Martha Finch. Lincoln: University of Nebraska Press, 2006, 109–24.

Putney, Clifford. *Muscular Christianity: Manhood and Sports in Protestant America, 1880–1920.* Cambridge, MA: Harvard University Press, 2003.

Reps, John W. *The Making of Urban America: A History of City Planning in the United States.* Princeton, NJ: Princeton University Press, 1965.

Reynolds, David S. *John Brown, Abolitionist: The Man Who Killed Slavery, Sparked the Civil War and Seeded Civil Rights.* New York: Vintage, 2005.

Riess, Steven A. *City Games: The Evolution of American Urban Society and the Rise of Sports*. Urbana: University of Illinois Press, 1991.

Robins, Natalie S. *Copeland's Cure: Homeopathy and the War between Conventional and Alternative Medicine*. New York: Alfred A. Knopf, 2005.

Rorabaugh, W. J. *The Alcoholic Republic: An American Tradition*. New York: Oxford University Press, 1981.

Rosenberg, Charles E. *The Cholera Years*. Chicago: University of Chicago Press, 1962.

Rydell, Robert W. "The Chicago World's Columbian Exposition of 1893: 'And Was Jerusalem Builded Here?'" In Rydell, *All the World's a Fair: Visions of Empire at America's International Expositions, 1876–1916*. Chicago: University of Chicago Press, 1984, 38–71.

Sanborn, F. B., and William T. Harris. *A. Bronson Alcott: His Life and Philosophy*. 2 vols. Boston: Roberts Brothers, 1893.

Sandage, Scott A. *Born Losers: A History of Failure in America*. Cambridge, MA: Harvard University Press, 2005.

Sandoval-Strausz, A. K. *Hotel: An American History*. New Haven, CT: Yale University Press, 2007.

Saxton, Martha. *Louisa May Alcott: A Modern Biography*. New York: Macmillan, 1995.

Scharf, John Thomas, and Westcott Thompson. *History of Philadelphia, 1609–1884*. Vol. 2. Philadelphia: L. H. Everts, 1884.

Scherzer, Kenneth. *The Unbounded Community: Neighborhood Life and Social Structure in New York*. Durham, NC: Duke University Press, 1992.

Schneirov, Matthew. *The Dream of a New Social Order: Popular Magazines in America, 1893–1914*. New York: Columbia University Press, 1994.

Schwartz, Richard. *John Harvey Kellogg, M.D.: Pioneering Health Reformer*. Battle Creek, MI: Review and Herald, 2006.

Sears, Clara Endicott, ed. *Bronson Alcott's Fruitlands*. Boston: Houghton Mifflin, 1915.

Sellers, Charles. *The Market Revolution: Jacksonian America, 1815–1846*. New York: Oxford University Press, 1994.

Shaffer, Marguerite S. *See America First: Tourism and National Identity, 1880–1940*. Washington, DC: Smithsonian Institution Press, 2001.

Shapiro, Laura. *Perfection Salad: Women and Cooking at the Turn of the Century*. Berkeley: University of California Press, 2008.

Shelley, Percy Bysshe. "Queen Mab: A Philosophical Poem." In *The Complete Poetical Works of Percy Bysshe Shelley*, edited by George Edward Woodberry. Boston: Houghton Mifflin, 1892, 1:73.

Shepard, Odell. *Pedlar's Progress: The Life of Bronson Alcott*. Boston: Little, Brown, 1937.

Silver-Isenstadt, Jean L. *Shameless: The Visionary Life of Mary Gove Nichols*. Baltimore: Johns Hopkins University Press, 2002.

Singer, Peter. *Ethics into Action: Henry Spira and the Animal Rights Movement*. Lanham, MD: Rowman and Littlefield, 1998.

Smith, Andrew F. *Eating History: Thirty Turning Points in the Making of American Cuisine*. New York: Columbia University Press, 2009.

Spencer, Colin. *Vegetarianism: A History*. New York: Four Walls Eight Windows, 2002.

Stampp, Kenneth M. *America in 1857: A Nation on the Brink*. New York: Oxford University Press, 1992.

Stavely, Kevin, and Kathleen Fitzgerald. *America's Founding Food: The Story of New England Cooking*. Chapel Hill: University of North Carolina Press, 2004.

Stern, Alexandra. *Eugenic Nation: Faults and Frontiers of Better Breeding in Modern America*. Berkley: University of California Press, 2005.

Stewart, Donald W. "Memoirs of Watson Stewart: 1855–1860." *Kansas Historical Quarterly* 18 (November 1950): 376–404.

Stuart, Tristram. *The Bloodless Revolution: A Cultural History of Vegetarianism from 1600 to Modern Times*. New York: W. W. Norton, 2008.

Tegeder, Vincent G. "Lincoln and the Territorial Patronage: The Ascendancy of the Radicals in the West." *Mississippi Valley Historical Review* 35, no. 1 (June 1948): 77–90.

Trachtenberg, Alan. *The Incorporation of America*. New York: Hill and Wang, 1982.

Vogel, Morris J. *The Invention of the Modern Hospital: Boston, 1870–1930*. Chicago: University of Chicago Press, 1980.

Volo, Dorothy Denneen, and James M. Volo. *The Antebellum Period*. Westport, CT: Greenwood, 2004.

Wade, Louise Carroll. *Chicago's Pride: The Stockyards, Packingtown, and Environs in the Nineteenth Century*. Urbana: University of Illinois Press, 2002.

Walters, Kerry S., and Lisa Portmess, eds. *Ethical Vegetarianism: From Pythagoras to Peter Singer*. Albany: State University of New York Press, 1999.

Walters, Roger G. *American Reformers, 1815–1860*. New York: Hill & Wang, 1997.

Warner, Sam Bass, Jr. *The Urban Wilderness: A History of the American City*. Berkeley: University of California Press, 1995.

Warren, Wilson J. *Tied to the Great Packing Machine: The Midwest and Meatpacking*. Iowa City: University of Iowa Press, 2007.

Watterson, John Sayle. *College Football: History, Spectacle, Controversy*. Baltimore: Johns Hopkins University Press, 2002.

White, Jon Ewbank Manchip. *Everyday Life of the North American Indian*. Mineola, NY: Dover, 2003.

Whorton, James C. *Inner Hygiene: Constipation and the Pursuit of Health in Modern Society*. New York: Oxford University Press, 2000.

———. "Muscular Vegetarianism: The Debate over Diet and Athletic Performance in the Progressive Era." In *Sport and Exercise Science: Essays in the History of Sports Medicine*, edited by Jack W. Berryman and Roberta J. Park. Urbana: University of Illinois Press, 1992, 297–318.

———. *Nature Cures: The History of Alternative Medicine in America*. New York: Oxford University Press, 2002.

Wiebe, Robert H. *The Search for Order, 1877–1920*. New York: Hill and Wang, 1967.

Williams, Robert Chadwell. *Horace Greeley: Champion of American Freedom*. New York: New York University Press, 2006.

Williams, Susan. *Food in the United States, 1820s–1890*. Westport, CT: Greenwood, 2006.

Wood, Clement. *Bernarr Macfadden: A Study in Success*. New York: Copeland, 1929.

The World Almanac and Book of Facts, 1915. New York: Press Publishing, 1915.

Young, Michael P. *Bearing Witness against Sin: The Evangelical Birth of the American Social Movement*. Chicago: University of Chicago Press, 2006.

Zelizer, Julian E. *Arsenal of Democracy: The Politics of National Security—From World War I to the War on Terror*. New York: Basic Books, 2009.

Zunz, Olivier. *Making America Corporate, 1870–1920*. Chicago: University of Chicago Press, 1990.

WEBSITES

"About NAVS." http://navs-online.org/about/index.php.

"About Us: Worthington Foods Company." http://www.worthingtonfoods.com/brand/worthington/about.shtml.

Cambridge Dictionary. "-arian." http://dictionary.cambridge.org/define.asp?key=3939&dict=CALD. Cambridge: Cambridge University Press, 2009.

Economic Research Service, U.S. Department of Agriculture. *Food Availability (per Capita) Data System*, http://www.ers.usda.gov/Data/FoodConsumption.

"Letter from John Milton Hadley to George Allen," April 25, 1855. http://www.kancoll.org/khq/1972/72_1_hadley.htm.

Loos, Anita, and John Emerson. *His Picture in the Papers*. Silent film. Directed by John Emerson (Los Angeles: Fine Arts Film, 1916). http://www.archive.org/details/His_Picture_in_the_Papers.

Mayo Clinic Staff. *Cholera: Symptoms*. http://www.mayoclinic.com/health/cholera/DS00579/DSECTION=symptoms.

National Park Service. "National Register Information System." *National Register of Historic Places*, http://nrhp.focus.nps.gov/natreghome.do?searchtype=natreghome.

Index

Cookbooks, 106, 125, 126, 131, 134–39, 145, 171, 175–76, 188–90
Cowherd, William, 11, 12
Critics of vegetarianism, 25, 27, 73, 94–97; in medical publications, 103–5, 209–10; in popular press, 97–102
Currier and Ives, 95, 96

Dabney, Charles W., 129, 132
Denton, Anne, 69
Dickens, Charles, 106–7
Dorrell, William, 3
Dwight, Henrietta Latham, 136–37

Earle, Sarah, 18
Eddington, Jane, 139
Eggs, 30, 63, 64, 67, 136
Emerson, Ralph Waldo, 30, 48, 50

Fairbanks, Douglas, 206, 208
Fisher, Irving, 196–98
Foote, E. B., 111
Foote-Henderson, Mary, 139–40
Forward, Charles W., 159–60, 183
Foster, Abbey Kelly, 32
Fowler, Orson, 80–81, 83, 86
Fremont, John C., 95–96
Fruitlands, 4, 6, 40, 47–55
Fulton, E. G., 136

Gage, Matilda, 72
Garrison, William Lloyd, 31, 71, 87, 108
George, W. S., 71
Goodell, William, 34
Goss, Roswell, 31
Graham, Ruth, 16
Graham, Sylvester, 28, 35–37, 39, 41, 46–47, 54, 58, 120, 132; and American Vegetarian Society, 60–63, 66; death of, 73–76; early career of, 16–26
Grahamites, 35–37; at boarding houses, 28–32; conversion narratives of, 33–34
Granola, 127, 130, 135, 136
Granose, 129, 135

Great Disappointment, 117–18
Greeley, Horace, 30, 34, 72, 78, 111–14
Grimké, Angelina, 20, 32
Grimké, Sarah, 20
Gunn, Thomas Butler, 93–94

Hadley, John Milton, 83, 87
Hanaford, J. H., 69
Hinduism, 97, 100, 105, 158
His Picture in the Papers (film, 1916), 206–8
Hog industry, 68, 150
Holmes, John H., 87–88
Humoral theory, 3–4, 20, 21, 45
Hunt, Harriet K., 70, 72

Jackson, James Caleb, 119, 127
Jefferis, Benjamin Grant, 144
Jesus Christ, 13, 14, 204

Kansas Vegetarian Settlement Company, 79–87
Kellogg, Ella, 125, 129, 134–35, 188
Kellogg, John Harvey, 5, 7, 115, 146, 147, 148; and Battle Creek Sanitarium, 119–22, 142–43; dietetic theories of, 123–25; and eugenics, 144–45; portrayal in His Picture in the Papers, 206, 207, 208; and proliferation of meat substitutes, 128–34, 168, 169, 170, 176; work with Vegetarian Society of America, 149, 152, 154, 165; and World's Vegetarian Congress, 158, 160, 161
Kellogg, Will Keith, 130, 143
Kemp, Francis G., 165

Ladies Physiological Society, 41
Lambe, William, 3
Lane, Charles, 48–54
Le Favre, Carrica, 151–54, 161, 177
The Liberator, 71–72, 109
Library of Health, 6, 37, 39–40, 42–47, 51, 52, 54, 56
Lovell, J. Harvey, 149, 150
Low, Gilman, 195

Tea, 20, 33, 49, 52, 194
Temperance, 34, 37, 79, 156, 168; and
  American Vegetarian Society, 60,
  65–66, 71–72, 146; of Bible Christians,
  11, 13–14; and Sylvester Graham, 18–19,
  28
Thoreau, Henry David, 48
Trall, Russell, 74–76, 108, 119–20
Transcendental Club, 48
Tyler, William, 28

University of Chicago football, 199, 201

Vegetarian equipment, 169–70
Vegetarian Federal Union, 155–56, 162
Vegetarian grocery stores, 8, 172–74
Vegetarian restaurants, 171–72, 173, 176,
  181, 185, 188, 190–93, 195, 207
Vegetarian Society of America, 5, 8, 140,
  142, 149–55, 165–69, 210; advances

consumerism, 170–71; and shift for
  vegetarianism, 177, 180, 183, 198, 204
Vegetarian Times, 1
Vegetarian Wherryman, 107–11
Volney, C. F., 106

Water cure, 40, 55–57, 79, 121, 123
Water-Cure Journal, 60, 68, 72, 77, 83, 86, 91
Weld, Theodore, 30, 31
Welsh, Fred, 194
Wheat gluten, 131, 135, 136, 173
White, Ellen Harmon, 118–21, 141, 142–43
Willard, Frances, 168, 180
Women's rights, 4, 7, 60, 69–70, 101
World's Vegetarian Congress, 5, 156–64,
  167, 183
Wright, Henry Clarke, 30
Wright, Lavinia, 33–34

Young, Cy, 194

CPSIA information can be obtained at www.ICGtesting.com
Printed in the USA
LVOW08s0223300615

444343LV00004B/4/P